CAMBRIDGE SO

THE M
OF BRIT1

CAMBRIDGE SOUTH ASIAN STUDIES

These monographs are published by the Syndics of the Cambridge University Press in association with the Cambridge University Centre for South Asian Studies. The following books have been published in this series:

THE MUSLIMS
OF BRITISH INDIA

P. HARDY

CAMBRIDGE
AT THE UNIVERSITY PRESS
1972

CAMBRIDGE UNIVERSITY PRESS
Cambridge, New York, Melbourne, Madrid, Cape Town, Singapore, São Paulo

Cambridge University Press
The Edinburgh Building, Cambridge CB2 8RU, UK

Published in the United States of America by Cambridge University Press, New York

www.cambridge.org
Information on this title: www.cambridge.org/9780521084888

First published 1972
Re-issued in this digitally printed version 2007

A catalogue record for this publication is available from the British Library

Library of Congress Catalogue Card Number: 77–184772

ISBN 978-0-521-08488-8 hardback
ISBN 978-0-521-09783-3 paperback

To Sir Herbert Butterfield

*in gratitude for his inspiration as a
teacher and for his example as a historian*

CONTENTS

A NOTE ON SPELLING

Absolute consistency in matters of transliteration and transcription in a more general work on Asia, spanning both the medieval and modern periods and drawing on source material in several European and Oriental languages presents many problems. Broadly speaking the system adopted here follows the lines of that advocated in the Report of the Sub-committee of the 10th Congress of Orientalists printed in the *Journal of the Royal Asiatic Society*, 1895, p. 888, with the minor modifications given in the key to the Glossary, in which the words explained are also given diacritical marks.

ACKNOWLEDGEMENTS

I am honoured that the Committee of Management of the Centre of South Asian Studies, University of Cambridge, have accepted this work for inclusion in their *South Asian Studies* series. The invaluable and sympathetic suggestions of Professor Eric Stokes and Dr Peter Reeves were a source of badly-needed encouragement and have been responsible for great improvements in the final revised text. Professor K. A. Ballhatchet meticulously read and commented upon an earlier and more extended version; I am greatly indebted to him. Mr Ralph Russell, Reader in Urdu in the University of London, selflessly gave me Urdu lessons beyond the call of his normal teaching responsibilities. May I also remember with sadness the late Mushtaq Husain Sahib of Aligarh, with whom I spent many happy hours of further instruction in Urdu. Dr Francis Robinson of Trinity College, Cambridge, generously allowed me to utilise several of his important and original findings in research work yet to be published. Over the years Dr S. R. Mehrotra and Dr Z. H. Zaidi have ungrudgingly given me of their specialised knowledge and advice. To acknowledge the willing and indispensable services of the staff of the India Office Library and of the British Museum is always a pleasure for any student of South Asia. I would like also to express gratitude to Mr ʿAbdur Rahim, librarian of the University of the Panjab, Lahore, and his staff for throwing open their valuable resources to me. At the proof stage Professor Masood Ghaznavi gave invaluable help with the life dates of some Muslim personalities.

Lastly, without the patience and forbearance of my wife, Diana, her help in typing the several revisions of the manuscript, in checking and arranging the text and in assisting in the preparation of the index, this work would never have been published.

P. HARDY

June 1972

1

INTRODUCTION: THE MEDIEVAL LEGACY

Writing in November 1888, the Viceroy of India, Lord Dufferin (1826–1902), described the Muslims of British India as 'a nation of 50 million, with their monotheism, their iconoclastic fanaticism, their animal sacrifices, their social equality and their remembrance of the days when, enthroned at Delhi, they reigned supreme from the Himalayas to Cape Cormorin'.[1] Lord Dufferin's etching of his image of British India's Muslims is worth disinterring from the records of British rule in India because it expresses vividly the image of themselves which modern-educated Indian Muslims came to have in the later nineteenth and twentieth centuries. It was an image which spurred them to demand first a special political position in British India and then, in the nineteen-forties, independent statehood should the British leave. But it was an image which would have startled the Muslims of that earlier, pre-British, period when Muslims were supposed to have 'reigned supreme from the Himalayas to Cape Cormorin'. Scattered unevenly over a subcontinent the size of western Europe, divided by sectarian beliefs, dietary habits and often by language, most under Muslim but some, as in the empire of Vijayanagar or in the coastal towns of the south, under non-Muslim rule, medieval Muslims did not think or act as a nation. As much subject as non-Muslim cultivators and weavers to domination by Mughal, Afghan and Turk, the Bengali Muslim cultivator or the Gujarati Muslim weaver was less engaged in a common enterprise of ruling India than members of the British working classes in the nineteenth century, for at least the latter were welcome as soldiers of the ruling power. Excluded from the mosque and from eating with 'respectable' Muslims, Muslim

[1] Dufferin's Minute of November 1888 on Provincial Councils, enclosed with letter dated 11 November 1888 to Viscount Cross, Secretary of State for India, Letters from Dufferin to Cross, vol. v, *Papers of the First Viscount Cross*, India Office Library, EUR E 243.

sweepers in many parts of India would not have recognised themselves as members of a nation or indeed of a community devoted to the practice of social equality. In so far as village Muslims occasionally made offerings to local Hindu deities, they could not be said to be more monotheistic than their non-Muslim neighbours.

In reality, the British began, in the eighteenth century, to rule over a Muslim community unified at best by a few common rituals and by the beliefs and aspirations of a majority – not the totality – of its scholars. How, by 1947, a very large number of Muslims in British India came to have Lord Dufferin's image of them as their own, and in religion and politics to act it out, is the history of Muslims under British rule. What the condition and *rôle* and aspirations of Muslims in India had actually been before they began to be affected by that rule must now be briefly sketched.

BRITISH INDIA'S MUSLIM POPULATION – ITS
DISTRIBUTION AND GROWTH

By the middle of the nineteenth century, when the East India Company had become supreme in India both north and south of the Vindhyas, Islam had pressed upon the peoples of the Indian subcontinent as a way of life and belief, if not as a political force, for twelve hundred years – from the moment when, not long after the death of the Prophet Muhammad in A.D. 632, Arab Muslims touched the shores of India as traders. Yet Muslims constituted but a fifth of British India's population, a minority most unevenly distributed and territorially consolidated only in Sind and in the western Panjab. The highest proportion of Muslim population was in Sind, where three out of four people were Muslim; the lowest was in the area of the Central Provinces and Madras, where Muslims were about one-fortieth and one-twentieth of the total, respectively. In the Panjab Muslims were rather less than half of the population, in Bengal proper (excluding Bihar and Orissa) about a half. In the North-Western Provinces and Awadh (the latter not annexed to British India until 1856) Muslims formed rather more than a tenth of the population. In the Bombay Presidency, minus Sind, rather less than that.

Within several British-formed provinces, the overall Muslim

population figure covered significant local variations in density. Thus in the western Burdwan division of Bengal proper perhaps one in seven of the population were Muslim, whereas in the eastern divisions of Rajshahi, Dacca and Chittagong two out of every three persons were Muslim. In the Panjab, the population proportion ranged from rather less than a third in the districts east of Lahore to over three-quarters in the districts to the west, reaching almost 100 per cent in the frontier areas. In the far south of British India, in the Presidency of Madras, in the western coastal districts of Malabar about one person in four was a Muslim, but in the eastern districts of the Carnatic perhaps not one in twenty. Then again in some areas Muslims were principally town-dwellers and in others principally country-dwellers. In the North-Western Provinces about a third of the town population was Muslim (about a quarter of all Muslims) but in Bengal proper not more than 3 or 4 per cent of Muslims lived in towns. In the west Panjab, although Muslims were three-quarters or more of the whole population, they made up less than half the population of the towns. In Sind the typical Muslim inhabitant was a cultivator. In Bombay city itself Muslims were one-fifth of the urban population – double the proportion for the whole Presidency excluding Sind.

The thrust and direction of Muslim conquests in South Asia certainly helped to determine the location of the Muslim population, but they were not wholly responsible for it. Furthermore, the numbers of Muslims in particular regions at the beginning of British rule did not provide an automatic index of the length and strength of Muslim rule in each region. The earliest Muslims in the subcontinent were Arab seafarers and merchants who settled as compradors on the Malabar coast under the protection of Hindu rulers. The Malabar coast did not experience Muslim rule until the eighteenth century, under Haidar ʿAli (1761–82) and Tipu Sultan (1782–99) of Mysore, and then only for a generation. The considerable Muslim population of Malabar, remarked upon by the Arab traveller Ibn Battuta (1304–78) in the fourteenth century, had grown under non-Muslim power. In Sind, however, the Arab conquests of the early eighth century had acted as a catalyst. Invading Arab armies formed military colonies but left the conquered people undisturbed in their religions. In the ninth century Arab missionaries of the *shiʿi* Ismaʿili sect made many non-Muslim converts to their version of Islam; Isma'ili princes ruled from Mansura and Multan in the next century and in lower Sind an Isma'ili dynasty survived until the fourteenth century. The gradual turning of both Muslim and non-Muslim in Sind to a more orthodox faith probably occurred subsequently.

In the Panjab, political vicissitudes had a considerable influence on the size and distribution of the Muslim population. The Turk, Mahmud of Ghazna, established a military headquarters at Lahore in the 1020s and an area of the Panjab as far east as Thanesar remained under Ghaznavid hegemony until it was taken over by the Ghurids in 1186. Muslim garrisons, administrators and scholars of Turkish Afghan, Iranian and even of Arab stock settled in the region, to be joined in the thirteenth century by Muslim fugitives from the Mongols. Further considerable migrations, this time of Afghans, occurred in the fifteenth century, following Amir Timur's whirlwind campaigns in what is now Afghanistan. These movements of population, coupled with seasonal migrations from the hills to the plains, gave the western Panjab the character of an area of consolidated Muslim settlement. In the central and eastern Panjab, regions which before the sixteenth century were but tenuously held, if held at all, by garrisons subject to the sultan of Delhi, the Muslim population pattern is more that of the Ganges–Jumna heartland of Muslim imperial power, with Muslims forming a higher proportion of the urban population and a lower proportion of the rural population. The presence of Muslim political power was probably felt more in the Panjab during the latter part of Akbar's reign (1556–1605) and in Jahangir's reign (1605–27), when Lahore was for long periods the working capital of the empire and sizeable Mughal military contingents were stationed in the province, watching events in central Asia.

The size and distribution of Muslim population in the area of the Indo-Gangetic plain, with its centre in the long fillet of land between the Ganges and the Jumna (the Doab), seem to be in inverse proportion to the period and to the power of the Muslim political impact upon that area. In 1881, Muslims were but 13 per cent of the population of the North-Western Provinces and Awadh, and this nearly seven centuries after the capture of Delhi by the Ghurid invaders in 1192 and the consolidation of the authority of the Delhi sultanate in the reign under Iltutmish (1211–36). Over the centuries, a professional *élite* of soldiers, officials, scholars and mystics from Central Asia and from the eastern Muslim world settled in the towns of 'Hindustan'. They created their own urban Muslim service society around them, but were content to treat the countryside not as an area for settlement or colonisation, but as an arena for the exercise of those military and diplomatic skills required to induce the non-Muslim rural population to yield up as much as possible of their produce for the use of Muslim rulers, their servants and their clients.

To the east, in Bengal, the situation was equally paradoxical. A Muslim sultanate with headquarters at Lakhnauti (Gaur) in the district of Malda had been established at the beginning of the thirteenth century. Following the Mughal conquest of Bengal in Akbar's reign, in 1612 Dacca became the capital of Mughal Bengal. In the eighteenth century Murshidabad became the centre of the Nawwab of Bengal's government. Yet according to the first British censuses in Bengal only Dacca district had more than half its population Muslim, and the proportion in Malda and Murshidabad districts was appreciably less. In contrast, in what British observers contemptuously described as the 'rice swamps', districts such as Bogra, Rajshahi, Noakhali, Pubna, Bakarganj, Tippera and Mymensingh, areas of no particular strategic importance in the maintenance of Muslim rule, from two-thirds to more than three-quarters of the population, mostly poor cultivators, were Muslim.

Muslims appeared in Gujarat (which became part of the Presidency of Bombay in 1817 after the third Anglo-Maratha war) centuries before its conquest by the forces of the Delhi sultan, ʿAla al-din Khalji, in 1299. Arab merchants and shippers settled in its seaports and moved inland to the capital, Patan. Not later than the twelfth century, Ismaʿili missionaries were active, their preaching being successful in creating two locally important convert communities, the Bohras and the Khojas, following different successions of spiritual leaders.

The growth of Muslims in any number in the Deccan south of the river Narbada followed the invasions of ʿAla al-din Khalji's forces between 1307 and 1312. With the establishment of a southern and second capital for the Delhi sultanate at Daulatabad in the reign of Muhammad bin Tughluq (1325–51), Turkish, Afghan and Persian soldiers and officials settled in the Deccan in sufficient numbers to create for themselves in 1347 the independent Bahmani sultanate. By the middle of the fifteenth century this had become the dominant power of the northern Deccan plateau. Acquiring control of the western coastline, the Bahmani sultanate attracted Muslim immigrants with professional military and administrative skills, as well as a large number of slaves, the property of Muslim traders, from Iran, the Arab lands and east Africa. The break-up of the Bahmani sultanate at the turn of the fifteenth century into the five successor sultanates of Ahmadnagar, Bijapur, Bidar, Berar and Golkonda, which were eventually absorbed into the Mughal empire in the seventeenth century, had little effect upon the Muslim population pattern in the Deccan. This was somewhat similar to that in the North-Western Provinces and Awadh, namely urban concentrations, though on a much smaller scale, supplemented by rather more scattered rural communities.

Of the fifth or so of British India's population who, in the period of the establishment of British supremacy, were Muslim, only a small minority could claim, for themselves or for their ancestors, membership of a 'ruling nation'. The vast majority of Muslims supported themselves as the vast majority of non-Muslims supported themselves – by 'husbandry' and by the provision of economic goods and services for others. It would be wrong of course to project backwards to the time of Plassey or even to the time (1803) of Lord Lake's (1744–1808) occupation of Delhi, such data on the occupational distribution of Muslims as appear in the early British census reports. However, in the absence of any strong traditions that particular humbly-occupied Muslim groups had fallen from a ruling estate, it would not be wrong to assume that, give or take a few score thousand of disbanded soldiery, the occupational split between the Muslim ruling classes and other Muslims was roughly the same in the eighteen-seventies and eighties as it was a century earlier, on the eve of the gradual British take-over.

In the area of the Indo-Gangetic plain, for all the claims to foreign descent and ruling status by its most educated Muslims, the mass of the Muslim population was composed of agriculturalists, artisans or members of the service occupations which grow around courts, as, for example, musicians, bards, perfume sellers and prostitutes. Such Rajput-descended cultivators as the Malkanas, the Khanzadas and the Lalkhanas and such skilled artisans as weavers, cloth-printers, dyers and cotton carders, in the aggregate out-numbered those who, by calling themselves *saiyids*, Pathans, Mug-hals and *shaikhs*, claimed foreign descent and thereby ruling status.[2] In the Panjab such pretensions were fewer; the 1881 census report found that, including the frontier districts under British rule, only twenty-one Muslims per thousand *claimed* foreign extraction. At that time of every 1,000 Panjabi Muslims 574 were engaged in agriculture, 274 as artisans, 36 as menials and 7 in some form of commerce.[3]

In the Presidency of Bengal (which included Bihar, Orissa and Chota Nagpur) the proportion of agriculturalists among Muslims was higher than in the Panjab – 628 per thousand – with 31 engaged in textile production and 73 as labourers. As in other pro-vinces, many Muslims in Bengal claimed foreign origin; a some-what speculative calculation in the Bengal census report of 1901, which, however, took account of recent Bengali Muslim protests against being considered as mainly of low indigenous origin, sug-gested that perhaps one-sixth of the population of the Presidency as a whole had some foreign blood in their veins.[4] Not all these would have had ancestors in official employment.

In Gujarat, the area of Bombay Presidency which had been longest under Muslim rule, apart from Sind, the occupation pattern was varied by the presence of the descendants of Arab traders and sailors and by sizeable communities of Muslim merchants. In the areas of the Deccan ruled by the sultanates of Ahmadnagar and Bijapur there were some Muslim social groups whose existence was attributable to their ancestors having acted as camp-followers to the armies of the Mughals or of the Deccan sultans, as for example armourers, elephant drivers and horse doctors. But they were heavily outnumbered by artisans and agriculturalists, though it is possible that some of the latter were descended from disbanded soldiers. In towns of the Deccan, after a century or more of Maratha supremacy, most Muslims were small traders, artisans and labourers.

In the Presidency of Madras, in the north-eastern districts of the

[2] A calculation in the 1931 census report for the then United Provinces put the number of Muslims there claiming foreign descent at 411 per thousand.

[3] D. C. J. Ibbetson, *Report on the Census of the Punjab 1881*, vol. 1 (Cal-cutta, 1883), p. 149.

[4] E. A. Gait, *Report on the Census of Bengal 1901*, part 1 (Calcutta, 1902), p. 169.

Carnatic and farther south in Tanjore, areas which had been ruled by the Mughal Aurangzib (1658–1707), or where in the eighteenth century the Nizam of Hyderabad and the Nawwab of the Carnatic had struggled with the French and the English for control, there was a sprinkling of Muslims in the towns claiming foreign and ruling status. However, the largest Muslim element in the eastern areas of the Presidency were cultivators, traders and boatmen of mainly Tamil origin. In the west, in Malabar, the principal Muslim community, the Mappillas (Moplahs), were fishermen, sailors and coolies along the coast, but inland, in the later nineteenth century, constituted a rapidly growing community of very poor tenant cultivators.

The British encountered then – although they were not fully aware of it until the first census reports of the 1870s and 1880s – a Muslim community widely dispersed, much the greater part of which was in fact of native Indian descent and which in most rural areas and in many towns was indistinguishable in occupation from surrounding non-Muslims. It is true that in northern India, Gujarat and the Deccan, Muslims shared the *lingua franca* of Hindustani, but they often learned first as their mother tongue the dialects of Panjabi, Bengali, Gujarati, Tamil and Malayalam spoken by the non-Muslims around them. How had such a medley of peoples become Muslims, at least by profession – 'census' Muslims? In seeking an answer, in so far as that answer is in terms of 'conversion', it is as well to be aware that in Indian life, 'conversion' means more a change of fellowship than of conduct or inner life – although the latter may in time occur. The 'convert' to Islam joins a new social group – never conterminous with the aggregate of all Muslims in India for the most intimate of social relations – for the purposes of marriage, interdining and ritual observance, leaving his old associates, but not necessarily his old ways, behind him.

Although, as has been observed, there was no necessary correlation between the location of Muslim political power and the location of Muslim population, the presence of Muslim rulers in India undoubtedly stimulated an increase in the number of Muslims in the country. Muslim rulers encouraged immigration. They endowed Muslim schools and colleges and conferred land grants and pensions upon Muslim scholars. Very occasionally, in the heat of a campaign, their forces made captives profess Islam on pain of death. Occasionally a Muslim ruler might offer a tributary chieftainship or rights over land on condition of conversion. But mostly Muslim rulers created situations where conversion was convenient. Professional Brahman or Kayastha administrators and clerks, wishing to preserve their hereditary status in government, and shunned perhaps by their fellows for their association with ritually polluting Muslims, might find it convenient to become Muslim, particularly if they could be assured of a high status in Muslim society. The large number of slaves taken in war and carried off to the homes and cantonments of their captors might find some protection and companionship, even some power, in the pre-Mughal sultanates at least, by becoming Muslim. They might after all, if, say, carried off from the Deccan, never see their families again. The children begotten by Muslim masters upon non-Muslim slaves would, furthermore, be brought up as Muslims.

The concentration of Muslim courtiers, troops, officials and scholars in towns encouraged the growth of court and cantonment 'service industries' – butchery, farriery, textile and fine gold and silver manufacture – not to speak of the concentration of such necessary servitors as palanquin or torch-bearers, water carriers, dancing girls, entertainers and musicians. Many so engaged might find conversion socially convenient. In the countryside, cultivating tribes or sub-castes might be encouraged to turn Muslim by the prospect of land settlement on advantageous terms under a Muslim ruler's protection.

In Indian society, with its rules of endogamous marriage and penalties of social ostracism for sexual misconduct, conversion often mitigated the consequences of passion, or made its gratification possible. Non-Muslim girls who solaced Muslim troopers and officials in town and country, and were therefore ostracised, avoided social isolation by conversion. Men of high caste or with money, forbidden by Muslim law and the custom of the country to marry Muslim girls, were sometimes acceptable as sons-in-law after conversion.

Much has been made, and rightly, of the *rôle* of Muslim saints in bringing about conversions to Islam by force of personal example. In Bengal particularly, but also in many areas away from courts and fortresses, their understanding, indeed sharing of popular religious psychology, their tolerance, their cultivation of inner religious experience, often with the aid of methods borrowed from yogic or tantric traditions,[5] persuaded many to enter the Muslim fold. Those unable to profit from arduous spiritual exercises or barred by illiteracy from penetrating the higher philosophy of mysticism might find their way to Islam through having their prayers granted at the tombs of saints, by hearing about their miraculous powers, or simply by finding a local saint a helpful and sympathetic person. Muslim saints did not always insist on a total and immediate abandonment of all old habits and social ties on accepting Islam and were tolerant of deviations from the letter of the Muslim law in, say, rules of inheritance. This made their form of Islam more attractive than the straiter and indeed more intellectual version of the scholar and the jurist, who were, in any case, perhaps less often encountered outside the small town. The density of Muslim population in the area which has become Bangladesh is probably attributable to the activities of Muslim saints among the cultivators and tribes in regions where, at the time of Muslim political penetration into Bengal in the early thirteenth century, Brahmanism had not succeeded in gaining dominance.

Muslims have claimed in modern times that Islam in India had a special attraction for lowly social groups because of its spirit of democratic brotherhood and equality. This hypothesis is more plausible than persuasive, not only because in modern times it is difficult to know what meaning to attach earlier to the concepts 'democratic brotherhood' and 'equality', but also because members of many lowly, indeed degraded, social groups in India, within reach of Muslim rulers, scholars and mystics, were not attracted to Islam. Furthermore, some converts found that if, for example, they were scavengers and sweepers, they still suffered some discrimination at the hands of other Muslims. But this is not to say that many members of low castes or of untouchable groups did not, by becoming Muslims, kick against particular acts of discrimination by higher castes or sub-castes as, for example, a denial of the use of the village well or exclusion from certain quarters in villages and towns.

Then again, it would be easier to maintain the traditional social

[5] On this see, for example, Momtazur Rahman Tarafdar, *Husain Shahi Bengal* (Dacca, 1965), pp. 163–237 *passim*.

and economic life of the village within the pattern of the traditional *jajmani* (patronage) system, with its exchange of gifts and services according to custom, if, when members of the dominant landholding families became Muslim, those in a *jajmani* relationship to them also became Muslim.

MUSLIMS AS RULERS IN MEDIEVAL INDIA; THE MUGHAL LEGACY

British servants of the East India Company were intensely conscious that they were the successors of Muslims as rulers in India. Certainly Muslims had been the empire builders of medieval India; by 1605 Akbar ruled over the whole of north India and by 1690 the power of Aurangzib reached as far south as the river Kauveri. In British India many Muslims' belief that they were the natural ruling aristocracy of the country gave them a confidence in politics all the greater because they knew the British shared their belief. The achievements of the Muslim rulers were indeed great, but, like the British in India, after the demonstration of initial military superiority, their achievements were more diplomatic than martial, perpetuated by the suggestion of unlimited force rather than by its use. Muslim rule in India, like British rule, was much more of a confidence trick played on the compliant populace than its authors would publicly concede.

The reason was that Muslim rule in medieval India was established by a heterogeneous professional immigrant *élite*, reinforced on occasion by further immigration (but equally on occasion threatened by it) and maintained by some co-option from among the conquered people. Muslim rule was neither a colonial rule from some central Asian homeland nor national rule by members of a victorious political nation domiciled in India. Armies of Turkish slaves and Afghans headed by the eastern Iranian chieftains of Ghur, east of Herat, conquered the Indo-Gangetic plains between 1192 and 1206. By 1221, however, the Ghurid power in Afghanistan had disappeared and the Ghurid troops in India were isolated by the Mongols under Chingiz Khan. Although the Delhi sultanate, established by the former Turkish slave Iltutmish (1211–36), received some infusion of new blood from Muslim fugitives from the Mongols in Central Asia, its existence was repeatedly threatened at the end of the thirteenth century by invaders led by Mongol chiefs. At its height, however, under the Khalji and early Tughluq sultans of the fourteenth century, when the process of intermarriage had brought into being a large 'mestizo' *élite* served by Afghans and military slaves, the Delhi sultanate made its power briefly felt over a vast area from the Bay of Bengal to the Indus and from the foothills of the Himalayas to Madura in the far south.

At the end of the fourteenth century however, the Turk, Amir Timur (1370–1405), sacked Delhi in a whirlwind raid and ensured that the process of disintegration of the Delhi sultanate into the regional sultanates of Gujarat, Malwa and Jaunpur, already apparent in the reign of Firuz Shah (1351–88), would not be reversed. (Delhi had lost paramountcy in the Deccan by 1347 when the Bahmani sultanate was founded.) After a period in which Delhi was a petty local principality whose chiefs, the Saiyid sultans, initially acknowledged the overlordship of Timur's successors in Central Asia, the Lodi Afghans were able in the second half of the fifteenth century to reassert the authority of Delhi over an area from the Panjab to Bengal. In 1526 they fell to the Mughal, Babur (1483–1530), ruler of Kabul, one of the several Mughal political entrepreneurs of Central Asia trying to pick up some pieces of the former Timurid empire.

Although Babur's son Humayun (1530–56) was expelled from India in 1540 by the Sur Afghan Shir Shah, he was able to make a comeback in 1555 from the Mughal base in Kabul, with the help of forces lent by the Safavid *shah* of Iran, Tahmasp (1524–76). His son Akbar (1556–1605) created an empire which included not only the Indo-Gangetic plains region, Malwa and Gujarat, but also all the Panjab, Bengal, Kashmir, Sind, Orissa, Khandesh, the northern Deccan and Kabul, the last becoming a dependency of an essentially Indian empire. His successors, Jahangir (1605–27) and Shah Jahan (1628–58), pursued intermittently a policy of expansion at the expense of the Deccan Muslim sultanates of Ahmadnagar, Bijapur and Golkonda until Aurangzib (1658–1707) succeeded by 1690 in occupying most of the peninsula as far south as the river Kauveri, though not without a continued guerrilla resistance by the Maratha chieftains, which ultimately fatally weakened the empire.

The authority of medieval Muslim rulers in India derived from their ability to control a racially, and under the Mughals religiously, heterogeneous *élite* and at the same time to organise successfully the internal military occupation of the country. At no time did Muslim rulers preside over a demilitarised society. A Muslim ruler was a chief of chiefs, a political ring-master; an entrepreneur who only for limited periods, under an Akbar or an Aurangzib, succeeded in becoming a monopolist. A Dutch factor, Pelsaert, writing of the time of Jahangir, graphically described political India as she was until the nineteenth century:

This king [Jahangir] possesses the largest area of all the kingdoms of the world. . .if all these countries were justly or rationally governed, they would not only yield an incalculable income but would enable him to conquer all the neighbouring kingdoms. But it is important to recognise also that he [Jahangir] is to be regarded as king of the plains or of the open roads only, for in many places you can travel only with a strong body of men or on payment of heavy tolls to rebels. The whole country is enclosed and broken up by many mountains and the people who live in, on and beyond the mountains know nothing of any king, or of Jahangir; they recognise only their Rajas, who are very numerous and to whom the country is apportioned in very small fragments by old tradition.[6]

In order to overawe this open competitive political society, Muslim rulers employed the instruments of the extended patrimonial household – servitors and clients linked to the family of the ruler not by ties of race, tribe or clan, but by memory of past dangers and adventures faced together, by the relationship of master and slave and by the charisma of the successful leader who is able to dispense generous patronage. Without the aid of traditional loyalties such as common ancestry may provide, and without the habits of obedience inherited from a long established dynasty (the Mughals almost succeeded in encouraging the formation of such habits), the ruler had to rely on extensive conquest to maximise the resources available for distribution among his followers and on a tactic of balance and rule between different groups of his followers. But there was always the danger that, if the patrimonial ruler's territories became over-extended, his clients and servitors would be tempted to set up on their own in areas remote from head-

[6] Francisco Pelsaert, 'Remonstrantie', translated as *Jahangir's India* by W. H. Moreland and P. Geyl (Cambridge, 1926), p. 58.

quarters, or that in his need to buy loyalty the ruler might deplete his own personal resources. He needed these resources to sustain his own personal army, which was used not only to control would-be rebels but also to resist outside attack. This danger became actuality in the later fourteenth century, when the governors of Gujarat, Malwa and Jaunpur broke away from Delhi; at the end of the fifteenth century, when the Bahmani sultanate became the five successor kingdoms of Ahmadnagar, Bijapur, Golkonda, Berar and Bidar; and in the eighteenth century, when the Mughal Muhammad Shah (1719–48) was unable to resist the Persian king Nadir Shah and was powerless to prevent the provinces from going their own way.

Akbar, the greatest of the Mughals, perfected an instrument of rule based on patronage in the *mansabdari* or office-holding system, which he opened to Rajput chiefs on the same terms as Muslims. The Mughals did not, as did the Ghurids, win north India with the aid of large contingents of military slaves; they relied upon mainly free forces of often quarrelsome and sometimes disloyal Mughals, Turks and Iranians; Akbar found it necessary to put Indian-born Muslims and (after he had subdued the principal chiefs of Rajasthan) Rajputs in the balance against his immigrant followers. In the *mansabdari* system (elements of which he inherited from the Delhi sultans) he founded an imperial service order offering dignity and prizes beyond the reasonable expectations of would-be rebels and fostering peaceful co-existence between diverse ethnic groups divided by religion. Officers were graded decimally, given a personal salary and usually (but not always) an additional rank expressed in terms of cavalry command, the emoluments of which would be related to the number of cavalrymen the *mansabdar* was commissioned to bring to muster.

A *mansabdar* was always at the disposal of the emperor, whether for military or for civil employ, and could be dismissed or trans-ferred to other employment at will. The *mansabdar*'s position was not hereditary, although his sons tended to enjoy some advantage in starting up the ladder of *mansabdari* promotion. The pay and emoluments of high-ranking *mansabdars* were such that rebellion was hardly worth the hazard; in the reign of Shah Jahan, for ex-ample, the income of a *mansabdar* with a personal rank of 7,000 and a cavalry rank of 7,000 could amount to thirty *lakh* of rupees, larger than the revenue to be realised from most Rajput principalities.

The methods adopted for paying the salaries of *mansabdars* encouraged them to co-operate in the subduing or overawing of rural chiefs, clans, tribes and other claimants on the resources of the soil. Although some *mansabdars* received a cash salary direct from the royal treasury, many, indeed until the end of Aurangzib's reign, received their pay in the form of a draft on the revenues of a specified rural area. This assignment (technically *jagir*) was usually managed by the agent of the assignment holder (*jagirdar*), but in time of external peace a *jagirdar* would see that the chiefs in the area of his assignment were compliant. The more important *jagirdars* were often given civil and military commissions (*faujdaris*) within the area of their *jagirs*.

The Indian countryside was extensive and Muslim agents of Muslim rulers comparatively few; their interest in local rural society was strictly a business interest in the peaceful collection with the minimum effort of the maximum share of the produce of the soil. When non-Muslim chiefs and other local claimants on the resources of the land discovered that Muslim rulers would be happy to be accepted as the latest generation of overlords and superior revenue-receivers, they hastened to co-operate or at least to acquiesce. These chiefs and local vested interests owed their position in the countryside to earlier movements of conquering peoples, to grants of land by Hindu kings, to the fact that they were leaders of tribes, clans and village brotherhoods who had cleared land for cultivation. Under the Mughals this rural aristocracy was accepted into the revenue collecting system as *zamindars* (landholders) of various grades. Some were allowed to pay tribute without a detailed inquisition into the revenue-paying capacity of the lands over which they had *zamindari* rights. Others, the majority, were employed as agents for the collection of revenue, in accordance with imperial regulations governing its assessment and collection. The revenue was raised by division of the crops or by payment of a fixed rate in cash per unit area under cultivation, according to the crop, average local yields and average local prices for the crop. Such *zamindars* were entitled to a percentage of the revenue and/or immunity from land revenue on their own holdings. These *zamindari* rights could be bought and sold as properties and were often conferred by the Mughal government to reinforce Mughal authority in a particular area. They did not extend to interference with the occupancy rights of the actual cultivator, so long as the latter paid the revenue demand.

The rural population under the Mughals was subject to an elaborate system of district and provincial administration, which the British were to inherit and not fundamentally to modify. When the area concerned was not in assignment to a *jagirdar*, but managed directly by officials of the imperial treasury (*diwan*), a subordinate collector or *ʿamil* was responsible for the collection of revenue from the *pargana* or group of villages. The *pargana* was retained for a long time by the British as a revenue unit, but was early superseded for general administrative purposes by the larger *tahsil*. Above the *ʿamil* was the *ʿamalguzar* or collector of the *sarkar*, the forerunner of the British district. The *sarkar*, however, had an executive officer or *faujdar*, who commanded the local military contingent and whose duty it was to ensure that the revenue officials did not meet with armed resistance from the retainers kept by many *zamindars*. He was also responsible for criminal justice. Above the *sarkar* was the *suba* or province, with its chief revenue officer or provincial *diwan* and the governor or *subadar*, *nazim* or (in the eighteenth century) *nawwab*; he was commander of the military forces of the province, and ultimately responsible, under the emperors, for the administration of justice. *Faujdars* and provincial *diwans*, and indeed some *jagirdars*, were appointed by the emperor himself or by his central officials, thus providing a check on the provincial governor.

Oppression and failure to obey the imperial revenue regulations in the districts were supposed to come to the notice of the authorities through the reports of news-writers and spies. Frequent transfers of appointments lessened the opportunities for *faujdars*, *jagirdars* and other officials to acquire local positions of strength. The ultimate sanction against rebellion on a provincial scale (other than the absence of a corporate spirit among provincial governors and their senior officers) was the emperor's personal army, in Akbar's time numbering 12,000 cavalry on cash salaries and 7,000 gentlemen troopers.

THE MUGHAL COURT CULTURE

In Mughal times Akbar and his successors presided over, where they did not personally foster, an imperial court culture, shared and contributed to by Muslims and non-Muslims alike. By the eighteenth century, the Mughal courts at Delhi and Agra had become schools of manners and good taste even for opponents and rebels. As Dr Percival Spear has well said, 'an observer who visited only the cities of Mughal India might have supposed that India was mainly a Muslim country... and that Persian was the current language'. Persian had been the language of the court under the sultans of Delhi and of the Deccan, but under the Mughals it also became the language of the Hindu political *élite* and higher civil servants.

Both Babur and Akbar revitalised Persian literature in India by attracting Persian poets to India, but Akbar extended its appeal to non-Muslims by having parts of the great Hindu epics, the *Mahabharata* and the *Ramayana*, translated into Persian from Sanskrit. By Jahangir's reign members of the Kayastha writer caste had attained proficiency in ornamental Persian epistolography. In the early eighteenth century, a Hindu mystic, the Khatri Bhopal Rai, expressed his spiritual experiences in a Persian *mathnawi* and Lala Anand Rai used Persian to express devotional themes from the *Ramayana* and *Bhagavad Gita*. A remarkable form of cultural syncretism expressed through Persian was historical writing by Hindu historians in a Muslim idiom. Ram Lal in his *Tuhfat al-Hind* (The Indian Present), 1735–6, followed Muslim convention so far as to state that the establishment of Muslim rule in India was divinely ordained and that when Shivaji, Aurangzib's Maratha antagonist, died, he departed to hell.

Mughal architecture, that architecture of drama and pageant, set the fashions of public building for the Rajput prince and for the British civil servant. Its unique combination of the Muslim tradition, outside India, of light and air, expressed by the vaulted arch, the dome, expansive courtyards and audience chambers, with Hindu traditions of massive solidity and ornate decoration, found expression in the triumphant structures of Akbar's palace city of Fatehpur Sikri, and of Shah Jahan's Red Fort in Delhi. Mughal influence is to be seen in the palace building of Maharaja Man Singh (1592–1615) and Raja Jai Singh (d. 1668) at Amber.

In painting, Mughal and Hindu princes and courtiers were to patronise a remarkable synthesis of Persian techniques and Indian preoccupations. The Mughals introduced to India the miniature style of Bihzad, painter at the court of Sultan Husain Baiqara of Herat (1470–1506), with its personal portraiture in three-quarter profile, its combination of garden landscapes and walled settings and its rich colour patterns. By the middle of Akbar's reign, Indian influences were becoming noticeable in greater attention to human and animal detail, in the introduction of Indian flora and fauna and in a largeness of construction reminiscent of Hindu mural decoration. Akbar had his own palace studio with over one hundred painters, of whom all but a handful were Hindu. By the beginning of the seventeenth century, a Rajput tradition of painting had appeared at the courts of Jaipur, Jodhpur and Bikaner and in the eighteenth century in the sub-montane centres of Kangra and Jammu. It adopted the dramatic composition of the earlier Mughal style and conveyed the same sense of air and space, but devoted its brilliant talent for drawing animals and plants to the expression of themes drawn from essentially Hindu mythology.

Despite some disapproval among Muslim theologians and lawyers, music flourished early in the thirteenth century among Indian Muslims under the auspices of the Chishti mystic order. All the Mughal rulers except Aurangzib were patrons of music. In 1666, a Muslim, Faqir Allah, compiled his *Rag Darpan*; partly a translation into Persian of a Sanskrit work, the *Rag Darpan* describes the principles of musical composition and the *rags* or melodies appropriate to different times of day and to different seasons. Muslim singers at courts of such broad-minded Muslim rulers as Ibrahim ʿAdil Shah of Bijapur (1535–57) would be expected to sing songs from Hindu mythology, while Hindu singers would be expected to sing Muslim songs. Probably it was in the sphere of music that Hindu and Muslim cultural traditions came nearest to a synthesis.

It was in the syncretic but none the less living language of Urdu that the court culture presided over by the Mughals bequeathed its most lasting legacy, one into which society outside the audience chamber and the courtyard also entered. The most acceptable theory today is that Urdu originated in the Ghaznavid province of the Panjab in the eleventh and twelfth centuries as an impregnation of Old Panjabi with Persian vocabulary and idiom, after which the new dialect was, so to speak, transported to Delhi by the Ghurid conquerors, who took over from the Ghaznavids in the Panjab in 1186. From Delhi it was conveyed by the armies of ʿAla al-din Khalji (1296–1316) to the Deccan, where it emerged in the sixteenth century as a literary and court language, particularly under Sultan Muhammad Quli Qutb Shah of Golkonda (1580–1611). With Aurangzib's conquest of Bijapur and Golkonda in the 1680s, literary Urdu was introduced to the northern cities of the Mughal empire (where members of the ruling establishment had continued to converse with the ruled in Urdu dialects, *Urdu-i Muʿalla*) and seized upon by Muslim poets already dissatisfied with the increasing formalism of the Persian *ghazal* or lyric. *Urdu-i Muʿalla* was purged of much of its popular Hindi vocabulary and more Persian idioms and metaphors introduced. With a vital new language, poets such as Khwaja Mir Dard (1720–84), Mirza Rafiʿ Sauda (1713–81) and Mir Taqi Mir (1733–1814) wrote to express their anguish and dismay at the spectacle of an empire and a cultured society in decay.

A gradual rejection or submergence of Mughal culture has been a feature of the modern history of India; it is well, therefore, to stress its hold over the imaginations and sensibilities not only of the Muslim and Hindu ruling *élite* but also, and particularly in northern India, over the general urban population. While the Muslim and Hindu *élite* showed a common fondness for the chase and for ostentatious living, the common people of the towns joined together in celebration of the Muslim festivals of *Nauruz* and *Shab-i Barat* and the Hindu festivals of *Dahsehra*, *Holi* and *Diwali*. All classes attended celebrations at the tombs and shrines of saints and enjoyed the showy displays of the great office holders with illuminations, jugglers, rope dancers, magicians, cock-fights and bear-fights. If, after the looting of Delhi by Nadir Shah (1736–1747) in 1739, the capital lost much of its splash and glitter, the court of Awadh was able to continue the old traditions in Allahabad and Lucknow.

THE DECLINE OF THE MUGHAL EMPIRE

For all its identification with the Indian scene and its willingness to intermarry with the 'select' people of the country, the Muslim ruling *élite* could only enact the *rôle* of the *kshatriya* or ruling element in Indian society with the acquiescence of those who themselves had a tradition of authority and influence in Indian society. In a political society of locally strong clan and tribal chiefs and of entrenched agrarian interests, domination was only one mistake away from resented domineering. Chiefs and *zamindars* were more ready to offer allegiance than to be forced into submission. Government needed to be a government of men much more than of measures, a confidence trick by the sincere and honest. This was why Akbar was indeed the greatest of medieval Muslim rulers. Combining wide-ranging curiosity and sympathy with decision and daring, tolerance with efficiency and industry, an acute sense of the possible with ruthlessness in emergency, Akbar had charm, the ability to win the hearts and fire the imagination of Muslim and Rajput, Kayasth and Khatri, and even, through his fiscal measures, of *zamindar* and peasant. It was no coincidence that the Mughal empire went 'over the hill' under Aurangzib, that Neville Chamberlain of the Mughal empire, with his business efficiency and unimaginative pedantry, and down the hill under such middle-aged gallants as Jahandar Shah (1712–13).

A British member of the Covenanted Civil Service once wrote, 'as every district officer knows, we rule India not by issuing orders but by cajoling the local groups'. Under the Mughal empire, substitute *zamindars* for 'local groups'. It was when Aurangzib failed to cajole the Maratha *zamindar* Shivaji (1627–80) into believing that his best interests lay within the Mughal system that he had to embark upon a war that permanently weakened the empire. After his Rajput general Jai Singh (d. 1668) had forced Shivaji in 1665 to a not-inglorious peace, Aurangzib failed during Shivaji's visit to Agra to turn him into a loyal *mansabdar* and ally against the Deccan Muslim sultanates. Perhaps Aurangzib's spirit was too narrow and unsympathetic to allow him to charm Shivaji by a generous *mansabdari* appointment, or the Mughal exchequer was unready for full war against Bijapur and Golkonda, or perhaps Shivaji was too greedy, but Aurangzib found that in the Deccan he had thrust his hand into an agitated ant-heap by not reaching an alliance with Shivaji against the Deccan Muslim sultanates. After 1681, when his son Prince Muhammad Akbar rebelled and fled for refuge to the Deccan, Aurangzib embarked upon a full-scale war of conquest against the Marathas and Bijapur and Golkonda. Although the capitals Bijapur and Golkonda were taken in 1686 and 1687 and Shivaji's son and successor Shambhaji captured and executed in 1689, Aurangzib's forces were still engaged, with diminishing success, in an attempt to scotch mobile Maratha guerrilla bands over a vast area from the southern borders of Gujarat to Jingi in the far south.

Aurangzib's Deccan imbroglio weakened not only the Mughal army as a fighting unit but also the *mansabdari* and *jagirdari* systems as instruments for ensuring the internal military occupation of the whole empire. Aurangzib subverted the Bijapur and Golkonda sultanates partly by offering Bijapuri and Golkonda officers *mansabs* and *jagirs*. Famine and devastation in the Deccan reduced the local resources for meeting the pay of the appointees, and *jagirs* in northern India were therefore assigned to former Deccani nobles. So many demands were made that Aurangzib himself is reported to have said that the area available for assignment was like one pomegranate among a hundred sick men.

On Aurangzib's death in 1707, the frustrations of the *mansabdars* encouraged them to support rival royal claimants to the throne and the latter to over-bid for that support. The royalty and cohesion of the ruling *élite* were fatally weakened; between 1707 and 1719 there were two wars of succession and two depositions of emperors. *Mansabdars* spent their energies in court intrigue, and *jagirdars*, fobbed off with small *jagirs* with inadequate revenue yields, or with *jagirs* which yielded much less than the official estimate, placed their assignments in the hands of revenue farmers who stirred up the *zamindars* with their exactions. Fewer troops were available to keep the countryside in awe, as many *mansabdars* were unable to meet their obligations to bring men to the muster. As emperors increasingly alienated the reserved areas under direct revenue administration to their supporters or favourites, their ability to maintain a body of personal troops sufficient to enforce their authority rapidly declined.

By the seventeen-forties the Mughal empire had been reduced to the ghost of the Delhi sultanate after Timur's invasion in 1398–9. Divided counsels and intrigues with Maratha chiefs had helped to lose most of Gujarat and Malwa to the Marathas. Preoccupation with trying to balance one cabal against another had obliged Muhammad Shah to watch impotently as the governors of Bengal,

Awadh, Panjab and Hyderabad converted their offices into personal and family properties. In 1739 the Turkoman Nadir Shah, ruler of Persia, brushed aside the inadequate Mughal forces belatedly mustered, and sacked Delhi, carrying off fifteen crore of rupees in cash besides vast quantities of jewels and the Mughal Peacock Throne itself.

During the next two decades the Panjab was lost to Nadir Shah's legatee in Afghanistan, the Afghan Ahmad Shah ʿAbdali (1747–73). Delhi was fought over by rival factions among the Mughal nobility, was plundered twice again, this time by ʿAbdali's forces, and witnessed the deposition and murder of two emperors, Ahmad Shah (1748–54) and ʿAlamgir II (1754–9) and the flight of a third, Shah ʿAlam (1759–1806). The Marathas intervened against Ahmad Shah ʿAbdali, only to be disastrously defeated at Panipat in 1761. The clamour of his troops for pay, however, forced ʿAbdali to withdraw from India, leaving a power vacuum at Delhi which his lieutenant, the Rohilla Afghan Najib al-Daula (d. 1770), tried to fill.

Although Shah ʿAlam returned in 1772 from the protection of the Nawwab of Awadh and of the East India Company, to preside over a resurgence of the local power of Delhi brought about by his Persian champion, the adventurer Najaf Khan (d. 1782). Nevertheless, in the seventeen-eighties, following the death of Najaf Khan, Shah ʿAlam was obliged to become a pensionary of the Marathas under Mahadji Sindhia of Gwalior (d. 1794). He changed masters in 1803 for the last time when, as an episode in the second Anglo-Maratha war, Lord Lake occupied Delhi. At about the same time the Sikh Ranjit Singh was founding a consolidated Sikh power in the Panjab. With the British entrenched in Bengal and Bihar after the battles of Plassey (1757) and Baksar (1764), and with the Nawwab of Awadh in subordinate alliance with the East India Company, paramount power over the heartlands of the empire which Akbar had created had passed, by the opening of the nineteenth century, into non-Muslim hands.

The ousting of members of the Muslim ruling *élite* from positions of political and economic advantage did not follow as a necessary consequence of the loss of Mughal imperial authority. The eighteenth century was the age of the able and adventurous soldier of fortune and in Muhammad Khan Bangash the Nawwab of Farrukhabad (1714–43) or in the Afghans of Rohilkhand, Muslims had their successful fortune hunters. In Awadh, and in Bengal before the age of Warren Hastings, the provincial *nawwab* continued to dispense patronage and to confer revenue-free lands upon scholars and former servants. In the countryside Muslims could still buy *zamindaris* and act as revenue collectors and even as revenue farmers. Indeed the weakening of imperial control meant in some cases that a *jagirdar* could really become a local chief with the support of local interests. The big man's descent was the little man's ascent. If, however, in Bengal the Muslim *nawwab* preferred to engage for the payment of revenue with mainly Hindu *zamindars*, as Murshid Quli Khan appears to have done, then that was a decision of the Muslim *nawwab* of Bengal. But in the areas of Gujarat, Malwa and the Deccan controlled by the Marathas, Muslims appear to have forfeited their local ruling status along with their *jagirs* and Muslim *zamindars* were fewer. After a century and more of Maratha domination, Muslims in Gujarat, Malwa and the northern Deccan appear to have lost aristocratic pretensions.

In the Panjab, despite the religious antagonism of the Sikhs, Ranjit Singh continued to accept Muslim village *zamindars* as engagers for the payment of revenue and recruited Muslims to his armies. Under the Sikh rule in the Panjab Muslims did not have power but they had modest careers and income from land. The British were to find a solid Muslim peasant interest in the Panjab, without the aristocratic pretensions of the Muslims of the Indo-Gangetic plains. Muslims suffered as did non-Muslims from the anarchy and confusion of the eighteenth century and where, as skilled artisans, they were dependent upon the maintenance of peace and security for the patronage of the nobles, they doubtless suffered much. However, it seems unlikely that their sufferings were peculiar to themselves. Politics were still an open-air tournament in eighteenth-century India; Muslims belonging to the service *élite* had apparently lost their skill as tournament managers, but why should they not continue to show their old skill as jousters?

THE RELIGIOUS LEGACY

In the religious sphere Akbar had set the tone of Mughal rule as one of public tolerance from a position of strength. Although in the earlier years of his reign he had bowed in the direction of Muslim

orthodoxy in order to win the support of the Indian-born Muslim
élite, by the middle years he had adopted a policy of 'peace with all'
and set his face – in the environment of the court at least – against
Muslim practices, such as cow-slaughter, which were offensive to
Hindu sentiment. Although Muslim judges (*qazis*) continued to be
appointed to give decisions according to the Muslim holy law
(*shariʿa*) in those spheres of family and property relationships which
had always effectively been their province, and although Muslim
scholars continued to be given pensions and land-grants for their
subsistence, the discriminatory poll tax on non-Muslims, the *jizya*,
was formally disavowed.

Akbar and his successors Jahangir and Shah Jahan were also
tolerant as between the principal Muslim sects, the *sunni* and the
shiʿa (who differed over the right of temporal succession to the
Prophet and over the right of authoritative interpretation of divine
law, the *sunnis* holding that right to inhere in the consensus of the
scholars, the *shiʿa* in an infallible *imam* or charismatic descendant
of the Prophet's son-in-law, ʿAli). With the foundation of a *shiʿi*
empire in Iran by Shah Ismaʿil Safawi (1501–24), and with Safawid
military assistance for Humayun's 'come-back' in 1555–6, it was
politic not to discriminate in official appointments against *shiʿi*
immigrants and their descendants in India. Before the reign of
Aurangzib, orthodoxy under the Mughals was a matter of private
practice, not of dynastic policy.

In the eighteenth century, the rueful chagrin with which the
strongly orthodox had acquiesced in Akbar's stance showed signs
of being supplanted by attitudes of a more puritan aggressiveness.
By the time the British acquired paramountcy in India voices
had been raised demanding, in effect, the rejection of the religious
modus vivendi of medieval India in favour of a classical and indeed
Arabic Islam. The history of British India was to reveal that such a
call could unite for common action India's Muslims, otherwise
divided by class, education, language and regional culture. ·

Muslim scholars and writers in India had preserved in their
writing the ideal of classical Islam, formulated at least four centuries
before the Ghurid conquests in India, that the truly Islamic
temporal order was that in which the holy law, *shariʿa*, as understood by the consensus of the scholars, was the sole law of the
dar al-Islam (abode of Islam) and was to be enforced by a godly

Muslim ruler whose sole *raison d'être* was such enforcement. He was to appoint pious judges, to collect the canonical taxes of *ʿushr* (tithe) and *zakat* (alms) and to ensure that the infidel was made to recognise his second-class status in this life by the payment of a poll tax or *jizya*. Until the twelfth century, *sunni* Muslim scholars laid down that this pious Muslim ruler should be the universal *khalifa* or caliph, elected or selected for his religious qualities from among the members of the Prophet's own clan, the Quraish, by god-fearing elders of the community. With the emergence of regional war-lords in the Islamic world (such as the Ghurids and their successors in India) Muslim scholars at first proposed that such *de facto* rulers should exercise the caliph's functions on his behalf and then, particularly after the Mongol destruction of the ʿAbbasid caliphate in 1258, that each *de facto* ruler or *sultan* should act as the caliph for his own territories – a conception dubbed by some modern scholars the 'pious *sultan*' theory.

The appearance of an identity of the fact and the ideal was kept up in pre-Mughal Muslim India. Sultans claimed, on their coins, to be lieutenants of the caliph; the levying of revenue from an overwhelmingly non-Muslim population could be made to look like the levying of *jizya*; sultans of Delhi did appoint *qazis*; Muslim scholars and teaching institutions were supported by royal subventions and grants. It was true that the sultan managed the revenue system and punished certain offences at his discretion and heedless of the holy law, but already outside India before the twelfth century scholars had in practice accepted that the sphere of the holy law would be limited to questions of belief and ritual, to family and certain property relationships, providing that the government did not formally deny the supremacy of the *shariʿa* in all spheres of life. Furthermore, since the sultans of Delhi employed Hindu chiefs, as auxiliaries commanding Hindu troops or as tributaries ruling over Hindu populations, the world still, to all appearances, remained in the hands of the faithful.

It was more difficult to preserve appearances under Akbar, Jahangir and Shah Jahan. Akbar formally abolished *jizya* (in fact it is doubtful whether it had ever been levied in the countryside separately from land revenue), and by appointing Rajput chiefs as provincial governors and a Khatri, Raja Todar Mal (d. 1589), as chief revenue officer he placed non-Muslims in authority over

Muslims. He allowed religious debate on an equal footing between Muslims and non-Muslims in his *'Ibadat-Khana* or house of Worship. In works on kingship written by his friend and confidant, Abu'l Fazl (1551–1602), no reference was made to the duty of a Muslim ruler to enforce the *shari'a*. Although in fact Akbar continued to maintain a Muslim religious establishment out of royal revenues and allowed the *qazis* to continue the application of Muslim law among Muslims, Islamic militancy found no official favour.

Orthodox ideals never lost their hold among the Muslim religious classes and in Aurangzib they found, for whatever reasons, a public champion. In 1657–8 Aurangzib had fought his way to the throne over the corpses of his eldest brother, Dara Shikuh, and his youngest brother, Murad, and on reaching it had imprisoned his father in Agra Fort until the latter's death in 1666. His earlier wars of expansion in the Deccan and Assam did not go well; between 1665 and 1672 he was faced by a number of local risings of Hindu *zamindars* and Afghan tribesmen. Even before the sixteeneighties the strain on his forces was considerable. Personally of an orthodox temperament, he began to make a bid for orthodox support. In 1665 he levied discriminatory internal customs tolls on Hindu merchants; in 1669 he issued orders for the destruction of Hindu temples and in 1679 he formally imposed *jizya* – and levied it – allowing members of the Muslim religious classes to enjoy some of the proceeds. He encouraged conversions to Islam and sponsored the compilation of a digest of *sunni* jurisprudence, the *Fatawa-i 'Alamgiri*, which, in Bengal at least, was operating in the penal sphere at the time the East India Company took over.

Although Aurangzib did not cease to employ Rajputs in his service, it seems he reduced their opportunities for executive office in the latter part of his reign. Within a decade of his death his successors had rescinded his measures, but his actions fostered powerful myths after his death – in the eighteenth century that powerful elements in the Muslim ruling *élite* could be rallied for a policy of discrimination against non-Muslims, and in the twentieth century that Muslims had once been great because they had been godly, and might be so again – by becoming godly again.[7]

---

[7] In 1910 Sir Muhammad Iqbal recommended that Muslim education in India should aim at fostering Aurangzib's type of character; *vide* lecture 'Muslim Community', an extract of which was published in *Punjab Census*

But the real challenge to purity of belief and practice in Islam in medieval India was to be found not in the ruler's court or in the raids of the Marathas but in the convert's countryside – in the ignorance of new Muslims of the requirements of Islam and in the insidious infiltrations of 'creeping Hinduism' into the daily life of the convert. Many conversions in such areas as eastern Bengal occurred far from centres of Muslim education, through the influence of Muslims not themselves well-versed in the law of Islam or personally committed to teaching its requirements. Thus 'census Muslims' might continue to worship Sitala, the goddess of smallpox, recite hymns to Lakhshmi, Hindu goddess of wealth, or make offerings to Narasinha, the leonine incarnation of the god Vishnu. In family and property relationships, old attitudes and customs died hard if at all: thus in many circles of Muslim society, widow remarriage was not permitted, divorce frowned upon and the *shariʿa* sanction for cousin marriage ignored. In parts of the Panjab and in modern Uttar Pradesh, Muslim women were denied the rights of inheritance guaranteed them under Islamic law, while among the Mappillas of Malabar matrilineal rules of succession were followed in defiance of the *shariʿa*.

As in other parts of the Islamic world, the mystics of Islam, the *sufis*, were regarded with suspicion as posing a threat to fundamental Qur'anic doctrines of God's transcendence and otherness to His creation. Seeking God through interior experience and direct intuition, the *sufis* often appeared to be denigrating the approach of the scholars through the study of Qur'an and *sunna* (the model behaviour of the Prophet). The ecstatic utterances of the great *sufis* at the moment of supreme insight sounded as if they were proclaiming that God 'like unto whom there is not anything' dwells in the mystic or that He alone has Being (the concept of *wahdat al-wujud* or the unity of being) and that the empirical world is but the manifested reflection of the sole Divine Existence.

Such language was the more disturbing to Muslim purists in India because it sounded similar to that in the Upanishads, to the effect that man in his deepest ground (*atman*) was identical with

Report 1911, part 1, p. 163. He also stated that Aurangzib saw that the strength of Islam in India depended not on the goodwill of the people of the land, as Akbar had thought, but on the strength of the ruling race; vide, Iqbal's *Stray Reflections*, 1910, quoted in Annemarie Schimmel, *Gabriel's Wing* (Leiden, 1963), p. 11.

the universe in its deepest ground (*brahman*). The formulation of the Arab-Spanish mystic Ibn al°Arabi (1165–1240), that phenomena are epiphanies of a Divine Being yearning to make Himself known, appeared to have analogies in the teaching of the early twelfth century *nath-yogi* (master yogi), Gorakhnath, that the urge for self-expression in the Perfect Existence was responsible for creation. The frequent friendly encounters between *yogis* and *sufis*, the *sufi* borrowing of yogic techniques, such as those of breath control, as an aid to spiritual experience, created an atmosphere unfavourable to religious militancy in medieval India.

Attempts were made from within the mystics' own fold to reassert the religious need for a positive rejection of mystical ideas smacking of pantheism and immanentism. Shaikh Ahmad Sirhindi (1564–1624) of the Naqshbandi order asserted as a mystic that God's overwhelming seizure of the mystic in ecstasy merely blinded the mystic to the existence of all else save He, but that that existence was not thus rendered illusory. That he failed to weaken the appeal of the doctrine of *wahdat al-wujud* is suggested by the eighteenth-century scholar-mystic Shah Wali-Allah's elaborate justification of a modified version of that doctrine.

The anarchy and despoliation of the eighteenth century and the evident loss of Muslim dynastic power to non-Muslim Maratha and Sikh began to gain a hearing for more purist Islam. The Qur'an proclaimed that God confided the world to his righteous servants; the eighteenth-century scene suggested that Muslims were losing command of the world: therefore, the religiously-inspired logic ran, they were doing so because they were no longer righteous. Much of the contemporary historical writing of the first half of the eighteenth century ascribed the troubles of the empire to the moral shortcomings of the Mughal nobility, to its members' disloyalty, dereliction of duty and greedy intrigues with Maratha chiefs. There was a school of thought, led by Chin Qulich Khan, 'first Nizam of Hyderabad' (1724–48), that saw salvation for the empire in greater discrimination against non-Muslims, including the levy of *jizya*. *Sunni* Muslims sometimes resented the rise to power of the *shi°i* *nawwabs* of Awadh, who made of Lucknow a *shi°i* capital. The situation was ready for a *sunni* revival.

In the encyclopaedic Delhi scholar Shah Wali-Allah (1703–62), eighteenth-century *sunni* Islam in India found its revivalist. He offered an integration of theology, philosophy and mysticism catholic enough to place the fervour of the mystics at the service of an essentially transcendent conception of the divine being and an active preaching of the mandates of the holy law. Writing in Arabic and Persian, after a prolonged stay in Mecca itself, he sought a world, rather than a merely Indo-Islamic, readership. In theology he held to the doctrine of a God transcendent in essence, the Creator who knows and is responsible for the universe, yet who is unlike it. God's relationship to the world of creation, in his language the Universal Self, is as the relationship of the number one to the number two, preceeding it, 'in' it, but not it. He recognised the force of the mystical experience of the oneness of being, but argued that the oneness is of the being of the universal self, or the world of creation, not of the oneness in substance of the universal self and the essence of God. In the daily practice of Islam, Shah Wali-Allah stressed a renewed study of the *hadith* or authoritative sayings of the Prophet, and preferred that authentic *hadith* should be followed rather than a doubtful ruling by a jurisconsult *(faqih)*. He would allow some choice of legal doctrines as between the four orthodox Muslim schools of law *(mazahib)*, but was far from proposing the abandonment of the authority of the consensus of the scholars.

Shah Wali-Allah actively criticised the practices of popular religion in India, the imputation of divine powers to saints, worship at their tombs and sacrifice of animals to any other than God. In a work directed against *shi'i* claims he reiterates the *sunni* doctrine of an elective caliphate and lays special emphasis on the duty of *jihad* or holy war against the infidel. His work in emulation of al-Ghazali's *Ihya al-'ulum al-din* (the Revivification of the Religious Sciences), namely *Hujjat Allah al-Baligha* (the Mature Proof of God), suggested that the mandates of divine law were also acceptable to human reason, though not accountable to it.

Although Shah Wali-Allah's teachings had little, if any, effect on the situation during his lifetime – indeed his efforts to see in the Afghan plunderer, Ahmad Shah 'Abdali, a potential saviour of Islam in India were satirised by the Indian Muslim poet, Sauda – nevertheless they did present a comprehensive statement of Islamic belief and practice, in which all Muslim scholars, within the *sunni* fold at least, could find guidance and inspiration. The temporal fortunes of Islam had appeared to Muslims to depend in the medieval period upon a tacit partnership between pious sultans and pious scholars; even if sultans had the will to shoulder their responsibilities they no longer now had the capacity; by deliberately seeking harmony within the entire *sunni* tradition, Shah Wali-Allah helped to prepare the scholars to defend Islam in India in a situation where Muslims were losing the physical power to do so. It was furthermore significant that by so doing, by writing his principal works in Arabic, by calling for greater regard for the Prophet's pronouncements and by openly criticising the influence of the Indian environment on the practice of Islam in India, Shah Wali-Allah was suggesting (as indeed others before him had done) that the less they shared with their non-Muslim neighbours the better servants of God Indian Muslims would be. As the religious appeal was to prove the most effective way of unifying the Muslims of British India, this was a suggestion with the profoundest political implications when, as was to happen under British rule, Muslims outside the old ruling circles came to have a hand in determining their political destiny.

2

THE EFFECTS OF BRITISH RULE
ON MUSLIMS BEFORE 1857

Writing in 1871, the Bengal civilian, W. W. Hunter (1840–1900), described 'the Musalmans' as 'in all respects...a race ruined under British rule'.[1] Ignoring his *caveat* that his remarks applied only to lower Bengal, most historians have not only accepted his judgement as valid for that region but have also extended it to depict the fate of Muslims throughout British India. Certainly British rule ruined the office-holding Muslim aristocrat of lower Bengal, but not all at once. British rule, or rather British manufactures, also ruined the Muslim weaver of Dacca, but not all at once. For other Muslims, in the Panjab for example, British rule brought security; for some in Bombay who were engaged in shipping it brought wealth; for some in British service in the North-Western Provinces, the centre of Mughal culture, it brought more land. The only generalisation possible is that gradually the British changed the form and style of success in Indian society from the military to the commercial. In so far as Muslims were left by the decline of the Mughal empire in a position to become capitalists, they could prosper just as non-Muslims could prosper.

THE EAST INDIA COMPANY, THE MUGHAL DYNASTY AND THE MUSLIM OFFICE-HOLDING CLASSES

For the many Muslims who wanted to preserve their illusions, the establishment of British supremacy in India wrought changes more real than apparent. Looking back over the period after the death of Aurangzib, the Mughal aristocracy could see that they had shared power to their increasing disadvantage with plebians –

[1] *The Indian Musalmans* (London, 1871), p. 149.

Marathas, Jats and indeed Afghan adventurers. Why should they not accommodate the British – who ranked somewhere between *banias* and Marathas? The British themselves in 1803 were rather awed by their own success and respectful towards Mughal culture. The British had indeed occupied Delhi, but so had the Marathas earlier. Meanwhile, there was still a descendant of Timur and Akbar in Delhi, and Muslim courts in Awadh and Hyderabad. Perhaps the British were prepared, having under Clive (1725–74) restored Shuja⁚ al-Daula (1731–75) to Awadh and having entered into alliances with the Nizam of Hyderabad, to accept the Indian political world of the mediatised prince and the nominal supremacy of Shah ⚈Alam. Indeed, early British historical writing on India, for example Alexander Dow's (d. 1779) *History of Hindoostan* (1768–72), Jonathan Scott's (1754–1829) *History of the Deccan* (1794) and Francklin's (1763–1839) *The History of the Reign of Shaw Aulum* (1798), had betrayed respectful admiration for the Mughal achievement coupled with pity for its end. The Mughal hope, and the dying of that hope, that the British were but white Marathas and that the dynasty had merely to wait for a turn of Fortune's wheel before again standing forth as the actual ruler of India, are best read in the story of the relations of the East India Company with the Mughal court in Delhi.[2]

On Lord Lake's capture of Delhi, Shah ⚈Alam and the servants of the East India Company engaged in a deadly serious contrapuntal political exercise. Lord Wellesley (1760–1842) praised Lord Lake to Shah ⚈Alam as the 'happy instrument of your Majesty's restoration to a state of dignity and tranquillity under the power of the British Crown'. Shah ⚈Alam replied by conferring upon Lord Lake the office of *sipah-salar* or Commander-in-Chief and when Lord Lake seized Maratha money from the Mughal treasury Shah ⚈Alam promptly offered it as a donation to Lord Lake's army. The British acted upon their thesis that Shah ⚈Alam was a crowned pensionary by settling upon him eleven and a half *lakh* of rupees, drawn from the land revenue of areas west of the Jumna, and allowing him to retain ruling powers within the area of the Red Fort. In the time of Shah ⚈Alam's son and successor, Akbar II (1806–37) the British reinforced their pensionary thesis by

[2] The following is based upon T. G. P. Spear, *Twilight of the Mughals* (Cambridge, 1951).

refusing to recognise his right to nominate his successor and by Lord Hastings (1754–1826) refusing when Governor-General to stand in Akbar's presence. In the eighteen-forties the British began to omit those courtesies due to a king which they had formerly shown. In 1844 Lord Ellenborough (1790–1871) abolished the presentation of *nazrs* (gifts from an inferior to a superior), dishonestly concealing the fact that the Directors of the East India Company had decided to continue them for the lifetime of the then king, Bahadur Shah (1837–57). Eventually, in 1851, Bahadur Shah received the monthly sum of 833 rupees in lieu of his *nazrs*. In 1849, Dalhousie (1812–60) agreed to recognise Mirza Fakhr al-din as heir-apparent on condition that at Bahadur Shah's death the royal family move out of the Red Fort, which Dalhousie wanted as a powder magazine. In 1856, however, Mirza Fakhr al-din died and the new Governor-General Canning would only recognise Mirza Muhammad Kolash as *shahzada* or prince of the House of Timur, that is as head of the family, but not as king. Had the Mughal family in Delhi not come to an end in death and exile after the British recapture of Delhi in September 1857, they would have ended their days as retired noblemen living in a 'grace and favour' residence near the Qutb Minar.

The British in India had, by 1857, persuaded themselves without difficulty that the Mughals in Delhi were an anomaly and their existence a matter of indifference even to the Muslim population of the East India Company's territories. The East India Company should 'rest satisfied with the degree of respect, submission and attachment which [its] strength and skill in arms, [its] wisdom and beneficence in governing may procure for [it]'; it was 'unnecessary to derive from the King of Delhi any additional title to the Allegiance of our Indian subjects'.[3] But as Bishop Heber (1783–1826) recorded in the eighteen-twenties, many Muslims believed that the East India Company ruled in the name of the Mughal emperor. Bishop Heber wrote,[4]

. . .if a fair opportunity offered the Musulmans more particularly would gladly avail themselves of it to rise against us. But this is from political not religious feeling; and it has been increased of late years by the conduct of Lord Hastings to the old Emperor of Delhi. . .Lord

---

[3] Quoted in Spear, *Twilight of the Mughuls*, p. 44.
[4] Reginald Heber, *Narrative of a Journey Through the Upper Provinces of India*, vol. I, 2nd ed. (London, 1828), pp. 393–4.

Hastings' refusal to pay him the same homage which all his pre-decessors [*sic*] had courted every opportunity of doing and which even the Maharattas did not neglect when the late Shah Aullum was their prisoner have awakened questions and scruples among the fierce Mohammedans about obeying an unbelieving nation which were quite forgotten while the English company acted as the servant and 'Dewan' of the House of Timur.

In 1830, after the accession of Nasir al-Daula as Nizam of Hyder-abad (1830–57), the new Nizam sent *nazrs* to Delhi and asked Akbar for the conferment of his father's titles, as from an overlord. No doubt the court in old Delhi, with its processions, its festivals, the pro-gresses of royal elephants through Chandni Chowk, the respectful attendance of the British Agent at public *darbar* in the *Diwan-i Khwas* (private audience chamber), the presentation of *nazrs* from visiting dignitaries and distinguished travellers, the unproductive life of poetry-reading and cultivated idleness, was to the British an anachronism, made all the more irritating by its background of *haram* intrigue and suspected sexual excess among the *salatin* or Mughal princes. But in 1857, the mutineers at Meerut, Muslim and Hindu alike, rode to Delhi, as if by instinct, to restore Bahadur Shah to the empire of India. Meanwhile, as long as a Mughal reigned in Delhi, aristocratic Muslims could persuade themselves that the old order was not dead and the East India Company was merely an occupying power.

For the Muslim *élite* in northern India, British conquest meant the destruction of a way of life more than the destruction of a livelihood. Under a Bangash Khan, a Najib al-Daula or a Ghulam Qadir (d.1789) the Muslim soldier had the same opportunities of finding his fortune by attaching himself to a successful adventurer as his forebears had had under the Lodis and Surs in the fifteenth and sixteenth centuries. For the ruthless, brave and enterprising, northern India in the eighteenth century was as open a society politically as it had been when Babur came to India. British rule changed all that, though not everywhere at once. The East India Company wanted the steady flow of revenue – and the presence of roving bands of horsemen engaging in forays against *zamindars* interrupted that. Moreover, changes in military technique had destroyed the usefulness of irregular – and ill-disciplined – cavalry. The well-drilled musketeer had ended the dominance of cavalry, whether heavy or light, on Indian battlefields. The Nawwab of Awadh, burdened by a subsidy for a British force, could not find employment for all the Muslim (and indeed other) cavalrymen seeking employment, and anyway, against whom would they be held ready to fight? An indication of the size of the problem is Siraj al-Daula's (1756–7) action in disbanding 80,000 troops (not all cavalry) after his defeat at Plassey. Service in the armies of the East India Company attracted few. What could the Company's service with its strict discipline hold for a cavalryman on twenty-seven rupees a month, or for a *subadar* or 'native officer' on sixty to seventy rupees per month (out of which both had to find their own horse) when in the old days both might have held whole districts to ransom? In any event, the Company could not have employed all.

Occasionally the Company softened for a minority the process of demilitarising Indian society, by the award of pensions or by taking some contingents into its forces. In the settlements in 1818 after the Pindari wars one Namdar Khan received a pension of Rs. 8,125 per annum, while Amir Khan (1768–1834) was made Nawwab of Tonk and had 3,000 of his cavalry and eight infantry battalions 'entertained' in the Company's army.[5] Some Muslim soldiers did find employment in the Company's police, but many more joined the Pindaris before they were crushed by the Company. Some were to join the *jihadi* movement of Saiyid Ahmad of Rai Bareilly, himself a former Pindari. Their fate as a class has not been properly studied, but Bishop Heber, writing in 1824 while passing through Rohilkhand, provides the ocasional *aperçu*.[6]

The Musalman chiefs, who are numerous, are very angry at being without employment under Government, or hope of rising in the State or Army, and are continually breaking out into acts of insubordination and violence. [Or again], the country [Rohilkhand] is burdened with a crowd of lazy, profligate self-called *suwars* [horsemen] who, though many of them are not worth a rupee, conceive it derogatory to their gentility and Patan blood to apply themselves to any honest industry, and obtain for the most part a precarious livelihood by sponging on the industrious tradesmen and farmers, on whom they levy a sort of 'blackmail', or as hangers-on to the few noble and wealthy families yet remaining in the province. Of these men, who have no visible means of

---

[5] Biswanath Ghosh, *British Policy Towards the Pathans and Pindaris in Central India 1805–1818* (Calcutta, 1966), pp. 297, 312.

[6] Bishop Heber, *Narrative*, vol. II (London, 1828), pp. 120, 139.

maintenance at all and no visible occupation except that of lounging up and down with their swords and shields like the ancient Highlanders, whom in many respects they much resemble, the number is rated at perhaps, taking all Rohilcund together, not fewer than 100,000; all these men have everything to gain from a change of Government.

In judicial and revenue employ, except in the highest posts, i.e. judgeships and collectorships, Muslims held their own, in Bengal until the middle of the nineteenth century, in the region of modern Uttar Pradesh for a generation thereafter. But now they held their posts at the pleasure of alien and infidel masters and, after the abolition of Persian as the language of the courts in 1837, in increasing competition with Hindus who had learnt English. In Bengal the East India Company at first acted as a revenue farmer for Shah ʿAlam and for the Nawwab. Until 1772 the Nawwab exercised full police and judicial powers, though ineffectively, through the Muslim *na'ib nazim* or deputy governor, Muhammad Riza Khan (1717–93), and the district Mughal officers, the *faujdar*, the *qazi* and the *mir ʿadl*. Muslim law continued to be administered by *qazis*, and by Muslim officers in the *Sadr Nizamat ʿAdalat* and *daroga-i diwani ʿadalat* (the superior and inferior criminal courts). In Bihar a similar system obtained. Although Warren Hastings' reorganisation of 1772 placed the new district courts for both 'civil' and criminal jurisdiction under European superintendence, *maulawis*, *qazis* and *muftis* continued to be attracted to them. Indeed, Muhammad Riza Khan's reappointment as *na'ib nazim* in 1776 was followed by a revival in the *faujdari* system and an increase in the number of *qazis* atached to the district criminal courts. In 1781, however, Hastings (1732–1818) supplanted Muslim *faujdars* by English magistrates and reduced the number of district criminal courts from twenty-three to eighteen, although he increased the number of civil courts from six to eighteen. The district criminal courts continued under Muslim *daroghas*. Under Warren Hastings Muslims in judicial service lost power but not employment. In 1781, Hastings founded the Calcutta Madrasa to maintain the supply of qualified Muslim law officers. A translation of a Muslim legal digest, the *Hidaya*, was also sponsored and completed in 1778.

In revenue administration, as money was the Company's principal concern, European control was established within five years of the

Company's becoming *diwan*, although from 1765 to 1772 Muhammad Riza Khan also held, along with the post of *na'ib nazim*, that of *na'ib diwan* or deputy collector of revenue. In 1769 European supervisors of revenue were appointed to the districts, and in the following year controlling Councils of Revenue were established at Murshidabad and Patna. In 1772 European Collectors were appointed to the districts and Muhammad Riza Khan was dismissed. Although the European Collectors were withdrawn in 1774 they were finally reinstated in 1785. The consequence of anglicisation of the revenue system for the Muslims in Bengal was not that they lost employment but that they lost income. Hindus, as C. J. Lyall (1835–1911) suspected in 1882,[7] had dominated revenue employment under the Mughals in Bengal. In Chittagong district in 1777 there were only five Muslim to forty-two Hindu employees in the revenue offices.[8] The Muslim *nawwabs* who had ruled Bengal before the Company, Murshid Quli Khan (1700–17) and ʿAliwardi Khan (1740–56), had preferred to confide revenue management to those Hindus (e.g. Brahmans and Kayasthas) best fitted by caste tradition for it.

Lord Cornwallis' (1738–1805) reorganisation of the Company's government in Bengal starkly revealed what Hastings' régime had disguised, namely that Muslims would not be subordinate partners of the British, but merely subordinates. In 1790, Cornwallis abolished the office of *na'ib nizam*. Muslim judges were dismissed, the *nizamat ʿadalat* moved to Calcutta and reconstituted with Europeans, and four courts of circuit established for Calcutta, Murshidabad, Dacca and Patna districts. In 1793, the Collector was divested of his judicial powers and European district judges appointed, who were also given charge of the police as magistrates. No Indian was in future to be appointed to a post carrying an annual salary of £500 or more. The 'career prospects' of Muslims (and Hindus) were limited to appointments as 'native commissioners' (*amins, salis* or *munsifs*) in minor civil suits (their jurisdiction was enlarged in the eighteen-twenties and thirties), as advisory *qazis* to

---

[7] *Home Dept. Correspondence on the Subject of the Education of the Muhammadan Community in British India and their Employment in the Public Service Generally, Selections from the Records of the Govt. of India*, no. ccv (Calcutta, 1886), p. 337.

[8] H. J. S. Cotton, *Memorandum on the Revenue History of Chittagong* (Calcutta, 1880), pp. 169–71.

the circuit criminal courts and to the Nizamat 'Adalat at Calcutta, or as *daroghas* of police in the district *thanas* under the control of European magistrates. However, it was not until the eighteen thirties, when the Company affirmed the principle that 'all natives of India' were eligible for judicial service and placed increasing emphasis on a knowledge of English, that the Muslim predominance in the judicial service in Bengal was challenged. By 1856, the Muslim disadvantage was overwhelming; of 366 persons listed as holding appointments in the judicial and revenue service in Bengal with salaries of fifty rupees and upwards, only fifty-four were Muslim.[9]

In the North-Western Provinces, composed of the territories ceded by the Nawwab of Awadh in 1801 and those obtained by the defeat of the Marathas in 1803, Muslims provided the great majority of subordinate judicial officials. In 1850 they held 72 per cent of the judicial posts open to Indians, that is, up to the post of *sadr amin* (judge for small causes) and including almost all the appointments in the latter part.[10] They were equally dominant in the subordinate revenue service. In 1853 Banda, Gorakhpur, Muradabad, Azimgarh, Gurgaon, Ghazipur and Bharathana are named as having Muslim deputy collectors,[11] and in 1856 Farrukhabad, Ghazipur, Jalaon, Meerut, Muttra, Aligarh, Mainpuri, Etawa, Gorakhpur and Shahjahanpur.[12] Muslims were very numerous too among the *tahsildars*, or Indian collectors of revenue, at the *tahsil* level. George Campbell (1824–92), writing in 1852, stated that the majority of inspectors of police in northern India were Muslim, as were a majority of the rank and file.[13]

THE EAST INDIA COMPANY AND THE MUSLIM LANDED CLASSES

British rule profoundly changed the relationship of the landed classes to the land in India. In some provinces, Muslims proved

[9] Azizur Rahman Mallick, *British Policy and the Muslims in Bengal 1757–1856* (Dacca, 1961), p. 50.

[10] Thomas R. Metcalf, *The Aftermath of Revolt* (Princeton, 1965), p. 301.

[11] Index to *North-Western Provinces Revenue Proceedings, 1853*, (India Office Library) Range 220, vol. 26, *s.v.* names of districts.

[12] Index to *N.-W.P. Rev. Procs., 1856*, Range 221, vol. 14, *s.v.* names of districts.

[13] George Campbell, *Modern India* (London, 1852), pp. 295, 443.

specially vulnerable to British-induced change, in others less so or not at all, as British agrarian policy varied from province to province. Much depended on how far Muslims in the eighteenth century had transformed themselves into *zamindars* and on whether they enjoyed incomes from *jagirs* or from grants of revenue-free land. In Bengal, Muslims did not become as significant a proportion of the new landlord class as their numbers among the population might suggest; in the North-Western Provinces a Muslim landlord class exercised an influence and power which persisted well into the twentieth century.

Muslim *jagirdars* along with other *jagirdars*, as for example in the Maratha country, found their *jagirs* subject to critical scrutiny, detailed inquisition and frequent resumption and commutation to pension. Nevertheless as an institution *jagirs* were not abolished, but were kept as a means of rewarding loyalty to the British, or of easing the transition to the new order.[14] A number of Pathan and Sikh chiefs who had served the British in the Maratha wars were given *jagirs* to the north-west and south-west of Delhi.[15] After the Pindari wars *jagirs* were conferred upon several Muslim Pindari chiefs. However, in the North-Western Provinces the British appear to have seized any opportunity of resuming *jagirs* upon the death of their holders. Sir Charles Metcalfe (1785–1846) sought to do so in the Delhi territory and by the middle of the century the Revenue Proceedings indicate a zeal for commutation.[16] In 1856, for example, twenty-five descendants of one Hussain ʿAli, originally granted a *jagir* by Lord Lake in 1806, were given life pensions in lieu of the proceeds of the *jagir*. The British agent at Farrukhabad was coldly informed in February 1854 that 'it is not desirable to keep together the members of a particular family trained to look to the receipt of a gross fixed amount of gratuitous support from the Government'.[17] The temporising and equivocal behaviour of the

[14] Kenneth Ballhatchet, *Social Policy and Social Change in Western India, 1817–1830* (London, 1957), pp. 52 *et seq.*

[15] J. Holmes, *The Administration of the Delhi Territory, 1803–1832* (unpublished doctoral thesis), London, 1955, p. 70.

[16] E.g. *N.-W.P. Rev. Procs.* nos. 287, 288 and 290 for 11 August 1856, *N.-W.P. Proc.*, 22 July–12 August 1856, Range 221, vol. 6.

D. N. Panigrahi, *Charles Metcalfe in India: Ideas and Administration 1806–1835* (Delhi, 1968), pp. 71–4.

[17] Proc. no. 43 for February 1845, *N.-W.P. Political Proceedings*, Range 230, vol. 69.

jagirdars of Loharu, Amin al-din (1814–69) and Ziya al-din (1821–1885) in 1857, and the rebellion of others, taken with the evidence of pernickety inquisition in the Revenue Proceedings of the North-Western Provinces in the last five years before the Mutiny, suggests that the *jagirdars* in the Delhi region had already become fearful of the future under British rule. In Sind, by contrast, the government of Sir Charles Napier (1782–1853) treated the Muslim *jagirdars* as 'the aristocracy of Sind' and despite reservations confirmed them in their incomes and privileges.[18] In Bengal, however, Muslim *jagirdars* were among the first to lose from resumptions.

A class of Muslim landholder commonly believed to have suffered greatly from British rule was the holder of revenue-free land or the recipient of land revenue from the cultivators of a specified area. These rights were granted not in return for service, but to support learning and education. Such grants (*la-kharaj* revenue-free and *muʿafi* grants) were made on a considerable scale by Muslim rulers and by their Hindu predecessors and were not confined to Muslims. In order to maximise receipts from land revenue, the East India Company issued, from 1793 onwards, regulations for the investigation and resumption of those holdings which did not possess unimpeachable title deeds properly registered with the Collector. According to W. W. Hunter and those modern writers who have accepted his conclusions,[19] Muslims in Bengal were worse hit than others by resumption proceedings, partly because they were a majority of grantees and partly because, as the ruling *élite*, they were careless in preserving their title deeds, if they had ever had any. Unfortunately it is today as difficult to prove or disprove this contention as when Hunter made it. The number and income of grantees, Hindu or Muslim, in Bengal during the period of resumptions has not been ascertained. Nor do we know the number and value of the resumptions, distributed by community. Muslims did suffer, but whether they suffered disproportionately to Hindus remains a matter of opinion, not knowledge. Hunter's contention was, however, challenged at the time it was taken up by Bengali Muslims. Sir Anthony MacDonnell (1844–1925), commenting on the

---

[18] Hamida Khuhro, *The British Administration of Sind 1843–1865* (unpublished doctoral thesis), London, 1965, pp. 73, 99–100, 123, 148.
[19] Hunter, *The Indian Musalmans*, pp. 181–3; Mallick, *British Policy and the Muslims in Bengal*, pp. 34–47.

Memorial of the National Muhammadan Association of February 1882, pointed out that possession for only twelve years before British rule had had to be proved, that *la-kharaj* lands were exempted from resumption proceedings if they were not over fifty *bighas* in extent, and that there was no explanation of why Hindus had survived the effects of resumption proceedings and not Muslims.[20] The Education Commission Report of 1882 also suggested that 'the result of even the harshest resumption case, was, not the dispossession of the holder but the assessment of revenue on his holding, and even that in no case at more than half the prevailing rate'.[21]

In the upper provinces, Muslim grantees were certainly not destroyed as a class before 1857. The Revenue Proceedings for 1859, recording confiscations of holdings for rebellion in 1857, mention, for example, 255 Muslim *muᶜafidars* in Shahjahanpur district and 109 in Shikarpur *pargana*.[22] In Meerut district, there were 350 Muslim and 21 Hindu *muᶜafidars* mentioned in a return of 22 November 1858.[23] Nevertheless, the Revenue Proceedings for the years immediately before the Mutiny suggest a detailed inquisition by officials into revenue-free tenures, followed by resumption where the titles were deemed invalid, or where more land was held than the deed of grant or *sanad* specified. It is noteworthy that in the revenue proceedings examined for the North-Western Provinces between 1850 and 1856, the majority of petitioners against resumption were Muslim, if only as the lists of 1859 show because the majority of grant-holders were Muslim.

The majority of Muslim cultivators and landholders were converts or descendants of converts whose relationship to the soil was the same as that of the non-Muslims among whom they lived. British land and revenue policies affected them in the same way as they affected non-Muslims of the same status and relationship to land. The British encountered a system of land tenure which, though

---

[20] *Selections from the Government of India Records*, no. ccv, pp. 275–7.

[21] (Hunter) *Education Commission Report, 1882* (Calcutta, 1883), pp. 498–9.

[22] Report, dated 25 Jan. 1859 by Collector Shahjahanpur, *N.-W.P. Rev. Procs.. 14–30 April 1859*, Range 221, vol. 24. Report by F. Williams of 13 April 1859, *N.-W.P. Rev. Procs.*, Range 221, vol. 29.

[23] Proc. no. 67, report dated 22 Nov. 1858, *N.-W.P. Rev. Procs., Jan.–Feb. 1859*, Range 221, vol. 22.

they did not always recognise it to be so, was complex in detail, but simple in principle, resting as it did on occupancy, enjoyment and use, rather than on possession. Land was occupied and cultivated by families, brotherhoods, clans and tribes, linked by a common ancestry in village communities, united by a relationship to a common founder or founders, and enjoying an hereditary claim to undisturbed use so long as the gross produce of the soil was shared with the *zamindar* (if there was one) and with the government. Where a member of a village community or brotherhood died without heirs his land was divided among his former co-sharers. It was unusual for his holding to be transferred to a stranger or outsider.

Although the occupiers were subject to land revenue, they were not tenants of the 'state', for the 'state' claimed no rights of regulating the disposal of tenures and the land revenue was more a wage for a protector than a payment for the use of the soil. Between the actual cultivator and the government might stand an intermediate *zamindar*, who could be a member of a descendant of a conquering clan, the manager (or his descendants) of the original colonisation, someone who had engaged to pay revenue from a specified area to the 'state' or someone who had purchased that right or had been introduced by the 'state' as its revenue agent. Such a *zamindar* would normally receive for his pains a percentage of the revenue collected and a grant of revenue-free land, but would not enjoy rights of ownership in the soil of the area for which he was a revenue-collecting agent. He could, however, be the landlord of his self-cultivated holding and let it out to tenants. A cultivator who defaulted on the land revenue could expect perhaps to be assaulted, perhaps in the last resort to be expelled from his holding, but not to have his holding compulsorily sold to the highest bidder.

The British desired a land system which would ease the task of collecting the state's traditional share of the gross produce of the soil, promote agricultural production and create a loyal class of landholders. They abhorred, and did not understand, an agrarian society based on custom and tradition, in which land supported a pyramid of imprecise qualified rights to a share in its produce, rather than a clear doctrine of unqualified and absolute possession. In Bengal, on assumption of the *diwani* or revenue collectorship in 1765, they first adopted the line of least resistance and sought the quickest returns by contracting for the revenue demand with the *zamindars* and tax farmers they found. In 1772, however, having found that too much revenue was retained by these intermediaries, the revenue was farmed out to the highest bidders for periods of five years. After an attempt at annual settlement, in 1786 the Court of Directors of the East India Company expressed a preference for a long-term revenue settlement with the *zamindars*. In 1789–90 a decennial settlement was made with the *zamindars* of Bihar and Bengal and declared by Cornwallis in 1793 to be permanent, with a net sum of Rs. 26,800,989 payable to the government. But Cornwallis went further. By Regulation I of 1793, the *zamindars* were empowered to transfer 'their lands' by sale, gift or otherwise, without sanction of government – that is they became landlords. Regulation XVII of 1793 empowered the revenue engagers to distrain the property or sell the land of under tenants and cultivators for arrears of payment of revenue to them.

It is true that Regulation VIII of 1793 attempted to give security of tenure to cultivators, by providing that those who had held their land for twelve years were not to pay more and that *pattas* or deeds were to be granted to self-cultivating and resident farmers. But at one stroke the *zamindar* of Bengal, whether originally coloniser, freebooter, Mughal revenue agent or tax farmer, was transformed into what Dr Irfan Habib has felicitously described as 'that "pukka loyalist" of British Raj, the modern Indian landlord'. Those responsible for the Permanent Settlement believed not only that the Company would be spared the inquisition into Bengal agrarian society that it was so manifestly unqualified to undertake, but also that capital investment in land could and would, as in England, be made only by a class of improving landlords secure in their property and guaranteed against capricious exactions by government.

The Permanent Settlement meant, in the circumstances of eighteenth-century Bengal, the virtual closing of the door to landlordism to Muslims. The majority of those who had engaged for the payment of revenue with the East India Company, whether because they were *zamindars* in the Mughal sense or because they were revenue farmers, were Hindus. Under Murshid Quli Khan, chief revenue officer *(diwan)* and governor *(subadar)* of Bengal 1700–1727, most of the revenue collectors and *qanungos* (revenue record-keepers) were Hindus; under him revenue was collected by both *ʿamils* and *zamindars*, most of whom were Hindu. N. K. Sinha opines that nine-tenths of the *zamindaris* in Bengal were held by Hindus.[24] Of the fifteen biggest *zamindaris* only two were held by Muslims.[25] In the eastern and predominantly Muslim regions of Bengal, only one-tenth of the managers of *zamindari* estates were Musim[26] and of thirty-nine persons who engaged in 1774 for the payment of revenue in the settlement of Chittagong district, only ten were Muslim.[27]

The Muslim rulers of Bengal, many of whom were immigrants from the area of modern Uttar Pradesh, had confided the collection of revenue to those best fitted for it. The Muslim cultivators of east Bengal were illiterate and unfitted for clerical and administrative work. Moreover when, after the Permanent Settlement, speculators moved in to buy the new proprietory *zamindaris*, few Muslims were among them. The East India Company's command of the treasuries meant that the Muslim military aristocracy no longer possessed the liquid resources which could have been used for land purchase. They were also excluded or had excluded themselves from trade. Within twenty years of the Permanent Settlement, at least one-third of the landed property of Bengal was sold for arrears of revenue. The Hindu Rajas of Nadia, Rajshahi, Bishnipur and Kassijara were badly affected.

The long-term effect of the Permanent Settlement was to depress the status of the cultivator, whether Hindu or Muslim. No proper attempt was made by Cornwallis to ascertain the extent of the lands to which *zamindars* were given proprietory titles, and this enabled the *zamindars* to deprive cultivators of their customary rights to graze the pasture land and to use the waste land. Many *zamindars* were unable to manage their estates on commercial lines and farmed them out to middlemen, who squeezed the cultivators. Few culti-

[24] N. K. Sinha, *The Economic History of Bengal from Plassey to the Permanent Settlement*, vol. II (Calcutta, 1962), p. 229.
[25] A. H. M. Nooruzzaman, *Rise of the Muslim Middle Classes as a Political Factor in India and Pakistan 1858–1947* (unpublished doctoral thesis), London, 1964, p. 42.
[26] A. K. N. Karim, *The Modern Muslim Political Élite in Bengal*, (unpublished doctoral thesis) London, 1964, p. 272.
[27] A. M. Serajuddin, *The Revenue Administration of Chittagong from 1761 to 1785* (unpublished doctoral thesis), London, 1964, p. 154.

vators sought *pattas* (a written confirmation of rights), as provided for under Regulation VIII of 1793.

Most cultivators were poor and illiterate and ignorant of the rights conferred upon them. The *zamindar* did not want to limit his opportunities for levying cesses by a written record of payments due to him; the cultivator did not always want all the land he cultivated to be fully recorded. Cornwallis also found that the terms offered by the *zamindars* were often too high and that under Regulation IV of 1794, *zamindars* were empowered to post up those terms in their offices and recover their rents accordingly from the cultivators. Even when he had secured his rights in writing, it was almost impossible for a poor cultivator to have them enforced by a distant court following a strange procedure which opened the way to bought testimony.

The balance was kept permanently tilted in favour of the landlord by the increase in Bengal's population in the nineteenth century, when human beings became cheap and land dear. There is no reason to believe that Muslim cultivators individually suffered more than Hindu cultivators in this process, but there were more of them to suffer. As the majority of *zamindars* were Hindu, however, communal antagonism could arise. Moreover, the moneylenders into whose grip they fell in order to pay their rents were Hindu. The Muslim revivalist movements in Bengal (see below pp. 55–8) took on the character of a Muslim peasant revolt against Hindu landlords and moneylenders.

Muslims were better able to bear the introduction of landed proprietorship, as the English understood it, in the North-Western Provinces than in Bengal. There they were less polarised into vulnerable *mansabdars* and *jagirdars* at the one extreme and illiterate cultivators at the other. Muslims were to be found alongside Hindus as tenants, occupancy cultivators, village *zamindars*, *pargana zamindars*, *ta'alluqdars* (collecting revenue from *zamindars*), revenue farmers, revenue officials and accountants. Benares provides a classic illustration of the interpenetration of Hindus and Muslims in rural society. The Raja of Benares was a Hindu chief, obliged to furnish troops and money for his Muslim overlord, the Nawwab of Awadh. He employed both Hindu and Muslim *'amils* to collect revenue from *zamindari* brotherhoods both Hindu and Muslim, who in turn received a proportion of the gross produce from occupancy cultivators and tenants, both Hindu and Muslim.[28] Unlike Bengal, Muslims were prominent as *zamindars*, as headmen and as revenue collectors ('amils). In Ghazipur in 1789 Jonathan Duncan (1756–1811) made settlements with both Hindu and Muslim 'tribes'.[29] In 1788, of the seven 'amils responsible for 85 per cent of the Raja of Benares' revenue, three were Muslim and four Hindu.[30] In a revenue settlement in Rohilkhand in 1802, eleven of the revenue engagers were Muslim and eight Hindu.[31]

By the early years of the nineteenth century, when they acquired the Conquered and Ceded Territories, the British were aware that by the Permanent Settlement in Bengal they were sacrificing increments in revenue and that hereditary occupiers were being dispossessed. They were also aware that in these provinces, brotherhoods of cultivators and village communities engaged for the payment of revenue direct with government officials without the interposition of large *zamindars*. They therefore did not hasten to conclude a Permanent Settlement or to single out a particular rural class for the endowment of landlord rights. They began with temporary annual settlements and declared the rights of all *zamindars*, *ta'alluqdars* and other 'proprietors' in the lands comprising their *zamindari*, *ta'alluqdari* and other forms of 'property' as confirmed and established, but without investigating what those rights were. A Commission appointed to inquire into the expediency of a Permanent Settlement advised in 1808 against one, on the ground that the resources of the country had not been assessed, and their report was accepted by the Court of Directors in 1811.

After years of controversy, Regulation VII of 1822 provided for a detailed record of rights. Settlements were to be made with members of village communities wherever possible and all persons enjoying 'the power of disposing of the land by sale, gift or mortgage' were to be recognised as proprietors and admitted to direct engagements for payment of revenue. Where a cultivator

[28] A. Shakespear, *Selections from the Duncan Records*, vol. 1 (Benares, 1873), pp. 170, 172, 178. See also: Bernard S. Cohen, 'Political Systems in Eighteenth Century India: the Banaras Region', *Journal of the American Oriental Society*, LXXXII, 3, July–Sept., 1962.

[29] Wilton Oldham, *Memoir of the Ghazipur District* (Allahabad, 1870), p. 41.

[30] Cohen, 'Political Systems', p, 420.

[31] *Bengal Revenue Consultations, 26 August–30 Sept. 1802*, (India Office Library) Range 54, vol. 27. Reference kindly provided by Mr Waheed al-Haq.

was a co-parcener he was not to forfeit his holding if the *malguzar* or fellow co-parcener singled out by the Collector to pay the revenue due from the whole partnership defaulted upon his obligations. Where a settlement was made with a large *zamindar* or *ta'alluqdar*, sub-settlements were to be made with hereditary occupancy cultivators and their due payments to the revenue engager and their rights recorded Although Regulation IX of 1833 speeded up the settlement by laying down simpler procedures and a definite rate of assessment (66 per cent of net assets of an estate) and by specifying thirty-year settlements, it did not change the rules for defining those with whom the settlement was to be made.

Although British policy in the North-Western Provinces did not, as in Bengal, create a class of large landlords receiving rent from increasingly unprotected tenants, it did have a similar effect in creating a market in land and in bringing about a wholesale transfer of landed rights between different classes, castes and tribes. (It must be emphasised that this transfer affected only the revenue- or rent-collecting right and did not normally bring about the eviction from the land itself of the actual cultivator or of the dispossessed previous revenue-engager.)[31a] There is no reason to believe, however, that before 1857 Muslims as such suffered more in this transfer than non-Muslims, or failed to take advantage of such opportunities of self-enrichment as were going.

For example, in the early years of British rule, *tahsildars* and Indian officials in the Collectorates conspired to keep some 'estates' in arrears of revenue, so that they could be compulsorily auctioned and purchased cheaply by themselves or their children. Later settlement reports reveal that the ancestors of many Muslims landholding families of the eighteen-seventies and eighties enriched themselves in this way. One Ahmad Bakhsh, *tahsildar* of Ghatampur, bought in the name of one of his servants estates yielding a revenue of nearly fifty thousand rupees for a mere Rs. 6,670. Nasir 'Ali, *diwan* in the collector's office at Cawnpore, bought eighty-one 'estates' for

[31a] Bernard S. Cohen, 'Structural Change in Indian Rural Society 1596–1885', chapter IV of Robert Eric Frykenberg (ed.), *Land Control and Social Structure in Indian History* (Madison, Milwaukee and London, 1969), pp. 90–1, 111–12. The detailed data given by Professor Cohen on the effect of compulsory auction-sales of *zamindari* rights in the Benares region support the contention here that Muslims did not, *as such*, fare unjustly as a result of such sales.

Rs. 79,968.[32] W. Irvine (1840–1911), in his Ghazipur settlement report, states that one Karimullah (Karim-Allah), a *tahsildar* of Zamania was an auction-purchaser between 1795 and 1807. He mentions other Muslims, pleaders, court officials and revenue men, who bought land in this early period.[33] The Azamgarh settlement report tells a similar story.[34]

The settlements following Regulation IX of 1833 greatly enhanced the revenue assessment and forced sales and transfers of land from defaulters. Examination of revenue proceedings in the five years preceding the Mutiny has not revealed that Muslims were at any special disadvantage, or were subjected to discrimination in the disposal of estates. For example, in August 1854 the Board of Revenue handed over an estate in the district of Banda to 'two respectable landowners in that district', one a Hindu and the other a Muslim.[35] In Rohilkhand division, land recorded as under the proprietorship of three Hindus was leased to two Muslims. In Allahabad division, land belonging to twenty-four Hindus was leased to five Hindus and one Muslim.[36] In the second quarter of 1855–6, also in Allahabad, the holdings of eighty-four named defaulting Hindu *pattadars* (lessees) were transferred to three named Muslims. Elsewhere in this return the holdings of defaulting Muslim *pattadars* (lessees) were transferred to Muslims and of Hindu *pattadars* to Hindus.[37] In a return for the first quarter of 1856–7 for Rohilkhand, Meerut, Agra and Allahabad divisions, forty-six Muslim defaulters had their holdings transferred to two Muslims and two Hindus and thirty-three Hindu holdings were transferred to four Hindus.[38]

---

[32] F. V. Wright, *Final Report on the Settlement of the Cawnpore District* (Allahabad, 1878), pp. 32–3.

[33] W. Irvine. *Report on the Revision of Records in the Ghazipur District* (Allahabad, 1886), pp. 32–3, 60.

[34] J. C. Reid, *Report on the Settlement Operations in the District of Azimgarh* (Allahabad, 1881), pp. 79, 81, 84.

[35] Procs. nos. 337–43, Index to *N.-W.P. Rev. Procs. 1854*, India Office Library Range 220, vol. 46 *s.v.* Banda.

[36] Procs. nos 734–6, *N.-W.P. Rev. Procs., 16–31 March 1855*, Range 220, vol. 51.

[37] *Abstract Statement of Transfer of Rights of Defaulting Pattidars* in second quarter of 1855–56. Proc. no. 400, *N.-W.P. Rev. Procs.*, Range 220, vol. 77.

[38] Proc. no. 561 for 31 December 1956, *N.-W.P. Rev. Procs, 11–31 December 1856*, Range 221, vol. 13.

Contemporary data on the effect of land transfers on the amount of land held by members of different communities is hard to come by. Such statistics as there are in the revenue proceedings before 1857 ignore community membership. Figures in the settlement reports of the eighteen-seventies and eighties often essay a percentage estimate of landholding by different castes and communities since the settlements of the eighteen-thirties and forties, but do not specify when transfers occurred. The figures include confiscations for rebellion in 1857–8. *Prima facie*, however, it does not appear that Muslims as such suffered unfairly. According to the settlement report for Agra of 1880, Muslims had lost 7,904 acres from all causes since the previous settlement in 1841. In the same period, excluding confiscation from rebellion, *thakurs* (Hindu landholders) lost 45,000 acres.[39] In the Allahabad district there was a fall of only 1.6 per cent in the land held by Muslims between 1839 and 1877.[40] In the trans-Gangetic tract of this division they lost over 13,000 acres, but in the trans-Jumna tract gained 23,000 acres.[41] In the Benares district between 1840 and 1887 there was a 1.39 per cent falling off in the number of Hindu landholders and a 1.41 per cent increase in the number of Muslim landholders.[42] It is not suggested that these figures and the settlement reports in general do more than establish a *prima facie* case that Muslims and non-Muslims alike shared a common lot under British revenue and agrarian policies and that before 1857 Muslims succeeded in maintaining their position as a substantial landed interest in the North-Western Provinces.

In sum then, the establishment of British rule in India affected different classes of Muslims in different ways. For a minority it destroyed not a livelihood, but a way of life, and damaged not so much their pockets as their pride. For the Mughal court at Delhi and the Muslim aristocracy attached to it, life under British patronage was probably materially no worse than life under Maratha patronage – but the patronage was made more galling by a

[39] H. F. Evans, *Report on the Settlement of the Agra District* (Allahabad, 1880), p. 43.
[40] F. W. Porter, *Final Report on the Settlement of the Allahabad District* (Allahabad, 1878), p. 54.
[41] Porter, *Final Report*, p. 53.
[42] F. W. Porter, *Final Report on the Survey and Revision of Records recently completed for the Benares District* (Allahabad, 1887), p. 7.

generation of British functionaries who put a low price upon the Mughal past and the Mughal present in the market of utility, who scorned gentility and poetry and those who did not live laborious lives (and could not because the British were there to prevent them living the only laborious lives they knew – of fighting and politicking). The Muslim *jagirdar*, subject to inquisition by office clerks in the North-Western Provinces, and removed in Bengal, knew that he now lived on sufferance in a closed society and that his opportunities to become a Nawwab of Farrukhabad were over. The Muslim soldier fared badly. At most he could look forward to a life in the service of a British magistrate, as a strong-arm man to a *zamindar* bullying cultivators in Bengal, in the Company's army, or, if he were very fortunate, in the small army of the Nawwab of Awadh on meagre pay and with no prospects of glory and fortune. The Muslim civil servant, at least in the upper provinces, could, however, expect a modest competence and, in the earliest days of Company rule, a chance of enrichment through his knowledge of British revenue regulations and courts and ability to rig land auctions. The Muslim cultivator, *zamindar* and *ta⁰alluqdar* did not suffer more than others from the introduction of landlordism, although in Bengal there were more Muslim cultivators to suffer. Probably more Muslim *mu⁰afidars* than non-Muslim *mu⁰afidars* suffered from resumptions, but again because there were more of them. Similarly, the handloom weavers of fine silks, muslins and cottons of Dacca, both Hindu and Muslim, suffered from Lancashire competition and as most were Muslim, more Muslims suffered.

THE MUSLIM REVIVALIST REACTION

But some Muslims were prepared to object publicly to the way history was going in early nineteenth-century India. They were those who as Muslim scholars did not care to see the express commands of God openly disregarded, those upon whom British rule was quicker to take effect and those who had no expectation, as the former ruling *élite* of the upper provinces (reasonably or unreasonably) had, that the British would recognise their merits.

Muslim scholars (*⁰ulama*) had been slow to react publicly to British rule, perhaps because the East India Company had only very gradually departed from the medieval *modus vivendi* between the religious and the political establishment. Until 1790, penal justice in Bengal continued to be dispensed according to the revived *shariᶜa* norms of Aurangzib's time, and Regulation II of 1772 had provided that 'in all suits regarding inheritance, succession, marriage and caste and other usages and institutions, the law of the Qur'an with respect to Muhammadans. . .shall be invariably adhered to'. But in the last decade of the eighteenth century and in the first decade of the nineteenth, the East India Company began by legislation to substitute its own rules of evidence, definitions of offences and penalties for those of the *shariᶜa*. The leading Delhi scholar, Shah ᶜAbd al-ᶜAziz (1746–1824), son of Shah Wali-Allah, protested at this formal interference with the substantive content of the Islamic Holy Law, by declaring those areas of northern India under British supremacy to be *dar al-harb* (the abode of war).[43] But this was an academic ruling by an academician to ease the consciences of those obliged to live under non-Muslim laws administered by non-Muslims. Saiyid Ahmad of Rai Bareilly (1786–1831) made a more active call to Muslims to stand up for Islam as a public way of life, but even he did not openly resist the East India Company in its territories.

Saiyid Ahmad was born into an obscure family, possibly in minor official service. Tradition has it that he found reading and writing difficult, but that in 1807 he had been accepted as a pupil by Shah ᶜAbd al-ᶜAziz and initiated into the Naqshbandi, Qadiri and Chishti orders. From about 1809 to 1818 he was a trooper under the Pindari chieftain, Amir Khan, later the *nawwab* of Tonk; probably there was nothing to distinguish him outwardly from other Pindari freebooters. The later story that he tried to influence Amir Khan against making peace with the British is apocryphal. After the suppression of the Pindaris, Saiyid Ahmad returned to Delhi where he attached himself to Shah ᶜAbd al-ᶜAziz. (The *Malfuzat* of Shah ᶜAbd al-ᶜAziz testifies to his being in the latter's company.) He formed ties with Shah Ismaᶜil (1781–1831) and Maulawi ᶜAbd al-Haiy (d. 1828) nephew and son-in-law respectively of Shah ᶜAbd al-ᶜAziz. Between the middle of 1819 and July 1821 he stayed in Rai Bareilly; Shah Ismaᶜil probably

---

[43] *Fatawa-i ᶜAzizi*, part 1 (Delhi, 1311/1893–4), p. 17.

compiled the *Sirat-i Mustaqim* (The Straight Path), a rendering of Saiyid Ahmad's ideas, during this period and preaching began.

In July 1821 Saiyid Ahmad started the journey to Mecca, to perform *hajj*, travelling by way of Calcutta. Arriving at Mecca in May 1822, he returned to India in November 1823. The next two years were spent in teaching, organising his followers and collecting funds in the upper provinces. In January 1826, however, he left Rai Bareilly and after a circuitous journey of nearly three thousand miles through Rajputana, Sind, Baluchistan and Afghanistan with his followers he reached Charsadda in the Hashtnagar district. From there he declared a *jihad* against the Sikh ruler of the Panjab, Ranjit Singh. In a night attack upon the Sikhs near Naushera the *mujahidin* were successful and Saiyid Ahmad was joined by neighbouring Pathan chiefs, including the *sardars* of Peshawar.

In January 1827 Saiyid Ahmad was declared *imam* and *bai*ʿ*a* offered to him. It was difficult to impose unity upon the Pathan tribesmen and after a betrayal by one of the Peshawar *sardars*, Yar Muhammad Khan, the *mujahidin* were defeated at Shaidu near Akora in March 1827. Saiyid Ahmad now toured the Pathan tribal areas gathering recruits and moved his headquarters to Panjtar. He defeated Yar Muhammad Khan and was able to establish himself at Peshawar in 1830. The local Pathans resented control by outsiders, even in the name of Islam, and rose against Saiyid Ahmad's tax collectors, murdering many and forcing him to return to Panjtar. In May 1831 at Balakot on the Kaghan river, in an area where he was trying to enlist the local chiefs against the Sikhs in Hazara and Kashmir, he, Shah Ismaʿil and nearly six hundred of his followers were killed.

It is not extravagant to see significant parallels between the career of Saiyid Ahmad of Bareilly and that of Muhammad the Prophet himself – indeed later Muslim historians and biographers may have sensed, or unconsciously suggested, certain structural similarities between them. Both were men of action rather than men of the pen; both migrated with faithful followers from an unpromising to a more promising locale; both had to work with unruly tribesmen and both struggled to establish an Islamic state on the fringe of powerful empires by defying the local powers by force.

But there any parallels end: Saiyid Ahmad's world was suffused by sufism and so were his teachings. Indeed he described his path as the *tariqa-i muhammadi*, the Muhammadan mystical path. Although he proclaimed the love of a prophet for God to be superior to that of a mystic, because a prophet is concerned to create the good society on earth whereas the mystic is concerned only with his own soul's welfare,[44] the path of sainthood and the path of prophethood are complementary. Saiyid Ahmad is himself represented as having first acquired the special graces vouchsafed through the Chishti, Naqshbandi and Qadiri mystic orders, before acquiring those vouchsafed through the *tariqa-i muhammadi*. Before he went on *hajj* in 1821, he preached a reformed sufism, purged of *shirk* or polytheism, of intercession of saints to perform acts that only God can perform, and of worship of all other than God. He and Shah Isma'il condemned pilgrimage to Hindu holy places, participation in Hindu festivals, consulting Brahmans and resorting to astrologers and fortune-tellers.[45] He tried to weaken the Indo-Muslim prejudice against widow-remarriage. But he did not set up as a *faqih* or canon lawyer.

It was the *sufi* idiom of Saiyid Ahmad's early reforming activities that distinguished them from those of the Wahhabis in near-contemporary Arabia, who attacked the *sufi* orders. Saiyid Ahmad of Bareilly, following the tradition of Shah Wali-Allah, wished to expurgate, not to expunge sufism in India. Arabian Wahhabism no doubt helped turn Saiyid Ahmad's thoughts towards an active military *jihad*, though precedents were not wanting in India itself for reforming brotherhoods to become military brotherhoods – as in the militant Raushaniyya movement on the north-west frontier in the sixteenth century, and indeed in Sikhism.

Saiyid Ahmad Bareilly left behind him among Indian Muslims what the Prophet had left behind him in Arabia, an affirmative rather than an affirmation, the affirmative of the Islamic society made actual. From February 1829 the Holy Law governed, or so it was recorded, the community of the *mujahidin*. As the Prophet, according to Muslim tradition, wrote letters to the great powers of his day calling upon them to accept his prophethood, so Saiyid Ahmad, according to reformist tradition, wrote letters to Muslim

---

[44] Shah Isma'il, *Sirat-i Mustaqim*, (Persian text) (Calcutta, 1823), pp. 58–60, 67–8.

[45] Mir Shahamat Ali, 'Translation of the Takwiyat ul-Iman', *Journal of the Royal Asiatic Society*, 1852, pp. 320–57, *passim*.

rulers in Central Asia under the title of *amir al-mu'minin* (commander of the faithful), calling upon them to recognise his *khilafat*. He described how Hindustan had fallen under the rule of Christians and how he would strive to free it and to establish the supremacy of the *shari°a* over it.[46]

In the event the new *umma* on the frontier fell prey to Pathan unruliness, to the hostility of Pathan chiefs (who felt as the Meccan oligarchy had felt, the threat from a charismatic religious leader to their own position) and to the superior military power of the Sikhs. But the new militant *umma* did not die with him on the field of Balakot. The surviving *mujahidin* eventually found a refuge in remote Sittana where they continued to obey mandates of the *shari°a* long fallen in desuetude in India – collecting the °*ushr* or tithe for benevolent purposes and levying fines for non-attendance at prayer. The organisation of an 'underground apparatus' in India for the transmission to the frontier of men and supplies (chiefly from Bengal), maintained the existence of the community. Before his death Saiyid Ahmad Bareilly had sent a number of deputies, including two brothers, Maulawi Wilayat °Ali (1791–1853) and °Inayat °Ali (1794–1858) of Patna, to organise the indispensable 'tail' of the army of the faithful on the frontier. They in turn sent 'missionaries on mission' to tour India both to preach and to organise 'fiscal circles' under collectors to collect funds which would eventually be forwarded to the *mujahidin* on the frontier.

The British were early apprised of Saiyid Ahmad's campaigns against the Sikhs, through their political agents in Sikh territory. After his death they correctly gauged that his followers intended the eventual overthrow of British rule, but recognising the reformist religious aims as not necessarily identical with the long-term political aims, they thought prosecution would savour of persecution.[47] The British noted in the early eighteen-forties that °Inayat °Ali was collecting funds and preaching *jihad* against the Sikhs. °Inayat °Ali, joined later by Wilayat °Ali, was active on the frontier between 1844 and 1847. They were both captured by the British when the latter took over control of the frontier region after the

---

[46] (Persian) *Correspondence of Saiyid Ahmad*, British Museum MS. Or. 6635, fols. 27a–27b.

[47] Proc. no. 29 of 14 August 1839, *India Secret Consultations*, India Office Library, vol. 23, for 7–28 August 1839.

first Sikh war. Both brothers were sent back to Patna and obliged
to take out a bond for good behaviour. Earlier, in 1839, the
brother of the Nizam of Hyderabad had been involved in a conspiracy to overthrow his brother and was alleged to have employed
followers of Saiyid Ahmad to suborn native troops of the Company
stationed in Hyderabad. The first direct clash between the *mujahidin* of Sittana and British forces occurred in 1852 at Kotla, after
the final British annexation of the Panjab, but it was no more than
a frontier skirmish. It seems that the *mujahidin* then numbered
some 600 men and were receiving between twenty and forty thousand rupees a year from the Nawwab of Tonk, as well as larger
sums from Bengal.

Contemporary with Saiyid Ahmad Bareilly there arose in Bengal
another religious movement, less chiliastic in aim and closer to the
daily struggle for existence of the Muslim cultivator – the *fara'izi*.[48]
Its founder, Hajji Shari°at-Allah (1781–1840) was born at Shamail
(now in the Faridpur division of Bangladesh), probably of a petty
ta°alluqdari family (that is, in Bengal, a small landholding family
who had also contracted to pay revenue on behalf of other small
landholders). After a traditional education in Arabic and Persian
in Hughli district, he accompanied his teacher, Maulana Basharat
°Ali, on pilgrimage to Mecca in 1799 and did not return to Bengal
until 1818.

After a second *hajj*, in about 1821 he began preaching, moving
about the districts of Faridpur, Bakarganj, Dacca and Mymensingh. His message was simple, but, in the context of popular Islam
in Bengal, revolutionary. It was that Muslims should observe strictly
the duties (*fara'iz* hence *fara'izi*) enjoined by Qur'an and *sunna*
and maintain God's unity (*tauhid*) and exclusive efficacy. A disciple
signified his readiness to accept his responsibility by respecting a
formula of repentance (*tauba*) after a spiritual guide and undertaking to live strictly according to the Qur'an and *sunna*. The
fara'izi must forswear any belief or action smacking of unbelief
(*kufr*) or innovation (*bid°at*), such as participating in Hindu cere-
monies and revering local deities or *pirs*.

Thus far there was nothing in Hajji Shari°at-Allah's programme

---

[48] The account of the *fara'izi* movement follows closely Muin-ud-din
Ahmad Khan, *History of the Fara'idi Movement in Bengal (1818–1906)*
(Karachi, 1965).

that a disciple of Saiyid Ahmad Bareilly or indeed of Shah ʿAbd ʿAziz could not accept. The *faraʾizis*, however, held that so long as the British ruled in Bengal, the congregational prayers on *jumʿa* (Friday) and at ʿid (festival) should not be performed, on the ground that they must not be performed anywhere except in a *misr al-jamiʿ* (a town where an *amir*, or governor, and a *qazi*, or religious judge properly appointed by an independent *khalifa* or *sultan*, are stationed). In this doctrine the *faraʾizis* claimed to be following *hanafi* doctrine and in legal matters they generally followed this *mazhab*.

Although the doctrine of the suspension of *jumʿa* and ʿid prayers implied that Bengal was *dar-al-harb*, Hajji Shariʿat-Allah did not preach *jihad* against the British, but concentrated on his mission of religious purification. His son Dudu Miyan (1819–62), however, turned to social and political militancy. The supporters of the *faraʾizi* movement were mostly depressed Muslim cultivators sinking into the sea of landless labourers, oppressed by their mainly Hindu landlords or by the new class of European indigo planters, who treated their 'native' labour almost as plantation slaves. Dudu Miyan asserted the equality of man before God and campaigned against the levy of illegal cesses by landlords, on the ground that money screwed from Muslim peasants might be spent on Hindu religious rites. He organised violent resistance to the levy of such cesses. Some landlords retaliated by torturing their tenants to discourage them from joining the *faraʾizis*. The British administration in Bengal, which was responsible for the Permanent Settlement which had conferred such advantages upon landlords over cultivators, held the balance tilted in favour of the landlords, by trying to enforce the 'law and order' of the *status quo*.

Dudu Miyan was repeatedly charged before the British courts, of plunder in 1838, of murder in 1841 and of unlawful assembly in 1844, but the prosecutions failed for lack of evidence, or rather of witnesses. However, in 1847 Dudu Miyan and sixty-three of his followers were convicted by the (European) Sessions Judge of Faridpur of setting fire to an indigo factory at Panch Char belonging to a Mr Dunlop. The conviction was quashed on appeal to the Calcutta *Sadr Nizamat ʿAdalat* (Chief Criminal Court), on the ground of the untrustworthiness of the prosecution's evidence.

Before he died, Dudu Miyan had turned a missionary brother-

hood into a military brotherhood. He organised a volunteer force of
fara'izi cudgel-bearers to fight the *zamindars* and established a
hierarchy of district 'commissars' called *khalifas* at village, town-
ship and district level, responsible to the *ustad* or chief of the
fara'izis, namely Dudu Miyan himself. Each *khalifa* was head of
an underground organisation, responsible for propaganda, the collection of funds and the settlement of disputes among members of
the movement. The *fara'izis* were not allowed to bring disputes before the British courts without permission from a senior *khalifa*
and it is claimed that in many districts of east Bengal a legal *imperium in imperio* came into existence. In the later nineteenth
century however, after the death of Dudu Miyan, possibly through
the introduction of tenancy legislation and partly through the
controversy aroused among Muslims by the *fara'izi* refusal to say
the *jum'a* and *'id* prayers, the strength of the *fara'izi* movement
declined, until today they are found in any numbers only in two
subdivisions of Dacca district and in two subdivisions in Tippera
district.

The most violent of these Bengali Muslim 'Lollard' movements,
and the one which required British military action for its suppression, was that led by Titu Mir. Born in 1782 in Chandpur in the
Twenty-Four Parganas, Titu Mir was described in government
records as a wrestler and as leading in the Calcutta district until
about 1815 the life of 'a bad and desperate character'. Apparently
he acted as 'a strong-arm man' for some Hindu *zamindars* at Nadia
and was imprisoned for an affray. But by 1827 he was campaigning
in favour of a purified Islam, in an idiom similar to that of Saiyid
Ahmad Bareilly and Hajji Shari'at-Allah. His sphere of operations was mainly in west Bengal. He directed his followers to grow
beards and to tie their *dhotis* in a distinctive fashion.

Some Hindu *zamindars* seized the opportunity offered by opposition to part of his message among their Muslim cultivators to fine
some of his followers on their estates for wearing beards. Appeal to
the British magistracy against this 'cess' having failed, Titu Mir's
followers attacked a village within the estate of one of the offending
zamindars, slaughtered a cow in a public place and defiled the
village temple with its blood. Open warfare between Titu Mir
and the *zamindars* followed and Titu Mir did not hesitate to
attack Muslim *zamindars* hostile to his movement. After several

districts of west Bengal, including the Twenty-Four Parganas, Nadia and Faridpur, had become a battleground between the *zamindars* and the followers of Titu Mir, the government intervened. The police and auxiliaries sent from Calcutta were defeated and the British authorities were obliged to despatch a regiment of native infantry to deal with what had become a *jacquerie*. In November 1831 they destroyed the insurgents' stockade at Narkulbaria in Baraset district, killed Titu Mir and fifty of his followers and arrested about three hundred and fifty. Muslim agrarian revolt in west Bengal was thus snuffed out.

The reform movement of Saiyid Ahmad Bareilly and of the *fara'izis* contributed to the gradual (and in the event incomplete) transformation of the Indian Muslim community from an aggregate of believers into a political association with a will for joint action. In medieval times, Muslim scholars had looked to the autocratic ruler to 'save Islam'. Shaikh Ahmad Sirhindi had written letters to notables; Aurangzib had used his autocratic authority; Shah Wali-Allah had looked to an Ahmad Shah ʿAbdali or a Najib al-daula to rescue India for Islam. The reformist movements of the nineteenth century enlisted Muslims outside the former ruling circles – of whom Saiyid Ahmad was openly critical for their willingness to act as collaborators of the British[49] – in effect trying to achieve a juster and more god-fearing society by popular co-operation.

Saiyid Ahmad Bareilly aimed not to restore the Mughals or the Mughal aristocracy, but to create a facsimile of the early Muslim community on the borders of India, in the belief that it would one day inspire Muslims to conquer India for God. His message appealed not to the higher but to the humbler strata of Muslim society in India, to the 'lower-middle' classes of pre-industrial society, to petty landholders, country-town *mullas*, to teachers, book-sellers, small shopkeepers, minor officials and skilled artisans. It was members of these classes who, when enfranchised after 1919 under British-sponsored constitutions, were to respond passionately to the call of religion in politics. The sympathisers with the militant reform movements in British India were the non-jurors of the Muslim community, galling the consciences of comfortable Muslims and helping to provide them with constituents and followers when such Muslims had learnt the power of a call to Islam in politics.

[49] (Persian) *Correspondence of Saiyid Ahmad*, fol. 54b.

Nevertheless, the contemporary force of the reformist movements of the nineteenth century should not be exaggerated. A tiny majority of the Muslim population at any time actively joined Saiyid Ahmad's movement or gave money, or indeed preached in favour of the purification of Indian Muslim belief and custom. The reformers themselves splintered ideologically as much as any Jacobins or Marxists; they encountered bitter opposition doctrinally from many *ᶜulama*. Wilayat ᶜAli, while preferring injunctions derived directly from the Qur'an and from the Prophet's *hadith*, was prepared to allow *taqlid* or obedience to the rulings of the *sunni mazahib* where the Muslim was not sufficiently learned to come to proper conclusions from Qur'an and *hadith* himself.[50] This was too much for Maulana Karamat ᶜAli (d. 1873) and his followers the *taᶜaiyunis* (those who identify themselves with the schools of law), who insisted that the rulings of the four *mazahib* must be followed, with preference for the school of Abu Hanifa. It was too little for the *ahl-i hadith* (the People of the Prophetic Tradition) who, led by Siddiq Hasan (d. 1890) and Saiyid Nazir Husain (d. 1902), campaigned from the eighteen-sixties for complete conformity to Prophetic Tradition, rejecting the rulings of the four *mazahib* if necessary. Furthermore, the *shiᶜa* remained aloof from the *tariqa-i muhammadi*.

The Muslim reform movements of the nineteenth century helped to transform Muslim attitudes towards Hindus. They were essentially rejections of medieval Islam in India in favour of early Islam in Arabia. They were not movements confined to the library and to the study; their exponents did not merely formulate intellectual positions against monism, but went out and preached against the customs which so many Muslims shared with Hindus – intercession at the tombs of saints, consultation of Brahmins, even vegetarianism and aversion to the remarriage of widows. Muslims in India were to be made aware of what they did not share with their non-Muslim neighbours. India could be made by the reformers to feel not like a home, but like a habitat. The religious and social activism of Dudu Miyan and Titu Mir in Bengal could result in a social and economic conflict assuming a communal guise. In the condition of Bengal under the Permanent Settlement, where the majority of *zamindars* were Hindu, the conflation of Muslim and of exploited tenant, of

50 Muin-ud-din Ahmad Khan, *Fara'idi Movement*, pp. liv–lv.

Hindu and exploiting landlord was inevitable, although in fact Muslim landlords treated their Muslim tenants no differently than did Hindu landlords.

The reform movements moreover dealt another blow to the composite upper-class Mughal culture, already waning as its chief centres came under British domination. Poetry, painting, the cultivation of the senses, the urbane nostalgia of gentlemen, whether Muslim or Hindu, for 'better days', all had to give place to the harsh exigencies of religious rectitude, as they were giving way to the harsh utilities of commercial rectitude.

The militancy of Saiyid Ahmad Bareilly's and Dudu Miyan's followers was to have profound long-term effects on British political strategy in India. It helped to reinforce the British belief after 1857 that Muslims were by nature fanatical and irreconcilable and could only be kept quiet by a judicious mixture of buffets and boons, not necessarily, however, to be administered to the same Muslims. For the reformist movements, with their attacks on landlords and their disrespect for family and position, alarmed the 'better-class' Muslim. The British saw this and by offering favours to those Muslims with something to lose were able to isolate and contain the actively disaffected.

Because, in thinking about Muslims after 1857, the so-called Wahhabis were for the British the great unthinkable that was always thought, the British were usually ready to meet the demands of 'respectable' Muslims more than half way. But it took the trauma of the Mutiny and Rebellion of 1857–8 to open up these political perspectives. Before 1857 British policies were generally speaking 'community-blind'; Muslims were members of 'a fallen race' or in George Campbell's words,[51] 'the most gentlemanly and well-mannered' of those seeking employment under the Company. By 1888 however, for the then Viceroy, Lord Dufferin, they had become 'one of the two mighty political communities' of 'our Indian "cosmos"'.[52]

[51] George Campbell, *Modern India*, (London, 1852), p. 291.
[52] Dufferin, Minute on Provincial Councils enclosed with the letter of 11 Nov. 1888, no. 25, Letters from Dufferin to Cross, vol. v, *Papers of the First Viscount Cross*, India Office Library, EUR E 243.

3

1857 AND ITS AFTERMATH

For both the Muslims of northern India and the British, the events of 1857 were a trauma. The savage British suppression of the Mutiny and Rising, with its destruction of Delhi as a centre of Muslim culture, and the dispersion of the descendants of Akbar and Aurangzib by execution and exile, at last forced educated Muslims to realise not only that the British were in India to stay, but also that they intended to stay on their own terms. The last illusions that they were the mayors of the Mughal palace were dissipated; the last illusions that an education in Persian and Urdu and in the Muslim religious sciences would serve both a Muslim's eternal and his worldly welfare were torn away. The British, though a mere handful of men, had successfully defied the hosts of Zion, or rather of Mecca. Their behaviour in 1857 showed that success owed nothing to superior virtue; it must therefore be success of a superior technique, the sources of which could no longer be ignored.

The British historian of British India often fails to appreciate how little British rule had touched the minds and still less the hearts of Muslims in India before 1857. Conscious that there was profound debate over whether the British should interfere with Indian custom and religious practices or whether they should introduce English education in English, the British historian often overlooks how British culture appeared to Indians and particularly Muslims before 1857. Eaters of pork and drinkers of wine, who paraded their women in the bare-shouldered evening fashions of the early Victorian age, builders of graceless bungalows, unskilled in the *ghazal*, always counting their – or worse, other people's – money and contemptuous of what they did not understand, the British added boorishness and arrogance, scandalous laxity and repulsive habits to their undoubted infidelity. It is not surprising, therefore, that before 1857 Muslims in India were more concerned to purify their own religion than to imitate or even to notice a culture in their eyes barely worth the

61

name. Now after 1857 that culture, however distasteful, would have to be considered, not for its worth, but for its worldly success. Perhaps 1857 was a divine punishment, if not for sin then for ignorance.

For the British, the effect of 1857 was to make them conscious of Muslims as Muslims and to endow them, at least in British thinking about them, with a corporate political character which in British eyes Muslims had not previously possessed. Not immediately and not quite decisively, but after a lapse of a decade, the Mutiny and Rising of 1857 were to usher in the period of balance and rule with the Muslims (and the British now began to think in terms of *the* Muslims as a collectivity) occupying one of the pans of the balance. Before 1857 the servants of the East India Company would have liked to treat India as if it were inhabited by rational individuals capable of pursuing their own enlightened self-interest; after 1857 the officials of the Crown began to regard India as inhabited by communities bound together by unreasoning sentiment and requiring not guidance but manipulation.

THE MUSLIM INVOLVEMENT

For most British observers in 1857 a Muslim meant a rebel. Dr Metcalf has recently summed up the typical British attitude.[1]

The first sparks of disaffection it was generally agreed, were kindled among the Hindu sepoys who feared an attack upon their caste. But the Muslims then fanned the flames of discontent and placed themselves at the head of the movement, for they saw in these religious grievances the stepping stone to political power. In the British view it was Muslim intrigue and Muslim leadership that converted a sepoy mutiny into a political conspiracy, aimed at the extinction of the British Raj.

Sir William Muir (1819–1905), whose *Life of Mohammed* (1858–1861) and *The Caliphate, its Rise, Decline, and Fall* (1891) helped to foster the myth of the Muslim as always armed with the sword in one hand and the Qur'an in the other, wrote to his brother in October 1857,[2]

[1] Thomas R. Metcalf, *The Aftermath of Revolt: India 1857–1870* (Princeton, 1965), p. 298.
[2] Sir William Muir, *Records of the Intelligence Department of the North-West Provinces of India during the Mutiny of 1857*, vol. 1 (Edinburgh, 1902), p. 46.

The Musulmans, while they thought their cause had a fair chance of final success have frequently compromised themselves by flagrantly traitorous acts. At Allygurh, for instance, the Mussulmans were for a considerable time dominant; they forcibly converted many Hindoos; they defied our Government in the most insolent manner; all the ancient feelings of warring for the Faith, reminding one of the days of the first Caliphs, were resuscitated.

'That the proclamation', he wrote, 'of the King of Delhi's reign should unsettle the allegiance of the Moslems was to be expected from the singularly close combination of the political and religious elements in the system of Islam.'[3]

John Lawrence (1811–79), on 14 June 1857, wrote to the Governor-General, Lord Canning (1812–62), 'The Mahommedans of the Regular Cavalry when they have broken out have displayed a more active, vindictive and fanatic spirit than the Hindoos – but these traits are characteristic of the race.'[4] Charles Raikes (1812–85), Collector at Agra, writing while passions were still raging, saw the Muslims as innately hostile to the British. 'The green flag of Mahomed too had been unfurled, the mass of the followers of the false prophet rejoicing to believe that under the auspices of the Great Mogal of Delhi their lost ascendancy was to be recovered, their deep hatred to the Christian got vent, and they rushed forth to kill and destroy.'[5]

It would have needed minds much less knocked off balance by fear and wounded pride than those of most Britons in India in 1857 to disregard the evidence of Muslim responsibility for mutiny and rebellion. The *suwars* (troopers) of the 3rd Native Cavalry, among the first units to be provoked into mutiny, were Muslim. It was they who rode off from Meerut to Delhi to set up Bahadur Shah at the head of the rebellion. Nor did the Mughals at Delhi appear reluctant to assume the *rôle* assigned to them. Bahadur Shah had no cause to love the Europeans, who were going to reduce his family after his death to retired gentlefolk living in a 'grace and favour residence' near the Qutb Minar, one of the earliest monuments to Muslim conquest in India. By nightfall on 11 May 1857, the day after the

---

[3] Muir, *Intelligence Records*, vol. II (Edinburgh, 1902), p. 258.
[4] Letter no. 61 of *Letters from Chief Commissioner Punjab, Canning Papers* (formerly in the Harewood Estate record office now in the City Library, Leeds).
[5] *Notes on the Revolt in the North-Western Provinces of India*, (London, 1858), p. 159.

mutiny at Meerut, a salvo of twenty-one guns at Delhi announced that Bahadur Shah had assumed the mantle of Akbar, Shah Jahan and Aurangzib and that he whom most Indians, Hindu and Muslim alike, regarded as the *de jure* ruler of India had come into his own again. Within Delhi itself, it seemed almost as if the great days of the Mughals had come again. A Mughal prince, Mirza Mughal, was commander-in-chief. The remaining Muslim *jagirdars* in the Delhi territory, for example ʿAbd-Allah Rahman Khan of Jhaggar, Amin al-din Ahmad Khan of Loharu and Ziya al-din Ahmad (all of whom were either hanged or imprisoned after the British recapture of Delhi) were summoned to attend the royal presence. A proclamation was issued in the Mughal name calling upon all who wished to save their religion to join the troops and not to leave their religion to join the troops and not to leave any unbelievers alive.[6]

Events in Awadh, too, seemed to confirm the Muslim character of the rising. There the sepoys rallied under the standard of Birjis Qadir, a minor son of the exiled King of Awadh, (Wajid ʿAli Shah, 1847–56) and his mother Hazrat Mahal (d. 1879), who was one of the Indian heroes of 1857. The Chief Commissioner of Agra, Colonel H. Fraser (d. 1858), advised against abandoning Lucknow after the British storm of Delhi in September, as it would be 're-occupied as the head of the Mahomedan rebellion'. The famous *Times* correspondent, William Howard Russell (1820–1907), spoke of Begum Hazrat Mahal as exciting all Awadh to take up the interests of her son and as declaring undying war against the British.

Events in the countryside pointed also to the Muslim character of the rising. 'The Mahomedan villages in the Doab and the people in the neighbourhood of [Aligarh] were by far the worst in the district. They seem to have risen as if by signal and certainly committed the greatest depredations.' In Aligarh 'the fanatical lower Mussalmans, Jooluhas [weavers]' raised 'the cry of "Deen Deen" '.[7] One Ghiyath Muhammad Khan proclaimed himself at Aligarh as *subadar* on behalf of Bahadur Shah II. The Muslim population of Rohilkhand, composed of the districts of Bareilly, Muradabad, Shahjahanpur, Bada'un and Bijnor, had strongly resented British rule since Company annexation in 1801. They had rioted against

---

[6] *Paper on Miscellaneous Subjects*, no. 131, *Canning Papers*.
[7] Muir, *Intelligence Records*, vol. ii, p. 6.

taxation in 1816 and troops had had to be called in. As already seen, Bishop Heber reported on the large numbers of unemployed Pathan cavalrymen in the area in the eighteen-twenties. Now, in 1857, Khan Bahadur Khan (1790–1859), grandson of Hafiz Rahmat Khan (1708–74), the last independent Muslim ruler of Rohilkhand, assumed the title of *Nawwab-Nazim* (provincial governor) on behalf of Bahadur Shah II and appointed a Pathan chief, Mubarak Shah, as governor of Bada'un. For nearly a year Khan Bahadur Khan ruled in Bareilly with a fighting force 'popularly estimated at 30 to 40 thousand' and composed mostly of 'impecunious Pathans'. At Allahabad, the old capital of a principal Mughal province, after the mutiny of the 6th Native Infantry stationed there, the discontented Muslim aristocracy and the Muslim city population joined hands and soon 'the green flag of Islam' was waving over the Kotwali. A member of the *ʿulama*, Maulawi Liaqat ʿAli (d. 1872), said to be a weaver by birth and a schoolmaster by profession, came forth to take charge in the name of the Mughal in Delhi.

Members of the Muslim religious classes were prominent in revolt. 'The Maulavi of Faizabad' Ahmad-Allah Shah (d. 1858), a natural leader of men, harassed Sir Colin Campbell's (1792–1863) forces during the hot season's campaign in 1858 for the conquest of Awadh, although he was without any formal military training. One Maulana Rahmat-Allah assumed leadership of the revolt in Muzaffarnagar. Suspicion naturally fell upon the followers of Saiyid Ahmad Bareilly. At Patna, on 20 June 1857, William Taylor (1808–1892) arrested by a subterfuge the leading reformist *maulawis*, Shah Muhammad Husain (1788–1860), Ahmad-Allah (1808–81) and Wa'iz al-Haq, claiming that they were plotting a rising. A chief of *jihadis* from Tonk, whose *nawwab* was an undoubted patron of the *mujahiddin* on the frontier, arrived in Delhi on 31 July 1857, to be followed by a contingent of Muslim warriors for the faith, who fought valiantly during the seige of Delhi.[8]

The case for a general Muslim conspiracy was strengthened by events hundreds of miles distant from the outraged sepoys of the Bengal army or the disaffected countryside of Rohilkhand. The Muslim *wilayatis*, mercenary retainers of the *rajas*, *nawwabs* and petty chiefs of Gujarat, were disaffected towards the British. In

[8] C. T. Metcalfe, (ed.) *Two Native Narratives of the Mutiny at Delhi* (Westminster, 1898), pp. 174–5.

July 1857 there was a Muslim rebellion at Fort Dohad in the Baroda area, followed by another in Soonth in September led by a Muslim sergeant (*jam^c dar*), Mustafa Khan.[9] Sir George Campbell describes the bitter British feelings towards Muslims which he encountered in the North-Western Provinces as follows:

It was at Meerut that I first realised the strong feelings against the Mahomedans which had grown up in the North-Western provinces. We thought that the Mahomedans had no excuse from the caste grievance which was the immediate occasion of the mutiny and were disappointed when the Mahomedan sepoys in the regular regiments went with the rest. Then we thought that the irregular cavalry, a superior class and largely Mahomedan, would have stood by us and when a good many of them went too we felt aggrieved. When our power was completely upset in the North-Western provinces and all signs of our rule had disappeared, it was not unnatural that in some places the Mahomedans whom we had succeeded within the memory of man should try to set up in our stead, the more as the Sepoy rule was nominally that of the old Emperor of Delhi. We were very bitter against those Mahomedan pretenders.[10]

Nevertheless, appearances were deceptive and were recognised as such by the Governor-General, Lord Canning, and others in high places, with profound consequences for the future of Muslims in India. The original military mutinies were sparked off by the Hindu sepoys' fear for their caste, their honour and their self-respect. The civil risings in Awadh, Bihar and Central India were mostly Hindu-led. The majority of the rebellious *ta^c alluqdars* of Awadh were Hindu. The Rani of Jhansi (d. 1858), Tatya Tope (*c.* 1819–59) and Nana Sahib (1820–59) were all Hindus. In the Gorakhpur region, the Commissioner, C. Wingfield (1820–92), noted that it was certain tribes of the higher castes of Rajputs who displayed the most marked hostility.[11] Sir James Outram (1803–63) failed to raise Hindus in Rohilkhand against the régime of Khan

---

[9] *Source Material for the History of the Freedom Movement*, (Bombay, 1957), pp. 194, 198–9, 266–7.

[10] Sir George Campbell, *Memoirs of My Indian Career*, vol. 1 (London, 1893), pp. 243–4.

[11] Report, dated 20 Dec. 1858 to the Sudder Board of Revenue. Proc. no. 31, *N.-W.P. Rev. Procs., 14–30 April 1859*, India Office Library Range 221, vol. 24.

Bahadur Khan and had to return money granted for the purpose unspent to the treasury.[12]

Muslims themselves were as divided by personal, ethnic, class and regional affiliations as were Hindus and felt the same pressures. Among Muslim princes and aristocrats, the Nizam of Hyderabad and the Nawwabs of Rampur, Karnal, Muradabad and Dacca remained 'loyal', while the Nawwab of Farrukhabad and the Nawwab of Danda turned 'rebel'. Some Muslim officials went one way, some the other. In the Aligarh and Rohilkhand areas they mostly joined the rebels;[13] on the other hand, the district of Muttra, a predominantly Hindu area, was held for the British by a Muslim Deputy-Collector and the loyalty of Sir Sayyid Ahmad Khan as *sadr amin* at Bijnor, in trying to hold the district for the British assisted by a Muslim *tahsildar* (Indian sub-collector of revenue), became part of the saga of the 'loyal Muhammadans' of India. Even at Patna, where Taylor was busy taking leaders of the *mujahidin* into custody, his principal *aides* were Muslims like Maula Bakhsh, Shah Kabir al-din, Qazi Ramzan ʿAli and Saiyid Wilayat Khan.[14] The Muslims of Bengal, who had certainly suffered most, economically, from British rule, did not stir. In the Panjab, Muslims joined with Sikhs and the Muslim tribesmen of Kohat to form part of the reinforcements for the British troops on the Ridge outside Delhi. Charles Raikes describes them as 'tall, sleek, good-natured quiet men, easily managed in the lines and ready to cut off the head of a brother Mahomedan in Hindostan [i.e. the North-Western Provinces] when required'.[15]

The remarkably perceptive and balanced observations of Sir George Campbell, written in July and August 1857 when the conflict was at its height, cannot be improved upon today. He emphasised that, apart from a few small risings which occurred after the British capture of Delhi in September 1857 and were provoked by British severity and persecution, the rebellion was essentially Hindustani in character, a rebellion of previously dominant classes, both Hindu and Muslim, in the North-Western Provinces 'who have been

[12] T. R. Metcalf, *The Aftermath of Revolt*, p. 299.

[13] Report of J. Inglis, Collector of Bareilly, dated 11 Jan. 1859, *N.-W.P. Rev. Procs., 14–30 April 1859*, Range 221, vol. 24.

[14] S. N. Sen, *Eighteen Fifty-Seven* (Delhi, 1957), p. 245.

[15] Charles Raikes, *Notes on the Revolt in the North-Western Provinces of India* (London, 1858), p. 133.

rejected by us'. It was not a general Muslim movement against the British.

The Pathans and Rajputs and Boondelas whose countries have been acquired within the last fifty years (in the decline of the Mahomedan power great Hindu *zamindars* were in much of the country the really powerful men) have made a considerable, but I believe it will be found not a really formidable figure; while the Mahomedans and *zamindars* of Behar and part of Benares whose subjection to us is of a date twenty years earlier, have generally not joined in the rebellion at all.[16]

He pointed out that the Muslim communities most given to religious fanaticism, the *fara'izis* in Bengal and the Mappillas in south India, had not stirred. He believed that there was no active sympathy on the part of 'the professors of the Mahomedan religion'. Even in the North-Western Provinces where, he conceded, 'the mass of the Hindoostanee race has wavered in their allegiance', he denied that Muslims rose in revolt as a body and as a matter of religion and class, although he thought that probably most of the 'native' civil servants who went over to the rebels were Muslim. 'The Mahomedans have, I think, behaved better than might have been expected, considering their antecedents and position; and that the result, far from bringing to light a chronic Mahomedan conspiracy, has been to show that we have not in that class of our subjects that formidable danger that has been sometimes apprehended.'[17] As for the Mughal at Delhi, Bahadur Shah 'was simply set up by our army' (that is, by the mutineers from Meerut).[18]

The Governor-General himself had, even earlier than Campbell, entered a *caveat* against interpreting the rising as essentially Muslim. Writing on 5 June 1857 to Vernon Smith (1800–73), President of the Board of Control, he said that the revolt began as a Hindu movement of men honestly afraid for their caste; although there is evidence, he says, that twenty-six regiments have bound themselves against the government, and that some outbreak was meditated,

it cannot have been such an outbreak as has now occurred, and which for a time took the shape of a caricature revival of the Mahommedan

[16] Sir G. Campbell, *Memoirs of My Indian Career*, Appendix to vol. II (London, 1893), pp. 398–9.
[17] Campbell, *Memoirs*, vol. II, p. 397.
[18] Campbell, *Memoirs*, vol. II, p. 399.

Empire. This phase of the affair is, I believe due simply to the fact that the men of the Regiments which were so grossly mismanaged at Meerut, and those who suffered punishment were chiefly Mahommedans and that Delhi unguarded by a single European, was close at hand...now that the rebellion has lost all distinctive character it is not more Mussulman than Hindoo.[19]

A formal assessment made for Canning early in 1859 under the title 'Note by L. Bowring [1824–1910] on the causes of the Mutiny and on the part taken in it by the Mahommedans'[20] held to the same judgement. 'Considerable prevalence', it noted,

has been given to the report that the Mahommedans were the prime movers of the revolts, that a conspiracy on their part of long standing has been concocted under the eyes of the Government and that the sepoys were their dupes and blind instruments. This is an assumption rather than a fact. It is true that the Mahomedans in many parts of India are ill-disposed towards the British Government and have at various times excited disturbances, as for example the Moplahs in Madras and the Ferazees in Bengal. It is also true that every Mahomedan would gladly see the day when his faith should again be in the ascendant and would infinitely prefer Mahommedan to British rule. But allowing this to be an accurate exposition of their secret aspirations, it cannot militate against facts which tend to show that the Mahommedans only took a partial share in the mutiny and that after its development.

Bowring then goes on to say that there is nothing in the correspondence seized since the first outbreak to prove the complicity of Muslim chiefs prior to the Barrackpore outbreak and that, although the rebellion took on a Muslim appearance when Delhi was seized by the mutineers from Meerut, 'there is nothing whatever to show that the sudden seizure of Delhi was anything but a fortuitous circumstance and there is evidence that the people and sepoys were quite unprepared for the arrival of the Meerut mutineers'. Bowring notes the quiescence of Muslims in Bengal and the active loyalty of Muslims in the Panjab and acknowledges the debt of the British to those Muslim chiefs, the Nizam of Hyderabad, the Nawwab of Murshidabad and the Nawwab of Rampur, who were distant

[19] Letter no. 67 of *Letters to the President of the Board of Control Jan.–Dec. 1857, Canning Papers.*
[20] No. 362 of *Papers on Miscellaneous Subjects, Canning Papers.*

from the British troops and could have done the British much injury had they not remained 'staunch'. The leaders of the rising were non-commissioned officers, not Muslims of rank, 'thus showing that the mutiny was in truth a military revolt and not a national insurrection'.

BRITISH TREATMENT OF MUSLIMS

'After 1857', wrote Jawaharlal Nehru (1889–1964) in his autobiography, 'the heavy hand of the British fell more upon the Moslems than on the Hindus'. This verdict, which has been generally accepted by modern historians,[21] has an ancestry going back at least to the generation after 1857.[22] While the rising was at its height, George Campbell expressed the fear that the British might degrade Muslims as a class[23] and William Howard Russell recorded in 1858 that, 'the Mahomedan element in India is that which causes us most trouble and provokes the largest share of our hostility. . .Our antagonism to the followers of Mahomed is far stronger than that between us and the worshippers of Shiva and Vishnu. They are unquestionably more dangerous to our rule'.[24] After the capture of Delhi in September 1857 a dire vengeance befell the Muslims there. As the famous Urdu poet Ghalib (1797–1869) wrote, 'Here there is a vast ocean of blood before me, God alone knows what more I shall have to behold.' Bahadur Shah was tried and exiled to Rangoon. Lieutenant Hodson (1821–58) summarily shot three Mughal princes and later twenty-four *shahzadas* (princes) were tried and executed. Catastrophe befell the Muslim intelligentsia in Delhi. Zahir Dihlawi (1835–1911) wrote in his *Dastan-i Ghadar*, 'The English soldiers began to shoot whomsoever they met upon the way . . .Mian Muhammad Amin Panjakush, an excellent writer, Moulvie Imam Bakhsh Sabhai along with his two sons. . .were

---

[21] See e.g. Tara Chand, *History of the Freedom Movement in India*, vol. II (Delhi, 1967), p. 349; I. H. Qureshi, *The Muslim Community of the Indo-Pakistan Subcontinent (610–1947)* ('S-Gravenhage, 1962), p. 233; Hafeez Malik, *Moslem Nationalism in India and Pakistan* (Washington D.C., 1963), p. 207.

[22] Sir Alfred Lyall, *Asiatic Studies*, second ed. (London, 1884), pp. 239–240.

[23] Campbell, *Memoirs*, vol. II p. 397.

[24] *My Diary in India in the Years 1858-9*, vol. II, (London, 1860), pp. 73–4.

arrested and taken to Raj Ghat Gate. They were shot dead and their dead bodies were thrown into the Jumna.'[25] During the weeks when the British military authorities held Delhi at their mercy, they made every citizen who wished to return to the city after expulsion pay a fine. Muslims were required to pay 25 per cent of the value of their real property, while Hindus had to pay only ten per cent.

Far away in the cool of an English October, the Prime Minister, Palmerston (1784–1865), wrote to Canning that every civil building connected with Mahommedan tradition (an oblique reference to the Jamaᶜ Masjid) should be levelled to the ground 'without regard to antiquarian veneration or artistic predilection'.[26] On 8 January the President of the Board of Control, Vernon Smith, reported to Canning that 'the *Times* has taken up the religious cry... which is not content with cramming Christianity down the throats of the Mussulmans, unless in taking up the Cross they insult the tenet of the Prophet'.[27]

Nevertheless, the call to wreak a special vengeance upon Muslims, however loud among the men on the spot in Delhi, Lucknow or other major Muslim centres, was not heeded at the very summit of the British government in India; however severely Muslims suffered, Canning was determined that they should not, as an act of State, suffer because they were Muslims. The military vengeance taken at Delhi and elsewhere may have been acquiesced in by the highest civil authorities, but it was not their doing or their wish. In the process of punishment by confiscation in the North-Western Provinces in 1858 and 1859 official policy was 'community-blind'. Muslims survived as a major social and economic interest in northern India, depressed in spirit and with their own image of themselves shattered, but a major social and economic interest group nonetheless, ready to form, when the wind of change should blow, one of the two great political communities of Lord Dufferin's Indian cosmos of the eighteen-thirties. They were not destroyed as a weight in the religious, social and political balance in British India;

[25] Quoted in S. N. Sen, *Eighteen Fifty-Seven*, (Delhi, 1957), p. 116. The text has been published by the Panjab Academy of Literature (Lahore, 1955), see p. 171.

[26] Letter no. 9, dated 9 Oct. 1857 of *Letters from H.M. Ministers Feb. 1856 to Feb. 1862, Canning Papers.*

[27] Letter no. 40 of *Letters from President of the Board of Control 26 Jan. 1856 to 9 May 1858. Canning Papers.*

moreover, as the following letter[28] from Canning to the President of the Board of Control, dated 21 November 1857, shows – it is almost a *locus classicus* for British policy in the next half-century – that outcome was not wholly unforeseen or unintended. Referring to Palmerston's effusion of 9 October 1857, Canning wrote,

I am quite opposed to touching the Jumna [*sic*] Masjid – which is a religious building – because I will do nothing which shall stamp this rebellion as being in the estimation of the British Government and people a religious one. I do not of course assert that religion has not been amongst the causes of it and beyond doubt it has kept alive and exasperated [*sic*] it. But the Hindoo religion has done this as well as the Mahomedan; and a crusade against one must be a crusade against both. The men who fought against us at Delhi were of both creeds; probably in about equal numbers. If we destroy or desecrate Mussalman Mosques or Brahmin temples we do exactly what is wanting to band the two antagonist *races* [author's italics] against ourselves. . .As we must rule 150 million of people by a handful (more or less small) of Englishmen, let us do it in the manner best calculated to leave them divided (as in religion and national feeling they already are) and to inspire them with the greatest possible awe of our power and with the least possible suspicion of our motives. . .But I beg you not to ask for anything to be done against the religion of either race. I do not wish to compliment or even to humour Mahomedanism or Hindooism nor that we should adapt our Military or any other usages to the prejudices of caste. But I do wish to leave both religions alone, and to treat them with indifference in the real sense of the term. It will be a bad day for England when an opposite policy is taken up in India whether under pressure from home or in deference to the howlings and yelpings of those who call themselves a 'British Public' here. . . The razing of the city could be accomplished only at great cost, or at great injustice. It was not the people of Delhi – certainly not the householders – who rebelled or abetted rebellion; but the sepoys who entered the Town and committed flagrant atrocities upon many of those whose property we should destroy. It would be monstrous to destroy it without compensation.

Few Muslims, even had they known of Canning's views on their fate, would have felt reassured at the difference between his outlook and that of the British press in Calcutta or of many of his

[28] Letter no. 93 of *Letters to the President of the Board of Control, January to December, 1857, Canning Papers.*

own junior civil and military officers. Indeed, in so far as they were educated in Islam, they would have found incomprehensible his distinction between the Muslim political and the Muslim religious identity in India. Nevertheless, however effectively disguised, there was hope for Muslims in what Canning had written. Their religion was to be left alone, if only as a counterweight to Hinduism. They were not to be ill-treated, so long as they did not hanker after past power, merely because they were Muslims. Their character as property-owners, not to be expropriated without compensation if peaceably behaved, was acknowledged. They were not, moreover, as another of Canning's letters shows, to be denied official employment. Writing to the Lieutenant-Governor of the North-Western Provinces on 20 September 1857, Canning gave his view that

all exclusion of Mahomedans, Rajpoots or even of Brahmins should be a matter of management rather than of rule; and indeed that it will be right to take an opportunity, though not just yet, to show, by an exception here and there, that the rule does not exist. It is desirable that no class should feel that it had henceforward nothing to expect from the Government.[29]

Muslims in India could have a future, but not on their own terms. They must be prepared in secular matters (a concept which they must now perforce adopt) to appear to think and act like Victorian Englishmen of property, to make the most of the security of their property and of the sanctity of contract assured to them by their alien government – to accept a régime of civil but not of political liberty. They could compete in the race of life, but not by using the old weapons of arms and statecraft. They were to take Samuel Smiles (1812–1904) or Cobden (1804–65) and Bright (1811–89), not Akbar or Aurangzib, as their paragons. They must substitute a capitalist's for a cavalier's ideal of life, or, to take an analogy from the history of Christianity, a Calvin's for a Loyola's. A surprising number of Muslims were, as will be seen, willing to make the transition and, somewhat against the conventional historical belief that Muslims suffered unduly from reprisals after 1857, economically able to do so.

Act XI of 30 May 1857 provided for punishment by death and by confiscation of property of all persons guilty of rebellion and

[29] Letter no. 18 of *Letters to Lt.-Governor, North-Western Provinces, March, 1856 to February, 1862, Canning Papers.*

Act XIV of 6 June 1857 extended these penalties to all who incited to mutiny and rebellion. Martial law, however, supervened district by district as the rising spread and troops meted out vengeance and retribution 'without any practical restriction upon their acts but the humanity and discretion of their commanding officers' – commodities in short supply in 1857 and 1858. Special Commissioners were appointed to dispense summary justice in reconquered areas; their jurisdiction was indeed special and summary and if they were guilty in their decisions of partiality between members of the different communities, that partiality has gone unrecorded. By the autumn of 1858, however, the regular civil administration had been reinstalled in most districts affected by rebellion in the North-Western Provinces and collectors and magistrates could turn their attention to a more measured and deliberate investigation of the conduct of individual *jagirdars*, pensioners, officials and landholders.

In their judgements officers were instructed to have regard only to the degree of an individual's complicity in murder, rebellion and active disaffection.[30] According to the official proceedings of 1858 and 1859, Canning's policy of no discriminatory punishment against Muslims as such was carried out. Discrimination by British military officers or special commissioners may have occurred when vengeful passions were at their height; it is impossible to judge from the records. However, if the official British records for the period 1858–1860 of the treatment of pensioners, *jagirdars*, *muᶜafidars* and landholders are examined, they betray no such policy carried out in cold blood. They show moreover that in the disposal of confiscated property Muslims were at no great disadvantage. The period of confiscation in the North-Western Provinces (and it must be remembered that the fate of the Muslims in the North-Western Provinces only is at issue here) left the Muslim community of those provinces more damaged in its prestige and its pride than in its pocket. Many indeed were killed or impoverished, but some too emerged with their fortunes made. The 'loyal Muhammadan' was no myth invented by Sir Saiyid Ahmad Khan and what some Muslim landholders lost other Muslim landholders gained.

Muslim pension-holders were particularly vulnerable to British

[30] See *Revenue Letters from India*, vol. II, 1859, pp. 348–9. India Office Library.

wrath. Yet in January 1859 the Governor-General sanctioned the continuance of a large number of pensions to members of the royal family of Awadh.[31] Shortly afterwards a large number of pensions were sanctioned for surviving members of the family of Bahadur Shah II. Hostile or equivocal conduct during the rising, however, brought a cancellation or reduction of pension.[32] A large number of Muslim pensions were forfeited, but then so were many Hindu. In Gorakhpur, for example, one proceeding records the loss of pensions by twenty-three Hindus as against six Muslims. In Jalaon district all the pensions listed as forfeited in one proceeding had been received by Hindus.[33] In Bareilly district, however, a consolidated return of forfeitures gives ninety-five Muslim forfeitures to two Hindu.[34] In other centres of Muslim disaffection, such as Bijnor, Moradabad and Bada'un, Muslim losses of pensions were also great.[35] In Aligarh district forfeitures of or confirmations of pension were more nearly balanced between Hindus and Muslims.[36] A cold determination to be severely just, rather than a deliberate seeking out of Muslim pensioners to do them harm, is suggested by these proceedings.

Jagirdars received similar treatment. The Nawwab of Dadri's *jagir* was declared forfeit to the Raja of Jhund, on the ground that the Nawwab sent cavalry to assist the rebels at Delhi. But as the Nawwab was old and feeble and had perhaps been coerced, Canning himself decided to award him a monthly pension of one thousand rupees.[37] The *jagirs* of Saiyid Atta-Allah Khan in Allahabad and Saharanpur districts were continued until his death, but they were then to be resumed, as his son had helped the rebels.[38]

[31] Letter of Secretary to Government of India to Chief Commissioner Oudh dated 11 January, 1859, *India Foreign and Political Proceedings for 14–21 January 1859*, India Office Library Range 203, vol. 32.

[32] *idem.*, Letter of 31 Dec. 1858 on behalf of G. G. and Consultation dated 14 January 1859.

[33] Proc. no. 105 of 9 Sept. 1859, *N.-W.P. Rev. Procs.*, *1859*, Range 221, vol. 30.

[34] Proc. no. 130 of 11 June 1859, *N.-W.P. Procs.*, *1859*, Range 221, vol. 26.

[35] Proc. no. 329, *N.-W.P. Rev. Procs.*, *1859*, Range 221, vol. 24.

[36] Report by F. B. Outram dated 23 June 1859, *N.-W.P. Rev. Procs.*, *3–30 June 1859*, Range 221, vol. 26.

[37] Canning to Court of Directors, 8 July 1858. *Collections to Despatches* nos. 3–17, 1858. India Office Library.

[38] *Revenue Letters from India 1859*, vol. II, p. 129.

Pensioners and *jagirdars*, however, made a very small proportion of the Muslim population of the North-Western Provinces. The fate of Muslim landholders, including *mu'afidars*, is a sounder index of British intentions towards Muslims as such. It has not been possible to survey the data in the official proceedings comprehensively, or to ascertain the total number of confiscations for each district for members of all communities, but it appears that where Hindu involvement in the rising was greater the number of confiscations of Hindu properties was greater and where Muslim involvement was greater the number of Muslim confiscations was greater. It is not claimed, however, that the following evidence does more than establish a *prima facie* case against the popular belief that Muslims as such suffered discriminatory treatment. Thus, in a proceeding of 12 November 1858 the Commissioner of Meerut, a centre of non-Muslim disaffection, lists 305 of 399 confiscated land holdings as belonging to non-Muslims.[39] On the other hand, in a consolidated return of forfeited pensions and *mu'afi* holdings for Rohilkhand division, an area of Muslim disaffection, 315 confiscations related to Muslims and only six to Hindus.[40] In the Shikarpur *pargana* of Bulandshahr district, seventy-two Muslim and forty-two Hindu *mu'afi* grants were recorded as confiscated,[41] while in three lists for the Etawa district collected in November 1858, thirty-nine of a total of fifty properties listed belonged to Hindus.[42] In Jhansi all twenty-eight and in Jabbalpur all forty of the holdings listed as confiscated in one return belonged to Hindus.[43] Some confiscations made by Special Commissioners in the autumn of 1857 were rescinded in quieter times in 1859; Muslims received the benefits of these second thoughts as well as Hindus. In the district of Benares, for example, sixty-nine Muslims along with sixteen Hindus had their holdings released to them in perpetuity, along with another sixty-nine Muslims and nine Hindus who had them released for their own lifetimes only.[44]

[39] Proc. no. 292, *N.-W.P. Rev. Procs., Dec. 1858*, Range 221, vol. 20.
[40] Proc. no. 130, *N.-W.P. Rev. Procs., 3–30 June 1859*, Range 221, vol. 26.
[41] Report by F. Williams, Commissioner Bulandshahr dated 13 April 1859, *N.-W.P. Rev. Procs.,* 1859, Range 221, vol. 29.
[42] Return by A. O. Hume, Collector, dated 24 Nov. 1858, *N.-W.P. Rev. Procs., January and February 1859*, Range 221, vol. 22.
[43] Proc. no. 359, *N.-W.P. Rev. Procs., 14–30 April 1859*, Range 221, vol. 24.
[44] List dated 8 Sept. 1859 signed by Charles Currie, *N.-W.P. Rev. Procs., October 1859*, Range 221, vol. 31.

In the disposal of confiscated properties it is difficult to detect anti-Muslim bias in the official proceedings. Apparently confiscated property was given to Hindu or Muslim loyalists or sold to the highest bidder. Of thirteen Muslim 'estates' confiscated in the district of Fatehpur, ten were handed over to other Muslims and Muslims also took over two Hindu estates.[45] Even in the districts of Bijnor, Bareilly and Bada'un, where Muslim disaffection was notorious, a few Muslims received the property of rebel Hindus.[46] Nawwab Jan-Fishan Khan was assigned villages in the Meerut Division, and in the district of Rai Bareilly three *parganas*, assessed at an annual revenue of Rs. 119,158, were granted to the Nawwab of Rampur.[47] The settlement reports of the eighteen-seventies and eighteen-eighties sometimes give actual figures for the acreages of confiscated lands and show clearly that Muslims had been allowed to participate, and participate successfully, at auction sales after 1857–8.

In Bijnor district, for example, 3,092 acres are mentioned as having been confiscated in *pargana* Keerutpur from Muslim *saiyids*, *mughals* and *shaikhs*. Of these, 1,415 acres were given to a Hindu Jat as a reward and the remainder was auctioned off and bought by *banias*, Jats, *saiyids* and Pathans. In *pargana* Afzalgarh 35,614 acres were confiscated from Rajputs. After 7,978 acres had been given to a Brahman and a large quantity reserved by the government, about 5,000 acres were auctioned and bought by (Muslim) *shaikhs* as well as Hindu *banias* and Chauhans. In *pargana* Chandpore, 13,246 acres were confiscated from *saiyids*, Pathans, Mughals and *shaikhs*, but after 4,549 acres were given to *saiyids*, Tagas and *thakurs* as a reward, most of the remainder was purchased by a mixture of Hindus and Muslims.[48] It is true that the acreages purchased by members of the different classes and communities are not specified, but even allowing for bias and sharp practice among junior officials, possible fearfulness among Muslims of obtruding

[45] Return by Collector of Fatehpur, dated 29 April 1858, *N.-W.P. Rev. Procs.*, Range 221, vol. 22.
[46] Enclosure with letter of 13 July 1859 from Officiating Under-Secretary, N.-W.P. on rules for confiscation, *N.-W.P. Rev. Procs., 1–20 July 1859*, Range 221, vol. 27.
[47] S. M. Moens, *Report on the Settlement of Rai Bareilly* (Allahabad, 1874), p. 4.
[48] A. M. Markham, *Report on the Tenth Division of Settlement of the District of Bijnour* (Allahabad, 1847), pp. 269–73, *passim*.

upon official attention by bidding at auction sales and Muslim poverty *vis-à-vis* the *bania* classes, it is difficult to sustain the hypothesis of an official policy of deliberate discrimination against Muslim landholders in the North-Western Provinces.

The settlement reports of a later generation reveal that in many areas of the North-Western Provinces Muslims held their own in the possession of land between the settlements of the late eighteen-thirties and forties and those of the eighteen-seventies. In the district of Aligarh, one of the principal regions of Muslim disaffection in 1857, in *tahsils* Ahrauli, Koil, Khair Hathras, Iglas and Sikandra Rao, *Nau-Mussulman* (recently converted) *zamindars* increased their holdings between the settlements of 1839 and 1868 from 47,822 acres to 72,218 acres, *saiyids* from 25,879 to 29,857, Pathans from 125,261 to 156,148 and *shaikhs* from 11,970 to 19,972 acres; only the 'Mughals' dropped from 7,873 to 4,368 acres.[49] In Agra district, the Hindu *thakurs* lost over 28,000 acres on account of their rebellious conduct, and although Muslims lost 7,904 acres from all causes after the last settlement of 1841, the (Hindu) *thakurs* lost 73,482.[50]

Probably what happened after 1857 was that there was a shift in landholding within the Muslim community itself, with those having a Mughal past losing to those with a British future. Already before 1857, the growth of a new Muslim class of landholders, composed of those who were ready to serve the British as deputy-collectors and *sadr amin* and who had done well at land auctions, was visible. After 1857, such Muslim 'loyalists' as Mahmud ʿAli Khan of Chhatari (d. 1898), Faiz Ahmad Khan, ʿAbd al-Shakur Khan, ʿInayat-Allah Khan of Aligarh and Imdad ʿAli of Muttra district were typical of those who had turned British rule to their profit and who were to follow Sir Saiyid Ahmad Khan in promoting Western education for Muslims and in collaborating politically with the British. Outside this circle, it is possible that those with fewer aristocratic pretensions, such as the Pathans and *shaikhs*, came to terms more easily with British revenue demands and a commercialised agriculture.

[49] W. H. Smith, *Final Report of the Revision of Settlement in the District of Aligarh* (Allahabad, 1882), p. 66.

[50] H. F. Evans, *Report on the Settlement of the Agra District* (Allahabad, 1880), pp. 43–4.

While the above data in no way discredit the received view that old Muslim families suffered, and suffered disastrously, from the consequences of 1857 – the pensions which the British granted to the scions of noble families were often paltry – they do suggest that Muslims remained a substantial landholding interest in the North-Western Provinces, with a nucleus of potential leaders in the loyalists who had done well out of the mutiny and rising. And it must always be remembered that the events of 1857 had little effect upon the fortunes of Muslims outside the North-Western Provinces. In so far as the Panjabi Muslim was faithful to the British he gained in grants of land and in so far as the Bengali Muslim was standing aloof from British education he continued to suffer exclusion from official employment. Muslims emerged from 1857 discredited in the eyes of their rulers (at least, the more junior officials), and with their traditional leaders dead or in exile, but with the economic position and social prestige of those who were not punished for rebellion or active disaffection no weaker than before.

THE BRITISH SETTLE FOR 'BALANCE AND RULE'

British attitudes towards Muslims for a decade after the suppression of the Mutiny and Rising express the dualism of Canning's letter of 21 November 1857 – acceptance of them as an important interest with expectations of fair treatment from their rulers, coupled with severe repression of any political pugnacity. As, however, any British acceptance was strictly on British terms, and as from the middle of the eighteen-sixties there was open British repression of the followers of Saiyid Ahmad of Bareilly, Muslims could see only British suspicion and antipathy; with the assassination of Chief Justice Norman (1819–71) of the Calcutta High Court by a Muslim in August 1871 and the assassination of the Viceroy, Lord Mayo (1822–72), by a Muslim in February 1872, it began to appear that the British and the Muslims of northern India were on a collision course. Nevertheless, before Norman's assassination, Lord Mayo had acted to assure Muslims publicly that an honourable place was theirs in British India if they were willing to accept it and the two assassinations, instead of killing conciliation, determined the British to confirm it.

The British recognised that political persecution of devoted

Muslims was no way to reduce Islamic passion and stopped the trials of actively-disaffected Muslims, the 'Wahhabi' trials, begun in 1864 (see below p. 84). They began, slowly at first, to offer educational boons to Muslims in the hope that more Muslims would then become qualified to compete successfully for the official and professional employment created by British rule. The premise of British policy was that it would be possible to balance and rule between the Hindu and Muslim communities, once significant elements of the latter had been convinced that they had more to gain by collaboration than by opposition.

In the years immediately following 1857–8 Muslims in the North-Western Provinces remained well represented in the subordinate services. On 1 July 1859, the number of deputy-collectors in these provinces was thirteen Hindu to nine Muslim, with six Hindu and three Muslim temporary deputy-collectors. By 1 October 1859 Muslims were predominant, with thirteen to eleven Hindu permanent deputy-collectors.[51] In 1864 Muslims still held half the deputy-collectorates in the North-Western Provinces; forty-three Muslims against thirty-four Hindus were *sadr amin* and ninety-three Muslims as against eighty-three Hindus were *tahsildars*.[52] Thirty-five per cent of the appointments carrying a salary of Rs. 150 *per mensem* made in 1871 in the North-Western Provinces were given to Muslims, and in the Panjab 38 per cent.[53] Nor were they excluded from the operation of Canning's policy of creating a solid 'native' vested interest in British rule by, for example, conferring magisterial powers upon prominent landowners. Of the fifty-six 'independent gentlemen of property and influence' who were selected in 1861 as honorary magistrates in the districts of Agra, Meerut, Rohilkhand, Benares, Ajmir, Jhansi and Gorakhpur, five were Muslims.[54] Of the forty-eight *taᶜalluqdars* in Awadh empowered in 1862–3 to try

[51] Proc. no. 176, *N.-W.P. Rev. Procs.*, *16 Aug.–7 Sept. 1859*, Range 221, vol. 29, and return dated 11 Oct. 1859 by J. B. Outram, *idem.*, for November 1859, Range 221, vol. 32.

[52] Rahmani Hassaan Begum, *The Educational Development of Sir Syed Ahmad Khan 1858–1898* (unpublished doctoral thesis) London, 1960, p. 174.

[53] Zafarul Islam and Raymond L. Jenson, 'Indian Muslims and the Public Service 1871–1915', *Journal of the Asiatic Society of Pakistan*, IX, 1, June 1964, pp. 88–9.

[54] *North-Western Provinces Government Gazette* (Allahabad) for 24 December 1861, pp. 2087–9. I am indebted to Mr Waheed al-Haq for this reference.

civil, revenue or criminal cases as honorary assistant-commissioners, fourteen were Muslim.[55] It is true, however, that Muslims in the North-Western Provinces in the decades after the rising lost the overwhelming advantages in official favour which they had enjoyed before 1857. Dr Metcalf quotes figures to the effect that Muslims held 45.9 per cent of the judicial posts in the North-Western Provinces and Awadh in 1885–1887, as compared with 72 per cent for the North-Western Provinces alone in 1850.[56] Official voices were heard demanding an improved educational (that is, an English) qualification for public office. Kempson (1831–94), Director of Public Instruction, North-Western Provinces, called in 1862 for the removal of uneducated officials, who he implied were Muslims not educated in government schools.[57] The Lieutenant-Governor ignored his animadversions against Muslims, but approved a tightening up of educational qualifications.

It is probable that without special measures to encourage English education among the Muslims of upper India, they would have found themselves where the Muslims of Bengal found themselves in 1871, holding a tiny minority of official appointments. (Muslims held only 4.4 per cent of the gazetted posts in Bengal in 1871 and were given only 11 per cent of the appointments made in that year.)[58] Official employment concerned only a tiny minority of Muslims, but in the heartlands of the old Muslim empires it was seen as the touchstone of British intentions towards those who regarded themselves as the natural aristocracy of the country. In the eighteen-sixties the educated Muslims of upper India were conscious of official suspicion and of an official disinclination to temper the wind of anglicisation to the shorn Muslim lamb.

Most Britons emerged from the events of 1857 with the conviction that Muslims were required by their religion to be antipathetic if not actively hostile to British rule, despite the active military assistance of Muslims from the Panjab and the loyal service of Muslim

---

[55] *Parliamentary Paper* no. 62 of 1865, 'Papers Relating to the Administration of Oude', pp. 71–2. I am indebted to Mr Waheed al-Haq for this reference.
[56] T. R. Metcalf, *The Aftermath of Revolt*, pp. 301, 304.
[57] Rahmani Hassan Begum, *Educational Development*, p. 178.
[58] Zafarul Islam and Raymond L. Jenson, 'Indian Muslims and the Public Service', p. 86.

officials. The *mujahidin* on the frontier seemed to express the real spirit of militant Islam and the presence of many *ulama* among the rebels in 1857–8 merely confirmed a belief that those who devoted their lives to studying the Faith knew what it demanded when opportunity offered. In the embittered and distrustful atmosphere which now prevailed, the British were constantly on the watch for 'rustles in the Muhammadan community', for an outbreak of that fanaticism and bigotry 'characteristic of the race'. Aware now of the precariousness of British rule, the earlier British attitude of complaisance towards the *mujahidin* on the frontier and their underground organisation in India disappeared.

Yet, notwithstanding the confidence of Commissioner Taylor of Patna in his own judgement, there is little evidence that the followers of Saiyid Ahmad Bareilly took a direct part, in British India proper, and as an organised brotherhood, in the rising of 1857. T. E. Ravenshaw (1827–1914) who was commissioned to make an exhaustive inquiry in 1865 was unable:

to ascertain that any of the Patna Moulvis took a direct part in the Mutinies or in the disturbances which occurred in Patna in 1857. . . but I am informed that although they were thoroughly disaffected towards Government, they had other schemes in hand and overtures were received by the Moulvies in Patna from their relatives at Sittana inviting them to proceed to the Hills and from thence to make an attack on the British Frontier. Their not doing so was probably on account of the fear of retribution so long as their families remained in Patna. . .It moreover appears to have formed a part of their creed to keep to the Hills as their basis of operations. This belief is said to be founded on a text in the Koran 'He who believes and leaves his village (Huzrut) to fight for God will be respected.' The Wahabeen interpretation is that they are bound to go beyond the Frontier to commence Jehad or Holy War.[59]

On the frontier, however, the *mujahidin* stirred up the Yusafzais to raid a British camp. Despite their other preoccupations in April and May 1858, the British sent an army of 5,000 men under Sir Sidney Cotton (1792–1874) to destroy the base at Sittana. This was the first full-scale war between the British and the *mujahidin* on the frontier.

[59] Undated (probably 9 May 1865) *Memorandum on Wahabis* in *Correspondence Relating to the Wahabee Movement* in *Mayo Papers* (Cambridge University Library Add. 7490), no. 29.

The latter, however, merely formed yet another settlement at Malka and kept the frontier tribes in turmoil. In the summer of 1863 they reoccupied Sittana.

In the previous year, the Panjab government had pressed for strong action against the *mujahidin*, employing some politically significant arguments.

These Hindustani Wahabis regarded as pilgrims from the land which bends to the yoke of infidels, self-exiled from their homes for religion's sake, the germs of a Crescentade in which the tribes of Islam shall be gathered together to wage a holy war against the Faringhi, meet with a ready sympathy. . .mysteriously supplied with money from Hindustan even beyond their wants. . .worshipping God after the strictest tenets of their religion, they are spoken of by all as *sans peur et sans reproche*.[60]

The avowed object of the fanatics is the restoration of the Muhammadan rule in India by the sword. . .They unite the sympathies of Muhammedans all over India and on its frontier. They are supplied with funds from Hindustan. It was ascertained that the Nawab of Tonk supplied persons with money to enable them to reach their settlements. They are believed to carry on correspondence with Bombay, Patna, Bareilly and other Muhammadan cities. In short their hostile position on our frontier is a rallying point for all those who long for the renewal of Muhammadan rule, an encouragement to the disaffected intrigues of that sect, and a stimulus of the worst sort to the unruly passions of the warlike and inflammable population on our frontier. In a time of difficulty their posture of defiance might not improbably serve as a beacon to the Muhammadans generally.[61]

In September 1863, the Viceroy, Lord Elgin (1811–63), sanctioned a major campaign against the *mujahidin* on the frontier and a force under Sir Neville Chamberlain (1820–92) advanced against Malka via the Ambela pass. The British troops, however, failed to force the pass and received a severe check, losing a tenth of their effectives. Although Malka was eventually burned, this was made possible more by tribal defections than by military victory.

---

[60] Deputy Commissioner Hazara to Commissioner Peshawar, 28 July 1862, *Selections from Government of Punjab Records*, Confidential Series no. A xiii (Lahore, 1884), p. 20.
[61] Secretary, Panjab Govt., to Govt. of India, 16 August 1862, *ibid.*, p. 23.

Baulked on the frontier, the British government attempted to destroy the organisation of the *mujahidin* in India, believing that it was the transmission of men and supplies via the 'underground' that maintained the threat on the frontier. In a series of trials at Amballa in the Panjab and at Patna, in 1864 and 1865, a dozen of the most active *mujahidin*, including two prominent *maulawis* of the Patna organisation, the brothers Yahya ʿAli (1828–68) and Ahmad-Allah (1808–81) were condemned to various terms of transportation to the Andaman Islands, on charges of conspiring to wage war against the Queen. There was a further wave of arrests in 1868 (a year in which there was a further indecisive frontier campaign), when twenty-eight suspects from Bengal were detained under Regulation III of 1818, providing for detention without trial for political reasons. At one time, in 1870, as many as fifty suspects were detained under Regulation III, some at least without the knowledge of Lord Mayo. In 1870 and 1871 a further series of trials took place at Rajmahal, Malda and Patna, at which further sentences of transportation were passed. The supply organisation of the *mujahidin* in India was practically destroyed after several years of intense police investigations.

On 20 September 1871, Chief Justice Norman of the Calcutta High Court was knifed by a Punjabi Muslim ʿAbd-Allah. The official records relating to the assassination in the Mayo papers show some circumstantial evidence, not of direct 'Wahhabi' complicity in the deed, but of indirect 'Wahhabi' influence upon the assassin. ʿAbd-Allah had been born near Peshawar, had studied in a mosque known as a centre of 'Wahhabi' teaching and numbered among his associates one who possessed a certificate of spiritual discipleship going back to Shah ʿAbd al-ʿAziz and Shah Wali-Allah.[62] Chief Justice Norman was believed to be a supporter of the executive against the *mujahidin*, having previously dismissed appeals against detentions under Regulation III of 1818. He was also about to hear appeals against the recent convictions at the Patna trials.

There were those high in the Government of India who were ready to believe in a general Muslim conspiracy, particularly as some Muslims were known to be actively debating between them-

[62] Letter from Sir George Campbell to Lord Mayo of 12 October 1871 and appendix 2 to memo. by A. H. Giles of 30 November 1871, *Bundle Wahabees I*, no. 28 of *Mayo Papers*, Cambridge University Library.

selves whether India was *dar al-harb* or *dar al-Islam*.[63] Sir George Campbell, now Lieutenant-Governor of Bengal, besought Lord Mayo 'not to let loose the people (of whom there are already too many) who may make such suspicions a cause for persecuting Mahommedans and bring about a feeling of great insecurity among all our subjects of that persuasion'.[64] It was hard, however, for the British in India at this time, confronted with open warfare with the *mujahidin* on the north-west frontier, grappling with what appeared to be an endemic conspiracy against their empire in India itself and themselves convinced that no sincere Muslim could willingly acquiesce in infidel rule,[65] not to believe that they were engaged in a trial of strength with the whole Muslim community.

Yet, several months before Norman's assassination Lord Mayo had recoiled, quite deliberately, from such a contest. On 30 May 1871 he asked a Bengal civilian, W. W. Hunter, to write a book 'on the burning question of the day: "Are Indian Mussulmans bound by their religion to rebel against the Queen?"'[66] On 26 June 1871 Mayo wrote a note[67] on means to persuade Muslims to enter government schools and colleges more willingly and to revive the Calcutta Madrasa, an action which issued in a Government of India Resolution of 7 August 1871, drawing special attention to the problems of Muslim education and calling for the encouragement of classical and vernacular Muslim language in government schools and colleges and the recruitment of English-speaking Muslim teachers in English medium schools.[68] Mayo and his officials drew back because they realised that not all Muslims were active sympathisers with the *mujahidin* and that the British and the Muslims were not alone in India. The British–Indian government had offended most sections of India's upper classes in the eighteen-sixties, notably by the imposition of an income tax, and evidence

[63] See no. 317 of *Letters Despatched, Oct.–Dec. 1870*, no. 41 of *Mayo Papers;* also *Bundle Wahabees II*, no. 29 of *Mayo Papers*, translation of article in *Journal of Scientific Society of Bihar*, 15 February 1871.

[64] Sir George Campbell to Mayo, 12 Oct. 1871, *Bundle Wahabees I*, no. 28 of *Mayo Papers*.

[65] W. W. Hunter, *The Indian Musalmans, Are They Bound in Conscience to Rebel Against the Queen?* (London, 1871), pp. 66, 75, 139.

[66] F. H. Skrine, *Life of Sir William Wilson Hunter* (London, 1901), p. 199.

[67] *Mayo Papers*, Education, 12/V.

[68] *Selections from the Records of the Home Department of the Government of India*, no. ccv (Calcutta, 1886), p. 152.

was not lacking of Hindu religious fanaticism.[69] It was time to stop antagonising all the people all the time.

For several years before Hunter (who was given full access to official papers in the writing of his book) publicised the fact, some officials had perceived that the 'Wahhabis' mainly belonged to the Muslim lower classes and that landowning and propertied Muslims were antipathetic to them unless British policies inclined them to discover a common antipathy to foreign rule. J. H. Reily, the Bengal police officer deputed to investigate the 'Wahhabi' underground, reported on 2 November 1868 that the appeal of the Wahhabis was to the landless rather than to the landed classes. 'One of the chief inducements held out to a ryot is the privilege of holding his land free of rent; it is not likely therefore that a *zamindar* or landlord would support such a movement.'[70] He stated that in the district of Malda and Rajmahal the movement did not include any influential *zamindar* or landholder. In the Madras Presidency the Inspector General of Police ascribed the spread of the militant reform movement to the failure of 'native officers' to command that position *vis-à-vis* the old orthodox gentry to which their official rank, in their eyes, entitled them. Sir William Muir, however, noticed a certain sympathy in the district of Aligarh between 'certain of our Mahomedan landholders and the disloyalists on the frontier'.[71] Two of his district officers – Court (1822–91) Collector at Meerut, and Jenkinson (1835–1919) Collector at Saharanpur – attributed some of the Muslim landholders' disaffection to the income tax introduced in 1860.[72]

Hunter later depicted in florid rhetoric the connection official circles saw between religious and social discontent.[73]

[69] On the general situation see: G. R. G. Hambly, 'Unrest in Northern India during the Viceroyalty of Lord Mayo 1869–72', *Journal of the Royal Central Asian Society*, XLVIII, 1961, pp. 37–55.

[70] Muin ud-din Ahmad Khan, *Selections from Bengal Government Records on Wahhabi Trials (1863–1870)* (Dacca, 1961), p. 320. Lord Mayo almost certainly saw the report; a copy is extant in the *Mayo Papers*.

[71] Muir to Mayo, 8 July 1870, no. 2, *Panic at Allahabad and Roorkee, Mayo Papers*.

[72] *Panic, Mayo Papers*, Letters from Court and Jenkinson to Muir dated 5 June and 24 July 1870, respectively.

[73] *The Indian Musalmans*, p. 107. In the preface to the second edition of *The Indian Musalmans* (London, 1872), Hunter specifically denies that the work was 'demi-official' in the sense that the government had attempted to influence his views or to assume responsibility for his conclusions. Those who are

In India, as elsewhere, the landed and clerical interests are bound up by a common dread of change. The Muhammadan landholders maintain the cause of the Mosque, precisely as English landholders defend the Established Church. Any form of Dissent, whether religious or political is perilous to vested rights. Now the Indian Wahabis are extreme Dissenters in both respects; Anabaptists, Fifth Monarchy men, so to speak, touching matters of faith; Communists and Red Republicans in politics.

Earlier several officials had thought a distinction could be made between the religious and the political passions inspiring the followers of Saiyid Ahmad Bareilly. They included John Wyllie (1835–70),[74] Sir William Muir and some of his subordinates. Sir William Muir wrote to Mayo, 'but as Court says Wahabees is a large word and includes the purely religious (or protestant) sect as well as the political fanatics'.[75] Others doubted whether the *mujahidin* were a serious threat to British power and suspected that it was persecution which gave them their appeal. A member of Mayo's Council, Fitzjames Stephen (1829–94), wrote to the Duke of Argyll (1823–1900), Secretary of State for India, on 19 August 1870.

I do not think that the Wahabee conspiracy is in itself very serious. It has been in existence for 40 years more or less and would probably become formidable only if it came to be connected with other causes of disaffection. I believe that the conspirators played no part, or at least no part of any importance in the Mutiny.[76]

'I am not at all sure', wrote the Commissioner at Peshawar on 24 January 1871, 'that they do not languish when ignored and flourish when persecuted.'[77]

Provincial officials repulsed any ideas that the Muslims as such

granted privileged access to confidential records are often, however, subtly if unconsciously influenced by the structure of events or the drift of policy revealed therein. Hunter never showed any signs of becoming a viper in the official bosom.

[74] Holograph minute at end of J. Talboys Wheeler's *Memorandum on the Wahabees* in *Bundle Wahabees II*, no. 29 of *Mayo Papers*. 'J. W.' – the initials of John Wyllie, Under Secretary and for a time Acting Secretary of the Foreign Department of the Government of India. Talboys Wheeler (1824–97) was an Assistant Secretary in the same department.

[75] Letter dated 18 July 1870, no. 2, *Mayo Papers*.

[76] Enclosed with no. 237 of *Letters Despatched July–Sept. 1870*, no. 40 of *Mayo Papers*.

[77] *Papers about Wahabees, Confidential Punjab Civil Secretariat (Annual) File no. 210*, Record Office, Lahore.

were ready to rise, though they did not doubt their dislike of British rule. Court wrote:[78]

I think it most probable there has been more than usual *movement* on the part of the Mahomedans [but] I cannot see any sign of disaffection (unusual) or of any belief in a struggle at hand. . .Everybody knows the Mahomedans regard us as usurpers and would gladly see us knocked on the head. That their religion and power will be restored and established everywhere and that all infidels will be destroyed, are matters believed in and hoped for by them, just as much as we believe in the second coming of our Lord and the establishment of His Kingdom. But in this there is nothing to take notice of, or to be fearful of.

Hunter, believing that 'an established government has always the worldly minded on its side' and that 'we have the support of the comfortable classes, men of inert convictions and of some property, who say their prayers, decorously attend the mosque and think very little about the matter', advised the Government of India that they 'can segregate the party of sedition in a nobler way [than by imprisoning dissidents] – by detaching from it the sympathies of the general Muhammadan community'. He proposed that the British:

should develop a rising generation of Muhammadans, no longer learned in their own narrow learning, nor imbued solely with the bitter doctrines of their medieval Law, but tinctured with the sober and genial knowledge of the West. At the same time they would have a sufficient acquaintance with their religious code to command the respect of their own community, while an English training would secure them an entry into the lucrative walks of life.[79]

Hunter was almost certainly acting as a receiving set for transmissions of an official policy in gestation while he was writing, for on page 204 of his book he writes 'the Government has awakened to the necessity of really educating the Musalmans' and Mayo had already, as will be seen, adduced somewhat similar arguments in his note of 26 June 1871, that is three days before Hunter completed his manuscript.[80]

[78] Enclosure, dated 17 July 1870, with Muir's letter of 21 July 1870 to Mayo, no. 2 of *Mayo Papers*.

[79] *The Indian Musalmans*, p. 209.

[80] Skrine, *Life of Sir William Wilson Hunter*, p. 199. Hunter, however (p. 210), hoped that English education might be a first step towards weaning Muslims away from Islam and towards 'a higher level of belief' i.e. Christianity. There is no hint in the *Mayo Papers* that such was Mayo's intent.

After 1857 the British believed they could only be driven from India – and this was never dismissed as impossible – by a union of the 'twin fanaticisms' of caste and Islam. If the religious temperature in India was kept as low as possible, there was scope for what the British believed to be the natural antagonisms of Indian society, principally those between Islam and Hinduism, to produce a need for an impartial umpire, namely the British government. Deliberately to seek a quarrel with militant Islam was to invite a repetition of 1857. Before 1857 it had been a British dogma that Hindus and Muslims had, and indeed could have, no political feelings in common. The great British historiographers, James Mill (1773–1836), Mountstuart Elphinstone (1779–1859) and Sir Henry Elliot (1808–53), had indeed all written on this assumption. The events of 1857 had shaken but not destroyed British complacency. Even before the outbreak at Meerut, Canning was hopeful of a split between the Hindus and Muslims of the disbanded 19th Native Regiment.[81] After it had occurred, Colvin (1807–57), the Lieutenant-Governor of the North-Western Provinces, was certain that 'bye and bye the Hindoos will regret us'.[82] Money was provided to raise the Hindus of Rohilkhand against the Muslim government of Khan Bahadur Khan. Khan Bahadur Khan's proclamation that, if Hindus joined him, the Muslims would abstain from cow-killing, and Bahadur Shah II's proclamation that the Holy War was against the British and not against the Hindus[83] did not wean the British from the belief, or perhaps it was the necesary orthodoxy, that co-operation between Hindus and Muslims was preternatural. Nevertheless it would not do deliberately to stir up religious and communal antagonism. Charles Raikes warned that 'every ebullient of religious rancour amongst the natives recoils upon ourselves. If we cannot soften we must not exasperate the jealousies of caste and religion.'[84] To balance and rule, not to divide and rule, was the instinctive British approach to politics in India.

During Mayo's viceroyalty, some British observers were well aware that the fierce government of the decade after the Mutiny

[81] Canning to Vernon-Smith, 9 April 1857, letter no. 60 of *Letters to the President of the Board of Control Jan.–Dec. 1857, Canning Papers.*
[82] Letter no. 33 of 22 July 1857 of *Letters from the Lt.-Gov. N.-W.P. 6 March to 31 August 1857, Canning Papers.*
[83] C. T. Metcalfe, *Two Native Narratives of the Mutiny*, p. 98.
[84] *Notes on the Revolt in the North-Western Provinces of India*, p. 176.

and Rising was straining the tolerance of many sections of Hindu as well as of Muslim society. The *Pioneer* recognised unrest among Hindu college graduates after Norman's assassination; R. Drummond (1820–87) at Bareilly acknowledged 'a great deal of religious excitement throughout the country. . .there is a great deal of preaching going on, and the Moulvees are buzzing about like wasps – and the Hindoos are not much better'.[85] In the course of an investigation into the causes of the prevailing unrest ordered by Mayo's successor Northbrook (1826–1904), Wauchope (1823–75), an Officiating Commissioner of Police reported that 'most Hindoos dislike and distrust us at present'.[86] British moves to mollify Muslim hostility were encouraged by an outbreak of Sikh religious fanaticism directed against Muslims in the Panjab. The *Kukas*, a sect fiercely opposed to cow-killing, made a number of attacks upon Muslim butchers in the Panjab in 1870 and 1871. In January 1872 they rose at Maler Kotla, but were hunted down by forces under the control of Cowan, the Deputy Commissioner of Ludhiana, who had forty-nine of his *Kuka* prisoners blown from guns, an act disavowed by Lord Mayo before his assassination in the following month.

Mayo's note of 26 June 1871 on Muslim education shows clearly that he and his senior officials recognised that politically the time had come for a change of course. After reviewing the statistics of Muslims attending government or government-aided schools, he wrote, 'there is no doubt that, as regards the Mahomedan population, our present system of education is, to a great extent, a failure. We have not only failed to attract or attach the sympathies and confidence of a large and important section of the community, but we may even fear that we have caused positive disaffection as is suggested by Mr O'Kinealy (1837–1903) [acting-secretary of the Home Department] and others'. He then proposed measures to attract the Muslim gentleman's son into government schools, coupled with a public expression of regret in a Government of India Resolution that Muslims, by standing aloof from the British educational system, lose the advantages both material and social

[85] Letter dated 6 October 1871 to Officiating Secretary, Government of Bengal, *Bundle Wahabees I*, no. 28 of *Mayo Papers*.
[86] E. C. Moulton, *Lord Northbrook's Indian Administration 1872–1876* (London, 1968), p. 13.

which others enjoyed. 'A resolution of this kind. . .would have an excellent effect on the feelings of the Mahomedan population at this moment.'[87]

Mayo's assassination by a Muslim in February 1872 did not bring about a change in the course to which the Government of India had publicly committed itself in its Resolution of 7 August 1871 on Muslim education. Northbrook ordered extensive investigations into the possibility of a Muslim rising and was reassured that it was unlikely.[88] Although Mayo's Private Secretary, O. T. Burne (1837–1909), was always convinced of a connection between Mayo's assassin, Shir ʿAli, and the 'Wahhabis', the official inquiry failed to establish it. Northbrook urged the provision of special facilities for Muslim education and in 1873 the government of Bengal issued resolutions reforming the Calcutta Madrasa and providing financial assistance for the foundation of the new *madrasas* in Bengal and for the education of Muslims in government institutions. The death of Mayo was the nuclear explosion which permanently rearranged the atoms of policy in a new pattern.

An article in the *Pioneer* of 24 February 1869, thought to have been written by W. W. Hunter, had informed Muslims that they must accept the fortunes of war but that:

in the meantime we can offer them much good compensation for the wound which our dominion inflicts upon their self esteem or religious prejudice. We can give them good government. . .developing sources of wealth and securing lives and property, and upholding their privileges as British citizens over mercantile Asia. The Muslim today may view this prospect with reluctance, but they cannot help themselves so long as we are masters in the arts of war and administration.[89]

Mayo had begun to fill the cup of reconciliation, Northbrook held it out; would the comfortable educated Muslim gentlemen, for whom it was intended, accept it whole-heartedly?

[87] Note by Lord Mayo dated 26 June 1871, *Mayo Papers*, Education 12/V.
[88] Moulton, *Lord Northbrook's Indian Administration*, p. 9.
[89] Quoted in Rahmani Hassaan Begum, *The Educational Development of Sir Syed Ahmad Khan*, pp. 185–6.

4

MUSLIMS COME TO TERMS WITH BRITISH INDIA AS MUSLIMS

The British government in India was now ready to offer the chalice of reconciliation – but was it poisoned? No doubt Muslims had suffered military defeat and political humiliation before in their history, both in India and elsewhere, but they had not been asked then to submit to a new syllabus of study for success in life, which appeared to ask them to deny Islam as the one true religion. To agree to see the future as the British painted it – was this not to deny their past and to acknowledge that Islam was not the true order of the universe? To accept that an education on English lines was a necessary passport to success and consideration was tantamount to recognising that Muslim education was out of keeping with the requirements of the age – perhaps that Islamic belief itself was an anachronism. To live on the British terms could mean acknowledgement in practice that history would never become Islamic, that the temporal order in the age of Western dominance had escaped God's will and pleasure. The Indian Muslim could be forgiven for thinking that the British were asking him to commit that same sin of *shirk* which traditional Islamic doctrine held the British to be committing in proclaiming the separation of religion and politics to be the principle of 'progress'.

The vast majority of Muslims in India were in no position to distress themselves over the religious issues at stake – they were sufficiently distressed over the problem of keeping alive. As cultivators they were as ever preoccupied with the perennial threat of drought, flood, scarcity and how to meet the demands of the tax-gatherer and the moneylender. Would they suffer from typhoid, cholera, malaria and dysentery this year or next? Would they even reach the age of thirty? As artisans they never knew when the competition of machine-made manufactures might destroy their livelihood. Nor were many of the Muslims with something to lose, those able to educate their children, willing to hold themselves completely aloof from the British system of education out of fear for their religion. Figures given for the numbers of pupils in government schools in 1871–2, that is before Mayo's special measures could take any effect, indicate that in the North-Western Provinces Muslims made up 17.8 per cent and in Awadh 25.3 per cent of the school population, although in these areas they composed 13.5 per cent and 9.9 per cent of the population respectively. In the Panjab, Muslims were 34.9 per cent of the school population, as against a population proportion of 51.6 per cent. However, the higher the category of educational institution, the fewer the Muslim pupils and students. Thus in the Panjab, while 38 per cent and 30 per cent of the pupils in the government village and higher vernacular schools respectively were Muslim, only 20 per cent and 5 per cent of those in higher English schools and colleges were Muslim. In the twenty years before 1878, of 1,373 Bachelors of Arts and of 326 Masters of Arts who emerged from India's colleges and universities, only thirty and five respectively were Muslims.[1]

As has already been seen, educated Muslims in the North-Western Provinces and the Panjab continued to hold a high proportion of official posts and numbers of Muslims were well rewarded with land for their services in 1857–8. This falling off in the numbers of Muslims in higher English education is not therefore wholly explained by the relative poverty of Muslims (particularly in Bengal); it was due, in part, as a number of Muslim witnesses before the (Hunter) Education Commission of 1882 themselves conceded, to a religious and cultural reluctance, or to a determination to complete their religious education first. No doubt the pressure of competition from English-knowing Hindus and, indeed, from other Muslims who could not afford niceties of conscience would eventually have forced the wealthy Muslim of lineage to forsake his traditions and send his son to a religionless government school, but as an individual concession to *force majeure* and with the inference that Islam was only for Fridays. Under pressure, the upper-class Muslim might have become an individual private citizen seeking only his personal advantage, an oriental Samuel Smiles. It is doubtful whether the British really wanted this; an atomised and anonymous

[1] (Hunter) *Education Commission Report (1882)* (Calcutta, 1883), pp. 291, 484, 493.

aggregate of comfortable Muslims was of no use to them politically, whether they believed that a political challenge was likely to come from the Muslim 'lower classes' or from the English-educated Hindu.

From the fate of an embittered and identityless retired gentry, the comfortable Muslims of northern India were rescued by Sir Saiyid Ahmad Khan and other members of the Muslim intelligentsia. By arguing that modern education was not merely opposed to Islam, but was actually Islamic, and by making provision, however limited, for the education of Muslims as a collectivity, they helped to create among upper-class Muslims a sense of corporate unity and of political community in Western terms, a sense which later spread to wider circles of Muslims. That the Muslim upper classes were able to enter into *rapport* with other Indian Muslims was made possible because Sir Saiyid Ahmad Khan and others like him conducted the conversation among Muslims in an Islamic religious idiom. However obnoxious some of their doctrines might be to the orthodox *ʿulama*, the latter at least could recognise that the dialogue between them and Sir Saiyid and his emulators was being conducted in the same language of Islamic conviction. Muslims were not to surrender their souls to the modern world or to lose their distinct religious personality.

SAIYID AHMAD KHAN AND ISLAM AS A RELIGION OF PROGRESS

Sir Saiyid Ahmad Khan was born in October 1817 into the circle of Muslim gentlemen, respectable but not eminent, attached to the Mughal court at Delhi. His father, Mir Muttaqi (died 1837), was something of a recluse, but his maternal grandfather, Khwaja Farid al-din (1747–1828), a mathematics scholar, had been Principal of the Calcutta Madrasa in the seventeen-nineties and had served the East India Company in Lord Wellesley's time on an embassy to Iran. Sir Saiyid received the conventional education of the Muslim gentleman of his day – Qurʾan-reading, the study of Persian through the *Gulistan* and *Bustan* of Saʿdi, a smattering of Arabic and some mathematics and astronomy. Until the death of his father in 1838, he led the gay and undirected life of the insouciant Muslim courtiers in Delhi, but after his father's death he entered the judicial service of the Company, rising by 1857 to the position of *sadr-amin* or Sub-Judge. As a young man in his thirties he took up again the dilettante studies of his youth and published works in praise of the Prophet, against religious innovations, on mechanics and compasses and in proof of the circulation of the sun around the earth. In 1847 he published an account of the antiquities of Delhi, the *Athar ul-Sanadid* (Remains of Princes), which later earned him honorary membership of the Royal Asiatic Society. He also produced an edition of the famous gazetteer of Akbar's empire, the *A'in-i Akbari*. His work before 1857 is a reminder of the cultural vigour and scientific interests of Muslims in Delhi, centring around Delhi College, in the eighteen-forties and fifties.

The year 1857 was a watershed in Sir Saiyid's life and thought. He himself tried to hold the district of Bijnor for the British and, though deeply moved by British atrocities, he resisted the urge to emigrate and determined to stay in India to work for Anglo-Muslim understanding. His *Asbab-i Baghawat-i Hind (Causes of the Indian Revolt*, 1859), his *An Account of the Loyal Mohammedans of India* (1860), his review of Hunter's book (1872), arguing that India was not *dar al-harb*, sought British good-will towards Muslims. His *Tabyin al-Kalam (Explanation of the Word*, 1862–3), his *Essays on the Life of Mohammed* (1870), his articles in his journal *Tahzib al-Akhlaq* (The Refinement of Manners) and his commentary on the Qur'an *(Tafsir al-Qur'an*, 1880–95), among other works, aimed to convince Muslims that Western thought was not anti-islamic, but might now express a correct understanding of Islam. Even today the inspiration of his ideas is by no means clear. His mind roved over the whole of Muslim thought and learning, selecting the arguments to support the conclusion he wished to reach and imposing a kind of teleological consistency upon his thought. He was undoubtedly influenced by the general reformist climate of thought in the nineteenth century, which was ready to go behind the *ijma*ᶜ of the schools of jurisprudence. His opponents were conscious of his debt to the Muᶜtazilites and a modern Indian Muslim *ᶜalim*[2] has suggested analogies between his ideas and those of the Zahiriyya school of jurisprudence, which would derive the law only from the

[2] Saᶜid Ahmad Akbarabadi, 'Sir Saiyid ka dini shᵉur o fikr', *Aligarh Magazine*, special Aligarh Number, 1953–5, p. 89.

literal text of Qur'an and *sunna*, rejecting *qiyas* (reasoning by analogy) and *taqlid* (imitation or acceptance of earlier decisions by jurists). Sir Saiyid's famous biographer Altaf Husain, 'Hali', (1837–1914) has listed forty-one points of difference between him and the orthodox ʿ*ulama* for which there were precedents in earlier Muslim thought and eleven points for which there were none.[3] Sir Saiyid appears to have had close associations with Protestant Christians and missionaries. His *Tabyin al-Kalam* refers repeatedly to the writings of Protestants, for example, the commentaries on the Bible by T. H. Horne (1780–1862), and by George D'Oyley (1778–1846) and R. Mant (1776–1848). Bishop J. W. Colenso's (1814–83) work (probably *The Pentateuch and Book of Joshua Critically Examined*)[4] had apparently been brought to Sir Saiyid's notice within a year or so of publication.[5] In his attitude to religious authority and to the miraculous, there are obvious analogies between Sir Saiyid's thought and that of the liberal Protestants who were beginning to respond to German 'Higher Criticism' and Darwinism in mid-Victorian England. The agenda of his theological concern, however, was entirely Islamic.

Sir Saiyid Ahmad Khan faced what many considered to be the challenge of nineteenth-century science (which he acknowledged to be responsible for the worldly success of the West) to Islamic belief, determined not so much to blunt and repulse it as to show that it did not exist. It has been said[6] that he fashioned an Islam compatible with progress, as a Victorian liberal understood it. In fact he aimed to show that Islam was modern progress and modern progress was Islam properly understood. Sir Saiyid never doubted the unique truth of Islamic doctrine, whether of God or of Prophethood; nothing in the modern world, and certainly not Christianity, impugned that unique truth. Muslims had temporarily failed to control their history because they had lost social efficiency by ossifying their law and usages, rendering them unresponsive to contemporary urgencies, and believing wrongly that God had ordained it so. They had rejected education in the truths of science because they believed that in accepting such education they would be guilty of polytheism. They had believed that obedience to God

[3] Altaf Husain Hali, *Hayat-i Jawid* (Lahore, 1957 ed.), pp. 604–12.
[4] London, 1862.   [5] *Tabyin al-Kalam*, vol. II (Ghazipur, 1863–5), p. 292.
[6] Wilfred Cantwell Smith, *Modern Islam in India* (Lahore, 1943), p. 15.

ended where the study of nineteenth-century natural science began. The laws of science, indeed of 'progress', contradicted the divine dispensation. It was impossible to be both successful and godly.

Sir Saiyid saw clearly that this was indeed *shirk* and that for Muslims to accept a modern education in this spirit was indeed for them to lose their souls. Moreover, for Muslims not to prosper in this world was in itself an affront to God,[7] for had He not singled out His Muslims to inherit the earth? Muslims were not serving God unless they were successful. Indeed, they were not to achieve temporal prosperity in order to obey God better, but in achieving temporal prosperity they *were* obeying God better. But if, as Sir Saiyid believed, following the Western pre-suppositions of his day, the laws of nature formed a closed and immutable system, and if a knowledge of these laws was indispensable for worldly success, how could a Muslim indeed be both successful and a Muslim?

Sir Saiyid met the problem squarely by a restatement of the doctrine of the unity of God (*tauhid*). Islam, he said, is *tauhid*.[8] God is the creator of all existences, the cause of causes and the Lord of Nature.[9] God is therefore responsible for the laws of nature, or, as Sir Saiyid puts its, for the promises of how nature will always behave. Sir Saiyid concedes that it may appear from this doctrine that there is more than one power-house (*karkhana-i qudrat*) in the universe and that therefore God's unity may appear in danger. He resolves the problem by a restatement of the relationship between God's essence *(zat)* and His attributes *(sifat)*. God's essence and what are necessary to His essence, namely His attributes, are as one. His essence decides His attributes and His attributes His essence. It is of God's essence to be the cause of causes and therefore He will have such attributes as are necessitated by this quality of His essence.[10] Among His attributes thus necessitated are the promises or laws by which He will be bound in nature. God's attributes are unlimited and untrammelled, except by His essence and the

---

[7] Speech (in Urdu) at Patna on 26 May 1873, *Mukammal Majmuʿa Lecturon o Speeches* (Lahore, 1900), p. 87.

[8] Lecture 'Islam' at Lahore, on 1 February 1884, *Mukammal Majmuʿa*, p. 288.

[9] Article, 'ʿAqa'id-i Mazhab-i Islam' in *Tahzib al-Akhlaq* for 1 Jumadi al-Sani (6 August 1872), reprinted in *Maqalat-i Sir Sayyid*, ed. by Maulana Muhammad Ismaʿil Panipati, vol. ıı (Lahore, 1962), pp. 8, 16.

[10] Saiyid Ahmad Khan, ' ʿAqa'id', p. 21.

reason why He cannot change those of His attributes which are the laws of nature is that to do so would be to admit a defect (*nuqsan*) in His essence, since essence and attributes are one, although it does not lie in human power to say how.[11]

Sir Saiyid avoids the imputation of setting up a closed system of natural law, separate from and partnering a system of religious law, by arguing that man's reason and knowledge cannot grasp the nature and number of God's attributes and certainly not in the manner in which God Himself understands them.[12] Thus what may appear to be an event under a jurisdiction separate from that of nature, for example a 'miracle', may be explicable as a natural event because it is a manifestation of a Divine attribute which we, as human beings, have failed to conceive as belonging to God. Nature, then, 'that law in conformity to which all objects around us, whether material or immaterial receive their existence and which determines the relation which they bear to each other',[13] is of God's attributes, which are one with His essence and exist from all eternity to all eternity.[14] The unity of God is therefore preserved and Muslims in studying the laws of nature are in effect studying God. Islam is Nature and Nature is Islam.

But Islam is a revealed religion. The Qur'an is the word of God and, according to Muslim belief before Sir Saiyid's day, it speaks of miracles. How can the worlds of revelation be reconciled with the laws of nature? Sir Saiyid answers that the phenomena of God's universe cannot be distinguished as either revealed or natural. Revelation is itself natural. Man receives revelation through that reason which is man's special endowment in the order of nature. Reason in man is itself a form of divine inspiration.[15] Moreover the Qur'an itself was revealed to the Prophet through a natural process; it was written on the heart of Muhammad, who was endowed with the faculty of prophecy by reason of the original excellence of his nature.[16] In a detailed exegesis, Sir Saiyid holds that

[11] *Tahrir fi usul al-tafsir* (Agra, 1892), pp. 35–8; lecture 'Islam', *Mukammal Majmuʿa*, p. 289.

[12] 'Aqa'id-i Mazhab-i Islam', *Maqalat*, vol. II, p. 20.

[13] *A Series of Essays on the Life of Mohammad* (London, 1870), preface, p. x.

[14] *Tahrir fi usul al-tafsir*, p. 35.

[15] *Tafsir al-Qur'an*, vol. III (Lahore, n.d.), pp. 12–13.

[16] 'Wahi-i Ilahi aur Nabuwwat ki Haqiqat', *Maqalat-i Sir Sayyid*, vol. XIII (Lahore, 1963), p. 69.

the text of the Qur'an does not support belief in the occurrence of events against a rational order of nature. He holds, for example, that the Qur'anic account of Moses crossing the Red Sea by dividing its waters with his rod refers to a crossing at the time of ebb tide and that, in any event, the Red Sea was not so deep in Moses' time as in his own. There can never be a conflict between the Word of God and the Work of God.[17]

Sir Saiyid established, to his own satisfaction and to that of many other Muslims, that to study differently was not against the will of God; he had also to establish that it was not disobedience to God to live differently. Christian controversialists informed Muslims that they were 'backward' not despite, but because of, Islam – that the greatest bar to their advancement was their obstinate belief that their laws and social institutions were divinely ordained. (Christian critics usually singled out for attack such institutions as slavery, polygamy, seclusion of women and easy divorce for men but, had they been arguing in economic terms, they might have addressed themselves more to the prohibition of usury and the Muslim laws of inheritance, where a case for a connection between these mandates of the Holy Law and a low rate of capital formation in Muslim countries can at least be made.) Westerners were successful because they were adaptable and dynamic and had learned to separate the laws of the State from the laws of the church. Law for them was a social convenience and as human needs and intentions changed, so could the laws. In the century since the French Revolution Western man, at least in Protestant countries, had assumed to an increasing extent that social problems were soluble by the application of will and intelligence to the social environment. Religion could claim only to inculcate a spirit; to prescribe a detailed and mandatory code of conduct was beyond its sphere. Such assumptions were against the spirit of classical Islam, because they introduced a dualism into the universe and denied the omnipotence of God. The *shariᵉa* was a comprehensive scheme or positively ordained divine law, to which man and society must conform. For Muslims, to assert the sovereignty of the general will, was to deny the sovereignty of God.

Sir Saiyid Ahmad Khan tried to resolve the dilemma facing

---

[17] *Tahrir fi usul al-tafsir*, p. 10 and lecture 'Islam', *Mukammal Majmu ᵉa*, p. 286.

Muslims who wished to adapt themselves to the world the British had brought into existence, by arguing that God's guidance for man in earthly society was not to be found fully spelt out in the verbal revelation of the Qur'an, in the practice of the Prophet or in the deductions which subsequent generations of Muslims had made therefrom. Rather, it was to be sought in the immanent revelation of man's reason applying itself to the changing circumstances of man's social existence. Enlisting Shah Wali-Allah as an authority, Sir Saiyid held that although the Prophets communicated one *din* or belief to mankind, they each brought a different *shari'a*, adapted to the circumstances of their times. There was a clear distinction between the mandates relating to *din*, which were eternal, and those relating to temporal affairs, which were mutable.[18] The Qur'an itself abrogated the laws brought by earlier prophets, because history had outgrown them.[19] The *'ulama* erred in thinking that the Qur'an underpins an unchangeable and divinely ordained code of temporal law. It is rather to be treated as a source of reflection and not of reference; it calls for consideration, not conformity. Sir Saiyid is not prepared to accept the legal authority of Prophetic tradition unless that tradition is in accord with the spirit of the Qur'an as he would interpret it and only then if it embodies a religious commandment; if the tradition refers to a matter of temporal expediency, then man is free to follow it or not as he wishes. Only the manifestly declared commandments of the Qur'an are to be regarded as the commandments of religion. All else is conjectural.[20] Muslims have wrongly come to regard the pronouncements of the *'ulama* as the commandments of religion. *Taqlid* must be abandoned and the gates of *ijtihad* reopened.[21] The character of the received mandates of the *shari'a* must be carefully scrutinised to see if in fact they were mandates of religion.

---

[18] *Tafsir al-Qur'an*, vol. III (Lahore, n.d.), pp. 19–21.

[19] 'Nasikh wa Mansukh ki Bahs', *Maqalat-i Sir Sayyid*, vol. XIII (Lahore, 1963), pp. 139–41.

[20] Letter to Pirji Muhammad 'Arif, printed as an *avant-propos* to Muhammad Qasim Nanotawi, *Tasfiyya al-Aqa'id* (Delhi, 1901), p. 4. This work has been translated in: Aziz Ahmad and G. E. von Grunebaum (eds.), *Muslim Self-Statement in India and Pakistan 1857–1968* (Wiesbaden, 1970), pp. 60–76.

[21] 'Ahl-i Sunna wa Jama'a ke liye Mujtahid ki Zarurat', *Maqalat-i Sir Saiyid*, vol. I (Lahore, 1962), pp. 290–1; see also 'Azadi-i Ra'y, *Maqalat*, vol. v (Lahore, 1962), pp. 213–37.

Sir Saiyid strongly criticised the contemporary Ottoman empire for stagnation through fear of infringing laws wrongly believed to have divine sanction.[22] He did not challenge in so many words the traditional Muslim belief that the mandates of religion should be penally enforced by the temporal government – it was after all an academic issue in an India which he believed would be ruled by the British for as far ahead as he could see – but his own definition of a religious government showed that he himself had abandoned or ignored it. For him a true religious government was one which upheld the rights of its subjects to free and equal expression of opinion, to free and equal exercise of their own religion and to peaceful enjoyment of their property.[23] Certainly this was far from the orthodox Muslim view that truth and right conduct were already fully revealed and recorded and that it was merely the responsibility of men and governments to ensure that that truth was protected and enforced.

Sir Saiyid Ahmad Khan was calling his fellow Muslims to look at themselves in a new light and to take part in a new form of social activity. Instead of the life of obedience to the Holy Law as already known, he was calling them to the strenuous life of free inquiry into what God required of them in the world of the nineteenth century. He called them to a life of joint endeavour rather than to a life of individual obedience. They were together to strive for the welfare of their community as a corporate body endowed with a common will.[24] They were to seek their salvation through serving their community. A dynamic exercise of *ijtihad* in the way that Sir Saiyid proposed would help to bring into being a sense of political community and of common purpose, even though the object of such an exercise was the discovery of the nature and demands of Islam as a religion. Muslims were once again to take command of their souls and then of their destiny in Islam. But the experience of active fellowship was unlikely to stop at the frontiers – and for Muslims there were strictly no such frontiers – of theology, ethics and education. Muslims would find it difficult under the conditions

[22] 'Na-mazhab Mulk aur Na-Mazhab Government', *Maqalat*, vol. ix (Lahore, 1962), pp. 3–4.
[23] Saiyid Ahmad Khan, 'Na-mazhab Mulk', p. 2.
[24] 'Hubb al-Watan', *Maqalat*, vol. v (Lahore, 1961), pp. 49–50; Lecture on 'Qaumi Ta'lim, Qaumi Hamdardi aur Bahami Ittifaq' at Ludhiana, 23 January 1883; *Mukammal Majmu 'a Lecturon o Speeches*.

prevailing in British India after 1857, more difficult than Sir Saiyid Ahmad Khan with his acute sense of the possible, not to extend their experience of dynamism in thought to action and to political action. Meanwhile, Sir Saiyid Ahmad Khan himself responded to his call for public action. He was able to take advantage of the extension of the railway and the telegraph to the chief centres of Muslim population – the railway reached Allahabad, Lucknow and Lahore in the eighteen-sixties – to create a receptive Muslim public for his projects. His position as a senior and respected 'native' servant of the British government (Lytton, as Viceroy, singled him out for special commendation to his successor Ripon in 1880)[25] gave timorous upper-class Muslims the assurance that British officials would not frown upon those who followed his lead. In January 1863, while serving at Ghazipur, he founded a Translation Society, later renamed the Scientific Society and transferred to Aligarh. Its aims were to introduce European sciences to the educated Muslim (and Hindu) of the upper provinces by means of translations of standard textbooks into Urdu, and to improve Indian agriculture by the purchase of more advanced tools and implements. Under Sir Saiyid's guidance it widened the range of its activities to offer friendly comment upon such public questions as the reform of railway management and the Native Marriages Bill of 1869. In 1866 Sir Saiyid founded the *Aligarh Institute Gazette* as an organ of expression for educated Muslims in the upper provinces. It was printed in both Urdu and English in the same issue. Both the Society and the *Gazette* emphasised the advantages to India of British rule and encouraged Europeans to attend meetings and contribute articles.

During and after his visit to England Sir Saiyid planned a 'Muhammadan Anglo-Oriental College', which would impart to Muslims an education along Western lines but concomitantly with Muslim religious teaching. He had originally preferred that the medium of instruction should be the vernacular, but he returned from England convinced that English should be the language of instruction, partly because of the difficulties of rendering scientific and technical terms into the vernacular and partly to avoid stirring up strife over the relative merits of Urdu and Hindi (he looked forward to Hindus attending the proposed college). He argued for a

---

[25] Lytton to Ripon, 8 June 1880, *Letters Despatched 1880, Lytton Papers*, India Office Library EUR E 218, 518/6.

separate and predominantly Muslim college, at which good-class Muslims would be assured of association only with boys of their own class. In the course of his campaign to raise funds for the proposed college, Sir Saiyid argued that better government provision for the education of Muslims in ordinary government colleges or in missionary schools would not suffice, as proper Muslim religious instruction would be lacking. Opposition to his religious views already published in the *Tahzib al-Akhlaq* was, however, so strong[26] among educated Muslims that he had to undertake that they would not be propagated in the proposed college and that religious instruction would be confided to orthodox instructors in whom the subscribers to the college funds had confidence.

With the assistance of the British administration (it helped obtain the land for the college at Aligarh and gave a grant-in-aid) and with the support of subscriptions from the Muslim princes and landed aristocracy, the Muhammadan Anglo-Oriental College started life as a primary school on Queen Victoria's birthday, 24 May 1875. On 1 January the Viceroy, Lord Lytton, formally laid the foundation stone of the college; in 1878 intermediate and in 1881 B.A. classes were started. In 1881, too, a Civil Service preparatory class was started for the many aspiring Muslim government servants and in 1887 the Aligarh college began to prepare students to enter the Engineering College at Roorkee. By 1895, when the college entered some lean years because of embezzlement of its funds, the number of students had risen to 565.

It is, however, important to recognise the limitations of Aligarh as an educational foundation. At no time did it educate a majority of the Muslim graduates even of the North-Western Provinces. Of 1,184 Muslims graduating in India between 1882 and 1892, Aligarh produced only 220, compared with 410 from the University of Allahabad.[27] What Aligarh did was to produce a class of Muslim leaders with a footing in both Western and Islamic culture, at ease both in British and Muslim society and endowed with a consciousness of their claims to be the aristocracy of the country as much in British as in Mughal times. Educated in a residential college which

---

[26] See, for example, letter from ʿAli Bakhsh Khan to Sir Saiyid of 11 July 1873, *Selected Documents from the Aligarh Archives*, ed. Yusuf Husain (London, 1966), pp. 251–60.

[27] T. Morison, *History of the Muhammadan Anglo-Oriental College* (Allahabad, 1903), p. 63.

imitated the English public schools of the time, with its emphasis on character, leadership and prowess in games, rather than scholarship, with debating societies and old boys' associations to maintain college *esprit de corps*, the Aligarh student was encouraged to work for the welfare of the Muslim community in India. Success in examinations and individual achievement were at a discount. According to Crosthwaite (1835–1915), Lieutenant-Governor of the North-Western Provinces, 'it is better for the future of your race. . .that ten men should be sent out than that a hundred should be sent out, able indeed to satisfy the examiners but otherwise imperfectly trained'.[28] The purpose of Aligarh was to further the temporal progress of the Muslim community as its founder visualised it, that is of the gentlemanly portion of it, particularly in northern India. The boys at Aligarh were not exhorted to an unhealthy anxiety about the fate of their souls, or indeed to an individual investigation of God's demands upon them in the modern world. Islam for them was a matter of cultural rather than of religious conviction. Whatever the founder's real intentions, Aligarh became an institution for coming to terms with the British-created world on a footing of equality, rather than for questioning that world from burning religious conviction.

OTHER MUSLIM BRIDGE-BUILDERS

Sir Saiyid Ahmad Khan was by no means alone in India in working for rapprochement between Islam and the nineteenth-century Western-dominated world, although significantly, as a member of the Muslim upper classes in the old centre of Muslim rule, he was alone in founding a gymnasium to train leaders to bring it about. In Bengal, where the problem was less one of Muslim pride and more one of Muslim poverty, ʿAbd al-Latif (1828–93), a government servant with an excellent knowledge of English, founded in 1863 the Muhammadan Literary and Scientific Society of Calcutta, 'to impart useful information to the higher and educated classes of the Mahomedan Community'. It met once a month in ʿAbd al-Latif's house for lectures and discussions. By the middle eighteen-seventies it had more than five hundred members. ʿAbd al-Latif,

---

[28] *Aligarh Institute Gazette* for 20 November 1894, quoted in M. S. Jain, *The Aligarh Movement* (Agra, 1965), p. 44.

however, felt less tension between his Islamic and his British allegiances and was inclined to emphasise the humble origins of the mass of Muslims in Bengal (in 1881 62.81 per cent of male Muslims in Bengal were classed as husbandmen) in explanation of their backwardness in modern education.[29]

Another Muslim of Bengal and Orissa who tended to preach to the converted, those for whom the learning of English posed no great issue of conscience, was Saiyid Amir ʿAli (1849–1928). He was a member of a Cuttack Orissa family, formerly in the service of the Nawwab of Awadh, which had been persuaded by local British officers to give its sons a modern education. Saiyid Amir ʿAli attended the Muhsin College, Hooghly, specialised in English literature and took an M.A. degree before studying law at Calcutta University. After commencing practice at the Calcutta Bar, he won a scholarship to England. He stayed in England between 1869 and 1873, when he was called to the Bar. On return to Calcutta he practised as an advocate, before appointment as a Judge of the Calcutta High Court. In 1873 he published in London *A Critical Examination of the Life and Teachings of Mohammed*, which formed the basis of his more famous *The Spirit of Islam* (1891). Both these works were intended more for a European than for an Indian Muslim readership, but many of their arguments found their way into the thinking of the English-educated Muslim. It is noteworthy that Saiyid Amir ʿAli made no effort to communicate with the Bengali-speaking Muslims of his own provinces, an indication of the social and educational distance between the minority of educated Muslims in Calcutta and other towns and the majority of cultivators, particularly in the rural areas of east Bengal.

Amir ʿAli (who was a *shiʿa*) eschewed theological dilemmas. A student of W. E. H. Lecky (1838–1903), he is a camp-follower of the 'March of Mind', whose vanguard, he asserts, has always been composed of Muslims. 'While the barbarians of Europe who had overturned an effete empire were groping in the darkness of absolute ignorance and brutality, the Moslems were occupied in the task of civilization.'[30] Religion is practical morality and Islam is the most practical morality.[31] 'Everything that elevates the heart of

[29] (Hunter) *Education Commission Report, 1882* (Calcutta, 1883), pp. 500–501.　　[30] Saiyid Amir ʿAli, *A Critical Examination*, p. 338.
[31] Saiyid Amir ʿAli, *A Critical Examination*, p. 204.

man is true, everything that leads to goodness is true.' Islam is a spirit, the spirit of the primal truths implanted in the human breast, 'the latest development of the religious faculties of our being'. It is the highest expression of the innate moral consciousness of humanity and the Prophet Muhammad is its mouthpiece. It 'combines all the highest principles which have actuated humanity from the time it saw light on earth because it combines a sense of virtue with a sense of sin, encourages self-denial, the practice of heroic virtues, self analysis and reliance upon an almighty power in the conflict between Good and Evil'. 'In Islam is joined a lofty Idealism with the most rationalistic practicality.' The Prophet is pre-eminently a moral teacher and the Qur'an is essentially an expression of the process of development through which the mind of Muhammad went.[32]

The various chapters of the Koran which contain the ornate descriptions of paradise whether figurative or literal were delivered wholly or in part in Mecca. Probably in the infancy of his religious consciousness Mohammed himself believed in some or other of the traditions which floated around him. But with the wider awakening of the soul, a deeper communion with the Spirit of the Universe, thoughts which bore a material aspect at first, became spiritualised. The mind of the Teacher progressed not only with the March of Time and the development of his religious consciousness but also with the progress of his disciples in apprehending spiritual conceptions.[33]

The precepts of Islam are adapted to all ages and nations and are in entire accordance with the light of reason. 'The compatibility of the laws of Mohammed with every stage of progress shows their founder's wisdom. The elasticity of laws is the greatest test of their beneficence and usefulness and this merit is eminently possessed by those of Islam.'[34] Islam is the best of religions because it 'introduced into the modern world civilization, philosophy, the arts and the sciences, everything that ennobles the heart and elevates the mind. It inaugurated the reign of intellectual liberty'.[35] Amir ʿAli implies that the Islamic revelation is not, however, uniquely necessary or uniquely true. Religion is necessary chiefly for the elevation

[32] Saiyid Amir ʿAli, *A Critical Examination*, p. 281.
[33] Saiyid Amir ʿAli, *A Critical Examination*, p. 282.
[34] Saiyid Amir ʿAli, *A Critical Examination*, p. 227.
[35] Saiyid Amir ʿAli, *A Critical Examination*, p. 345.

of the masses, 'virtue for its own sake can only be appreciated by minds of superior development'. If all minds were 'superior', Amir ʿAli implies, religion would not be necessary. Furthermore he looks forward to the time when Islam will join hands with the Christianity of 'the devoted Prophet of Nazareth' and 'will march together in the world of civilization' for both religions aim at the same results, namely 'the elevation of mankind'.[36]

It is evident that Amir ʿAli owed more to the rationalism of one of his favourite authors, W. E. H. Lecky, to the Hegelianism of D. F. Strauss' (1808–74) *Life of Jesus* (1835), in which Jesus is represented as expressing an Idea which propels humanity towards perfection, and to popular Darwinianism, than to the Islam of revelation and servanthood. Islam is a useful lubricant for the engine of progress. Conservatism and *taqlīd* must give way before the spirit of the religion of reason and rationality; polygamy and slavery as practised in Islam worked for the progress of mankind and represented a higher stage in human evolution than what had gone before, in Iran or under the Byzantines. Islam elaborated a fundamentally republican political system, which stressed the freedom and equality of those who lived under it.[37] In presenting Islam, however, as a religion with all the modern virtues, Amir ʿAli was presenting it as a religion which the ʿulama and the mass of Muslims could not recognise as their own. Sir Saiyid Ahmad Khan discussed fundamental issues of belief in a manner which, however heretical, was demonstrably Islamic. Amir ʿAli evaded such issues and presented Islam as a successful historical phenomenon and a world force. Not only did he encourage a sterile narcissism among English-educated Muslims, but he helped to create that educational chasm between the modern-educated and the traditionally-educated Muslim, where the one does not know the religion he is defending but defends it all the same, and the other knows his religion but does not know against what he is defending it.

BRITISH RULE IS ACCEPTED AS LAWFUL

Proof that Islam was a modern religion, or rather a religion for the modern world, was the obverse of the coin of Anglo-Islamic

[36] Saiyid Amir ʿAli, *A Critical Examination*, pp. 345–6.
[37] *The Life and Teachings of Mohammad or the Spirit of Islam* (London, 1891), p. 425.

reconciliation. The reverse was proof that Muslims were not obliged by their religion permanently to remain disaffected subjects of the British empire or wage an armed struggle against it. Hunter and others had charged Islam with being essentially a political religion, which must resent actively any rule by the infidel over the believer. There is no doubt that many Muslims had examined their consciences on this issue in the late eighteen-sixties, when the 'Wahhabi' excitement was at its height, and had given somewhat equivocal answers. Although the issue might appear dead, as several generations of Muslims had given their loyal service to the British since the establishment of British rule in Bengal after Plassey, nevertheless the events of 1857 were bound to revive it. Not only had many Muslims fought against the British, but the British had also destroyed the last illusions that they were acting as the *locum tenens* for the Mughal. British forces had taken by storm and then savagely looted a Delhi defended by Muslims under Muslim command; they had slain many members of the Mughal family and they had tried and exiled Bahadur Shah, after a degrading imprisonment. They must indeed have appeared in Muslim eyes as a new wave of Mongols.

The *mujahidin* on the frontier were merely defending an outpost of Islam, in the same way as the forces of the Delhi sultanate had done from the reverse direction in the days of Sultan Balban (1266–1287). Yet in 1857–8 the British had won and in winning had shown that the source of their power lay far across the seas, beyond the reach of Indians to destroy; furthermore they were ruling India in such a way that only non-Muslims could benefit from any display of utter Muslim intransigence. There were many English-educated Hindus willing to step into Muslim shoes in the official services. After 1857 it was a favourite British epigram that 'we rule India by British bayonets and native *tahsildars*'[38] and there were plenty of potential as well as actual, non-Muslim *tahsildars*. Must Muslims for ever be condemned to spit impotently into the wind? In the India of the Crown the British would visit the consequences of acting upon any *fatwa* that India was *dar al-harb* upon the Muslim office-seeker, who was already falling behind in the 'race of life' through backwardness in learning English.

[38] C. L. Tupper, in *Notes on Local Self-Government*, on 6 July 1882 found in loose *Proceedings of the Panjab Home Dept. (General) 1883*, Lahore Record Office.

In the predicament of Indian Muslims the *shariᶜa* provided only some indications, but no indisputable conclusions, as to where their duty lay. The Muslim *fuqaha* or jurists had formulated their position under the Ummayads and ᶜAbbasids, that is in the imperial phase of Islamic history, when it was not inconceivable that the Caliphate would become a universal state. In postulating a condition of permanent war between the abode of Islam and the lands of the infidel, the jurists were acting from a position of military strength. God's pleasure that the whole world should become Muslim was possible of fulfilment. If non-Muslims refused, if 'People of a Book', to acknowledge Islam's political supremacy by payment of poll-tax (*jizya*), or, if polytheists, to accept Islam itself, then *jihad* or Holy War was to be declared upon them.

It is true, however, that certain conditions limited this obligation: the obligation to wage *jihad* was *farz al-kifaya*, that is a duty which could be performed by some on behalf of all Muslims, rather than *farz al-ᶜain*, that is an absolute obligation on the individual believer, unless there was a sudden and unexpected attack on *dar al-Islam* by unbelievers. (It might therefore be argued that Muslims resident in India need not themselves take up arms against the British, since the *mujahidin* were fulfilling the *farz al-kifaya* on the north-west frontier.) Then again, *jihad* should be declared by a properly qualified *imam* and the identity of such an *imam* was obscure in British India. Some Hanafi jurists, evolving their doctrine outside India, were ready to accept a region as *dar al-Islam* as long as even one commandment of the *shariᶜa* was obeyed there. But the weightier doctrine was that a *dar al-Islam* conquered by infidels became *dar al-harb* when the law of the infidels was enforced in it, when the region in question directly adjoined an existing *dar al-harb* and when Muslims and their non-Muslim *zimmis* no longer enjoyed any protection there.

Muslim jurisprudence could offer no clear prescriptions, however, where a large Muslim population lived permanently under a non-Muslim government of which many Muslim princes (for example the Nizam of Hyderabad or the Nawwab of Awadh) had been active allies and under which many Muslims had loyally served; where the world balance of power was permanently tilted in favour of the infidel; where there was no generally accepted Muslim *imam* or *khalifa*, and where, it might be said, there was a large non-Muslim majority ready to take advantage of any Muslim mishandling of relations with their foreign rulers.

Without a religious hierarchy and without a recognisable political centre, the Muslim community in India could only be seen to be accepting or rejecting British rule by its reactions over a period to the pronouncements of individual Muslims. No general consensus of all sections of the community in fact emerged; those with expectations or hopes of British favour accepted the favourable arguments put forward in Bengal and in the upper provinces under the aegis of the Muhammadan Literary Society of Calcutta, or by Sir Saiyid Ahmad Khan; those without such expectations and the traditionally educated accepted the reserved *fatawa* of prominent *ʿulama*; others, such as the *faraʾizis* and the active followers of Saiyid Ahmad of Bareilly, retained the conviction that India was *dar al-harb*, but after the eighteen-seventies avoided open conflict with their rulers. British officials knew very well that the issue would be decided on political, social and economic, rather than upon theological considerations.

It is said[39] that Mayo in 1870 induced a group of *ʿulama* to issue a *fatwa* declaring India *dar al-Islam*; his papers themselves give no grounds for this statement. The government was approached in November 1870 by Maulawi ʿAbd al-Latif to know if the British would consider desirable a lecture by Maulawi Karamat ʿAli of Jaunpur (1800–73) *(see below)*, proving that *jihad* in the circumstances of British India was unlawful. Mayo replied through Sir John Strachey (1823–1907), a member of the Viceroy's Council, that he could not see why the matter was referred to him. 'I object to any mention of this Govt. *authorizing* a discussion of this kind, or assuming any responsibility on its account and I think it would be sufficient to say that we feel confident that the respectable Mahomedan gentlemen named would not lend themselves to the discussion of any subject which would give any opportunity to the evil-disposed to advocate resistance to the powers that be.'[40] Hunter was probably speaking for British officialdom when he expressed suspicion that any declaration that India was still a *dar al-Islam* was insincere.[41]

[39] Anil Seal, *The Emergence of Indian Nationalism* (Cambridge, 1968), p. 13, n. 5.
[40] No. 370 of *Letters Despatched Oct.–Dec. 1870*. No. 41 of *Mayo Papers*.
[41] Hunter, *The Indian Musalmans*, pp. 120–3.

He would rather have Muslims openly acknowledge that India was *dar al-harb*, but that they lived there as *musta'min* or as residents under protection and therefore had an obligation under the *shari*ᶜa to live peaceably under British rule.[42] A similar view was expressed a decade later, in 1881, by another British writer N. B. E. Baillie (1799–1883).[43]

The lecture given by Maulavi Karamat ᶜAli, referred to above, was given under the auspices of Maulawi ᶜAbd al-Latif's Muhammadan Literary Society of Calcutta on 23 November 1870. The lecturer was already a critic of the *fara'izi* doctrine that the Friday and ᶜid prayers should be suspended under British rule and had debated the question with the *fara'izi* leader ᶜAbd al-Jabbar at Barisal in 1867. He was a follower of the Hanafi school of jurisprudence. In his lecture at ᶜAbd al-Latif's house in Calcutta, he argued that British India was *dar al-Islam* and that therefore *jihad* was unlawful, as the three conditions laid down by Abu Hanifa for the conversion of a *dar al-Islam* into a *dar al-harb* were not satisfied. He asserted that most of the injunctions of Islam in the sphere of marriage, divorce, dower and inheritance were in force under British rule, that Muslims enjoyed full religious liberty and that the countries to the north-west of India were Muslim. He supported his argument by citing the authority of such legal digests as the *Fatawa-i ᶜAlamgiri*, the *Hidaya* and the *Durr al-Mukhtar*.[44] His audience had less taste for jurisprudential than for political arguments, for ᶜAbd al-Latif preferred to invoke British support for Ottoman Turkey in the Crimean war and in 1870, when Russia repudiated the clauses of the Treaty of Paris (1856) forbidding Russian military and naval establishments on the Black Sea, as proof that the British were defenders of Islam and therefore ought not to be the victims of *jihad*.[45] Probably few Muslims were convinced by Maulavi Karamat ᶜAli's lecture who did not already wish to be convinced.

Sir Saiyid Ahmad Khan's arguments for acceptance of British rule as legitimate were drawn from the armoury of Muslim theories

[42] Hunter, *The Indian Musalmans*, p. 137.
[43] N. B. E. Baillie, 'On the duty of Mohammedans in British India', *Journal of the Royal Asiatic Society*, 1881, pp. 430–4.
[44] *Abstract of the Proceedings of the Mahomedan Literary Society of Calcutta on 23rd November, 1870, Lecture by Moulvie Karamat Ali* (Calcutta, 1871), pp. 2–5.
[45] *Abstract*, pp. 14–15.

of the sultanate, as well as from Muslim jurisprudence. In a speech delivered at Muradabad in 1858 praying for the welfare of the Viceroy and Queen Victoria, he addressed God as one who had given dominion over Muslims to the British, who were just rulers. In 1862, in a prayer of thanksgiving for the recovery of the Prince of Wales from a serious illness, Sir Saiyid asserted that Islam teaches thankfulness and a sense of obligation to a just ruler. Since the government of Queen Victoria ruled in India without communal or religious bias *(qaumi aur mazhabi tarafdari)*, Muslims should acknowledge their gratitude.[46] He did not go further than this.

In answer to Hunter's book, however, Sir Saiyid deployed arguments drawn, like those of Maulavi Karamat ʿAli, from the Hanafi school of jurisprudence. *Jihad* against infidels is not lawful where Muslims have left their families and their property under the protection of the infidel, or where Muslims are living in peace and security under non-Muslim government, where there exists a treaty between Muslim and non-Muslim and where Muslims have no chance of success in war.[47] If India were invaded by another power, Muslims would be sinners against their faith if they assisted the invader, for they live in India with every sort of religious liberty. They are able to call the faithful to prayer, to preach and write openly, to resist the propaganda of Christian missionaries and to make converts themselves from Christianity. However, Sir Saiyid goes on to pronounce that India is neither *dar al-Islam* nor *dar al-harb*, but something of both, and adds significantly – and let it be said with honesty – that although there is no religious obligation upon Muslims to fight the British, their behaviour in any crisis affecting the survival of British rule will depend upon their 'national circumstances' *(mulki halat)*.[48] Sir Saiyid and Hunter meet in the middle under the star of political expediency. Sir Saiyid's review of Hunter's book was, however, published in London and was addressed more to the British than to his fellow Muslims; again it was unlikely to have convinced those who were not already convinced.

Chiragh ʿAli (1844–95) resembled Saiyid Amir ʿAli in that his arguments for the reinterpretation of Islam were more likely to

---

[46] *Mukammal Majmuʿa Lecturon o Speeches* (Lahore, 1900), pp. 3, 7.
[47] Syed Ahmed Bahadoor, C.S.I., *Dr Hunter's Our Indian Musalmans* (London, 1872), pp. 9–10.
[48] *Dr Hunter's Our Indian Musalmans*, pp. 77, 86–7.

appeal to Muslims who had already opted for a modern education. In his *Proposed Political, Legal and Social Reforms in the Ottoman Empire and other States*,[49] he affirmed that the Qur'an taught certain religious doctrines and general rules of morality, but did support a detailed code of divinely sanctioned and immutable 'civil law'. Legislation, he said, is a science experimental and inductive, not logical and deductive. The Qur'an is the revealed law and the *shari°a* or *fiqh* is the 'Muhammadan Common Law', which is distinct from the revealed law both in content and in authority. The books of *fiqh* take little from the Qur'an.[50] No doubt Muslim jurisprudence was well-suited to early Muslim society, but now 'there are certain points in which the Mohammedan Common Law is irreconcilable with the modern needs of Islam and requires modification. The original teachings of the Prophet must be quoted against subsequent usages' – in particular polygamy and slavery. As for the question of *jihad* and whether India is now *dar al-Islam* or *dar al-harb*, this is purely a question of jurisdiction in the law courts, and has nothing to do with religious rebellion or the prosecution of a religious war of aggression. As 'British India has no Mohammedan sovereign, no Mohammedan courts of justice, it is superfluous for the Mohammedan or Christian inhabitants of India to discuss the question.' Chiragh °Ali states plainly that *fiqh* was worked out on the assumption that Muslims were a conquering rather than a conquered people. India is neither *dar al-Islam* nor *dar al-harb*, it is simply British India and, as Muslims therein are subject to and protected by the British government, a subtle casuist may call it a *dar al-aman* or *dar al-zimma*, that is a home of security or of protection.[51] In his *A Critical Exposition of the Popular Jihad*, Chiragh °Ali argued that the 'fighting injunctions' of the Qur'an were not to be considered as religious precepts for all time; the wars of the Prophet were wholly defensive and 'had every justification under the natural and international law'. Muslim jurists had wrongly authorised the levy of *jizya* which 'mostly consists of uncertain traditions, Arabian usages and customs, some frivolous and fortuitous analogical deductions from the Koran and a multitudinous array of casuistical sophistry of the canonical legists'.[52]

---

[49] Bombay, 1883.   [50] *Proposed Political, Legal and Social Reforms*, p. 8.
[51] *Proposed Political, Legal and Social Reforms*, p. 25.
[52] *A Critical Exposition of the Popular Jihad* (Calcutta, 1885), pp. 159–60.

Chiragh 'Ali brushes aside twelve centuries of authoritative interpretation with a casual wave of his pen.

More typical of the common-sense and matter-of-fact Muslim,
who was not prepared to act so cavalierly towards his past and yet
who wished to make the best of the second best, was Maulawi Nazir
Ahmad (1833–1912), the Urdu novelist, who rose to be a deputy-
collector in the British service before becoming a member of the
Board of Revenue in the state of Hyderabad. As there is no mention
of the English in the Qur'an, he said, Muslims need to consider
yielding obedience to them most carefully. It is true that God and
the Prophet have commanded obedience to the powers that be, but
the command is to obey Muslim, not Christian, powers. If non-
Muslim rulers oppress their Muslim subjects, they should migrate
to *dar al-Islam*, but the English protect Muslims' rights, without
special regard to their own religion. It is true that many of the
mandates of the *shari'a* have fallen into abeyance and a new mode
of Islam has appeared, in which the *shari'a* is 'half partridge, half
quail'.[53] The fundamental purpose of the *shari'a* is to provide
security and this the English laws do, only in a different way. For
Indian Muslims the English laws are the *shari'a*: if this is not so,
then Hindustan is *dar al-harb* and therefore a place from which
Muslims should migrate, but then no *sunni*, no *muqallid* or *ghair-
muqallid*, no *sufi*, no *shi'a* or member of the *ahl-i hadith* proposes
this. It is therefore common sense for Muslims to accept British
rule.

Even traditionalist 'ulama, hostile to the modern world and antipathetic to the British, pronounce *fatawa* which permit Muslims to
live quietly under British rule and to accept service under them.
'Abd al-Haiy (1848–86), a prominent '*alim* of the Farangi Mahall,
the famous seminary at Lucknow founded in Aurangzib's reign,
quotes Abu Hanifa's three conditions for the conversion of *dar
al-Islam* into *dar al-harb* and implies they do not exist in British
India, and that consequently it would be wrong to rebel.[54] Although
it is better, he says, to avoid social intercourse with *kafirs*, he considers the acceptance of British pensions and employment and the
learning of English to be lawful as long as no harm to Islam results.[55]

[53] *Al-Huquq wa al-Fara'iz* (Delhi, 1324/1906), p. 131.
[54] *Majmu'a-i Fatawa*, Urdu trans., vol. II (Cawnpore, 1373/1953), p. 151.
[55] *Majmu'a-i Fatawa*, II, pp. 179, 218–19, 233.

Other *ulama* preferred silence when bluntly asked to give a decision. As late as 1309/1891–2, the Deobandi *alim* Rashid Ahmad Gangohi (1828–1905) refused to give a clear answer when bluntly asked for a *fatwa*.[56]

Thus educated Muslims in Mayo's time and after moved only as far towards the British as was necessary to encourage their rulers to continue the process of conciliation started by Mayo's education resolution. Neither party, however, mistook the coquetry of courtship for real affection. Even Sir Saiyid Ahmad Khan, as his private letters show, never forgot that the British were rebels against God. The British never weakened in their conviction that Muslims believed themselves created to rule and that Muslim discontent was more to be feared than any other in India. Moreover, there was no Muslim intellectual capitulation to the Western world. Sir Saiyid Ahmad Khan and other Muslims who wished for a *modus vivendi* argued from Muslim premises and from Muslim authority. That the Qur'an was in some sense Divine Revelation, perfect and whole, was never challenged. The source of law was in some sense God. Sir Saiyid intended to be a *mujtahid* whose *ijtihad* would be accepted by the whole community. Although his ideas were related to the problems of the comfortable and educated minority, he spoke as if to all Muslims. Merely in speaking as if they were leaders of a community with a corporate *rôle* in a play about the destiny of great societies, Sir Saiyid and his fellow moderns helped to create the sense among Muslims that they were a great self-determining all-Indian association, at least for purposes of religion.

[56] *Fatawa-i Rashidiyya*, vol 1 (Muradabad, n.d. [1906]), p. 87.

5

MUSLIMS MOVE TOWARDS POLITICAL COMMUNITY 1871-1901

Lord Mayo had recognised before his assassination that Muslims formed a distinctively dangerous class of Her Majesty's subjects in India, which it would be politic to conciliate. His papers on education indeed suggest that for him they were Her Majesty's Catholic Irish subjects in India, requiring for political reasons recognition of their peculiar cultural traditions. Lord Mayo saw them as a collection of private citizens whose religion happened to be Islam, whose educated classes had formerly acted as a ruling *élite* in certain areas of India, and whose lower classes were currently given to religious revivalism. He did not visualise them as an active political association or community upon an all-India scale. Muslims were to be the passive recipients of limited British favours; indeed not all Muslims were to be such recipients, but only those who could be persuaded to accept a British-conceived future. Within fifteen years of the Mutiny and Rising, no British statesman accepted the Muslims or indeed any other grouping of their Indian subjects as politically activist, still less as politically self-determining. By the eighteen-nineties, however, British statesmen and officials were prepared to see in the Muslims a great and separate political community and, what is more important, many Muslims were only too willing, for their own reasons, to see themselves likewise.

BRITISH RULE ENCOURAGES COMMUNITY-CONSCIOUSNESS

The very idiom of British rule after 1857 encouraged the development of political consciousness by religious communities. The proclaimed British intention of maintaining impartially the right of each religion to the free public practice of its observances encouraged co-operative action within communities to seek redress for any infringement of that right. Government through a civil service to which, in the lower ranks at least, Indians were recruited on the basis of educational qualifications and professional skills, introduced new arenas of competition for power, patronage and social prestige. But, as Sir Saiyid Ahmad Khan was to say, competition was now in the exercise of the pen, not of the sword. Books like Hunter's, and the shared experiences of classroom, examination-room and collector's '*daftar*', taught Muslims that they were at some disadvantage as a group in this new form of social competition. In areas like the Panjab,[1] where British fears of Muslim discontent resulted in the maintenance of a balance between communities on local government boards, whether by official nomination or, after the extension of the elective principle under the Ripon reforms of 1882–3, by the introduction of separate electorates, Muslims were naturally encouraged to organise themselves as an avowedly Muslim pressure group to win further concessions from the government. The British practice of appointing commissions of inquiry, which then invited the submission by Indians of oral or written evidence, encouraged the idea that the ruled should actively participate in the process of governmental decision-making.

All this was for the Muslims (as indeed for the non-Muslims of British India) the beginning of a sea-change in the life of their community. In terms of Islamic theory, ideally the common life of Muslims under the *shariᶜa* was politically speaking a passive life; so long as the caliph or sultan was enforcing the Divine Law, it was not for Muslims to come together to take political initiatives. Moreover, in practice, although the Muslims of the Panjab, Gujarat, or Bengal, could be said to have lived under one and the same political system in the seventeenth century, they had lived passively as subjects of an autocratic government and not as active participants, on however limited a scale, in the process of political decision-making. But now they lived under a government seen to profess a belief in self-improvement to be attained by joint action in consultation and co-operation with their rulers. How were Muslims to present themselves to the attention of government? Social and economic, regional and linguistic divisions between Muslims in

---

[1] The Panjab situation is discussed in N. Gerald Barrier, 'The Punjab Government and Communal Politics 1870–1908', *Journal of Asian Studies*, xxvii, 3 May 1968, pp. 523–39. This article is a useful warning against the assumption that 'British policy was put into effect by a monolithic bureaucracy'.

British India ran deep. Apart from religion it was difficult to see what tie associated the Mappilla (Moplah) cultivator of the Malabar coast and the descendant of Mughal office-holders in the North-Western Provinces, or the Muslim cultivator of eastern Bengal and the Muslim lawyer of Calcutta. Moreover, as has been seen in Chapter 2, British rule had not provided the Muslims of widely-separated provinces with the bond of common grievances. It would not be surprising therefore if Muslims asserted that the aspiration to be Muslim was the highest common factor of political unity among them, particularly as the British themselves were always asserting that this religious aspiration must necessarily, in the nature of Islam, have political implications.

In the eighteen-seventies and eighteen-eighties, when, through involvement in the defence of the Ottoman empire against Russia, the acquisition of Cyprus and intervention in Egypt, Britain was becoming a colonial power in the centre of the Muslim world, British statesmen began to depict the British empire in India as a 'Muhammadan' power and to consider the Muslims of India as one of the balls to be kept in the air in the jugglery of world-policy. Indian Muslims themselves also began to show interest in the fortunes of Muslim countries under European political pressure. It was the novelist-Viceroy, Lord Lytton (1831–91), who first introduced the Indian Muslims into the consideration of Middle-Eastern policy, where indeed they remained until the days of Churchill, sometimes as a ghoul, sometimes as a phantom, sometimes as a Frankenstein's monster, but always as a bogy.

In May 1877, within a month of the Russian declaration of war on Turkey, Lytton wrote to Lord Salisbury (1830–1903), then Secretary of State for India,

So far as I can judge the feeling of our Mahomedan subjects at the present moment is eminently satisfactory, more loyal than it has been at any former period perhaps. But all the Government officers whose special business it is to study and watch Mahomedan feeling in India are strongly of opinion that, were we suspected by our Mahomedan subjects of active connivance with Russia in the spoliation of Turkey, and yet more, did they see us openly sharing the plunder, we should probably be at once confronted by an internal embarrassment sufficiently serious to paralyse all external action on our part; we should not only have to reckon on a *real* jehad all around our frontier, but in every Anglo-Indian home there would be a traitor, a foe and possibly an assassin. Such a danger might possibly be more difficult to deal with than the mutiny which cost us such an effort to suppress.[2]

Later Lytton entreated Salisbury not to rely on assurances from men like Sir George Campbell, that Indian Muslims cared nothing for the fate of the Ottoman sultan.

It is my strong impression that, at the present moment, the lives of all your officers and European subjects in India mainly depend on the course of your Eastern policy and its freedom from all appearance of subserviency to Russia. . .There is no getting over the fact that the British empire is a Mahomedan power, and that it entirely depends upon the policy of Her Majesty's Government, whether the sentiment of our Mahomedan subjects is to be an immense security or an immense danger, to us.[3]

The 'Indian Muhammadan' bugaboo in British foreign policy had been born. For all that the Viceroyalty of India had turned Lytton from a novelist into a writer of thrillers, there was in this period increased interest among Indian Muslims in the fate of international Islam. Turkish successes against the Russians in the war of 1877–8 were celebrated in India and money collected and sent to Turkey. Saiyid Ahmad Khan himself had popularised the use of the Turkish *fez* in India, had sent a copy of his *Essay on the Life of Mohammed* to the Ottoman sultan ʿAbd al-ʿAziz (1861–76) and had praised several Ottoman sultans as social reformers.[4] Chiragh ʿAli in 1883 dedicated his *The Proposed Political, Legal and Social Reforms in the Ottoman Empire and other Mohammedan States* to the Ottoman ʿAbd al-Hamid (1876–1909) and addressed him as *amir al-muʾminin* and *khalifa*. In 1879 the journalist, political promoter and under-cover agent[5] Jamal al-din al-Afghani (1838–97), whose articles in his journal *Al-ʿUrwa al-Wuthqa* (The Indissoluble Link) called for the unity and common action of all Muslims against European imperialism, visited India. Although some of his articles were published in Muslim journals in Lucknow and Calcutta, it is

[2] Lytton to Salisbury, 21 May 1877, *Lytton Papers, Letters Despatched 1877*, vol. II, pp. 405, 519–20.
[3] *Letters Despatched 1877*, vol. II, p. 519.
[4] Aziz Ahmad, 'Sayyid Ahmad Khan, Jamal al-Din al-Afghani and Muslim India', *Studia Islamica* (Paris), XIII, 1960, p. 68.
[5] See Elie Kedourie, *Afghani and Abduh* (London, 1966).

doubtful whether he made much stir amongst persons of consequence.

W. S. Blunt (1840–1922), who toured India in the winter of 1883–1884, found many of the Muslim intelligentsia, including Chiragh ʿAli and Saiyid Husain Bilgrami (1851–1911) of Hyderabad, hostile to Gladstone's policy in Egypt. Blunt says the old British alliance with the Ottomans was popular and cast Russia as Islam's chief enemy. But the Treaty of Berlin, the British acquisition of Cyprus, the abandonment of Tunis to French occupation in 1881 and the defeat of ʿUrabi (1841–1911), a staunch Muslim freedom fighter, at Mers al-Kebir in 1882 had wrought a change in some Muslim minds.[6] Blunt dined in Calcutta with a *maulawi* and his students, who did not conceal their hatred for England or their hope that the Mahdi in the Sudan would drive the British out of Egypt. 'It is clear that they would welcome any deliverer here, Russian or French or from the Devil.'[7]

Hali's (1837–1914) famous poem *Musaddas* (1879) evoked and expressed Indian Muslim nostalgia for the time when Islam was the great world force. Probably Sultan ʿAbd al-Hamid was the first Ottoman sultan in whose name the *khutba* was read in Muslim India. It was ironic that British foreign policy directors in London were beginning to move away from diplomatic and military support for the Ottoman empire in favour of physical control of the Muslim lands along the route to India just at the time when British administrators in India were trying to give Indian Muslims a stake in British rule.

Although British officials concerned in education were far from accepting that Hunter's rhetorical account of and explanations for Muslim backwardness in education had any solidity outside Bengal, the cumulative effect of discrete decisions in the eighteen-seventies and eighteen-eighties was to establish the myth that Muslims were all over India, an educationally deprived community, needing protection and patronage. Figures for 1871–2 showed that Muslims in the three provinces longest exposed to English education, Madras, Bombay and Bengal (with Assam), formed 4.4 per cent, 8.2 per cent and 14.4 per cent respectively of the school and college population and in 1881–2, 6.5 per cent, 14.7 per cent and 23.8 per cent.

---

[6] W. S. Blunt, *India under Ripon* (London, 1909), pp. 294–5.
[7] Blunt, *India under Ripon*, pp. 112–13.

This represented a considerable improvement both absolutely and relatively to their proportion of the population in those provinces, which in 1881–2 was 6.1 per cent, 10.9 per cent and 28.6 per cent.[8] In the North-Western Provinces and the Panjab in 1871–2, Muslims were 17.8 per cent and 34.9 per cent of the school and college population respectively and in 1881–2 16.8 per cent and 38.2 per cent.

It is true that Muslim proportions fell off sharply at the higher levels of instruction, though most unevenly province by province. Thus in 1881–2 in Awadh only 5.5 per cent of those who went to English colleges were Muslim and in the Panjab 12.6 per cent,[9] in relation to population proportions of 10.0 per cent and 48.2 per cent. On the other hand, 45.1 per cent and 58.1 per cent respectively of those who went to Oriental colleges were Muslim. Between 1881–1882 and 1885–6 the percentage of Muslims to the whole body of students in Arts colleges increased from 9.3 per cent to 13.6 per cent.[10] This increase occurred in a period before the government had taken more than verbal action on the recommendations of the 1882 Education Commission's report. The Education Commission itself conceded that the poor showing of Muslims in the education statistics had, except in college education, been exaggerated; as early as 1871 officials were quick to point out that in the upper provinces Muslims at school were more than holding their own in comparison with Hindus.[11] Nevertheless the Education Commission committed itself to 'a leaning towards generosity' in the treatment of Muslims, recommending *inter alia* the recognition of Hindustani in primary and middle schools as the Muslim vernacular, (which in the Panjab, Madras or Bengal it was not) the teaching of Persian and Hindustani in middle and upper schools, the adoption of special standards in Muslim primary schools, the encouragement of higher education for Muslims, a graduated system of scholarships for Muslims, the recruitment of more Muslim inspectors of schools, a special section on Muslim education in the annual official reports on public instruction and, going outside the Commission's terms of

[8] *Education Commission Report (1882)*, p. 484; Sir Alfred Croft, *Review of Education in India in 1886* (Calcutta, 1888), p. 314.

[9] *Ed. Com. Report*, pp. 496, 494.

[10] Croft, *Review*, p. 315.

[11] *Selections from the Records of the Govt. of India (Home Dept.)*, ccv, pp. 191, 212.

reference, that provincial governments should be asked to consider appointing by patronage a proportion of Muslim public servants.[12] Somewhat over-ready to confuse the aspirations of its upper-class Muslim witnesses with those of humbler Muslims, the Commission in its report did not question the propriety of spending the little public money available on teaching Persian to aspirants to minor government employment or to the sons of middling landholders. It appears to have assumed that the Muslim community was an academic gymnasium in which the humblest day-labourer of East Bengal aspired to fit himself to compete for public appointments (an assumption criticised by Nawwab ʿAbd al-Latif)[13] and to acquire the accomplishments of a Muslim savant. Disregarding the evidence submitted by several provincial British officials that whole classes of Muslims did not regard and had never regarded themselves as contestants, the Commission's report spoke of 'the Muhammadans' as a 'class' who 'have fallen behind in the race of life under British rule'.[14] Although the provincial governments themselves showed every awareness of the varied educational needs and aspirations of different classes of Muslims, the Government of India resolutions of 23 October 1884 (which spoke of it being desirable to give Muslims 'in some respects exceptional assistance') and of 15 July 1885 (which assumed that 'the Muhammadans' as such aspired to rival Hindus in state employment) helped to endow the Muslims with a separate social as well as religious personality, which needed to be recognised in British policy.

The Resolution of 1885, indeed, was emphatic that a special section of the annual education reports should be devoted to Muslim education so that the Governments might be kept fully informed of 'the state and progress of the Muhammadan community'. If educated Muslims could supply leaders, the Government was ready to grant them followers. Although in 1886–7 the governments of the North-Western Provinces, Madras, the Panjab, Central Provinces, Assam and Berar all declared that they required to take no special measures to promote Muslim education,[15] the *suggestio falsi* that

---

[12] *Ed. Com. Report*, pp. 505–7.
[13] *The Present Condition of the Indian Mahomedans and the Best Means for its Improvement* (Calcutta, 1883), p. 4.
[14] *Ed. Com. Report*, p. 6.
[15] Croft, *Review*, pp. 318, 322.

the special disabilities of certain classes of Muslims in Bengal and Bombay affected all Muslims in British India everywhere, was given official respectability in Government of India resolutions and thereafter proved beyond the power of facts to expose.

In official employment, Muslims in the three original territories of British India, Bengal, Bombay and Madras, were doing relatively badly and Muslims in the upper provinces and the Panjab relatively well. Those in the first group had nothing to gain by simultaneous examinations and open competition by written examination with certain classes of Hindus and those in the second group had everything to lose. In 1886 in Bengal, Muslims held 12.9 per cent of the executive and 3.1 per cent of the judicial positions in the uncovenanted civil service, although they formed 31.2 per cent of the population. In Bombay and Sind the percentages were 7.4 and 0.8 respectively, in relation to a population proportion of 18.3, and in Madras the percentages were 5.4 and 1.6, in relation to a population proportion of 6.2 per cent. In the North-Western Provinces and Awadh, however, Muslims held 44.8 and 45.9 per cent respectively of the executive and judicial appointments, in relation to an overall population proportion of 13.4 per cent.[16]

In the Panjab, Muslims held 41.8 and 33.6 per cent of these appointments as against a population proportion of 51.3 per cent, but their position was better than it appears, for the population figures included the tribesmen of the British-administered areas of the frontier, who were hardly aspirants to a settled life let alone to office under a régime they detested. A less misleading picture is given in a Panjab Government return of 1883, where fifty-four Muslims are recorded as holding the executive post of extra-assistant-commissioner as against thirty-eight Hindus, and of a total of 312 of extra-assistant-commissioner, *tahsildar*, *munsif* and superintendent of settlement, 141 or 45 per cent, are held by Muslims. However, in those posts where professional and examination qualifications were required, such as those of assistant-surgeon and professor and headmaster in the education department, Muslims fared as badly in the Panjab as elsewhere, holding only 23.1 per cent of such posts.[17]

[16] *Report of the Public Service Commission 1886-7* (Calcutta, 1888), p. 38.
[17] Proc. no. 5, 'Present Condition of the Muhammadans in the Panjab', *Panjab Home Department (General) Proceedings* for April 1883.

In the Central Provinces, where Muslims were only 2.4 per cent of the population, they held 18.1 per cent of the executive and judicial positions combined. It was in Bengal that they provided the basis for the generalisations of woeful backwardness which Hunter had popularised. There, for example, in 1887 only one Muslim subordinate judge was to be found as against forty-six Hindu, and only eight Muslim *munsifs* as against two hundred and twenty-seven Hindus.[18] Only in Bengal were Muslims under-represented in appointments to the Statutory Civil Service, instituted in 1879 to provide entry by nomination to Indians of good family. There they numbered but two of a total of eleven, whereas in the North-Western Provinces and Awadh they numbered five out of eleven.

In 1885 and 1886 a movement among English-educated Hindus, headed by Bengalis, to change the rules of entry to the services and to abolish the Statutory Civil Service, led to the appointment of the Public Service Commission under the presidency of Sir Charles Aitchison (1832–96), formerly Lieutenant-Governor of the Panjab. Among the demands made were the raising of the age limit for entry to the examination for the Covenanted Civil Service, the institution of simultaneous examinations in England and India and entry to the uncovenanted services by examinations in which the holders of university degrees would have an advantage. Educated Muslims in Bengal and the upper provinces combined in their evidence before the Aitchison Commission to resist these demands, but for very different reasons – the Bengali Muslims because they were already at such a disadvantage *vis-à-vis* their Hindu competitors and the Muslims of the upper provinces because they feared the undermining of their superior position by competition from Bengali *babus*. Allahabad University, for example, produced no Muslim graduates between 1882 and 1887 and only fifty-three between 1888 and 1892. The figures for Aligarh were ten and seventeen respectively. The figures for the University of the Panjab were eleven and forty-four.[19] The total of graduates, both M.A.s and B.A.s and both Hindu and Muslim, who passed in the North-Western Provinces and Awadh in

---

[18] *Proceedings of the Public Service Commission*, vol. VI (Calcutta, 1887), p. 43.

[19] T. Morison, *History of the Muhammadan Anglo-Oriental College*, p. 63. In the period 1876 to 1886, India's universities produced 3,219 Hindu B.A.s and M.A.s and only ninety-eight Muslim. Appendix M of *Appendices to the Report of the Public Service Commission 1886–7* (Calcutta, 1888), pp. 78–9.

1886–7 was only thirty-four, as against 275 for Bengal.[20] Sir Saiyid Ahmad Khan, speaking for the Muslim upper classes in the upper provinces, and Amir 'Ali, speaking for the National Mahommedan Association with its predominantly Bengali Muslim membership, were able to join hands across provincial boundaries and personal rivalries to form a communal political tie against the Bengali Hindu 'examination-wallah'.

A perceptive Muslim of the educated classes could see in the eighteen-seventies and early eighties that the British were ready to treat Muslims as a distinct political interest in India. Muslims were nominated to serve on the Viceroy's Legislative Council and on the Education and Public Service commissions. Before the Ripon reforms (1883) introduced an elective principle into the constitution of rural local governments, Muslims were officially nominated to such bodies, sometimes, as in the North-Western Provinces, in a dominant proportion. Thus in 1882 the Saharanpur District Committee consisted of five Hindus and eleven Muslims and the Bulandshahr District Committee of two Hindus and five Muslims. In the North-Western Provinces Muslims were also nominated to municipal committees; in 1882 the Jaunpur Municipal Committee was composed of three Hindus and eight Muslims and the Bada'un Municipal Committee of two Hindus and five Muslims.[21] Official nomination of Muslims to the Corporations of the great presidency towns of Calcutta and Bombay, where the elective system in force operated against Muslim representation at least betokened official determination that a Muslim personality should be recognised. The selection of witnesses before the Public Services Commission was designed to ensure that Muslim views and interests were heeded. Although the Commission's report did not propose communal representation in the services, Panjab officials were asked to ensure in their official establishments that no important community went unrepresented.[22]

[20] Calculated by Anil Seal, *The Emergence of Indian Nationalism* (Cambridge, 1968), p. 118.

[21] *Parliamentary Paper* no. LI of 1883, *East India (Local Government)*, Pt. II, Appendix, fols. 455a, 426b, 574b, 590b.

[22] See Confidential demi-official letter from Secretary, Panjab Government to the principal officials in the Panjab, dated 2 August 1887. File no. 16, Employment of Muhammadans in the Public Service, *Home Dept.* (Panjab) *Procs. for February 1889*, Government Record Office, Lahore.

MUSLIMS BEGIN TO ADOPT
PUBLIC AND POLITICAL POSTURES

The revival in Muslim self-confidence and the new Muslim search for self-expression, commented upon in the Census Reports of 1881, for example, found expression in the adoption of modes of public life popular in contemporary Victorian England, in particular the public society or association and newspapers aimed at a wide and diverse public. The most famous Muslim association was the National Mahommedan Association, founded in 1877 by Saiyid Amir ʿAli. Its members were Muslims who had been educated in government colleges and generally knew English, preferring to advance Muslim interests by representations to the government rather than by themselves promoting Muslim education and self-help. It was that association's memorandum of 1882 to the Education Commission, using many of the arguments of Hunter's *The Indian Musalmans* to account for Muslim 'backwardness', that provoked sustained official investigation into the position of Muslims both in government employ and education and revealed that Hunter's explanations were perhaps valid only in Bengal and not always even there. Branches of the National Mahommedan Association were founded outside Bengal, in Amritsar, Lucknow, Madras and Bombay.

A number of local associations were also founded in the eighteen-eighties to promote Muslim culture and/or the diffusion of Western knowledge among Muslims. Such were the *Anjuman-i Islam* of Amritsar (1883), the *Anjuman-i Islam* of Bareilly, the *Anjuman-i Muhammadi* of Lucknow, the Muhammadan Association of Ellore and the *Anjuman-i Himayat-i Islam* of Lahore. Rivalling the latter in importance was the *Anjuman-i Islam* of Bombay, founded by the Tyabji family to improve educational facilities for poor Muslims.

In journalism Sir Saiyid Ahmad's *Tahzib al-Akhlaq* (1872) was followed by the *Awadh Punch* of Lucknow (1877), the *Rafiq al-Hind* of Lahore (1884) and the *Paisa Akhbar* of Lahore (1888). Unlike the Muslim newspapers and journals of the earlier nineteenth century, which flickered momentarily and were then extinguished for ever, these journals were influential well into the twentieth century. They brought into being, rather than were brought into being by, a Muslim reading public of province-wide if not India-wide range, and helped to make possible a Muslim public opinion on contemporary affairs which overstepped provincial boundaries. Soon Muslims were to be presented with an all-India issue on which educated Muslims from all the provinces of British India were required to adopt a decisive political stance.

On Monday 28 December 1885 the Indian National Congress met for the first time in Bombay. A retired Indian civilian, Allan Octavian Hume (1829–1912), capitalising on the emotion in support of Lord Ripon (1827–1909) over the Ilbert Bill among English-educated Indians and building upon such associations as the Indian Association (1876), the Bombay Presidency Association (1885), the Poona Sarvajanik Sabha (1870) and the Madras Mahajana Sabha (1884), persuaded such leading figures of these associations as Pherozshah Mehta (1845–1915), K. T. Telang (1850–93) and Dadhabhai Naoroji (1825–1917) to sponsor the first all-India political association. Of the seventy participants only two were Muslim, both Bombay lawyers and members of the Bombay Municipal Corporation. The Congress had, however, been organised at short notice and Bombay was not well-placed for Muslim travellers from northern India. Muslims, however, were not allowed merely to look the other way, even had they wished, for the organisers of Congress made an open bid for Muslim support. This stimulated a measured debate of the utmost significance among Muslim leaders about the nature of both Muslim interests and Muslim identity.

After thirty-three Muslims had attended the Congress session of 1886 in Calcutta, Hume wrote on 3 December 1887 to ask Badr al-din Tyabji (1844–1906), the Sulaimani Bohra Muslim leader in Bombay, to preside over the next Congress to be held at Madras. Meanwhile, Saiyid Amir ʿAli had asked Tyabji to attend a conference of Muslims separately from Congress. Saiyid Amir ʿAli's National (since 1883 'Central') Mahommedan Association had refused to participate in the Calcutta Congress in 1886. In his letter of 3 December to Amir ʿAli, Tyabji states his belief that 'in regard to political questions at large' Muslims should 'make a common cause with their fellow countrymen of other creeds' and deprecates any Muslim body rivalling Congress.[23] He developed this argument further in his presidential address at Madras and in letters written

[23] *Tyabji Papers*, microfilm in possession of the history seminar library, School of Oriental and African Studies, London, reel 2.

early in 1888 to Amir ʿAli, Sir Saiyid Ahmad Khan and the *Pioneer* of Allahabad.

Replying on 13 January 1888 to a letter from Amir ʿAli of 5 January, in which the aims of the proposed Muslim conference were defined as to bring about 'some degree of solidarity among the disintegrated masses of Mahommedan society' and 'to safeguard our legitimate and constitutional interests under British government', Tyabji held that the purposes of Muslim advancement could best be achieved in harmony with 'our fellow subjects' rather than separately from them. No doubt Hindus are 'more advanced than ourselves' and would profit by any concessions made by the government to educated Indians but 'surely it is our duty if possible to raise ourselves in the scales of progress rather than to prevent other people from enjoying rights for which they are qualified'.[24] Tyabji, however, significantly concedes that Muslims as such have their 'own peculiar interest' and it is for this reason that, with the aid of Hume, he is promoting a standing rule for Congress proceedings that no proposition or resolution to which Muslims as a body object should be considered by Congress. On 5 January 1888 Hume had written to the secretary of the Standing Congress Committee about the fears of numerous Muslim gentlemen that 'the Hindus being numerically strongest might at some time press and carry in Congress some Resolution directly hostile to Mahommedan interests . . .You will remember the worthy gentleman who desired to press a resolution on the Congress that cow-killing should be made penal.'[25] He had therefore drafted a rule (which later was adopted as Congress Resolution XIII) which would prevent such resolutions even being debated by Congress.

Badr al-din Tyabji, writing to the *Pioneer* in a letter which was published on 2 April 1888, in effect acknowledged that national Indian politics would have to occupy only the interstices left by the religious communities. 'The principle on which the Congress had been worked is that only such questions of general public interest affecting the whole of India at large should be brought forward in regard to which there is either absolute or at least practical unanimity on the part of the Hindus and Mussalmans.'[26] In a letter dated 18 February 1888 to Sir Saiyid Ahmad Khan, Tyabji asserted

[24] *Tyabji Papers*, microfilm, reel 2.
[25] *Tyabji Papers*, reel 2.   [26] *Tyabji Papers*, reel 2.

that Muslims could by united action confine Congress to such topics as they, the Muslims, deemed safe for discussion, instancing the possibility of suggesting an alternative to election to Legislative Councils as an example.

My policy, therefore, would be to act from *within* rather than from *without*. I would say to all Mussulmans 'act with your Hindu fellow-subjects in all matters in which you are agreed but oppose them as strongly as you can if they bring forward any proposition that you may deem prejudicial to yourselves'. We should thus advance the general progress of India, and at the same time safeguard our own interests.

Sir Saiyid Ahmad Khan entered the lists against Badr al-din Tyabji, with a forthright assertion that there was no such thing as 'the general progress of India' or 'India as one nation'. There could not be a National Congress of equal benefit to all the peoples of India. 'Is it supposed', he wrote to Tyabji on 24 January 1888, 'that the different castes and creeds living in India belong to one nation or can become one nation, and their aims and aspirations be one and the same? I think it is quite impossible and when it is impossible there can be no such thing as a National Congress.'[27] Earlier in the letter he disclaimed any intention of retarding the national progress of India, but it was not obligatory for Muslims 'to run a race with persons with whom we have no chance of success'.

In a series of speeches in the North-Western Provinces and Awadh,[28] Sir Saiyid Ahmad Khan spelt out the challenge to the Muslims of the upper provinces represented by Congress politics and Congress demands for representative government and free competition for government employ by written examination.

The Congress is in reality a civil war without arms. We also like a civil war but not a civil war without arms; we like it with arms. If Government wants to give over the internal rule of the country from its own hands to those of the people of India, then we will present a petition that before doing so she pass a law of competitive examination, namely that that nation which passes first in this competition

[27] *Tyabji Papers*, reel 3.
[28] Published under the title, *On the Present State of Indian Politics* (Allahabad, 1888).

shall be given the rule of the country; but that in this competition we be allowed to use the pen of our ancestors which is in truth the true pen for writing the decrees of sovereignty.[29]

Sir Saiyid argued that representative government in India would result in the permanent subordination of Muslims to Hindus. At Lucknow he said:

Let us suppose first of all that we have universal suffrage as in America, and that everybody, *chamars* and all have votes. And first suppose that all the Mahomedan electors vote for a Mahomedan member and all Hindu electors for a Hindu member. . .It is certain that the Hindu member will have four times as many because their population will have four times as many. . .and now how can the Mahomedan guard his interests? It would be like a game of dice in which one man had four dice and the other only one.[30]

Sir Saiyid appealed to the ruling traditions of the Muslims (and of some classes of Hindus too) of the upper provinces against the Bengal 'competition-wallah'. The British are the hope of the Muslims, 'the Bengalis can in no way assist our progress'. God has made the British rulers over Muslims and Muslims should so behave that British rule remains permanent 'and may not pass into the hands of the Bengalis'. 'If', Sir Saiyid warned his audience at Meerut, 'we join the political movement of the Bengalis, our nation will reap loss, for we do not want to become subjects of the Hindus instead of subjects of the "people of the Book".' In advocating loyalty to the British, Sir Saiyid held out the prospect that one day 'Pathans, Syeds, Hashimi and Koreishi whose blood smells of the blood of Abraham, will appear in glittering uniforms as Colonels and Majors in the army. But we must wait for that time. Government will most certainly attend to it, provided that you do not give rise to suspicions of disloyalty.'[31]

In the course of his exchanges with Sir Saiyid Ahmad Khan, both public and private, Tyabji acknowledged that he too accepted that India was a community of communities. 'If you read my inaugural address [at the Madras session of Congress], you will find it distinctly stated that there are numerous communities or nations in India which had peculiar problems of their own to solve,

[29] *Present State of Indian Politics*, pp. 27–8.
[30] *Present State of Indian Politics*, p. 12.
[31] *Present State of Indian Politics*, p. 21.

but that there are some questions which touched all those communities.'[32] That Tyabji himself, in the last resort preferred his Muslim allegiance to that of the National Congress, and that he himself assumed that Muslims should have a distinct political personality in India, is brought out in correspondence with Hume in October and November 1888. Tyabji believes that events in 1888, brought about by Sir Saiyid's open stand against Muslim participation in Congress, have shown that 'an overwhelming majority of Mohammedans is against the [Congress] movement. Against 'this', he goes on, 'it is useless saying that the intelligent and educated Muslims are in favour of the Congress. If then the Mussalman Community as a whole is against the Congress, rightly or wrongly – it does not matter – it follows that the movement *ipso facto* cannot be a general or National Congress.' As a result of the public disputation between the supporters and opponents of Congress, 'not only have the Mahomedans been divided from the Hindus in a manner they never were before, but the Mahomedans themselves have been split into two factions, the gulf between whom is becoming wider and wider every day'. The Congress movement may be continued by the force and determination of some men, 'but it is not the same thing as if the Mahomedans had joined it as a body. . . The peculiar state of Mahomedan society renders it necessary that we should act together in all political matters, but this friction [between leading Muslims] comes in the way and I already find that even in Bombay we are not able to act in the same way as we did before.'[33] Tyabji therefore proposes that annual Congresses should not be held until feeling has subsided.

The future relationship of Muslims to Congress and the political posture of Muslims were by no means decided during the controversies of the years 1886 to 1888. Sir Saiyid Ahmad Khan did not lack opponents even in his own provinces; of the 254 Muslims who attended the session held at Allahabad (despite official disfavour) in 1888, ninety came from the Allahabad and Lucknow districts. In the 1889 Congress, held at Bombay, 254 Muslims attended, of whom 125 were from Delhi and the United Provinces – and it cost money to travel from upper India to Bombay. In 1889 at Lucknow 300 of the 798 who attended the Congress were Muslim.

[32] Letter of 18 February 1888, *Tyabji Papers*, reel 3.
[33] Letter of 27 October 1888, *Tyabji Papers*, reel 2.

In analysing Muslim attendance at Congress meetings it should be appreciated that the venue of the meetings and the expense of travel always affected Muslim numbers. Nevertheless, it must be concluded that the older generation of Muslim landlords and service families in the upper provinces rejected Congress politics and were joined in that rejection by most, though not all, of the modern educated and the conservatively educated Muslims of Bengal and the Panjab.

In June 1889 Sir Auckland Colvin (1838–1908), Lieutenant-Governor of the United Provinces, admittedly no friend to Congress, analysed the social character of the Muslims from Allahabad and Lucknow districts who attended the 1888 Congress at Allahabad and found them to be mainly small landed proprietors and, he said, dismissed minor officials. He said that the Muslims (he is referring to those in his own province)

as a body feels that their numbers are so inferior to the Hindus and their capacity of acquiring the kind of information which pays best in the market of the day is so inferior, that, with rare exceptions, they have made up their mind to oppose all those who ask for a further voice in the Councils. They are animated by the bitterness of a class which has hitherto been dominant; but which finds itself in danger of being set aside by methods for which it has the heartiest contempt which are opposed to its own notions of polity.[34]

Dr Francis Robinson has recently shown that in the western districts of the North-Western Provinces Muslim landholders were beginning to lose land at this time to *bania* and *khattri* money-lenders and traders.[35] In eastern districts, however, the more substantial Muslim landlords were able to hold their ground. These economic changes could explain the greater interest shown by Muslim lawyers with landed connections and smaller landlords in Congress demands for more openings for Indians in the executive and judicial services. But in the eighteen-eighties and nineties any local threat to the privileged position of Muslim landlords was only

[34] *Memorandum on Provincial Councils* enclosed with letter dated 28 June 1889 from Lansdowne to Cross, vol. 1 of *Letters from Lansdowne to Cross*, letter no. 31, *Cross Papers*, India Office Library, EUR E 243, no. 26.

[35] F. C. R. Robinson, *Municipal Government and Muslim Separatism in the United Provinces 1883–1916*. Unpublished paper presented at the Second European Conference on Modern South Asian Studies at Elsinore in July 1970, pp. 24–9.

just beginning to take shape. The Western-educated Muslims of Bombay, without a solid political base, or the Western-educated Muslims of Bengal, out of touch with the submerged mass of illiterate Bengali Muslim peasants, could only speak for themselves. In the Panjab, where Muslims were conscious of being engaged in a three-cornered religious rivalry with Hindus and Sikhs, and where as late as 1911 less than half of one per cent of the population were literate in English, there was as yet no tradition of political activity. There and elsewhere in British India there was no real challenge to the conviction of Sir Saiyid Ahmad Khan and his followers in the North-Western Provinces, that the best hope for Muslim office-seekers was still favour from a British Indian government likely to be looking for counter-weights to Congress.

Indeed the British Indian government soon decided that it was expecting such counter-weights to present themselves. Soon after his arrival in India as Viceroy and before the foundation of the Congress, Dufferin proclaimed that 'It is both the pride and the desire of the Imperial Government to provide impartially for every class and section of Her Majesty's subjects in India' and described Muslims as 'one member of the body politic'.[36] In reply to an address from the Central National Mahomedan Association on 22 January 1885, he said that, while it was his supreme duty to display impartiality, 'naturally my liveliest sympathies will be for those who through any circumstances over which they have no control, have fallen behind in the race of progress and advancement'. However, when in January 1887 signs of some Muslim abstention from Congress were already evident, Dufferin wrote to Cross (1823–1914) the Secretary of State for India that such abstention was, he understood, 'entirely in accordance with their own views of what is politic and not at all under any pressure from officials'.[37]

In the following October he specifically denied allegations, in 'the extreme section of the Radical press' in India, that the opposition offered to Congress by the Muslims and many of the higher Hindu classes was in any way the result of his 'Machiavelian cunning'. 'Of course it is needless to say I have in no sense or degree

[36] Reply to an address from the *Anjuman-i Islam* of 9 Dec. 1884, enclosure to letter no. 116, vol. v of *Letters from Dufferin to Cross*, no. 25 of *Cross Papers*.

[37] Letter no. 22 of 4 Jan. 1887, vol. II of *Letters from Dufferin to Cross*, no. 22 of *Cross Papers*.

shown the slightest partiality towards them, and I have steadily refused to grant them the concessions they demanded on the ground that we can make no difference in favour of one community over another in the Regulations under which persons are admitted to Government employment.'[38] Earlier, in a reply to an address presented at the Town Hall, Calcutta, in March 1888, he said, 'God forbid that the British Government should ever seek to maintain its rule in India by fomenting race hatreds among its subjects. Its antecedents, its strength, its self-confidence and its dignity will for ever render a recourse to such expedients unnecessary and impossible.'[39] For all that Dufferin might disclaim the intention to foment divisions in India or the fomenting of such divisions, he nevertheless accepted the fact of such divisions with the air of a man struggling joyfully in the grip of a benevolent fate. It was impossible in the best interests of Indians themselves to accept the policies of Congress.

To hand over, therefore, the Government of India either partially or otherwise to such a body as this would simply be to place millions of men, dozens of nationalities, and hundreds of the most stupendous interests under the domination of a microscopic minority, possessing neither experience, administrative ability nor any adequate conception of the tasks before them. Already it looks as if the Mahomedans were rising in revolt against the ascendancy which they imagine a rival and less virile race is desirous of obtaining over them, while there are signs that the Native Princes, Magnates and Land-holders are becoming seriously alarmed at the thought of a small class of Barristers, Native Newspaper editors and University Students intervening between them and the just, impartial and powerful administration of the British Government.[40]

Dufferin's growing antipathy to Congress and that of his senior officials, such as Colvin, owed much to the efforts of the Congress leaders at popular contact in the winter of 1887–8. A statement of Congress demands was drawn up in the vernaculars and mass meetings were held in Bengal. The prospect of the English-educated

[38] Letter no. 116, of 29 Oct. 1888, vol. v of *Letters from Dufferin to Cross*, no. 25 of *Cross Papers*.
[39] Enclosure to letter no. 86, vol. iv of *Letters from Dufferin to Cross*, no. 24 of *Cross Papers*.
[40] Minute by Dufferin on Provincial Councils enclosed with letter no. 118 of vol. v of *Letters from Dufferin to Cross*, no. 25 of *Cross Papers*.

Congressmen establishing *rapport* with the 'voiceless millions', whom the British told each other they were in India to protect, moved Dufferin publicly to excoriate Congress as the organisation of a 'microscopic minority', having earlier in private proposed an enlargement of the provincial councils of Bombay, Bengal and Madras in which all the major interests, the 'hereditary nobility', the 'superior and influential landed classes', the Muslims, the Parsis and the European planting and commercial interests would be re-presented.

India for Dufferin and for the civil servants was a patchwork of interests to be placated and protected. The refusal of the Muslim aristocracy of the upper provinces to merge their sectional and class interests with those of the English-educated middle class, whether of Bengal or indeed of their own provinces, was in keeping with the official belief that if British rule had not existed it would have had to be invented, in order to maintain justice and equipoise in India. The Government of India were not going to encourage a political unity in India which would destroy a plausible justification for British supremacy. Upper-class Muslim requests for special repre-sentation of their substantial interests would fall upon sympathetic official ears. Representation in India, as a Panjab official pontifi-cated during the discussion in 1882 on Ripon's local self-govern-ment reforms, should be of the real atoms of which Indian society was composed, namely religious communities, castes and classes, not of opinions and geographical areas.

SAIYID AHMAD KHAN'S POLITICAL IDEOLOGY

Sir Saiyid Ahmad Khan's opposition to Congress was founded upon the same assumptions about the character of Indian society as those of British officials. After the revelation of British power in 1857, confirmed by his visit to England in 1869–70, he too assumed that British rule in India was irremovable. The most that In-dians could aspire to was to advise the British of Indian sentiment, so that they could avoid the mistakes which had produced the con-flagration of 1857. His *Asbab-i Baghawat-i Hind* (1859) held an Indian Parliament to be impossible, because of Indian ignorance and irregularity,[41] and when in 1864 he forecast a time when

[41] *Asbab-i Baghawat-i Hind* (Aligarh, 1958 ed.), p. 41.

someone from every district (*zilla*) might enter the Indian Legislative Council, he did not suggest that entry should be by election, but merely by educational qualification.[42] Sir Saiyid was thinking in terms of the *darbar* system of consultation established in effect by the British themselves in 1861 by the Indian Councils Act, which empowered the nomination of Indians to the Viceroy's Legislative Council.

Sir Saiyid saw the peoples of India as composing a geographical, but not a cultural or political, nation, sharing a common subjecthood under the Queen. India was the common habitat of two great religious communities, the Hindu and the Muslim.[43] As long as Indians were politically inert, he was prepared to accept neighbourhood as a criterion of nationhood. In 1873, in a speech to the *Anjuman-i Panjab*, given before an audience of both Hindus and Muslims, he declared that he did not care for religion to be regarded as the badge of nationhood. If black and white lived in a common domicile at a high level of civilisation, or if people lived happily together clearing jungles, he would consider them one brotherhood and one nation.[44] On 27 January 1884 he told an audience at Gurdaspur that Hindu and Muslim were religious words, but since Hindu and Muslim and Christian lived together in one country they formed one nation. Hindus and Muslims should try to be of one mind in matters which affected their progress.[45] On 3 March 1884 he told the branch of the Indian Association at Lahore that the word *qaum* had two meanings, one applied to Hindus and Muslims as religious communities and the other having the connotation 'nation'. Hindus and Muslims lived together in the same land under the same ruler; the term 'Hindu' or inhabitant of Hindustan should apply to both.[46] When Sir Saiyid was a member of the Viceroy's Legislative Council he strove for the welfare of both Hindus and Muslims.

Sir Saiyid Ahmad's stand against Congress in 1887 and 1888 and his foundation of the United Patriotic Association in August

---

[42] Speech at Ghazipur, *Mukammal Majmuʿa Lecturon o Speeches* (Lahore, 1900), p. 18.

[43] Speech to the Banares Institute on 20 Sept. 1867. *Mukammal Majmu ʿa*, pp. 40–2.

[44] Speech to *Anjuman-i Panjab* on 30 Dec. 1873. *Mukammal Majmuʿa*, p.137.

[45] *Mukammal Majmuʿa*, pp. 246–7.   [46] *Mukammal Majmuʿa*, p. 270.

1888 in order to oppose Congress claims to be representative might appear to have been a *volte-face*. But in his earlier speeches quoted above he is speaking of Hindus and Muslims as one nation under foreign rule, not of Hindus and Muslims as constituting a political nation with the power and freedom for self-determination. He was describing passive subjects, not active citizens. Sir Saiyid declined to accept, before the foundation of the Indian National Congress, that the political interests of the various communities were the same under any system of government where Indians were, after a process of popular election, decision-makers.

In his often-quoted speech in January 1883 on a Bill before the Viceroy's Legislative Council to extend local self-government in the Central Provinces, which included the principle of joint electorates of both Hindus and Muslims, Sir Saiyid said:

The system of representation by election means the representation of the views and interests of the majority of the population. In countries where the population is composed of one race and one creed, it is no doubt the best system that can be adopted. But, my Lord, in a country like India, where caste distinctions still flourish, where there is no fusion of the various races, where religious distinctions are still violent, where education in its modern sense has not made an equal or proportionate progress among all sections of the population, I am convinced that the introduction of the principle of election, pure and simple, for representation of various interests on the Local Boards and District Councils, would be attended by evils of greater significance than purely economic considerations. So long as differences of race and creed, and the distinctions of caste form an important element in the socio-political life of India, and influence her inhabitants in matters connected with the administration and welfare of the country at large, the system of election cannot safely be adopted. The larger community would totally override the interests of the smaller community, and the ignorant public would hold Government responsible for introducing measures which might make the differences of race and creed more violent than ever.[47]

There is no doubt that Sir Saiyid Ahmad Khan preferred a system of separate electorates where Muslims, even where they formed a small minority, as in the Central Provinces, would be sure of a voice,

[47] Quoted in Reginald Coupland, *India, A Restatement* (London, 1945), p. 93, from *Proceedings of the Council of the Governor-General*, 1883.

however feeble, in the counsels and councils of government, as a separate interest. It would not matter that the voice might be, in particular areas with a small Muslim population, a single voice, for ultimate responsibility for law and policy would not rest with Indians but with the British. The geometry of interests would thwart the arithmetic of population. But interests must be mobilised to be effective; the controversy over the participation of Muslims in Congress had shown even educated and comfortable Muslims in different provinces to be not so much out of step as unaware that they belonged politically to the same army. They needed to be recruited for some campaign in the all-India theatre which would not arouse the fears and suspicions of the British as the Congress movement had done.

That campaign was sought in Muslim education. In 1886 Sir Saiyid Ahmad Khan founded the Muhammadan Educational Conference, designed to gather together Muslims from the different provinces upon a common platform of public activity. Its stated aims were to encourage the study of Western sciences and literatures by Muslims, to revive traditional Muslim religious education in *madrasas* and *maktabs* and to encourage Muslim historical research. It was intended to be an educational parliament for the Muslim community, but never became more than a debating society. The number of teachers of any kind among the membership never exceeded 5 per cent and the bulk of the membership were *nawwabs*, lawyers, government servants and landholders. The Muhammadan Educational Conference at first did little more than pass resolutions in favour of Islamic religious instruction in government schools, against the exclusion of Persian from university curricula, in favour of elementary schools for Muslims and in favour of the translation of English books into Urdu. Its only significant activity between annual meetings was in 1892, when it set on foot an inquiry into the number of Muslims abstaining from school and the reasons therefor. It might not unfairly be described in its first years as little more than a front-organisation for Aligarh. After 1896, however, annual meetings were held in Calcutta, Madras and Bombay and local and central standing committees were established to further the scheme for an independent Muslim University. Muslims from the different provinces did begin to think of themselves as an all-India interest and it was no coincidence that the All-India Muslim League was founded in 1906 at a meeting of the Muhammadan Educational Conference.

THE GROWTH OF COMMUNAL FEELING

Modern education, places in the services, representation on local and provincial boards and councils – these were the secular concerns of a minority; they aroused concern but hardly passion and they did not make for contact between the modern-educated and the mass of traditionally-educated or uneducated Muslims. They were the concern of Muslims as worldlings, not as Muslims. Such an observer as Sir Anthony MacDonnell believed that the antagonism between the English-educated classes of the Hindu and Muslim communities was exaggerated and that it partook 'more of political jealousy than of fanaticism and is readily subordinated to common aims'.[48] He found a stronger antagonism 'among the lower strata', an interesting observation in the light of the later contention that communalism was an upper- or middle-class phenomenon. The anti-cow-killing agitation of the eighteen-eighties and eighteen-nineties among certain classes of Hindus stirred the religious feelings of Muslims of the artisan and shop-keeping classes in the small towns of the Panjab and of the United Provinces, and appeared to give upper-class Muslim politics that popular sub-soil they needed for established growth in an elective system. It could also be used as an argument against majority rule and for safeguards for Muslims in employment and in local representative government.

In the last quarter of the nineteenth century Hindu India, like Muslim India, was seeking renewal by a reinterpretation of its title-deeds as a religion. The Western-inspired reform movements of Ram Mohan Roy (1772–1833) and of Keshub Chandra Sen (1838–84), which accepted much of the ethical teaching of nineteenth-century Protestant Christianity and rejected some of traditional Hinduism, were too esoteric and utilitarian to appeal to more than a very small minority of English-knowing Hindus. Of wider appeal were the teachings of Swami Dayananda Sarasvati (1824–1883), founder in 1875 of the *Arya Samaj*. He preached against

---

[48] *Memorandum on the Growth of Local Self-Government*, dated 5 Sept. 1887, *MacDonnell Papers*, Bodleian Library Oxford, Eng. Hist. c. 335.

the practices of orthodox Hinduism in the name not of modern enlightenment but of the pure teachings of the Vedas. Untouchability, child-marriage, idol-worship and the subjection of women find no justification in the Vedas. His society devoted itself to aggressive proselytising and forcible defence of the cow.

The gentler and mystical Ramakrishna (1836–86) sought to lead others to realisation of the Divine that lay in themselves and brought home to many Westernised Hindus that true goodness was being, not doing, and that true happiness was not to be found in emulating the restless getting and spending of the West. His disciple Swami Vivekananda (1863–1902) became the missionary to the world of Ramakrishna's philosophy of God-realisation. At the World Parliament of Religions at Chicago in 1893 he offered Hinduism as a universal faith, the mother of religions. He challenged the Christian preoccupation with sin and offered instead the divinity of man and his capacity for self-liberation. Within India he founded the Ramakrishna Mission to call the young men of India to the work of uplifting the masses, if necessary by the adoption of Western science and technology. All these religious movements had a similar effect upon Hindus as did the movements of Saiyid Ahmad of Bareilly and of Sir Saiyid Ahmad Khan upon Muslims. It gave them a similar feeling of self-respect, fired them with zeal for the purification of their religion and sharpened their resentment against the attacks of the followers of other religions. The Census Reports of 1881 and 1891 note an increasing assertiveness and self-confidence among Hindus, particularly in the towns.

This assertiveness expressed itself in violent defence of the cow. It was politically not possible to defend the cow against the British – who were careful to avoid gratuitous offence to Hindu sentiment by killing cows only where they hoped Hindus would not notice, in certain cantonment areas – but it was possible to defend her against the Muslim knife – although many Muslims did not themselves eat beef (which was usually more expensive than goat). In 1882, Dayananda founded a *Gaurakhshini Sabha*, or Society for the Protection of Kine. In the following year there were anti-cow-killing riots in Lahore, Amballa district, Firuzpur and Delhi. Again in 1886 there was a rush of rioting at Ludhiana and Delhi and in 1889 a severe outbreak at Rohtak, following the establishment of a branch of the *Arya Samaj* there. In the early nineties, rioting spread to the United Provinces and Bihar and in August 1893 there was a major disturbance in Bombay, in which several hundred people were killed or injured.

The British were very fearful lest the leaders of Congress were utilising popular Hindu feeling about cow-slaughter to establish *rapport* between the Hindu masses and themselves and were inclined to credit stories of M.A.s and B.A.s disguised as ascetics roaming the countryside dwelling on the blessings of Congress as well as on the sanctity of the cow.[49] The Lieutenant-Governor of the Panjab, Fitzpatrick (1837–1920), however, was quite certain that the Congress leaders did not desire to set Muslims and Hindus against each other but rather to unite both against the British.[50] Panjab officials blamed the *Arya Samaj*, which they thought was willing to use the cow-killing issue in order to gain a hearing for doctrines of reform hitherto above the heads of the Hindu masses.[51] All, however, remarked upon an unwillingness of both Hindus and Muslims to turn the other cheek and a determination to stand upon their rights as protected by the Penal Code. Upper-class Muslims were not themselves personally involved in the riots or indeed personally affected – they could afford to eat mutton anyway – but they knew of attempts in the early days of Congress to pass a resolution against cow-killing and could argue plausibly for special safeguards for Muslim interests, which were demonstrably different from Hindu. That they were safeguards which protected themselves rather than the poor Muslim did not matter: the anti-cow-killing agitation could be used to show that rich and poor Muslim had more in common with each other than with the Hindus.

The force of Hindu revivalism was felt also in southern India, in Bombay, in an upsurge of a Maratha feeling of pride in the exploits of Shivaji against the Muslim sultans of Bijapur and against the Mughals. The Maratha journal, *Kavyetihas Samgraha Patra Yadi*, which made its appearance in 1878, had popularised the reading of the old Maratha chronicles (*bakhars*). Maratha archivists and historians, such as Rajwade, Khare and Ranade, fired Maratha

[49] Enclosure to letter of 18 Sept. 1893 from Crosthwaite to Lansdowne, *Lansdowne Papers*, India Office Library, EUR D 558, vii, vol. x.
[50] Fitzpatrick to Lansdowne, 9 Sept. 1893, *Lansdowne Papers*, vol. x.
[51] Mackworth Young to Elgin, 15 July 1897, *Elgin Papers*, India Office Library, EUR F 84/71.

pride in the past. The great nationalist, Bal Gangadhar Tilak (1844–1920), organised a festival in honour of Shivaji, which, though not intended by Tilak to exacerbate Hindu–Muslim relations – he himself proclaimed that had he been a north Indian he would himself have adopted Akbar as a hero for both Hindus and Muslims – provoked a Muslim defence of Bijapur and of Aurangzib. The Muhammadan Educational Conference held a debate upon the responsibility of Aurangzib for the decline of Mughal power. This quarrelling over the past all helped to foster the conclusion that Hindus and Muslims were two great monolithic political communities divided by memories of masterhood and subjecthood, and by the pride of the one at the humiliation of the other.

A concern in the United Provinces, which the Aligarh leadership could share both with the smaller Muslim *zamindars* and with minor but literate Muslim government employees, was the fate of Urdu as the language of the lower courts and the lower administration. The centuries of Muslim rule in the upper provinces had left Urdu, with its Arabic script and Persianised and Arabicised vocabulary, as the *lingua franca*. In the eighteen-sixties a movement in favour of Hindi, written in the *devanagari* script and with a vocabulary drawn more from Sanskrit, started from Benares. The argument was that Urdu was the language of an urban minority, and that its use for most purposes of legal and official contact with the Indian population discriminated against Hindus in favour of Muslims. British officials were inclined to see the demand for Hindi in the North-Western Provinces and Awadh as a ploy by Bengalis to gain employment there, as they would find it easier to work in *devanagari*, but this was an exaggeration; Babu Shiv Prasad, a Hindu member of Sir Saiyid Ahmad Khan's Scientific Society from the North-Western Provinces, demanded that the proceedings of the Society be conducted in Hindi and published a periodical to further the cause of Hindi. A number of memorials were received by the Hunter Education Commission in favour of Hindi from both the upper provinces and the Panjab.

Although in the eighteen-seventies Hindi was adopted as the language of the lower courts, first in Bihar and then in the Central Provinces, British officials in the upper provinces resisted the demand, partly on the ground that Urdu was the vernacular at least in Awadh, and partly because they did not wish to cause Muslim disaffection.[52] Moreover, recent research has suggested that, as a subject of study in the schools of the North-Western Provinces and Awadh, Urdu had gained ground relative to Hindi. In 1860–1 11,490 boys were studying Urdu in government schools and in 1873 48,229, a percentage increase of over 219. The equivalent figures for Hindi were 69,134 and 85,820, a percentage increase of rather over twenty-four.[53] In the Panjab the British themselves had been largely responsible for promoting Urdu as the language of day-to-day dealings with the 'native' population.

In 1900, however, without consulting Muslim opinion, but after receiving in March 1899 a Hindu deputation to press for the change, the Lieutenant-Governor of the United Provinces, Sir Anthony MacDonnell, issued orders permitting the optional use of the *devanagari* script in court documents and requiring a knowledge of both scripts by court officials. Although these orders did not enforce the use of Hindi in place of Urdu, but merely permitted it, they provoked a strong Muslim agitation led by Muhsin al-Mulk (1837–1907) and Wiqar al-Mulk (1841–1917) of Aligarh, who founded an Urdu Defence Association. Sir Anthony MacDonnell, who feared too much official reliance upon Muslims and played off Hindus against them,[54] intervened to force Muhsin al-Mulk to choose between the presidency of the Urdu Defence Association and the secretaryship of the Muhammadan Anglo-Oriental College at Aligarh, by threatening withdrawal of government financial support for the college. Muhsin al-Mulk resigned the presidency, but after MacDonnell's departure from the United Provinces organised the *Anjuman-i Taraqqi-i Urdu* in 1903, as an adjunct of the Muhammadan Educational Conference. Muslim fears of a relative loss of ground of Urdu to Hindi proved justified. In 1891 twenty-four Hindi newspapers had an estimated circulation of about 8,000, whereas sixty-eight Urdu newspapers had a circulation of over 16,000. In 1911 eighty-six Hindi newspapers had a

---

[52] Nandalal Chatterji, 'The Government's Attitude to Hindi–Urdu–Hindustani in the Post Mutiny Period', *Journal of the Uttar Pradesh Historical Society*, III, 1, 1955, p. 18.

[53] Paul R. Brass, 'Muslim Separatism in the U.P.', *Economic and Political Weekly* (Bombay) *Annual Number*, January 1970, p. 181.

[54] *Minute by Sir Anthony MacDonnell for his Successor as Lt. Governor of the North-Western Provinces and Oudh*, October 1901, *MacDonnell Papers*, Bodleian Library, Eng. Hist. c. 355.

circulation of over 77,000, about 1,000 more than the 116 Urdu newspapers.[55]

Realisation that, to the British, the educated Muslim of the United Provinces was expendable, came at a time when that Muslim had more hopes under the British system to disappoint than earlier – and more occasions for their disappointment. In 1891 0.08 per cent of Muslims were literate in English, compared with 0.17 per cent of Hindus. By 1901 the Muslim percentage had increased to 0.22, an increase of 225.5 per cent, and the Hindu to 0.36, an increase of 176 per cent. In vernacular literacy the rise in the same period had been Muslims 4.52 per cent to 5.62, an increase of 16.4 per cent, Hindus 5.06 per cent to 5.61, an increase of 9.2 per cent.[56] In 1911, the percentage of literates in the vernaculars among Muslims was to surpass that among Hindus.

Nevertheless the U.P. Muslim position in local government, in official service and in the legal profession was weakening. Dr Robinson has calculated that between 1884–5, with the wider introduction of the elective principle under the Ripon reforms, and 1907–8, the gap between the proportion of seats held by Hindus and Muslims on the municipal boards widened to the Muslim disadvantage by some 6 per cent. In 1911 Muslims were a majority of the population in twenty-one of eighty-four municipalities, but had a majority of voters in only ten. Dr Robinson suggests that with a municipal franchise based on income and property fewer Muslims than Hindus were able to register as voters, since Muslims were more dependent upon income from service and real property and were therefore worse hit by the sharp rise in prices from 1880 to 1910 than urban Hindus engaged in trade.[57] In government employ at monthly incomes of Rs. 200 and upwards the Muslim proportion was diminishing. In 1887 Muslims in the uncovenanted provincial service held 45 per cent of judicial appointments; in 1913 the proportion had dropped to just under 25 per cent. In the same period there was an 8 per cent drop in the proportion of Muslims in executive appointments.[58] In the legal profession out-

[55] F. C. R. Robinson, *The Politics of U.P. Muslims 1906–1922*, Cambridge University doctoral dissertation, 1970, p. 74.
[56] Paul R. Brass, 'Muslim Separatism in the U.P.', pp. 172, 173, 178.
[57] F. C. R. Robinson, *Municipal Government and Muslim Separatism in the United Provinces 1883–1916*, pp. 41–2.
[58] F. C. R. Robinson, *The Politics of U.P. Muslims, 1906–1922*, pp. 57–8.

side government service Muslims were also losing ground over the whole province. Between 1889 and 1909 the number of Hindu lawyers more than doubled, whereas the number of Muslim increased by about a third.

Before the educated Muslim of the Panjab or of Bengal could associate politically with the upper-class Muslim of the United Provinces he too must have some vested interest to defend. The aristocratic leadership of the United Provinces needed to create the impression that it spoke for the provinces where the decennial Census Reports were now showing that Muslims were in a local, albeit small, majority and that there was a Muslim political interest uniting the Muslims of the minority and the majority provinces. The creation of the new Muslim-majority province of East Bengal and Assam after Curzon's partition of 1905 provided the Muslims of one Muslim majority area of India with just that vested interest. The anti-partition campaigner in Bengal, the Hindi-promoter in the upper provinces and the Shivaji hero-worshipper in Bombay were all heads of that *hydra*, the upstart Hindu penman and speechifier.

The twentieth century found Indian Muslims politically 'on edge'. They wanted to play a distinctive *rôle*, but did not know what that *rôle* should be. The older generation educated by Sir Saiyid Ahmad Khan had rejected Congress politics, but, as the Muslim attendance of three hundred and thirteen at the 1899 Congress at Lucknow showed, it was by no means certain that the younger English-educated Muslims would always follow their lead. The Panjab and east Bengal were politically leaderless. In the Panjab Muslims appeared tolerably satisfied with the obvious efforts of British administrators to maintain a communal balance in the services and in local government;[59] the relatively small urban Muslim middle class had yet to enter into *rapport* with the Muslim peasantry of the province. Tyabji, after his appointment as a High Court Judge, was out of politics in Bombay and even in the United Provinces Sir Saiyid Ahmad Khan's successors at Aligarh were behaving like ranker officers newly commissioned – bent on displaying their mastery of Sir Saiyid's manual of tactics, rather than their capacity for original dispositions in a novel campaign.

[59] N. G. Barrier, 'The Punjab Government and Communal Politics 1870–1908', *Journal of Asian Studies*, xxvii, 3 May 1968, pp. 534–8.

Muslims of many different backgrounds had been irritated by the attitudes and policies of their non-Muslim rulers and fellow countrymen – and as a result had drawn closer together in political sympathy. The English-educated had been irritated by the Congress demand for an examination meritocracy and elective government in India and by British behaviour towards the Muslim countries of the Middle East and North Africa, the vernacularly educated by the pro-Hindi agitation and the uneducated by the anti-cow-killing agitation. They could all see, however, that, despite the occasional Sir Anthony MacDonnell, the British wished to treat them as a counterweight in a political balance to the new Hindu intelligentsia (and even MacDonnell merely thought that the balance had been tipped towards the Muslims in the United Provinces) and that their rulers needed them as much as they their rulers. The British were ready to grant that Muslims had their own separate identity; it rested with Muslims to assert and define that identity in a context of active all-India politics and to win constitutional recognition for it.

6

MUSLIMS ACQUIRE
A CONSTITUTIONAL IDENTITY
AND ENTER ALL-INDIA POLITICS

Indian Muslims formally entered politics and acquired, in the grant of separate electorates under the Indian Councils Act of 1909, a separate constitutional identity, as the outcome of the actions of a Viceroy who had come to India believing that he could end all Indian political activity and deny all Indians, not merely Muslims, any constitutional identity. George Nathaniel Curzon (1859–1925) came to India in 1898 to rule her as though she were a dominion of packages rather than a dominion of men. Efficiency in administration and state action to improve the lot of the voiceless millions, fondly believed – or pretended – to be Britain's 'bloc vote' in India, would expose the frivolity of the loquacious *babus* for all, including themselves, to see. Politics would be seen to be the luxury of the comfortable minority. There would be no need to balance and rule; the silent majority would be kept politically torpid and made sleekly content by a policy of 'development' under a benevolent autocracy.

But Curzon left political India raw and smarting, more inflamed than at any time since 1857, and with a bomb-throwing underground movement active in Bengal. The British need to play politics, to balance between the various communities and classes in India, had been made more exigent than before. It was necessary to appease educated India, but educated India was not all educated in the same way, was not all at the same stage of instruction, and did not all share the same interests. Different prizes might have to be handed out to different classes. Curzon's successor, Minto, was given scope for the policy of balance by the fact that, in loosing-off wildly at Curzon, his Hindu opponents had forced the Muslim bystanders to join together to seek the cover which the British were only too ready to give. The Muslims of Bengal were able to find sufficient common ground with the Muslims of the upper provinces, despite personal and regional rivalries, to form an All-India Muslim League and then to demand separate electorates for the expanded provincial councils which Minto (1845–1914) and the Liberal Secretary of State, Morley (1838–1923), proposed to introduce into all the major provinces of British India except the new North-West Frontier Province, created in 1900.

The granting of this demand endowed Muslims, albeit at first only a small minority of propertied Muslims, with a vested all-India political interest and a legal personality which other classes of Muslims might round out or take over. Paradoxically, Muslims became the *zimmis* or protected people of British India, a welcome counterweight to Congress in British eyes for as long as the British believed they were in India to stay, a tiresome responsibility when they saw an end to that stay approaching and then a wilful nuisance when Muslim leaders repudiated client status and asserted the Muslim claim to determine their own destiny as a nation. Whether separatist politics bred separate electorates or separate electorates bred separatist politics is a version of the question about the chicken and the egg, but separate electorates at provincial level did enable leading Muslims to behave as the plenipotentiaries of a separate political community when they wished to do so.

THE PARTITION OF BENGAL 1905 AND MUSLIM POLITICS

Lord Curzon had not intended to divide Hindus and Muslims, only Bengalis. Under the British the province of Bengal was as large as France and on the eve of partition in 1905, with a population of seventy-eight and a half million, nearly as populous as contemporary France and Great Britain combined. It included Bihar and Orissa and, until 1874, Assam. The eastern region was notoriously undergoverned; indeed the revelation of a Muslim majority there in the early censuses came as something of a surprise to officialdom. From the time of the Orissa famine in the eighteen-sixties, desultory discussions for the redrawing of the province's boundaries had occurred within the official machine. In 1892 a proposal to hive off the Chittagong region and to join it to Assam ran into strong opposition from officials whose careers might be affected and from Bengali pleaders whose fees might be reduced.

In 1902 Curzon set on foot a general discussion of provincial boundaries in India, affecting not only Bengal but also Berar, the Central Provinces, Madras, Bombay and Sind.[1] In 1903 a plan emerged for severing the eastern and predominantly Muslim regions of the Bengali-speaking area and uniting them with Assam, giving a new province with a population of thirty-one millions, of whom 59 per cent would be Muslim. However, as details of the plan leaked out Bengali dismay mounted. In the reduced province of West Bengal with a population of forty-seven million, Bengali speakers would be in a minority in relation to Biharis and Oriyas. Led by Surendra-nath Bannerjea (1848–1925), Jatindra Mohan Tagore (1831–1908), Narendranath Sen (1843–1911) and Motilal Ghose (1847–1922), the English-educated Bengali middle class held demonstrations in both town and countryside and brought about genuine surge of feeling among the vernacularly educated and illiterate Bengali. Some Muslims of the professional classes joined in the agitation and at first the Muslim *nawwab* of Dacca, Salim-Allah, was also hostile to the proposed partition. A boycott of British goods followed and, as popular feeling became indistinguishable from religious fervour, a call by young extremists for the assassination of British officials as an offering to the goddess Kali gave the movement a revivalist character.

As the agitation against partition grew in force, Curzon and his senior officials, who had begun by seeing the whole exercise as one of simple administrative efficiency, argued for the political merits of the partition scheme. If, Curzon wrote, the British were weak enough to yield to the clamour of the Bengalis 'who like to think themselves a nation and who dream of a future when the English will have been turned out of Calcutta and a Bengali Babu will be installed in Government House Calcutta' it would be impossible to dismember Bengal again and the British would be cementing and solidifying on the eastern flank of India 'a force already formidable and certain to be a source of increasing trouble for the future'.[2] On 21 April 1904 Sir Andrew Fraser (1848–1918), Lieutenant-Governor of Bengal, in a note on the political aspects of partition, argued that the separation of eastern Bengal 'will have the tendency

---

[1] For the genesis of the plan see the unpublished but authoritative thesis, Z. H. Zaidi, *The Partition of Bengal and its Annulment, 1902–1911*, Ph.D. (London), 1964, pp. 50–1.

[2] Z. H. Zaidi, 'The Political Motive in the Partition of Bengal', *Journal of the Pakistan Historical Society*, XII, 2 April 1964, p. 113.

to reduce the influence of the Calcutta wirepullers' and that the Muslims of that region should not be dominated by the Congress party.[3] H. H. Risley (1851–1911), a member of the Viceroy's Executive Council, acknowledged that Congress fears that Bengal divided would pull in different directions were 'perfectly correct' and that this indeed formed one of the great merits of the partition scheme. The creation of 'wholesome centres of provincial opinion' should be one of the aims of British policy.[4] Risley did not suggest that 'wholesome' meant Muslim, but rather 'antipathetic to Calcutta lawyers and *babus*'. Curzon himself made an open bid for Muslim support in February 1904 with a visit to Dacca, where he courted the Muslim landowners and spoke of partition as investing 'the Mohammedans of Eastern Bengal with a unity which they had not enjoyed since the days of the old Mussulman Viceroys and Kings'.

Articulate Bengali Muslim opinion did not with one accord accept British views of Muslims' own best interests. Muslim lawyers attached to the Calcutta courts shared Hindu lawyers' fears of loss of briefs from litigious landlords; the National Central Muhammadan Association expressed doubts about the wisdom of partition; the family of the Nawwab of Dacca was divided, partly through a family quarrel, it is attitude. It was the fact rather than the prospect of partition which crystallised Muslim opinion against the anti-partition agitation. In order to stir the Hindu of the countryside the opponents of partition, both before and after it had occurred, appealed to popular Hindu religious sentiment. The chanting of *Bande Mataram*, of 'Hail to the Motherland' (a cry taken from a poem of that name in Bankimchandra Chatterji's (1838–94) novel *Anandamath*), during processions was unpopular with some Muslims, by reason of its association with the plot of the novel and with the Hindu goddess Kali. The story of the novel is that of a group of Hindu ascetics devoted to Kali, whom they call the mother of their country; the ascetics fight victoriously against Muslim rulers and their British allies after pledging themselves to set up a Hindu state.

Muslim shopkeepers (though not Muslim weavers) were often opposed to the boycott of British goods. Muslim tenants were sometimes pressed to join the agitation by their Hindu landlords. These

[3] Z. H. Zaidi, 'The Political Motive', p. 137.
[4] Z. H. Zaidi, 'The Political Motive', pp. 141–2.

irritations were played upon by the administration of the first Lieutenant-Governor, Sir Bampfylde Fuller (1854–1935), of the new province of East Bengal and Assam. Fuller openly expressed favouritism towards Muslims, speaking of the Muslim as his favourite wife and exempting Muslims from bearing the cost of the punitive police force stationed in the Bakarganj district to combat the anti-partition movement. One of his district judges, after trying cases of communal rioting at Comilla, was censured by the Calcutta High Court for accepting the evidence of Muslim in preference to the evidence of Hindu witnesses out of preconceived sympathies.

Once the new Muslim majority province was established, leading Muslims began to see its advantages to them. In undivided Bengal Muslims, particularly in the eastern region, were lagging badly in middle-class education. In 1901 the total amount spent on education in Calcutta alone was more than that spent in the whole of the Muslim majority areas of East Bengal. In 1905 only Dacca and Rajshahi offered courses leading to the M.A. degree. In the same year, in those same areas, only four of fifty-four inspectorships of police and only 60 of 484 sub-inspectorships were held by Muslims. Taking undivided Bengal as a unit, in 1903–4 only 463 of the 8,009 students in arts colleges were Muslim, only 73 of 284 Bachelors of Arts and only 5 of 79 Masters of Arts.[5] The administration of the new province held out the prospect of more government money for Muslim education (and indeed between 1906 and 1911, with increased grants-in-aid, the number of Muslims in high schools in the new province rose from 8,869 to 20,729 and in middle English schools from 14,100 to 38,702) and undoubtedly attracted some Muslim middle- and upper-class support.

The Hindu anti-partition agitator appeared to be 'interfering' in what was 'their' (that is the Muslims') province. Minto's acceptance of Fuller's resignation in August 1906, over the Government of India's refusal to support reprisals against schoolboy agitators in Serajganj, appeared to be a victory for the Hindu 'agitator', just when Muslims in a Muslim majority province were basking in the unaccustomed sun of official favour. Muslims in East Bengal were coming closer to Muslims in the upper provinces, in that they were slowly acquiring something to lose.

[5] Education statistics quoted in Z. H. Zaidi, *The Partition of Bengal and its Annulment 1902–11*, pp. 348–9.

In the Panjab the local situation did not favour political initiatives in an all-India arena by Panjabi Muslims. Congress activity in the province was intermittent, with the local Hindu leadership more concerned with consolidating provincial Hindu unity than with forming a common front of Indian politicians to demand more self-government from the British. In the Panjab communal rivalries were undoubtedly bitter, but their objectives appeared attainable by action within the province. Having abandoned in the late eighteen-eighties its former policy of impartiality for one of action to create balance between communities, in 1901 the Panjab government had decided to reserve 30 per cent of civil service appointments for Muslims. The extension of the elective principle in local self-government, as a consequence of the Ripon reforms of 1882–1883, had been followed by fierce communal conflicts on municipal boards and by Hindu electoral victories resulting from their large educated urban electorate.

To redress the balance and to assuage bitterness, the government introduced communal representation in such towns as Amritsar, Hoshiarpur, Multan and Lahore. The government also intervened to prevent transfers of land, by foreclosure and compulsory sale for debt, from cultivating tribes and castes to moneylenders and other urban financial interests. In some areas of the Panjab a third of the land had been transferred to moneylenders in the period from 1878 to 1896.[6] The government's motive in passing the Panjab Land Alienation Act of 1901 was the maintenance of a contented peasantry – deemed necessary for the continuance of the Panjab's *rôle* as the principal recruiting ground for the Indian army – rather than to protect Muslims as such. Indeed individual Hindu cultivators as individuals had suffered as much from moneylenders as had Muslim cultivators as individuals. But as there were more Muslim cultivators suffering at the hands of Hindu moneylenders than Hindu cultivators at the hands of Muslim moneylenders, the measure appeared to be more in the Muslim interest. Thus at the turn of the century a modern style of politics and association with other Muslims outside the Panjab seemed to offer the Panjabi Muslim less than reliance upon official action within the province.

---

[6] S. S. Thorburn, *Appendices to Report on Peasant Indebtedness and Land Alienation to Moneylenders in certain parts of the Rawalpindi Division* (Lahore, 1896), p. 25.

Once again the political initiative rested with the Muslims of the United Provinces. (No significant Muslim leadership had emerged in Bombay since Badr al-din Tyabji had retired from politics after accepting a judgeship in 1895.) The Urdu–Hindi issue had aroused open questioning of Sir Saiyid Ahmad Khan's tradition of confidence in the British. A 'young Muslim' element emerged to challenge the conservatives, drawn from lawyers and professional men, often members of landowning families, but of less wealthy ones, whose estates were often encumbered with debt. It included Muhammad ʿAli (1878–1931) and his brother Shaukat ʿAli (1873–1938), Saiyid Wazir Hasan, Saiyid Hasan Bilgrami, Saiyid Zahur Ahmad and Hakim Ajmal Khan (1863–1928). Of them Muhammad ʿAli was the most scintillating; educated at Aligarh and Oxford, he had a brilliant command of English and great sensitivity to the emotions of his own generation of educated Muslims. The conservatives had been alarmed at the vehemence of their protests when Muhsin al-Mulk backed down before the government over the language issue and this alarm probably accounts for Wiqar al-Mulk's (a member of the Aligarh College Committee) abortive efforts between 1901 and 1903 to found a Muslim political association in the United Provinces under conservative leadership. He may have been trying to head off the more radical.[7] But all these various pieces of the Muslim kaleidoscope required a severe jolt if they were to tumble into a new political pattern.

THE SIMLA DEPUTATION AND SEPARATE MUSLIM ELECTORATES

The British gave just that jolt. John Morley, the Liberal Secretary of State for India, and Minto, the Viceroy, were determined to win over moderate Indian opinion to a policy of association in the Government of India. In May and June 1906 Morley discussed the Congress demands for the reform of the Secretary of State's Council, the executive councils of the Viceroy and of the governors, and the legislative councils with the moderate Congress leader, Gokhale. On 20 July 1906, in a speech on the Indian Budget in the House of Commons, he announced that he would consider proposals

[7] This paragraph draws heavily upon F. R. C. Robinson, *The Politics of U.P. Muslims 1906–1922.*

for reform, the initiative to come formally from the Government of India.

On 4 August 1906 Muhsin al-Mulk, the secretary of the Aligarh college, wrote to his Principal, Archbold (1865–1929), then staying in the Government of India's hill station, Simla,[8]

You must have read and thought over Mr John Morley's speech on the Indian Budget. It is very much talked of among the Mohammedans of India and is commonly believed to be a great success achieved by the National Congress. You are aware that the Mohammedans already feel a little disappointed, and young educated Mohammedans seem to have a sympathy for the 'Congress' and this speech will produce a greater tendency in them to join the Congress. . . I have got several letters drawing attention particularly to the new proposal of 'elected representatives' in the Legislative Councils. They say that the existing rules confer no rights on Mohammedans; and no Mohammedans get into the Councils by election. . .If the new rules now to be drawn up introduce 'election' on a more extended scale, the Mohammedans will hardly get a seat and no Mohammedans will get into the Councils by election.

Muhsin al-Mulk asked Archbold to advise him whether Muslims should submit a memorial to Minto and ask him to receive a deputation. Minto saw Mushin al-Mulk's letter on 8 August and sent it on to Morley with the comment, 'I have not had the time to think over the advisability of receiving the proposed deputation but am inclined to do so.' But he went on to add that care should be taken to give full value to the importance of other interests besides those represented by Congress. On 10 August Archbold was able to inform Muhsin al-Mulk that Minto would receive a Muslim deputation.

On 1 October 1906 Minto received a deputation of thirty-five Muslims, from all the provinces of British India except the North-West Frontier Province. They presented an address on behalf of 'a large body of the Mohammedan subjects of His Majesty the King Emperor in different parts of India'. The address claimed for Muslims a 'fair share' in such extended representation as was now being considered for India, that fair share to be computed not merely by reference to the numerical strength of Muslims in India, but also by reference to their political importance, and to the

[8] Enclosed with letter of 8 August 1906 from Minto to Morley, *Morley Papers*, India Office Library, EUR D 573, no. 9.

contribution which they made to the defence of the empire. After remarking that representative institutions of the European type were new to the Indian people, the address stated that such representation as Muslims had hitherto been granted in the Legislative Councils had been inadequate and without the approval of those whom the nominees had been selected to represent. Furthermore, a Muslim was unlikely, the address added, to be selected by the electoral bodies as now constituted, unless he was in sympathy with the majority which, it was implied, would be necessarily Hindu. He would not be a true representative of Muslims. The Muslims, however, 'are a distinct community with additional interests. . .which are not shared by other communities and these have hitherto suffered from the fact that they have not been adequately represented'. The address proposed that a fixed proportion of Muslims on Municipal and District Boards should be returned by separate electorates, that the proportion of Muslims on provincial councils should be established with due regard to the Muslim community's political importance, that proportion to be returned by an electoral college composed of Muslims only, and that a similar arrangement should be adopted for the Imperial (Viceroy's) Legislative Council, appointment by election being preferred over appointment by nomination.[9]

In his reply, Minto welcomed 'the representative character of your deputation as expressing the views and aspirations of the enlightened Muslim community of India'. 'The pith of your address, as I understand it', he went on,

is a claim that in any system of representation whether it affects a Municipality, a District Board or a Legislative Council, in which it is proposed to introduce or increase an electoral organization, the Mahommedan community should be represented as a community. . . I am entirely in accord with you; please do not misunderstand me. I make no attempt to indicate by what means the representation of communities can be obtained, but I am firmly convinced as I believe you to be that any electoral representation in India would be doomed to mischievous failure which aimed at granting a personal enfranchisement regardless of the beliefs and traditions of the communities composing the population of this continent.

[9] The text of the Simla deputation's address and of Minto's reply is given in full in: Ram Gopal, *Indian Muslims, A Political History (1858–1947)* (London, 1959), pp. 329–38.

Thus Minto acknowledged and decisively encouraged the *nisus* towards a separate Muslim political personality in India, which had been growing since Sir Saiyid Ahmad Khan refused to have anything to do with the Indian National Congress. But had the British done more than acknowledge and encourage? Had they in fact incited? Was the Simla deputation, in Maulana Muhammad ʿAli's words, 'a Command Performance'? Before 1947 most Indian nationalists would have said 'yes'; in both independent India and independent Pakistan the answer is now commonly 'no' – in India in order to blame Muslims and in Pakistan in order to praise them.

In its crudest formulation of a British summons, a calling up of puppets to counter-balance Congress, the 'command performance' hypothesis is almost certainly false. On present evidence, the first step towards the Simla deputation was taken by Muhsin al-Mulk; on 8 August 1906 Minto wrote to Morley in terms which suggest that Archbold's approach to him was unexpected. On 2 September 1906 Muhsin al-Mulk wrote to Harcourt Butler (1869–1938), then Deputy-Commissioner at Lucknow, that Muslims had decided to present a petition to the Viceroy and enclosing a draft which would be laid before Minto 'if permitted'.[10] On 16 September 1906 Butler criticised the Muslims meeting at Lucknow to draft the Simla address for not following his advice in presenting their demands; he had advised them against demanding separate electorates and against demanding a fixed proportion of Muslim appointments in the civil services. He goes on to add, 'the whole business since Fuller's retirement to now has been organized by Muhsin al-Mulk and Imad al-Mulk [Nawwab Imad al-Mulk of Bilgram] in a hurry'. Furthermore the gist[11] of Archbold's letter of 10 August, replying to Muhsin al-Mulk, and supposed to contain instructions from Minto or his private secretary, Dunlop Smith (1858–1921), on how the Simla address should be framed, advises that Muslims should seek representation by nomination rather than by election.

Nevertheless, the members of the Simla deputation knew that they would receive a sympathetic hearing from the British government in India. If the deputation was not a command performance it was guaranteed box-office success in advance. In his letter of 8

---

[10] *Harcourt Butler Papers*, India Office Library, EUR F 116/65.
[11] Given in Tufail Ahmad, *Mussalmanon ka Raushan Mustaqbil* (Delhi, 1945), pp. 349–50.

August 1906 to Morley, Minto wrote that it was necessary to give full value to the importance of other interests besides those so largely represented by Congress. Sir Denzil Ibbetson (1847–1908), then Lieutenant-Governor of the Panjab, wrote to Dunlop Smith *on 10 August 1906,*

I have heard from other quarters also what Mohsin ul-Mulk says about the aspirations of the younger generations of Mohammedans. Their aspirations are perfectly natural. But it would be a calamity if they were to drive those who feel them into the arms of the Congress party; for at present the educated Mohammedan is the most conservative element in Indian society.[12]

The members of the Simla deputation were the self-appointed representatives of Muslims – and even they themselves did not claim in the Simla address to represent the Muslim community as such. The Panjab and Frontier provinces, with their fourteen million Muslim population, had seven members on the Simla deputation and East and West Bengal, with their twenty-five and a half million Muslim population, one, Nawwab °Ali Chowdhry (1863–1929). The U.P., with its seven million Muslim population, had eleven. The deputation included eight members of princely families or states' ministers and six *zamindars*. The middle-class professional man of the U.P. was 'represented' by two lawyers.

Yet high British officials rushed to assure Minto of the representative character of the kind of Muslim who presented himself at Simla, and of the great threat to the stability of British rule of any Muslim discontent. 'The Mahommedan organization, through the Moulavis and based on religious practices', wrote Sir Lancelot Hare (1851–1922), Fuller's successor as Lieutenant-Governor of East Bengal and Assam, 'is far and away in advance of the Hindu organization which is only a political organization.' Afraid that Morley might dispute the representative character of the Muslims who approach government, he added,

unless these leaders go counter to the Maulavis, which would only be in some religious or quasi-religious question, the Mohammedans will follow their leaders to a man without question and to a man almost. They can easily organize a mass meeting of a million if they understand this is required as evidence [of their representative character]. . .

[12] Quoted in: Martin Gilbert, *Servant of India* (London, 1966), p. 51.

If the Govt. can do so [accept the claims of leading Muslims to be representative] and if it can say it does so, I think it will have a great political effect. It is then unnecessary for the Mohammedans to start a campaign of political agitation.[13]

Hare, in effect, is arguing that the British should accept at their face value the claims of any self-styled Muslim leaders to be representative.

The Viceroy's private secretary, Dunlop Smith, shivered to himself at the thought of Muslim disaffection. He recorded in his diary,[14]

I can see him [Sir Dinkar Rao (1819–96)] now saying. . .'What you Sahibs have to fear is first the Mussulman when he preaches Jihad – Holy War. Then you will be in a worse plight than you were in the Mutiny'. . .what I want to stop is these young Mohammedans forming small societies all over India. Once they start that game they can make us really anxious. The Bengalis are a low-lying people in a low-lying land with the intellect of a Greek and the grit of a rabbit. It's the Mussulman with the green flag calling for blood and the Mahratta Brahmin – not the Mahratta but the Brahmin – whom we have to watch.

Harcourt Butler, however, knew that the seed of Muslim political organisation needed the sun of British favour to grow into an all-India force. Writing to Erle Richard, Law Member of the Government of India, on 16 September 1906, he held that anti-Hindu feeling was 'about the only common platform' on which the Muslims gathered at Lucknow to draft the Simla address could meet. 'I have been in touch with several movements of late years but I have not yet come across so sketchy a movement as this. However it will grow.'[15]

The Simla deputation was the outcome of a marriage of convenience between British political necessity and upper-class Muslim interests – and those of the Muslim of the United Provinces above all others. It was a match made on the assumption that British rule in India was there to stay – before the war of 1914–18, not an over-optimistic assumption. Minto's pledge, that the political per-

[13] Hare to Minto, 1 Sept. 1906. Enclosure to Minto's letter to Morley dated 10 Sept. 1906, *Morley Papers*, India Office Library, EUR D 573, no. 9.
[14] Entry of 10 Sept. 1906. Martin Gilbert, *Servant of India*, p. 56.
[15] *Harcourt Butler Papers*, EUR F 116/65.

sonality of the Muslim community in a land of communities would be recognised, was no more than the logical outcome of the presuppositions of British policy in India after 1857, namely that the British should act as arbiters between substantial interests believed – or hoped – to be irreconcilable, and that safety for British supremacy lay in alliance with the substantial landholding classes.

The intention of British officials under Minto to have not just members, but representatives, of the Muslim community and not any representatives, but essentially conservative representatives, on the expanded provincial and imperial legislative councils, gleams through the official papers composed between Minto's undertaking on 1 October 1906 and the passage of the Indian Councils Act in 1909. The Government of India amplified the weakest call for help from conservative Muslims into an alarm siren shrieking in the ears of the Secretary of State in London. As early as 11 September 1906 the acting-Lieutenant-Governor of Bengal, Slacke (1853–1940), suggested that if Muslims were elected by a mixed electorate then 'the great probability is that the Mohammedan elected would be one of the Congress party' and he claimed to know that that kind of Muslim would not be a true representative of his community.[16] The scheme for Muslim representation through electoral colleges, devised in 1908 by a committee of the Council of India in London, would have returned a fixed ratio of Muslim voters for members of the expanded Councils in proportion to population, but it would have provided for Hindu electoral college voters to take part in the election of Muslim council members and the converse. This scheme was strongly resisted by Minto and his officials. There was, Minto held, 'a fear that the cleverness of the pleader class may enable them to manipulate the machinery of the electoral college so that whenever representatives or minorities are elected, they will be, whether Mahommedan or otherwise, as a matter of fact representatives of the political pleaders section'. He told Morley that Muslims said that large Hindu majorities would enable Hindus not only to elect their own man but a Mahommedan as well, and that, that being so, a Muslim might be elected representative of advanced Hindu inclinations and not at all of bona fide Mahommedan interests. 'The old fashioned Mahommedans who are such

[16] Quoted in: M. N. Das, *India under Morley and Minto* (London, 1964), p. 229.

a loyal mainstay to us, are not likely to push themselves forward and will be left in the lurch if opportunity is given for the election of manipulated Hindu voters to secure seats for a younger Mahommedan generation that is being drawn into a vortex of political agitation.'[17]

In insisting on the necessity of separate Muslim representation, British officials believed that they were merely recognising the facts of life in India.

> By virtue of their position as representatives of former rulers who had ousted the Hindus by the continuous tradition of authority existing among them and by the influential position which is still held by large numbers of them, they are without doubt entitled to a consideration in matters of comparative representation far greater than that which the mere number of their community as compared with the rest of the population would give them. . .

wrote an official of the U.P. government on 27 January 1909.[18] He then went on to argue that the proportion of better-class Muslims to the whole Muslim population of the United Provinces was higher than that of better-class Hindus to the Hindu population and that allowance in any system of representation should be made accordingly.

Indeed, in the United Provinces and in the Panjab, the government was not so much engaged in creating a special Muslim interest as in maintaining it. In January 1909 183 of 663 non-official members of District Boards and 310 of 965 members of Municipal Boards in the United Provinces were recorded as Muslim and in the same month in the Panjab, where a system of separate electorates already existed in some of the principal cities, such as Lahore and Amritsar, a return showed that in eleven municipalities there were seventy-eight Muslim municipal councillors for a Muslim population of 544,473 and sixty-six Hindus for a Hindu population of 442,769.[19] A Muslim gentleman in the United Provinces specifically stated that the electoral college scheme contained the danger that the landhold-

---

[17] Minto to Morley, 31 Dec. 1908; M. N. Das, *India under Morley and Minto*, p. 233.

[18] *Home Department Public Procs. for Jan. 1909*, no. 224. *Political and Secret Letters from India*, vol. 8150 for 1909, India Office Library.

[19] Letter from Lt.-Gov. U.P. to Govt. of India of 27 Jan. 1909, *Home Dept. Pub. Procs. for Jan. 1909.* Also, Appendix to minute by Maclagen, Chief Secy., Panjab Govt., Proc. no. 225, *ibid.*

ing aristocracy in those provinces would be under-represented 'owing to the revolutionary ideas prevailing at present and the levelling tendencies of the times'.[20]

In Bengal, however, there was hardly a Muslim position to preserve. A proceeding of 21 January 1909 of the (west) Bengal government stated that in the Burdwan division, one of the most advanced divisions of the province, the Muslims numbered just over 13 per cent of the population.

Yet in the last three years out of 88 persons elected to Local Boards only 6 are Muhammadan; and of 52 persons nominated by local Boards as their delegates to District Boards, only one is a Muhammadan. In the municipal towns of the Division, there are 230 elected commissioners of whom only 9 are Muhammadans. . .In the great town of Howrah, with a population of 157,594 of which just over a quarter is Muhammadan, amongst 20 elected Commissioners there is not a single Mussulman. The same is the case in Serampore, a town with a population of 44,451 of which 19 per cent is Muhammadan.[21]

To the charge that the principle of separate representation for Muslims would exacerbate, if indeed it did not create, communal differences, the official reply at the time was that such differences already existed. In a draft prepared for Minto to reply to an address by the *Hindu Sabha* of Lahore against separate electorates, Dunlop Smith suggested that the Viceroy should tell the *Hindu Sabha* that 'any government fit to rule the country for a day must take into account the differences in religions which exist' and that the answer to the claim that the political interests of Hindus and Muslims and other communities were identical was that Muslims and others did not think so.[22]

The government of the Panjab claimed that politics in its province were already communal in character. For this reason it preferred nomination to Councils to all schemes of election. 'There is in the Punjab a special danger of introducing schemes of election, as party cleavage is in this province on religious lines and parties constituted on the basis of religion are proverbially more bigoted and therefore more politically undesirable than parties dependent

[20] Proc. no. 224, *Home Dept. Pub. Procs. for Jan 1909, Regulations for the Nomination of Members of the Local Legislative Councils.*
[21] Proc. no. 223 for 25 Jan. 1909, *Home Dept. Pub. Procs. for Jan 1909.*
[22] Martin Gilbert, *Servant of India*, p. 189.

on some other dividing principle.' The Panjab government went on to compare politics in the Panjab with politics in Ulster. The discussions which had so far occurred in the province on the proposals for reform of the Councils had 'left no doubt that the arrangements for the improvement of the councils provide an area in which the champions of the two religions will not be slow to bring their forces into collision!'[23] The author of this letter to the Government of India, the Chief Secretary E. D. Maclagan (1864–1932), went on

I am desired to add that a person chosen from a purely religious electorate is likely to be a person who will represent exclusively the pro-Muhammadan and anti-Hindu view of public questions, whereas nomination is likely to secure a legislator who besides being a Muhammadan will have breadth of view and variety of ideas. For this reason the Lt. Governor would deprecate the extension of any electoral system in this province now or in the near future for the selection of candidates to represent the interests of special religions.

Two days later the government of the United Provinces argued that, although there was an apparent truth in the proposition that class representation only accentuates class differences, yet

the fact remains that these differences do exist at the present time and that there is no immediate prospect of their disappearance. If in the course of time they tend to disappear, it would always be possible to revise the system of election. What we have to do is to devise a means for representing existing interests. As matters stand, the different classes view many of the questions that arise in public administration in different ways.[24]

Here and there in the official proceedings there are suggestions that the granting of separate electorates to Muslims would be more likely to improve rather than worsen Hindu–Muslim relations.

Minto's (and his officials') successful stand against the electoral college scheme and for separate Muslim electorates owed much to the desire to divide and rule between Muslims themselves. Like Dunlop Smith (but perhaps Dunlop Smith caught the infection from him), Minto was fearful of Muslim disaffection. He passed on to Morley with alacrity Harcourt Butler's views, that at heart many Muslims were against the British government in India, that

---

[23] *Home Dept. Public Procs. for Jan. 1909*, Proc. no. 225 for 25 Jan. 1909. *Political and Secret Letters from India*, vol. 8150 for 1909.
[24] Proc. no. 224, *Home Dept. Pub. Procs. for Jan. 1909*.

the Muslim landowning classes and the Muslim lawyer and professional classes were drifting apart and that 'out of the tangle of warring ideas are slowly emerging or re-emerging the two persistent parties in Indian politics – the party for the Government and the party against it'.[25] Earlier Minto had informed Morley that 'though the Mahommedan is silent he is very strong'. However, after he had won Morley's acceptance of separate electorates and when Muslims began to demand a number of seats on the Councils above what Minto thought appropriate and to object to the proposal that Muslims should also have votes in general constituencies, then he was quick to join with Morley in reminding Muslims of their client status, and to intimate to them that they were not alone in India. Important to British interests as the conservative Muslim was believed to be, Hindus were after all the best organised elements in India, whatever Sir Lancelot Hare might say. As Morley put it, the British had to be careful lest in picking up their Muslim parcels they drop their Hindu.

British policy must be acquitted of deep Machiavellian cunning, for it must be seen against the assumption, made by all except a tiny minority even of Indians themselves, that ultimate executive responsibility in India would remain with the British for as far as men could see ahead. From Morley, with his well-known declaration in the House of Lords on 17 December 1908 that 'If I were attempting to set up a Parliamentary system in India, or if it could be said that this chapter of reforms led directly or necessarily up to the establishment of a Parliamentary system in India, I for one would have nothing at all to do with it' downwards to the Officiating Chief Secretary of the government of East Bengal and Assam, who wrote that 'as it is not a question of obtaining executive power' the objections to special or double representation for special interests which 'have so much force in England' did not hold to anything like the same extent,[26] the British rulers would claim that they were only applying their self-proclaimed national virtue of common sense to the Indian situation as it existed in 1909, not in 1919

[25] Harcourt Butler to Minto, 22 July 1909, enclosure to letter of 25 July 1909 from Minto to Morley, *Morley Papers*, India Office Library EUR D 573/21.

[26] Off. Chief Secretary, East Bengal and Assam to Secy. Home Dept. Govt. of India, 23 Jan. 1909, *Home Dept. Proc.*, no. 227 for Jan. 1909, vol. 8150 for 1909 of *Political and Secret Letters from India*.

or 1929. Moreover to expect them to encourage the ideals and growth of non-communal nationalism and thus to hasten their own demise as the rulers of India, with all that that would mean for the British political and economic position in the world,[27] was to expect a degree not merely of altruism but also of prophetic insight out of the world of the history of governments.

THE FOUNDATION OF THE ALL-INDIA MUSLIM LEAGUE

Minto, in his reply to the Simla deputation, had stated the British recognition that Muslims formed a distinct political community in India. It remained for Muslims to endow that distinct political community with its own political organisation. Self-appointed Muslim leaders from all over India had gathered together for the Simla deputation; it was convenient that a formal Muslim political organisation should emerge from the Simla deputation. On 30 December 1906 the members of the Mohammedan Educational Conference meeting at Dacca turned themselves into the All-India Muslim League. Although the members of the Simla deputation were prominently represented on the 'provisional' Committee of the League appointed at Dacca, the foundation of the League did not go altogether smoothly. Nawwab Salim-Allah of Dacca (1884–1915), who had been absent from the Simla deputation on account of an eye operation, in early December 1906 circulated a scheme for a 'Muslim All-India Confederacy'.

Muslims from the United Provinces were not prepared to yield the van to the Muslims of Bengal, and the young lawyer element, well represented at Dacca (twenty-five members of the fifty-five strong Provisional Committee were lawyers), were not enthusiastic supporters of the loyalist line favoured by the landlords and government pensioners. There were differences over such issues as proportionate reservation of posts in the government service – a minimum reservation which might benefit Muslims in a minority province would cramp Muslims in a majority province as they acquired the requisite educational skills. The young Agha Khan (1877–1957) claimed a *rôle* in Muslim politics more commensurate with his position in gay Edwardian society than with any personal

---

[27] For a recent interpretation, see: E. J. Hobsbawm, *Industry and Empire* (London, 1968), pp. 123 *et seq.*

aptitude for, or devotion to, grass-roots political work. Minto was to describe him as more an authority on *café chantants* than on Indian reforms. To paper over the cracks, personal and provincial, an anodyne resolution, proclaiming the League's loyalty to the British empire in India, its intention to protect and promote Muslim political interests in India and its desire to prevent the rise of any Muslim feelings of hostility towards other communities, was adopted. No attempt was made to spell out the nature of the Muslim political interests to be protected and promoted.

The All-India Muslim League remained a feeble and underweight suckling for several years after its nativity. At the first of its annual sessions at Karachi in December 1907, a constitution was drawn up providing for a maximum membership of four hundred. Financially it was dependent upon the subventions of princes such as the Agha Khan and the Nawwab of Arcot. In 1908 a London branch of the League was formed, led by Saiyid Amir 'Ali, who had retired to England, and this London branch behaved as an independent Muslim plenipotentiary-extraordinary in discussions with the Secretary of State over the council reforms. The tail wagged the dog. In the agitation in 1909 against the electoral college scheme, many of the telegrams calling upon the government to hold fast to a scheme for separate electorates were sent on behalf of local Muslim *anjumans* rather than on behalf of the Muslim League. In 1910 in the first elections to be held under the Morley-Minto reforms, the Muslim League failed to act as an organisation; it did not present itself to the new Muslim electorate as a political party and had no political platform. Such of its members as were elected to the enlarged Legislative Councils were elected by reason of their personal and local prestige and not because they were members of the Muslim League. The most dramatic revelation of the League's political limitations was its impotence to affect the British decision, widely construed as a blow to Muslim interests, to revoke in 1911 the partition of Bengal; indeed it was not accounted a factor in the discussions leading to that decision.

Earlier than 1911 the British Indian government had shown its indifference to the Muslim League when its demands were inconvenient to British interests. Its very foundation in December 1906 had passed without much comment in official circles. At its Amritsar session in 1908 the Muslim League protested against the electoral college scheme and protest meetings were held in India to pass resolutions against it. Minto, however, was not unduly disturbed by the League's agitation, rather it seconded his own preference. The League's agitation was useful to him in dissuading Morley against the scheme. The real pressure was felt in London by Morley, with the London Branch of the Muslim League, supported by *The Times* and a few Members of Parliament, urging him to fulfil the spirit of Minto's undertakings to the Simla deputation and with Minto in India drumming up official opinion against the scheme and forwarding with alacrity telegrams from protesting Muslims.

But when, having gained the principle of separate electorates, members of the Muslim League demanded separate electorates exclusively, that is with no Muslim participation at all in general electorates, Minto summoned a hand-picked collection of Muslim Leaguers to Simla and persuaded them, perhaps by holding out personal inducements, to accept the government's proposals. One of them, ʿAli Imam (1869–1932) of Bihar, summoned a special meeting of the Muslim League at Lucknow in July 1909 to accept the government's plan, but it broke up in confusion. With Muslim Leaguers divided and Morley brushing aside the opposition of Amir ʿAli in London, Minto pressed on with the plan for Muslims to vote both in mixed and separate electorates. When, in November 1909, the proposals were published as Regulations for giving effect to the Councils Act passed in the previous July, the Agha Khan was induced to give them his unqualified blessing in a telegram to *The Times*. The government was still strong and adroit enough to take the measure of any Muslim League claims to real power; indeed, writing in February 1910 to Hewett (1854–1941), the Lieutenant-Governor of the United Provinces, Minto specifically refused to accept the League as the only spokesmen for Muslims in India, although 'we should of course always accept the League as a very representative Mahommedan body to which we should naturally refer for an opinion on any question of importance'.[28]

Before 1911 the All-India Muslim League was an amateur theatrical company playing not in a command performance perhaps, but to an invited audience. Minto's remark in 1906 about any nationalist movement in India applied equally to the League in

[28] Minto to Hewett, 15 February 1910, cited in S. R. Wasti, *Lord Minto and the Indian Nationalist Movement 1905 to 1910* (Oxford, 1964), pp. 86–7.

its earliest years: 'there is no popular movement from below. The movement, such as it is, is impelled by the leaders of a class very small indeed in comparison with the population of India.'[29] It is to be remembered that the largest constituency under the Indian Councils Act of 1909 had only 650 voters and that there were only 4,818 electors for the twenty-seven elective seats on the Imperial Legislative Council, of whom 2,406 were landowners and 1,901 were Muslims. The British and the conservative Muslim had succeeded, as they thought, by separate electorates on a very narrow property franchise (e.g. payment of land revenue of Rs. 3,000 per annum or income tax on Rs. 3,000 per annum), in isolating the 'young Muslim' element both from radical Congress politicians and from Muslims outside the charmed circle of *darbar* invitees. But they underestimated the willingness of the 'young Muslims' (who often had votes as graduates) both to seek more popular support, through co-operation with those who had the ear of Muslims outside the British educational system, namely the ʿ*ulama* or Muslim religious scholars, and to bid for the leadership of the Muslim League. By conceding separate electorates the British had cast Muslims for a distinctive political *rôle* in British India. Now the British were to find the writing of the script for that *rôle* taken out of their hands.[30]

[29] Minto to Morley, 4 November 1906, *Morley Papers*, India Office Library, EUR D 573, vol. 10.
[30] For a valuable new account of the internal politics of the League after 1911 see: Matiur Rahman, *From Consultation to Confrontation* (London, 1970), chapter VIII.

7

RELIGION ENTERS POLITICS 1910-24

The Muslims who engineered the Simla deputation and who, with eager British assistance, secured separate electorates, were concerned to preserve their quality against the lower orders, a mixed bag of 'agitators', for the most part noisy talkative intellectuals and professional men, mainly Hindu, but including some Muslims. Such Muslims did not claim that an assured political identity would serve Islam, or enable Muslims to fulfil more fully the demands of their faith. They accepted that public life in India would continue to run on British lines with purposes – more trains and more drains – agreeable to the contemporary Western ethos. More Indians, it was clear from British pronouncements, were to be co-opted to help their rulers to run India as a westernised dependency and so they, the Muslims of the Simla deputation, wished to be certain of co-option. The possibility of ethical and ideological independence from the West they did not, for all their emphasis on their Muslimness, seriously contemplate. Like comfortable Christians somewhat relieved to be told that real Christianity died with Christ, the founders of the Muslim League were probably somewhat relieved to hear from some ʿulama that the true Islamic state had died with the Caliph ʿAli in 661 – or was it with the Prophet himself in 632? They could busy themselves with regaining, or defending, their status as the 'natural' aristocracy of India. Anyway, Sir Saiyid Ahmad Khan had shown that the modern world was 'islamic', though some of his arguments were perhaps rather quaint.

THE WORLD OF THE ʿULAMA

But Sir Saiyid Ahmad Khan had not convinced all Indian Muslims that in the modern world traditional Islam was an anachronism, that religion and politics should be separated, that British rule was divinely ordained for the welfare of Indian Muslims, or that Muslims should settle for being a major interest group in an India which was forced to ape the West. There were also the 'fanatical' or 'bigoted' Muslims of British official parlance, members of that underworld of which the British were subconsciously aware and which exercised a subtle pull upon all their policies towards Muslims, rendering them always more than half ready to meet 'moderate' and 'loyal' Muslim petitions. It is not easy to define this Muslim underground, except negatively. It was poor rather than rich, respectable rather than rufflanly, school-educated rather than university- or college-educated, traditionally- rather than modern-educated. It was drawn from the lower middle class of a pre-industrial society, printers, lithographers, booksellers, teachers, retail shopkeepers, skilled craftsmen and petty *zamindars*, men literate in the vernacular, able and willing to read the large annual output of Muslim devotional literature in Urdu. Politically they were unorganised and lacking in sense of direction, but, as the 'anti-cow-killing' riots of the eighteen-eighties and nineties, the Cawnpore mosque disturbances of 1913 and the Khilafat movement of 1919–22 showed, they were quick to be seized by religious passion.

Outside the collaborating classes, religious passion among Muslims had grown since 1857. The preaching of the followers of Saiyid Ahmad of Bareilly and of Hajji Shariʿat-Allah and Karamat ʿAli Jaunpuri continued to do its work. The learned might dispute the content of the Holy Law of Islam, but the reformers rammed home to the ordinary Muslim that it alone was the touchstone of the fully Islamic life. Modern methods of printing, improved communications by rail and protection of the rights of free expression by the Criminal Code indeed provided a wider readership for the ʿulama than perhaps they had enjoyed under Muslim rule. The official British policy of religious neutrality enhanced the position of the ʿulama in the Muslim community. If Christian missionaries were free to attack Islam, so the ʿulama were free to defend Islam. To the ʿulama, the 'ghair-mazhabi' or la-dini (religion-less) state meant freedom to preach more religion, not less, and they took full advantage of that freedom. Probably too because the challenge from the West was intellectual and ethical, rather than emotional, and capable of being countered by dialectical methods, the ʿulama rather than the *sufis* stood forth as the protectors and exponents of

Islam. The activist philosophy of the West stimulated the activists among the Muslim religious classes.

The most vital school of *ʿulama* in India in the second half of the nineteenth century was that centred upon Deoband, the *dar al-ʿulum* (seminary) founded in 1867 about ninety miles to the north-east of Delhi in the Saharanpur district. The suppression of the Rising of 1857 had scattered the *ʿulama* of the North-Western Provinces: many were killed, some migrated to Hyderabad and some, such as Hajji Imdad-Allah (1817–99), left India for good and settled in Mecca. In 1867 Maulana Muhammad Qasim Nanotawi (1832–80), a descendant of a *jagirdar* of Shah Jahan[1] and Rashid Ahmad Gangohi (1828–1905), raised a small *maktab* (school) at Deoband to a *dar al-ʿulum*. They doubtless found an area antipathetic to British rule more suitable for a traditional Muslim seminary than British-dominated Delhi or Lucknow.

Although the *dar al-ʿulum* was supported entirely by voluntary contributions, numbers of 'graduates' rose from 15 in the period 1867–73 to 395 in the period 1903–11 and 949 in the period 1922–1931.[2] The students were drawn from the respectable poor of Muslim society, petty landholders' sons, small shopkeepers' sons, not only from the upper provinces but from the Panjab, Bengal and even from Afghanistan and Iran. The course of study was strictly traditional – Arabic, prosody, rhetoric, logic, *kalam* (dogmatic theology), *fiqh*, *tafsir*, *tibb* (medicine) and a little philosophy. The medium of instruction was Urdu: no English was taught and no modern science. Cut off thus from government employment and by tradition from the small crafts, except printing and book-binding, the Deobandi *fazil* or graduate manned the *madrasas* (schools) and *maktabs* of Muslim India, maintaining a dual system of education and a bifurcated Muslim educated class.

The *ʿulama* of Deoband prided themselves (and still pride themselves) on being *ahl al-sunna wa'l jamaʿa* (people of the practice of the Prophet and of the community), accepting the authority of the four orthodox *sunni mazahib*, opposed to the *Ahl-i Hadith*,[3] to the *ʿulama* of the Bareilly school – not to be confused with the followers

[1] Manazir Ahsan Gilani, *Sawanih-i Qasimi*, vol 1 (Deoband 1373/1953), p. 113.

[2] From graph seen in the *Daftar-i Dastar-bandi* at Deoband, December 1960.

[3] See, for example, Rashid Ahmad Gangohi, *Fatawa-i Rashidiyya*, vol. 1 (Muradabad, n.d. [c. 1906]), pp. 5, 93.

of Saiyid Ahmad of Rai Bareilly – with their acceptance of the intercession of saints and worship at tombs and their ascription of semi-divine qualities to the Prophet – to the teaching of Sir Saiyid Ahmad Khan, to the *shiᶜa* and to the Ahmadiyya. Particularly important in discrediting Sir Saiyid Ahmad Khan's doctrines among the traditionally-educated was Maulana Muhammad Qasim's (1832–80) *Tasfiyya al-Aqua'id*.[4] In this work, employing the dialectical methods of *kalam*, the author argues for the Ashᶜarite doctrine of God's exclusive and immediate sovereignty over His creation, the 'laws of nature' not intervening, for the subordination of reason to the Tradition of the Prophet, for the authority of certified reporters of *hadith* and for the necessity of accepting the *ijtihad* of earlier scholars and jurists when accepted by *ijmaᶜ*. Qasim further argued that that which God commands is good, rather than that God commands what is good, and that the mandates of Islam are not necessarily in conformity with nature.[5] Maulana Muhammad Qasim also employed his talents as a controversialist against Christianity, Judaism and Hinduism, notably in his *Taqrir-i Dil-Pazir*.

The Deobandi ᶜ*ulama* offered practical guidance on daily behaviour for those who consulted them. Between 1911 and 1951 it is said that they issued 147,851 *fatawa* on points of law and practice.[6] The collections of *fatawa* by Deobandi ᶜ*ulama* are of immense importance for understanding the preoccupations of Indian Muslims outside the charmed circle of those whom the British met socially. Rashid Ahmad Gangohi, for example, gave rulings on request that it was lawful to learn English if there was no danger to religion,[7] that it was unlawful to take interest from a Christian, to use money orders and bills of exchange in which the element of interest enters,[8] that it was not lawful to pay money into a bank, and that although it was not lawful for a Muslim landlord to take interest from a bank, even with the intention of applying it to such good works as the digging of a well, God might not call the landlord to account if the banker's money has been acquired by exploiting cultivators.[9] Rashid Ahmad Gangohi also ruled the wearing of a cross or of a topi to be sinful.

---

[4] Delhi, n.d. (1902?).   [5] *Tasfiyya al-ᶜAqa-id*, pp. 7, 11–12, 17–18
[6] Saiyid Mahbub Rizvi, *Ta'rikh-i Deoband* (Deoband, 1953), p. 131.
[7] *Fatawa-i Rashidiyya*, vol. I, pp. 90–1.
[8] *Fatawa-i Rashidiyya*, vol. II (Muradabad, n.d. [c. 1906]), pp. 40–1, 172,
[9] *Fatawa-i Rashidiyya*, vol. II, pp. 174–5.

A less legalistic exposition of Islamic practice was written by the later Deobandi *'alim*, Ashraf 'Ali Thanvi (1863–1943). He argued that the minutiae of the *shari'a* were not devised by the *maulavis* to worry tender consciences, but were essential to the godly life. He was aware of the strong temptation facing the Muslim to ape the wealthy and powerful European and was prepared to allow a place for modern science in man's acquisitive life, seeing no danger to the religious life in science's basic intellectual assumptions.[10] European virtues were borrowed from Islam and anyway a bad Muslim was always better than a good *kafir*.[11]

The prestige of Deoband as the active, confident and watchful guardian of *sunni* Islam was enhanced by its struggle against a new interpretation of Islam which appeared in the late nineteenth century – the Ahmadiyya. In March 1889 Mirza Ghulam Ahmad (*c.* 1839–1908), a landholder of Qadian in the Gurdaspur district of the Panjab, announced that he was receiving revelations from God. He claimed to perform miracles – notably to cause the death of opponents by prayer. What enraged orthodox opinion was Mirza Ghulam Ahmad's apparent challenge to the fundamental doctrine of *khatm-i nabuwwat* – that Muhammad is the last of the Prophets. Mirza Ghulam Ahmad claimed to be a *zilli-nabi* (shadow-prophet) and to receive inspiration (*ilham*) from God, though not, the majority of his followers claim, of the kind vouchsafed to Muhammad. Prophets are, it is argued, of two kinds, those like Muhammad who are lawbearers and those, like Mirza Ghulam Ahmad who come to interpret the law and to clean away the corruptions that creep into religion with the passage of time.[12]

Mirza Ghulam Ahmad also claimed to be a *masih* (messiah). The orthodox Muslim view is that Jesus did not die on the Cross and that he is alive in the fourth heaven, whence he will descend to earth before the Day of Resurrection. Mirza Ghulam Ahmad held that Jesus was saved from the Cross to die a natural death in Kashmir and that the promised Messiah before the Day of Resurrection will be someone with the attributes of Jesus, namely Mirza Ghulam Ahmad. The latter also claimed to be the promised *mahdi* who will

---

[10] Ashraf 'Ali Thanvi, *Huquq o Fara'iz* (Multan, 1960 ed.), pp. 206–8.
[11] *Huquq o Fara'iz*, pp. 575, 706.
[12] Mirza Bashiruddin Mahmud Ahmad, *Ahmadiyyat or the True Islam*, 5th ed. (Rabwa, 1959), pp. 17–18.

conquer the world for Islam, but not by the sword – rather by reasoned argument. *Jihad* by means of the sword is only permitted in self-defence.[13] Mirza Ghulam Ahmad claimed to have received a revelation permitting him to accept disciples and from this point his disciples became a separate community, refusing to marry its womenfolk to other Muslims outside the fold and referring to such Muslims with a variety of opprobrious epithets. The *'ulama* of Deoband and indeed of other religious centres devoted much energy to refuting the claims of Mirza Ghulam Ahmad.

The cause of traditional Muslim education was also furthered by institutions less combative than Deoband. The famous seminary founded at Lucknow in 1694 in the reign of Aurangzib, the Farangi Mahall, sheltered some distinguished scholars, notably 'Abd al-Haiy. His *Majmu'a-i Fatawa*[14] is a rather more academic compendium of legal rulings than the collections of the Deobandi *'ulama*. He pronounces upon such problems as the duties of Muslims when travelling as *musta'min* (persons under safe-conduct) in a *dar al-harb* (India is not meant), whether the owner of a male slave may arrange the marriage of his slave and whether a man accidentally touching, in conditions of domestic overcrowding, his foster-brother's wife's mother's thigh is guilty of *zina* (unlawful intercourse).[15] Of a total of 1,307 *fatawa* in his collection, only about thirty directly or indirectly relate to problems created by the British presence in India. 'Abd al-Haiy does, however, advise avoiding all social intercourse with unbelievers but considers, like most other *'ulama*, that it is permissible to learn English so long as there is no danger to religion.[16]

The *'ulama* shared the political attitudes towards British rule of the mass of educated Muslims outside the circle of large landlords, aspirants to deputy-collectorships and would-be *Khan-Bahadurs*, that is, antipathy, sometimes hatred, but not active underground resistance. The followers of Saiyid Ahmad Bareilly continued to maintain an active guerrilla war on the north-west frontier in the region of the Black Mountain, the scene of British expeditions in

---

[13] Mirza Ghulam Ahmad, *Islam aur Jihad*, (1900) 3rd ed. (Lahore, 1954), pp. 5–6, 9, 11.

[14] Urdu translation in two volumes (Cawnpore, 1373/1953).

[15] 'Abd al-Haiy, *Majmu'a-i Fatawa*, vol. II, p. 23.

[16] *Majmu'a-i Fatawa*, vol. II, pp. 179, 218–19, 233, 293.

1888 and 1891, and participated in the frontier wars of 1897–8. Few men and supplies reached them from British India after Mayo's time. An investigation into so-called *Wahhabis* in the Panjab in 1876 showed that there were few political activists then among the many religious reformers. The *ulama* were circumspect in their pronouncements when asked whether India was *dar al-harb* or *dar al-Islam*, as indeed with the threat of prosecution they had need to be. Asked this question in 1309/1891 and 1312/1894, Rashid Ahmad Gangohi merely hedged;[17] earlier ʿAbd al-Haiy simply quoted Abu Hanifa's (c. 699–767) conditions for the transformation of a *dar al-Islam* into a *dar al-harb* and left it for his listeners to decide whether those conditions obtained in British India.[18]

Nevertheless, despite this circumspection, some British in India were aware that the *ulama* were a potential political force and that it was necessary to divide them politically from the supporters of Saiyid Ahmad Bareilly. In a letter to Badr al-din Tyabji on 7 May 1888, Beck (1859–99) wrote that 'Wahhabi' sentiment was by no means dead and that 'thousands' would obey the call to action. Allan Octavian Hume appears to have thought that the 'Wahhabis' would support Sir Saiyid Ahmad Khan's stand against Congress, on the ground that a constitutional movement with Hindu participation was death to any hope of overthrowing British rule by force,[19] and he argued that the *maulawis* were already being won over to Congress, particularly in the Panjab. He believed himself to be 'digging a mine under these Wahhabi traitors' and felt that Sir Saiyid Ahmad Khan did not know the real motives of some of the men around him.[20] Hume's claim to have had the support of influential *ulama* is sustained by a modern historian (writing in Urdu) of the *ulama*. Maulana Muhammad Miyan writes that Rashid Ahmad Gangohi delivered a *fatwa* in October 1888 in favour of Muslim political association, on conditions, with Congress, and against association with Sir Saiyid Ahmad Khan.[21]

[17] *Fatawa-i Rashidiyya*, vol. I, p. 87; vol. II, p. 151.
[18] *Majmuʿa-i Fatawa*, vol. II, pp. 151–2.
[19] Letter to Tyabji dated 5 November 1888, *Tyabji Papers*, microfilm reel no. 2.
[20] Letter to Tyabji dated 5 November 1888, *Tyabji Papers*, reel no. 2.
[21] Muhammad Miyan, *ʿUlama-i Haq*, vol. I (Delhi, n.d.), p. 101.

THE RISE OF 'PAN-ISLAMISM'

Developments both in scholarship and in international politics eased the way towards emotional *rapport* between the ʿulama and the modern-educated Muslim, so that they were both ready to spring together to the defence of Islam even though they had different ideas about the Islam which they were defending. As English education spread, so the Muslim graduate of Aligarh, Calcutta, Lahore and Allahabad became aware of the cool, if not hostile, tone of nineteenth-century Western orientalism towards Islam and islamic civilisation. Writers such as Sir William Muir, in his *Life of Mahomet* (1858–61), and Aloys Sprenger (1813–93), in his *Das Leben und die Lehre des Mohammad* (1861–5), impugned the Prophet's sincerity. Wellhausen's (1844–1918) picture of the Arab empire until A.D. 750 in his *Das arabische Reich und sein Sturz* (1902) and Noldeke's (1836–1930) *Aufsätze zur persischen Geschichte* (1887) and *Sketches from Eastern History* (1892) displayed the seamier side of Islamic civilisation. Ernest Renan's (1823–92) *Averroès et l'Averroïsme* (1852) and *L'Islamisme et La Science* (1883) held the Arabs to be incapable of philosophy, and independent thought in Islamic countries to have been non-existent since the thirteenth century of the Christian era. General historians of Europe, such as Leopold von Ranke (1795–1886) and Jacob Burckhardt (1818–97), treated Islam as the great foe of Christian Europe and, for Burckhardt, the enemy of art. The work of Ignaz Goldhizer (1850–1921), whose *Muhammadanische Studien* (1889) is the foundation of Western *hadith* study, was far from welcome to all Muslims, since it cast doubt on the authenticity of prophetic traditions accepted by Muslims for almost a millennium.

The work of most European orientalists in the second half of the nineteenth century, even that of British orientalists, treated Islam as a world religion with its centres in Arabia and the Middle East, in confrontation with Christian Europe both medieval and modern. The response in India to denigration of Islam as a world civilisation was defence of Islam as a world civilisation. In this defence the modern educated Muslim took the lead, partly because, unlike the ʿulama, they could read what Europeans wrote, and partly because they could talk the same Hegelian and Darwinian language about the 'spirit' and the 'evolution' and the 'progress' of cultures.

Amir ʿAli's *Short History of the Saracens* (1889) glorified the first two caliphs, Abu Bakr and ʿUmar, although the author was a *shiʿa*. He celebrated the rule of the first four caliphs of Islam as embodying the Muslim ideal of state. A liaison-officer between the traditionally- and the modern-educated Indian Muslim was the famous Shibli Nuʿmani (1857–1914), educated in *madrasas* and eventually appointed to the Arabic department at Aligarh in 1883. Seized of European orientalism, Shibli wrote biographies of the Prophet, of the Caliph ʿUmar and of the Persian poets depicting them as great historical figures and indeed civilisers. His life of al-Ghazali emphasises his contribution to *kalam* or dogmatic theology as a means of defence against modern rationalism. His friend ʿAbd al-Halim Sharar (1860–1926) wrote romantic novels on the splendid achievements of Muslims outside India, for example his *Malik-i ʿAziz Varjana* (1888), a rejoinder to Sir Walter Scott's picture of Muslim life in *The Talisman*, and his history of the Crusades published in his journal *Dil-Gudaz* between 1901 and 1905. In 1898, Saiyid ʿAli Bilgrami published an Urdu translation of the work of an admirer among European scholars of Islamic civilisation, namely Gustav Le Bon's (1841–1931) *La Civilization des Arabes*. Thus in the cultural sphere Indian Muslims in the generation before the First World War, stimulated and indeed often helped by the works of European orientalists, were reasserting their independence from the intellectual and moral imperialism of the West, and in doing so were finding what common ground was shared between the product of the *madrasa and dar al-ʿulum* and the product of the government college and school.

Politically too, by 1900 Indian Muslims were illustrating the truth of Marshal Lyautey's (1854–1934) later simile that the Islamic world was like a gigantic drum, the reverberations from one end being felt at the other. From about 1880 European pressure upon the Muslim world steadily grew. Tunis was occupied by the French in 1881, Egypt by the British in 1882, Eritrea by the Italians by 1885 and the Sudan by the British in 1898. It appeared, correctly, that Britain had lost interest in defending the Ottoman empire against Russia at the Bosphorus, now that she was directly safeguarding the Suez Canal route to India by the physical occupation of Egypt (with the Franco-Russian alliance of 1891–2 she had also lost the naval ability to intervene in the Bosphorus). Indian

Muslims were dismayed by Britain's aloofness towards the brief Graeco–Turkish war of 1897 and the outcry in England against the Turks during the Armenian massacres of 1894 and 1896. Support and sympathy for the Ottoman sultan, whose own emissaries had not been inactive in India, began to worry the British government in India by about the middle of the nineties. They were also disturbed lest the Amir of Afghanistan show his teeth when British forces were committed against the Pathan tribes on the north-west[22] and there was fear of unrest in Hyderabad state, coinciding with a call to *jihad* on the frontier.[23] In July 1897 Maulawi Hidayat Rasul an activist in Lucknow was sentenced to a year's imprisonment for making seditious statements at a public meeting, while congratulating the Sultan of Turkey and the Amir of Afghanistan on their championship of Islam.

Sir Anthony MacDonnell, the Lieutenant-Governor of the United Provinces, reported the circulation of a book preaching *jihad* and quoted to the Viceroy, Lord Elgin (1849–1919), a leaflet describing the Ottoman sultan as *Amir al-Mu'minin* and *Padshah-i Mussalmanan*. In the same letter he reported signs of Hindu-Muslim rapprochement in Rohilkhand.[24] In a later letter, MacDonnell passed on reports that Rampur is said to contain 'a large number of vigilantes and Turks'. He added:

there can be no doubt that there is great sympathy with Turkey and that the prevalent feeling partakes of the nature of an Islamic revival. This I believe to be partly due to incitement from outside India and partly spontaneous, and I think it has been growing for some time and is fostered in Mahommedan schools. The Commissioner of Agra tells me that many more people than formerly have taken to wearing the Turkish *fez* and this is perhaps a straw indicating how the wind is beginning to blow.[25]

In a memorandum specially devoted to an analysis of the 'panislamic' movement, officials recorded their suspicions of Maulana

[22] C. J. Alder, *British India's Northern Frontier 1865–1895* (London, 1963), p. 313.
[23] Elgin to Hamilton, 20 November 1895, *Hamilton Papers*, India Office Library, EUR D 509/1, p. 357.
[24] MacDonnell to Elgin, 16 July 1897, *MacDonnell Papers*, Bodleian Library, Eng. Hist. c. 353, fols. 172a–3.
[25] MacDonnell to Elgin, 22 August 1897, *MacDonnell Papers*, Eng. Hist. c. 353.

Shibli's *Nadwat al-'ulama*, the teaching institution established at Lucknow in 1894 to encourage a dialogue between the *'ulama* of all shades of opinion and the modern-educated. Fears that this institution had a pan-islamic influence helped to deny Shibli a C.I.E. in 1911.[26]

The strength of feeling in India in favour of the Ottoman sultan's claims to be the *khalifa* of all Muslims and in favour of *jihad* against the British may be gauged by the reactions of loyalist Muslims. Mirza Ghulam Ahmad's pamphlet *Islam aur Jihad*, published in 1900 and calling for loyalty towards the British, suggests that many *'ulama* were actively disaffected towards British rule. In the last years of his life Sir Saiyid Ahmad Khan was so worried by the wave of antipathy towards the British and of support for the Turkish sultan that he wrote a number of essays denying the latter's claim to be *khalifa*. He argued that a ruler who could not in practice protect Muslims and enforce the mandates of the *shari'a* could not be considered *khalifa*. Sultan 'Abd al-Hamid had no effective power in British India and therefore could not be the *khalifa* for Indian Muslims. All the latter might do was to wish the sultan well as a Muslim ruler. Sir Saiyid further argued that historically Muslims had known three caliphates at one time, the 'Abbasid in Baghdad, the Fatimid in Egypt and the Ummayad in Spain; Sir Saiyid claimed that there was no Quranic text or *hadith* which enjoined a universal caliphate.[27] Muslims lived in British India as *musta'mins* of their non-Muslim rulers, enjoying freedom of religion, freedom of conversion to Islam and security of life and property. In other essays in *Akhiri Mazamin*, Sir Saiyid urged his fellow Indian Muslims to show realism, for they could not aid the Ottoman sultan. In May 1897 MacDonnell reported to Elgin a conversation he had with Sir Saiyid at Aligarh, in which Sir Saiyid warned of the alienation of Muslim feeling; apart from the bad feeling over England's attitude towards Turkey, the prospect in the United Provinces of domiciliary visits by British troops and officers to combat plague (which would infringe *parda*) 'was creating more ill-

[26] L. A. S. Porter to Du Boulay, Letter no. 104 dated 25 July 1911 of *Letters from Persons in India*, June to Dec. 1911, no. 82 of *Hardinge Papers*, Cambridge University Library, pp. 148–9.

[27] Article 'Khilafat' in *Akhiri Mazamin* (Lahore 1898), reprinted in *Maqalat-i Sir Saiyid*, vol. 1 (Lahore, 1962), pp. 157–8, 161–3.

will against us than anything he had known since the Mutiny'.[28]
Similar measures had already been adopted to combat plague in
Bombay, resulting in the murder of two British plague officers.
To the end of his days, Sir Saiyid Ahmad Khan believed it was
necessary for Indian Muslims to allow the British to define the
terms and conditions of their political life. The memory of 1857,
and of the technical and organisational prowess of Western states
which he observed during his visit to Europe in 1869–70, walled in
his political imagination. The generation of Muslims that came to
manhood in the decade before the First World War were not
equally prepared to accept colonial status in their political thought.
They began to advocate Islam as providing a higher ideal of political organisation than the contemporary Western national state.
Politics should aim not merely at social peace, but at a social peace
cast in a particular ethical form. Society should not just provide the
opportunity for virtue, but should *be* virtuous. Moreover, Islam
offered a higher ideal than Western racialism and racial domination. After his return from Europe, Sir Muhammad Iqbal (already
in 1911 described by the Panjab Census Report as a force among
the Muslims of the Panjab) delivered a lecture to the effect that:[29]

the essential difference between the Muslim community and other
communities of the world consists in our peculiar conception of
nationality. It is not the unity of language or country that constitutes
the basic principle of our nationality. It is because we all believe in a
certain view of the universe and participate in the same historical
tradition that we are members of the society founded by the Prophet
of Islam.

Elsewhere, Iqbal (1876–1938) wrote that membership of the Muslim
nation is determined by 'like-mindedness not by domicile' and that
'the ideal territory for such a nation would be the whole earth'.[30]
    The young Abu'l Kalam Azad (1888–1958), whose famous Urdu
journal *Al-Hilal* (The Crescent) commenced publication in 1912,
also refused to see the nation state as the final political destiny for

[28] MacDonnell to Elgin, 9 May 1897, *MacDonnell Papers*, Eng. Hist. c. 353,
fols. 123b–5a.
    [29] Lecture 'Muslim Community' delivered at Aligarh in 1910 and quoted
in extenso in the *Punjab Census Report, 1911*, part I, p. 162.
    [30] Article 'Political Thought in Islam', *The Sociological Review* (Man-
chester), I, 1908, p. 251.

Muslims. The community which acknowledges the One God and His Prophet Muhammad must model its life on the pattern prescribed by them. Politics should be infused with the spirit of religion. Muslims should make obedience to the mandates of Islam their only aim in life. Islam will open the way to political life for Muslims, will order their system of education and will transform their morals.[31] In Europe it is the word 'nation' that makes a thousand hearts beat as one, but among Muslims it is 'God' or 'Islam'. The Muslim who wishes to separate religion and politics is an apostate who works silently.[32] Although Iqbal and Abu'l Kalam Azad and the *ʿulama* might not agree upon the manner in which the Holy Law of Islam was to be interpreted and applied in the twentieth century, or indeed who was to interpret it, they were at one in rejecting the secular territorial state and a political life founded upon Western assumptions.

ʿULAMA AND YOUNG MUSLIM POLITICIANS JOIN FORCES

Evidence of growing political co-operation between the *ʿulama* and the Western-educated Muslim mounted under Minto and his successor Hardinge. In the aftermath of the partition of Bengal, there were reports that *mullas* were whipping up anti-Hindu feeling in the new province of East Bengal and Assam. Many *ʿulama* attended meetings in 1909 to protest against the scheme for electoral colleges under the Morley–Minto reforms and to demand separate electorates.[33] In 1910 the *ʿulama* and the conservative leadership of the Muslim League joined in a movement to persuade the government of India to pass an Act overriding a Privy Council decision in 1894 that family *waqfs* (pious foundations) were invalid on the ground that ultimate reversion of benefit to the poor was illusory. In 1911 there was a similar combination against the Special Marriage Bill, which *inter alia* allowed an unconverted Hindu man to marry a Muslim woman, an act forbidden by the *shariʿa*. Over *waqfs* the *ʿulama* were concerned about the interference by non-Muslims with

---

[31] *Al-Hilal*, 9 October 1912, p. 7.
[32] *Al-Hilal*, 23 October 1912, p. 6.
[33] *Home Department Proceedings, July 1909*. Enclosure to despatch of 22 July 1909, vol. 8151 of *Political and Secret Letters from India*, pp. 522 and 572–90, *passim*. India Office Library.

divine law; but also they shared with the rich Muslim Leaguer a similar vested interest in *waqfs* as a source of income. A further straw in the wind was the foundation at Deoband in 1910 by Maulana ʿUbaid-Allah Sindhi (1872–1944) of a *Jamiʿat al-Ansar* (Society of Helpers) intended to further greater fraternity between the alumni of Deoband and Aligarh.

General Muslim disillusion with what Sir Muhammad Shafiʿ (1869–1932) of the Panjab called 'the Anglo-Muhammadan school of politics' set in with the revocation, announced by King George V at the Delhi *Darbar* in December 1911, of the partition of Bengal. Although Muslims found themselves in a small majority in the re-constituted province of Bengal and although the old Muslim capital, Delhi, was made the new capital of British India, even conservative Muslims regarded the revocation as a British concession to Hindu agitation and as a sign that their interests were no longer safe in British keeping. The *Raj* suddenly began to look a little vulnerable and a little less than eternal. The advice of the absentee would-be leaders of the All-India Muslim League, the Agha Khan and Amir ʿAli, that Muslims should not agitate against the revocation, turned many against conservative politics.

Maulana Shibli who, in 1908, had signed a *fatwa* calling upon Muslims to support the government in suppressing disturbances by 'polytheists',[34] now published in 1912 an article soon to become famous, calling for the Muslim League to become more popular, to attend to the welfare of the Muslim cultivator and to seek political co-operation with Hindus.[35] He questioned whether Muslims should any longer follow in Sir Saiyid Ahmad Khan's footsteps. The famous Muslim journalist, Maulana Muhammad ʿAli (1878–1931), argued in an article in *Comrade* that Islam could not teach Indian Muslims 'to keep aloof from a majority in this country even though its ideas are not their ideas and its gods not their gods'. 'We think it possible', he went on, 'to evolve out of the jealousies of today, a political entity on federal lines, a unique constitution, be-cause in accordance with our unique situation, it would have to be

---

[34] Proc. no. 615B in February 1909 of *Home Department Proceedings, 1909*, vol. 8159.

[35] 'Mussalmanon ki Politikal Karwat', originally published in the *Muslim Gazette* of Lucknow. *Maqalat-i Shibli*, vol. III (Azamgarh, 1357/1938), pp. 171–172.

a federation of faiths.'[36] Although Muhammad ʿAli still saw a *rôle* in India for the British (indeed, he described the existence of the British government in India as 'providential'), he was clearly looking forward to internal autonomy for India and an active partner-ship between Hindus and Muslims.

Muslim chagrin with the British government was boosted by a renewed surge of emotion over further European attacks upon Muslim countries. The Italians had attacked Libya, then a province of the Ottoman empire, in 1911. The French declared a protectorate over Morocco in 1911 and the Balkan war of 1912 practically extruded the Ottoman empire from the European mainland. The British and the Russians had divided Persia into spheres of interest by the Anglo–Russian agreement in 1907 and in 1912 the Russians had bombarded the holy city of Mashad. Maulana Muhammad ʿAli perceptively observed in *Comrade* that the British Foreign Secretary, Sir Edward Grey (1862–1933) was so apprehensive of German hegemony in Europe that he was ready to acquiesce in the aggrandisement of the other major European powers and of the pro-Russian Christian Balkan states at the expense of Muslim interests.[37] Abu'l Kalam Azad took the lead in calling for support for the Ottoman sultan, not merely as the head of the greatest surviving independent Muslim state, but also as caliph of all Muslims. The enemy of the Ottoman, he said, was the enemy of Islam.[38] A Red Crescent Society was formed to provide medical aid for Turkish troops in the war of 1912 and a medical mission of doctors and nurses was sent from India.

The Viceroy, Lord Hardinge (1858–1944), thought it politic to subscribe to Turkish relief. Earlier he had tried to impress the Home Government with the strength of 'pan-islamic' sentiment in India over the Italian attack upon Tripoli. 'I hear from the North-West Frontier Province where practically the whole population is Mahommedan', he wrote to Lord Crewe (1858–1945), the Secretary of State for India, 'that the war between Italy and Turkey is the sole topic of discussion in the villages and among the tribes and the

---

[36] 'The New Order. Change of Capital and After-Effects of the Partition of Bengal', *Selections from Maulana Mahomed Ali's Comrade*, selected and compiled by Syed Rais Ahmad Jafri Nadvi (Lahore, 1965), p. 268.
[37] Article dated 14 October 1911, *Selections*, pp. 250–6.
[38] *Al-Hilal*, 6 November 1912, p. 20, col. 2.

bazaar version is that we have conspired with Italy to help her to seize Tripoli.'[39] In August 1913 Hardinge told Crewe that he did not think the Foreign Office in London sufficiently appreciated the difficulties which the Government of India were having with the Indian Muslims over Turkey;[40] a month previously he regretted to Crewe that the latter had not allowed him publicly to express his sympathy with Turkey.

Hardinge and his senior officials realised that the conservative Muslims were losing ground to those whom they inelegantly described as 'Mahomed Ali and his gang'. But their own policy and actions and those of the Liberal Secretary of State, Lord Crewe, were not likely to stiffen conservative Muslim backbones. In 1909 the Muslim League had passed a resolution in favour of the foundation of a Muslim university with power to affiliate colleges and in 1911 subscriptions had been collected by no less a conservative leader than the Agha Khan. The British-Indian government, fearing that such an all-India Muslim educational institution would propagate pan-islamic ideas and become an instrument of the 'young Muslim' element, was antipathetic, although not openly so. In July 1912 the Secretary of State for India, Lord Crewe, disallowed the scheme. Although conservative Muslims at Aligarh thwarted Muhammad °Ali's attempt to divert the money collected for the Muslim university project to the purchase of Turkish bonds, Muslim feeling against the government in all educated circles ran high.

In December and January 1912–13 Muhammad °Ali's supporters dominated the session of the Muslim League at Lucknow and succeeded in passing a resolution calling for a 'suitable' system of self-government for British India. Within six years of its foundation even such an 'upper-class' organisation as the League had passed from a desire to be consulted by the government to a willingness to confront it. Hardinge reported to Crewe,

The Mahommedans are at this moment in a hopeless and very tiresome position. The young men are creating a separatist tendency away

---

[39] Letter dated 12 October 1912. No. 64a of *Letters of Secretary of State*, Nov. 1910 – Dec. 1911, no. 117 of *Hardinge Papers*, Cambridge University Library, p. 261.
[40] Letter dated 14 August 1913. No. 40 of *Letters to S. of S.*, Jan.–Dec. 1913, no. 119 of *Hardinge Papers*, p. 108.

from Aligarh in the minds of the more sober men and it is not impossible that we may see a breaking away from and collapse of the Moslem League. . .the All-India Moslem League preached at their meeting the union with the Hindus for purposes of agitation.

Then, after the usual official whistling to keep up spirits 'All this is I believe mere pretence. Were it not for the presence of the Government the relations between the Hindus and the Mahommedan community are so strained that they would be flying at each other's throats',[41] he confesses to Crewe that 'we can no longer count on the loyalty of the Mahommedan community as a whole. The extreme faction of that community will now join any other faction in opposition to the Raj.'[42]

The government furthermore collided with Muslim opinion in July and August 1913, in a religious incident which ended in the strengthening of the political position of Muhammad ʿAli and his 'gang'. As part of a road-widening scheme, the Cawnpore Municipality proposed to remove a washing place attached to the side of a mosque. In the ensuing riots twenty-three people were killed and thirty wounded. Meston (1865–1943), the Lieutenant-Governor of the United Provinces, saw the whole affair as a 'test case between (1) the domination of the false leaders who are gradually paralysing the best instincts of the Indian Mahommedans and (2) the traditional reliance of the community on the British government'. He believed the 'entire forces of the new Mahommedan machinery for agitation were being dishonestly used on a false cry of religious sentiment in order to show that the demagogues who now aspire to lead the Mussulman community can defeat the Government and wring concessions from it by mere shouting'.[43]

But aristocratic Muslims too joined in the outcry against the government of the United Provinces; the Raja of Mahmudabad (1877–1931) begged Hardinge to release those arrested for rioting; in the Panjab 'rabid feeling' among Muslims was reported and the newspaper *Zamindar* was so hostile that the Panjab government ordered the forfeit of its security. The Panjab government noted

---

[41] Letter dated 3 April 1913. No. 15 of *Letters to S. of S.*, Jan.–Dec. 1913, no. 119 of *Hardinge Papers*, p. 25.

[42] *Letters of S. of S.*, Jan.–Dec. 1913, letter no. 40, dated 14 August 1913.

[43] Letter from Meston to Hardinge dated 25 August 1913, enclosed with letter no. 43 of *Letters to S. of S.*, Jan.–Dec. 1913, no. 119 of *Hardinge Papers*, p. 117.

that the Cawnpore mosque incident had given 'the extreme or neo-Muslim section of the community composed of the young and hot-headed literati, editors, schoolmasters and journalists' their head. Hardinge was able to bring the affair to a close and, as he thought, to take the wind out of Muhammad ʿAli's sails,[44] by visiting Cawnpore himself and releasing 106 prisoners awaiting trial, in return for an apology by prominent local Muslims. Nevertheless, the government only just emerged from a head-on collision with Muslims with its face saved. In the Cawnpore mosque incident (where, as Hardinge found, the local government's hands were hardly clean) all sections of Muslim opinion could combine against the *Raj*.

THE FIRST WORLD WAR AND THE KHILAFAT MOVEMENT

The war of 1914–18 merely added more thrust to the converging courses in politics of the modern- and the traditionally-educated. Maulana Muhammad ʿAli, in his famous article on 26 September 1914 in *Comrade* entitled 'The Choice of the Turks', proclaimed that with the outbreak of war 'all truly loyal people have closed the chapter of civil controversy with the officials', but that nevertheless, if the war was really a war of right against might then Britain should evacuate Egypt.[45] (Hardinge's government thereupon declared the security deposit of *Comrade* forfeit and the journal had to cease publication.) On the outbreak of war between Britain and Turkey, in November 1914, the Council of the Muslim League passed a resolution of loyalty, but the government was well aware of the sympathy for Turkey, especially 'amongst the lower Mahommedan classes'.

In March 1915 Meston sent Hardinge from the United Provinces an interesting analysis of Muslim sentiment and of the 'young Muhammadan party's hopes of a common front among Muslims against British rule:

First there is the bigot who regards all Christians as anathema and hates us accordingly. He is very little in evidence at the present juncture as he cannot conceal his contempt for the lip service which the

---

[44] Hardinge to Crewe, 19 November 1913, *Letters to S. of S.*, Jan.–Dec. 1913, letter no. 58, no. 119 of *Hardinge Papers*, p. 152.
[45] *Selections from Maulana Mahomed Ali's Comrade*, p. 533.

forward party are rendering to religion. He would use them if he could thereby smite us, but he does not associate with them.

Meston did not, however, include the Deobandi *ʿulama* in this category. On a recent visit to Deoband he had found 'the whole tone was one of abstention from politics and genuine gratitude to the British government for its protection and sympathy'. But then 'there is the lower type of priest. . .who thinks more of power than of godliness. It is this section alone that contributes to our present difficulties.' Meston saw *ʿulama* of this stamp and the young Western-educated Muslims drawing closer together. The latter's 'quest is for a cause':

this he finds in his religion. It gives him a link with great traditions. It may not be an ethical ideal but it is a militant bond. . .at this point he comes into touch with the priest of the arrogant domineering type, whose ambition lies in swaying the passions of the ignorant masses. Hence arises Pan-Islamism, the ideas of the Muslim 'nation' and many of the fantasies generated from it.

The younger Muslims 'try to work with the priests, hoping through them to influence the mob. . .For the time being, however, it would be idle to deny that they have attained success; Mahomed Ali is the popular hero of every Islamic school and college in the province'.[46] Meston, however, doubted the capacity of the Muslim of the United Provinces for 'subterranean work' and did not believe he was in touch with the (non-Muslim) revolutionary movements in Bengal or with the *ghadr* (largely Sikh) revolutionary movement in the Panjab.

Despite Meston's complacency in 1915, some Muslims from among the *ʿulama* did engage in 'fifth column' work against the British during the war of 1914–18. A leading *ʿalim* belonging to Deoband, Mahmud al-Hasan 'Shaikh al-Islam' (1851–1920), left for the Hijaz in 1915 in order to make contact with the Turks. After meeting Enver Pasha (1881–1922) and Jamal Pasha (1861–1922) he was detained by Sharif Husain's (1853?–1931) men when they rose in revolt against the Turks and handed over to the British, who interned him in Malta between 1917 and 1920. One of

[46] Letter dated 25 March 1915, *Letters from Persons in India*, vol. IX, part I, from 2 Jan. to 30 March, 1915, no. 64 of *Hardinge Papers*, pp. 623–43 *passim.*

his *aides*, Maulana ʿUbaid-Allah Sindhi, went to Afghanistan and worked with German and Turkish agents there to stir up the tribesmen against the British on the north-west frontier.[47] Such open opposition, however, was confined to a very few; when Edwin Montagu (1879–1922) visited India as Secretary of State his impression was that the ʿulama were politically quite unorganised and indeed unaccustomed to political life.[48] It is doubtful, however, whether their attitude towards British rule was ever, during the period of Britain's war with Turkey, warmer than non-belligerent. When Harcourt Butler met the ʿulama at Deoband in May 1918, unlike Meston three years earlier, he described them as sympathetic to Turkey with a small number hostile to the British government. The *maulawis* of Deoband, he added, 'are rather notorious for their duplicity'.[49]

Although Muhammad ʿAli and Shaukat ʿAli had been interned after the outbreak of war with Turkey, the tide of Muslim politics flowed strongly in the direction they desired and towards an accommodation with Congress designed to hasten constitutional and political change at the all-India level. In December 1916, at simultaneous meetings at Lucknow of Congress and of the All-India Muslim League, attended by about 400 Muslims from Lucknow and district, a political pact was entered into by the 'young Muslim' leadership of the League and Congress. Under this famous 'Lucknow Pact', a formula for future Muslim representation in any expanded provincial legislative councils was drawn up. Congress accepted separate electorates for Muslims and agreed that in the Muslim minority provinces of U.P., Bihar, Bombay and Madras, Muslims should have 30, 25, 33 and 15 per cent of the elected Indian membership respectively. In the Muslim majority provinces of Bengal and the Panjab, however, they should have 40 and 50 per cent respectively.

Although Jinnah (1876–1948) played a prominent part in the negotiations, this 'pact' was essentially a deal between the 'young Muslim' U.P. leadership and Congress. It sacrificed the interests

---

[47] Cf. accounts in Urdu, e.g. *ʿUlama-i Haq*, I, pp. 139–70, Husain Ahmad Madani, *Naqsh-i Hayat*, vol. II (Deoband, 1954), pp. 145–81 and Sir Michael O'Dwyer, *India as I Knew It* (London, 1925), pp. 178–80.

[48] ed. Venetia Montagu, *An Indian Diary* (London, 1930), pp. 45, 118.

[49] Harcourt Butler to Chelmsford, 6 May 1918, *Harcourt Butler Papers*, India Office Library, EUR F 116, no. 49.

of the Muslim majority provinces to those of the minority provinces, and to those of the U.P. in particular. It was not, however, popular with the conservative U.P. Muslim, who would have preferred a 50 per cent proportion of legislative council seats in the U. P. with permanent British rule, without thought of a united Congress–League stand against the British at the all-India level. But with Muslim emotions stirred by the war between Britain and the Ottoman empire, the 'young Muslim', with his growing *rapport* with some of the *ʿulama*, held the political initiative. In any event, with the Panjab in the grip of the Lieutenant-Governor O'Dwyer (1864–1940) and the recruiting sergeant, and the Muslim League leadership in Bengal (in the hands of Fazl al-Haq (Fazlul Huq 1873–1962 who signed the 'pact') only too gratified to gain a 30 per cent increase over the Morley–Minto percentage of Muslim seats in the provincial legislature, there was no challenge to the dominance of the U.P. Muslim politician.

For all Hardinge's earlier warnings, British policy in London, not in Delhi, immediately after the victory of 1918 detonated an explosion of Islamic sentiment in India, which blew into each other's arms the very classes it had been the aim of British policy before 1914 to keep apart, that is, the modern- and the traditionally-educated. Religious passion took command. In October 1918 Turkey, completely defeated by Allenby's armies, sued for an armistice. Constantinople was occupied by Allied forces. The Treaty of Sèvres, signed in August 1920, deprived Turkey of all rights in Cyprus, Egypt and the Sudan, transferred the Arab areas of her empire to British and French mandate, gave certain Aegean islands to Italy and allowed Greece to administer Izmir (Smyrna) for five years. Italy was to have development rights in southern Anatolia and Adalia and France in Cilicia and western Kurdistan. Although the Sultan was to retain Constantinople, the shores of the Sea of Marmora, the Gallipoli peninsula and the interior of Anatolia, he became in effect a British puppet. Mecca and Medina were to be left under the control of the Arab rebel against the Ottoman and ally of the British, the Sharif al-Husain.

When, in May 1919, Greek troops landed at Izmir and advanced into the interior of Anatolia, it began to look as if the Byzantine empire was to be re-created on Turkish soil, in regions indisputably Turkish in population. Given Lloyd George's (1863–1945) sudden homage to his Welsh Non-conformist upbringing in a number of 'crusading' statements, the Muslim world might be forgiven for believing that, in its moment of triumph and with Russia in the midst of revolution, the Christian West was determined to reverse the verdict of the medieval crusading wars.

The mounting evidence of Allied and particularly of British intentions to smash Turkey enraged nearly all sections of Muslim opinion in India. Already in December 1918 leading *ʿulama*, including ʿAbd al-Bari (1878–1926) of the Farangi Mahall, attended the annual session of the All-India Muslim League. A Khilafat Conference was held in November 1919, which then gave birth to an All-India Khilafat Committee. The Khilafat Conference embraced conservative Muslims, the 'young Muslim party' and members of the religious classes – for example, ʿUmar Hayat Khan Tiwana (1874–1944) of the Panjab, Nawwab Zuʾl-fiqar ʿAli Khan (1875–1933), Fazl al-Haq of Bengal, ʿAbd al-ʿAziz Ansari, Maulana Hasrat Mohani (1878–1951) and ʿAbd al-Bari. They were joined by Abuʾl Kalam Azad, Maulana Muhammad ʿAli and his brother Shaukat, as soon as they were released from the internment to which the Government of India had consigned them during the war. In November 1919 *ʿulama* from Deoband and Farangi Mahall founded the *Jamʿiyyat al-ʿulama-i Hind* (Society of the *ʿulama* of India), which held its first meeting at Amritsar in November 1919.

Now Mahatma Gandhi (1869–1948) intervened. Eager to enlist Muslims in the cause of Indian independence, Gandhi attended a joint conference in November 1919 at Delhi of Muslim and Hindu leaders on the *Khilafat* question. The publication of the Rowlatt Bill, giving the British–Indian executive wide repressive powers against sedition and the Amritsar massacre of April 1919, when General R. E. H. Dyer (1867–1927) fired on a crowd of demonstrators killing at least 375 and wounding at least 1,200, had inflamed almost all sections of Indian opinion irrespective of community. In February 1920, Gandhi formally broached a non-co-operation campaign, and in June 1920, after an all-parties Hindu–Muslim conference at Allahabad, joined with Abuʾl Kalam Azad, the ʿAli brothers, Maulana Hasrat Mohani and others to draw up a detailed programme of non-co-operation with the government. In September 1920 the Indian National Congress, meeting at Calcutta, formally adopted non-co-operation as its policy. In July 1921 at Karachi the All-India Khilafat Conference, presided over by Muhammad ʿAli, passed a resolution that it was religiously unlawful for Muslims to continue to serve in the British army and that if Britain attacked Turkey the Muslims of India would declare India an independent republic. In October 1921 the Congress Working Committee passed a resolution confirming the Karachi resolutions and launching a civil disobedience campaign. Hindus and Muslims were fairly launched upon a struggle to free their native land from British rule.

MUSLIM POLITICAL THEORY IN THE PERIOD OF THE KHILAFAT MOVEMENT

But Hindus and Muslims were fairly launched not upon a common struggle but upon a joint struggle; they worked together, but not as one. The philisophy of the *Khilafat* movement was not that of territorial nationalism, but of community federalism, and of a federalism wherein one party, the Muslim, looked outside the common habitat, India, for the *raison d'être* of the federal relationship. To adapt Muhammad ʿAli's later simile,[50] the wider Muslim world and India were to be two non-concentric circles, with an overlapping segment in which the Indian Muslims had their being. It would be wrong indeed to believe that all Muslims who supported the *Khilafat* movement were imbued with the same ideas and purposes. Conservatives wished merely to influence the British government towards a more lenient treaty of peace with Turkey and to escape the odium of standing aloof from the popular cause; the conceptions of Dr Ansari (1880–1936) and ʿAbd al-Bari, Mazhar al-Haq (1866–1929) and Abu'l Kalam Azad, as to how and by whom the law of Islam was to be interpreted, were as different as those of Sir Saiyid Ahmad Khan and Maulana Muhammad Qasim. Some Muslims had reservations about the demand for immediate independence for India. The Bareilly ʿulama and the *Bahr al-ʿulum* ʿulama at Farangi Mahall were hostile to non-co-operation. Nevertheless, the Muslim leaders of the *Khilafat* movement came together on a religious platform; their appeal to their followers was in religious

[50] Speech at Fourth Plenary Session of the Round Table Conference, 19 November 1930. ed. Afzal Iqbal, *Selected Works and Speeches of Mahomed Ali* (Lahore, 1944), p. 465.

terms – that only by joining to support the independence of the Ottoman *sultan* as *khalifa* of all Muslims could they hope to live as Muslims in obedience to God.

Abu'l Kalam Azad's *Masla-i Khilafat* (The Question of the Caliphate), written in 1920, is an interesting amalgam of the orthodox *sunni* theory of the *khilafat*, the 'pious *sultan*' theory, and plain political expediency.[51] It argues that God entrusted the vicegerency of this earth to a succession of different communities, until finally it was entrusted to the community of the Prophet Muhammad. Only through obedience to God can good and right be manifested in the world.[52] The caliphate was instituted by God to secure obedience to Him in this world. Islam teaches that religion and the world, the Holy Law and government are not separate; 'true government and conformity with the will of God is that which the *shari'a* has itself brought into being'.[53]

Abu'l Kalam Azad holds that true Islamic government, in which the enforcement of the Law of God is the sole preoccupation and ground of government, existed only during the time of the Prophet himself and of the first four *khalifas*[54] and that thereafter the caliphate became a worldly monarchy. Nevertheless, he says, continued recognition by all Muslims of the caliphate remained a religious obligation. In a somewhat contrived argument, he states that God has ordained a special form of organisation for every category of created beings, which may be interpreted as a centre of law, or a legal centre (*qanun-i markaz*), on which a circle of being is dependent. Without obedience to this directional centre, existence will fall into confusion. The life and health of Islam is dependent upon there being a centre of law. Belief in the unity of God *(tauhid)* is the centre around which all other beliefs form a circle.[55] The political caliphate is the outward expression of man's acceptance of *tauhid* as the centre of Muslim life.

Abu'l Kalam Azad holds that the ʿAbbasid caliphs in Egypt were the recognised caliphs of the Muslim world and that the last of them, al-Mutawakkil (1508–17), handed over his rights to Salim,

---

[51] For a fuller treatment of the political theory of the Khilafatists see: P. Hardy, *Partners in Freedom and True Muslims* (Lund, 1971).

[52] *Masla-i Khilafat* (Lahore, n.d. [1958]); India Office Library, Urdu B. 4222, pp. 7–9.

[53] *Masla-i Khilafat*, p. 26.   [54] *Masla-i Khilafat*, pp. 10–1.

[55] *Masla-i Khilafat*, pp. 36–7.

the Ottoman sultan, in 1517. Only the Ottoman sultans had the power thereafter to be universal caliphs. As for the allegiance of Muslims in India, Azad says the sultans of Delhi recognised the caliph in Baghdad before the Mongol catastrophe and thereafter acknowledged the ʿAbbasid caliph in Egypt. He concedes that under the Mughals, Akbar and his successors considered themselves as *imams* in India, but they did not claim theirs to be a universal Muslim caliphate. Azad holds that if Akbar had performed *hajj* he would have heard the *khutba* read in the name of the sultan of Turkey just as if he was an ordinary Muslim. 'Rationally and religiously' this would have been tantamount to an acceptance of the caliphate of the Ottomans.[56] However, as long as there were effective Muslim powers in Safawid Iran and in Mughal India, it was not necessary for the enforcement of the mandates of the *shariʿa* that there should be any overt and formal link between these countries and the central caliphate of the Ottoman sultan. But as soon as the Mughal emperors lost authority in India, then the obligation of the Indian Muslim towards the Ottoman caliph, which had lain dormant so long as Muslims ruled effectively in India, revived. This had occurred at the time of the débâcle in 1857 and the obligation has persisted ever since.

Azad lays down that it is the individual duty (*farz al-ʿain*) of every Muslim to come to the aid of any Muslim government under attack from non-Muslims, but *a fortiori* it is their duty to do so when the *khalifa* himself is threatened.[57] The *Jazirat al-ʿArab* (the Arabian peninsula) must at all times be free of non-Muslim control and if it has escaped from the control of the *khalifa* of Islam then it must be restored to him by force, force to which all Muslims all over the world must contribute.[58] If the British government has been told by Muslims what the religious obligations of Muslims are and if it chooses to ignore such instruction, then Muslims must begin non-co-operation, not only towards the British but also towards any Muslim supporting the British government. Abu'l Kalam Azad justified Muslim co-operation with non-Muslims against a non-Muslim government by the argument that the Qur'an distinguishes between two sorts of unbelievers, those who commit aggression against Muslims and those who do not. It is not sinful to

[56] *Masla-i Khilafat*, p. 202.   [57] *Masla-i Khilafat*, pp. 221–9.
[58] *Masla-i Khilafat*, p. 301.

have close relations with friendly unbelievers and particularly with Hindus, as they have never attacked Muslim countries or killed Muslims as a matter of religion.[59]

The kind of independent India visualised by some of the less politically sophisticated (and therefore more typical) *ʿulama*, should the *Khilafat* and non-co-operation movements be successful, was spelt out in a number of proposals drawn up by a sub-committee appointed by the *Jamʿiyyat al-ʿulama-i Hind*, which met at Bada'un in December 1921. It proposed that it should be the duty of an *Amir-i Hind* to implement the mandates of the *shariʿa*, including those which had not been applied in India for a long time, owing to the presence of an infidel government. It should also be the duty of the *Amir-i Hind* to preserve the unity of Muslims in India and to discourage religious controversy. He should also establish a treasury *(bait al-mal)*, *qazis'* courts, an organisation for pious endowments and appoint officials to promote and supervise Muslim education. The *Amir* should, pending the liberation of the Ottoman *khalifa*, be elected and dismissed only at a general meeting of the *Jamʿiyyat al-ʿulama-i Hind*. He must be a scholar of *tafsir*, *fiqh* and *hadith* and be of high moral character. He should also, however, be aware of the political needs of the time. He was to be assisted by a *majlis-i shura* or body of counsellors numbering seven, five of whom were to be *ʿulama* and two non-*ʿulama*, experienced in politics. He might be dismissed for apostasy, the commission of acts forbidden by the Holy Law, incapacity exceeding his powers and cravenness towards the infidel (British) government. He could be replaced by a better qualified person, but only if there was no danger in his replacement of division within the Muslim community. When the (Ottoman) *khalifa* of Islam was freed from tutelage he would have the power to appoint and dismiss the *Amir-i Hind*, but only in consultation with the *Jamʿiyyat al-ʿulama-i Hind*.

The *Jamʿiyyat* committee also proposed the formation of an Assembly of the Select (Notables) and a General Assembly, the first to be composed of four pious and god-fearing men, one of whom must know English. The General Assembly was to be composed of members of the provincial organising committees of the *Jamʿiyyat* and of the 'ministers' superintending the *bait al-mal*, education and *auqaf* (pious endowments) and their assistants. There should also be

[59] *Masla-i Khilafat*, pp. 315–18.

a Law Assembly of five members. Questions of *shariᶜa* law would not in any event be settled by majority voting, but by the strength and superiority of the arguments adduced.[60]

On co-operation with Hindus the members of the *Jamᶜiyyat al-ᶜulama-i Hind* were confident, as Mahmud al-Hasan, Shaikh al-Islam, said in his presidential address at Delhi in November 1920, that it was no tragedy that Hindus and Muslims did not mix in social life, so long as they struggled together against the British. Mahmud al-Hasan considered Hindu–Muslim co-operation vital and said that God had strengthened the Hindus so that Muslims could attain their aims.[61]

It should now be evident that Abu'l Kalam Azad and the members of the *Jamᶜiyyat al-ᶜulama-i Hind* saw free India as a minimal federation of religious communities, with little or no common political and social life; they did not conceive India being ruled by a sovereign government enjoying authority over citizens sharing a national life which extended to most of the concerns of daily intercourse. The freedom of India, the ᶜ*ulama* declare, is necessary so that Muslims may be free in their religious and legal (*sharᶜi*) life and so that there may be no obstacle to enforcing the Holy Law of Islam. The ᶜ*ulama* visualised a free India in which Muslims would live in a juristic ghetto, for Muslim law applies only to Muslims. Moreover, since the ᶜ*ulama* advocated strict prohibition of usury and of commercial and industrial activity founded on the giving and taking of interest, in effect they were opting out of active co-operation with non-Muslims for the industrial and commercial development of India within a market economy. Common economic policies to raise the standard of living of all Indians irrespective of religion were to be rendered almost impossible of devising. Since the ᶜ*ulama* did not openly claim a monopoly of political and military power for Muslims in a free India (and how could they in the circumstances of 1919–22?) they were really advocating for Muslims a life of subsistence agriculture and skilled handicrafts.

The purport of the resolutions of the *Jamᶜiyyat al-ᶜulama-i Hind* and of Abu'l Kalam Azad's *Masla-i Khilafat* was that in the most vital concerns of life Hindus and Muslims shared nothing except a

[60] Maulana Muhammad Miyan, *Jamᶜiyyat al-ᶜulama Kya Hai?*, part II (Delhi, 1946), p. 88.
[61] *Jamᶜiyyat al-ᶜulama Kya Hai?*, part II, pp. 40–1.

habitat, that the good life could not be shared with non-Muslims and that Indian Muslims were an unfortunate section of the world-wide Muslim community, doomed to live in a non-Muslim majority area. The message of the *Khilafat* movement, as Azad and the *ulama* of the *Jamʿiyyat* conveyed it, was that India could win freedom from the British but that Muslims would co-operate only if, in free India, they were to be allowed to become members of an *imperium in imperio*. They were not to form a separate state, or a nation in any sense acceptable to Western political thought – for Indian Muslims were members of a world-wide religious fraternity under the jurisdiction of a *khalifa* – but they were to form a separate legal and religious community with self-governing institutions of its own. In 1920–2 Abu'l Kalam Azad and the *Jamʿiyyat* were advocating the mental partition of India.

That India would not easily settle down to becoming a federation of the two communities of Muslims and Hindus became evident even during the height of anti-British feeling in 1920 and 1921. The Muslim leaders of the *Khilafat* movement did not find con-genial Gandhi's vision of India under *swaraj* as enjoying a parlia-mentary constitution devised by a constituent assembly elected on an adult franchise (i.e. including women). Muslims moreover – Muhammad ʿAli was frank about this – accepted Gandhi's doc-trine of non-violence only as a political expedient.

The Muslim attitude towards the Anglo–Afghan war of 1919 was disturbing to many Hindus. Muhammad ʿAli's address to the court which sentenced him in 1921, on a charge of conspiracy to seduce Muslim troops from their allegiance to the Crown, gave colour to their fears that the Ghaznavid invasions could be repeated with Indian Muslim support. If, he said, it was the Amir of Afghanistan's aim to wage *jihad*, then the clear law of Islam required that no Muslim should render any help against him and if the *jihad* approached India then Muslims should join it.

The Mappilla (Moplah) rebellion from August to December 1921 revived old Hindu–Muslim antagonisms. The Mappillas, the Muslim cultivators on the west coast of Madras, rose against their oppressive landlords, who happened to be mainly Hindu. They killed or converted by force many Hindus. Although Hakim Ajmal Khan (1863–1928), in his speech as Acting-President of the Congress session at Ahmedabad, publicly regretted 'these deplorable incidents', his example was not followed by Hasrat Mohani, who opposed a Congress resolution condemning the Mappillas.

Some who have regretted the partition of India in 1947 have criticised Mahatma Gandhi for having encouraged the religious passions of Muslims in a cause which could only revive, if not create, a sense of alienation from India. He should have seen, it is hinted, that Muslims could be roused politically only for a cause that was not India's, namely the independence of the Ottoman sultan. His reported remark that 'I have been telling Maulana Shaukat Ali all along that I was helping to save his cow, i.e. the Khilafat, because I hoped to save my cow thereby' was no earnest of a union of hearts among Hindus and Muslims. It should be stressed, that Gandhi was only encouraging emotions that were already raging and which had been growing in intensity for at least two decades. Indian Muslim concern for the fortunes of the outside Muslim world was an expression of the revival of the morale and self-confidence of the community, already visible in the eighteen-nineties.

Moreover, although Sir Shafaʿat Ahmad Khan (1893–1947) was no doubt justified as a practical politician in describing the *Khilafat* and non-co-operation movement as essentially a destructive force, in which subconscious impulses, lofty idealism, youthful indiscretion and desire for power and leadership were mixed in a most incongruous manner, and although no doubt it was 'devoid of constructive thought and was purely negative in its aims, methods and policy',[62] nevertheless, as Muhammad ʿAli Jinnah was to say, the game of politics has to be played with the pieces actually on the board. The pieces on the Muslim board were religious feelings; indeed, given the social, regional and linguistic divisions among Muslims (as equally among Hindus), religion was the force most likely to fuse the disparate Muslim elements together. By 1919 Muslim politics had ceased to be the preoccupation of gentlemen and office seekers – even the Muslim League in 1913 had committed itself to self-rule for India according to modes suited to the country – and outside the charmed circle of aspirants to prestige in British eyes the only common language for political communication was religious.

The poetry of the *Khilafat* movement in India was fated to be deflated by the prose of political and military events in Turkey

[62] Sir Shafaʿat Ahmad Khan, *The Indian Federation* (London, 1937), p. 330.

itself. In September 1919 Mustafa Kamal (1881–1938) formed the Association for the Defence of the Rights of Anatolia and Rumelia, which became the instrument of the Turkish people's struggle against the Western powers and the captive sultan. In April 1920 an extra-legal Grand National Assembly met at Ankara and defied the authority of the sultan. In August 1921 the Greeks were badly defeated near the river Sakarya and by September 1922 Mustafa Kamal's forces had completed the reconquest of Anatolia. On 1 November the new Turkish National Assembly separated the office of caliph from the government of the Turkish state, and in March 1924, after an unfortunate plea by the Agha Khan and Amir ʿAli to the Turkish Prime Minister, Ismet Pasha (Ismet Inönü 1884–), to reassure the Muslim world that Caliph could perform his functions properly, the Turkish National Assembly abolished the caliphate altogether. Although the Khilafat Committee in India lingered on, making its platform the liberation of the Hijaz from foreign influence, its programme had been destroyed by events. Disillusion similarly overtook the Khilafatists in their relations with Gandhi and the Hindu leaders of the non-co-operation movement. The psychological atmosphere after the collapse of this first, and, as it proved, last effort at a Hindu–Muslim alliance against the foreign ruler was *post coitum omne animal triste.*

8

THE PERIOD OF FRUSTRATION 1924-35

The calling off of the non-co-operation campaign and the abolition of the caliphate by the Turkish National Assembly left Muslims politically 'all dressed up and nowhere to go'. The *Khilafat* agitation had been conducted in the spirit of an apocalyptic and not of a political movement. So much energy and passion had been mobilised, and the upshot was that Muslims appeared not only rather foolish but also rather dangerous in the eyes of their Hindu fellow-countrymen; foolish for pursuing an ideal which other Muslims in the pure Muslim lands of Arabia and Asiatic Turkey did not share, and dangerous because it seemed they could only be actively enlisted for causes which had little to do with India and into which the majority of India's population could not enter. Apparently Muslims of India did not mind being ruled by the British as long as the British did not ill-treat the Turks; worse still, the refusal of many middle-class Muslims to resign from appointments in the public and education services, or to forgo titles and pensions, suggested that they did not mind British rule so long as the British did not ill-treat *them*. Muslims had hitched their wagon to the crescent of the caliphate and it had dragged them 'up the garden path'.

The outlook for the Muslim comfortable classes, even for those who had shown little enthusiasm for the *Khilafat* movement, was uncertain. The era of politics in the *darbar* and on the commissioner's or collector's veranda was nearly over. For all their hesitations, concern for their commercial interests, backward glances and preference for the backing of conservative classes, the British now appeared to be stumbling along a road that could only end in responsible government and eventual majority rule. In a despatch as long ago as 12 December 1911, the Viceroy, Lord Hardinge, had looked forward to provincial autonomy as the only way in which the Indian demand for more power could be reconciled with the responsibility of the Governor-General in Council.

With the outbreak of the war in 1914, despite the quite remarkable outburst of loyal sentiment, all, including the British themselves almost as quickly as the Indians, realised that the British empire in India would never be the same again. By the end of the second year of war it was seen, in Dr Spear's words, that Britain was neither all-powerful nor all-wise. On 20 August 1917, Lloyd George's government, in a statement by Edwin Montagu, the Secretary of State for India, committed Britain to 'the gradual development of self-governing institutions, with a view to the progressive realisation of responsible government in India as an integral part of the empire'. Whatever esoteric meaning the phrase 'responsible government' may have had for Curzon, its author, it was taken by educated Indians to foreshadow parliamentary government with an executive responsible to an elected legislature on the English model.

The Montagu–Chelmsford Report of 1918 looked forward first to responsible government in the provinces; 'over this congeries of states [i.e. provinces] would preside a central Government increasingly representative of and responsible to the people of all of them, dealing with matters both internal and external of common interest to the whole of India'. The Reforms Act of 1919 gave the provinces increased financial discretion. Revenue from irrigation, land, excise and stamps was allotted to them, leaving the revenue from income tax, post, salt and railways to the centre. In the provinces the new principle of dyarchy was introduced. Some subjects of administration were kept in the hands of councillors (usually members of the I.C.S. responsible only to the governor of the province) and others were transferred to ministers responsible to the provincial legislatures. Broadly speaking 'law and order' subjects and those essential to the maintenance of ultimate British supremacy were 'reserved' and 'nation-building' subjects such as local self-government, education, public health, public works, and agriculture (but not land revenue) were 'transferred'. The provincial legislative councils were enlarged and at least 70 per cent of their numbers were to be non-official.

At the centre, power was taken to enlarge the Viceroy's executive council, which now normally remained responsible only to the Secretary of State for India and to the British Parliament. The Imperial Legislative Council was replaced by an enlarged Legislative Assembly with an elected majority, sitting for three years. In addition a Council of State was created, with an unofficial majority and sitting for five years. The electoral franchise for the Provincial Legislative Councils was based on a property qualification, the payment of land revenue in the countryside and of income or house tax in the towns. There were a number of special qualifications, such as possession of a university degree or membership of a chamber of commerce. Constituencies were divided into 'special' and 'general'. The former were composed of voters from such interests as big landholders, industry, commerce and the universities, and the latter of voters qualified as stated earlier. These latter 'general' constituencies, however, included separate constituencies for Muslims. The Morley–Minto principle of separate electorates for Muslims was extended to the enlarged provincial and central legislatures. The advancing wave of majorities was to be broken up by the rocks of special interests.

Under dyarchy Muslims were to continue to have their individual political personality, but they were unlikely to be able effectively to protect it in the Muslim minority provinces or to express it in creative action in the Muslim majority provinces. In the United Provinces, where Muslims had twenty-nine out of the hundred elected members of the Provincial Legislative Council, it would need the support of all the eleven representatives of special interests and of the twenty-three nominated members to protect them against the other sixty general constituency representatives. In the Panjab, on the other hand, with its 55.2 per cent (1921 census) Muslim majority, there were under dyarchy thirty-four elective Muslim seats, twenty-one Hindu and thirteen Sikh. For a majority the Muslims in the Panjab Legislative Council were dependent upon the support of the official *bloc*, as they found in 1923 at the end of a debate censuring the conduct of the Muslim minister Fazl-i Husain (1877–1936).[1] In Bengal, although Muslims numbered 54.6 per cent of the population, they formed only 45.1 per cent of the electoral roll by reason of poverty and illiteracy, and in the Legislative Council they held only thirty-nine of the 114 seats.

Muslims then were a political minority both in those provinces where they were in a population minority and in those where they were in a population majority. This, however, had come about

[1] *Report of the Indian Statutory Commission*, vol. x (London, 1930), pp. 57–8.

through the actions of Muslim political leaders themselves, in concluding the Lucknow Pact of December 1916. The reforms of 1919 accepted the Lucknow Pact percentages and, if anything, worsened their implications for Muslims in the Muslim majority provinces, by adding a number of special seats to the legislatures usually (though not necessarily) occupied by Hindus.

THE GROWTH OF COMMUNAL ANTAGONISM UNDER DYARCHY

With the experience of Hindu–Muslim co-operation during the period of the non-co-operation and *Khilafat* movements, with the avowed determination of Congress to enlist Muslims in a national struggle against the British and Mahatma Gandhi's personal commitment to Hindu–Muslim brotherhood, it might have been expected that Muslim fears of the majority Hindu community would fade with the experience of working dyarchy. Indeed, Hindu and Muslim legislators on the provincial legislative councils often co-operated, as for example in the Bengal Legislative Council's refusal of leave to introduce the Criminal Law Amendment Bill (1925) giving powers of preventive detention; or in the debates on the Oudh Rent (Amendment) Bill of 1921; or over the Agra Tenancy Bill of 1926; or the Panjab Acquisition of Land (Industrial) Bill in 1922, when Hindu and Muslim rural members combined against urban interests in fear that the Land Alienation Act of 1901 might be whittled down.

Nevertheless, the manner in which the reforms of 1919 shaped political life tended to sharpen communal awareness and antagonism. Although the total electorate for the provincial councils under the property qualifications was over five million, individual constituencies were small enough to give politics a personal flavour; in Panjab urban constituencies the electorate varied between 6,170 and 12,810[2] and also in the Panjab a higher proportion of the urban as against the rural population was enfranchised – an eighth as against a thirty-fifth. A candidate could therefore rarely ignore the sentiments and interests of local persons of wealth and influence and most tenants were obliged to vote according to their landlords' wishes. In Sind 'the Pir or Sayed or the big local zamindar became the most useful canvasser and no candidate could succeed without

[2] *Report of the I.S.C.*, vol. x, p. 41.

the assistance of such persons'.[3] The responsibility of elected ministers for the transferred subjects of local government and education offered scope for political patronage, which was often preferentially dispensed to members of the minister's own religious community or caste. Furthermore, in his choice of ministers the British provincial governor aimed at communal representation and balance, and once appointed, ministers, like those in eighteenth-century England, needed to establish their indispensability by gathering a following; this they could do most easily by dispensing patronage to members of their own community or caste.

In the Muslim majority provinces Muslim ministers used the power and influence that dyarchy granted them to equalise the scales between the Muslims and other communities in official employment, local government and education. In the Panjab Fazl-i Husain used his influence to bring the number of Muslims in government service into line with their proportion in the population. His Village Panchayat Bill of 1921 aimed to give Muslims in the western rural regions of the Panjab that preponderance which their numbers claimed for them. The Hindu preponderance on municipal boards in the Panjab was reduced by applying the principle that the number of seats held by members of different communities was to be in proportion not to their numbers on the voters' roll but to their numbers in the total population. The advantages of Hindu commercial and banking wealth were thus diminished. When Fazl-i Husain was Education Minister he used the grant-in-aid system for schools to further primary education in the villages, a move which tended to benefit, though not exclusively, the predominantly Muslim rural areas. In Bengal, A. K. Fazl al-Haq, when Minister of Education, forced the councillors in charge of finance to allot funds to start the Islamia College in Calcutta and pressed for more government aid for *madrasas*. Hindu ministers in Hindu majority provinces similarly used the power and patronage at their disposal to benefit caste-fellows and their extended family groups.

Communal antagonism between classes of Hindus and Muslims in those provinces where the reforms of 1919 had been introduced growled incessantly throughout the nineteen-twenties. At the Legislative Council level, the passing in the Panjab of the Courts Amendment Act (1922) was made the occasion for an attack by

[3] *Report of the I.S.C.*, vol. VII, p. 424.

Muslim members of the Council upon the High Court in Lahore – Hindus were alleged to dominate the Bench. The Moneylenders Bill of 1926 produced an unparallelled outburst of communal rancour as Muslims tried to pass a measure to control the way in which moneylenders kept their own and their debtors' accounts. Lower down, the business of the local elective boards was often carried on in an inflamed communal atmosphere. In 1922, at Hoshiarpur, the District Commissioner tried (unsuccessfully) to nominate an American missionary as President of the Municipal Committee to resolve a deadlock between its Hindu and Muslim members.[4] An Indian Christian member of the Panjab Legislative Council described municipal administration in the Panjab as 'an organized, continued and sustained Hindu–Muhammadan quarrel', and said that he did not know of a single instance where it had been possible to dismiss a corrupt or inefficient Hindu or Muslim municipal servant, since the members of his community sheltered and supported him.[5]

At the street level, there were serious communal riots at Multan in September 1922, at Panipat in July 1923, at Rewari in February 1926 and at Lahore in May 1927. In Bengal there was a bitter quarrel in the Legislative Council in 1923 between Hindus and Muslims, over a move to insert a sub-clause in the Calcutta Municipal Bill which would have prohibited cow-killing in the city. Voting on this sub-clause was entirely along communal lines. In April 1926 there was a major communal riot in Calcutta, with sixty-six killed and several hundred injured, followed by another outbreak in July, with twenty-eight killed and 226 injured. In the Bombay Presidency communal tension existed not only between Hindus and Muslims, but also between Brahmans and non-Brahmans, Marathas and non-Marathas, untouchables and 'touchables'; a number of Hindu–Muslim disorders occurred between 1924 and 1927 over such abrasive matters as the playing of music before mosques and the possession of sacred places.

In the United Provinces, British encouragement of an inter-communal landlord's party tended to prevent open communal encounters in the provincial legislature (although Muslims walked out in 1926 over the District Board's Primary Education Bill, in protest

[4] *Official Report, Punjab Legislative Council*, 2 March 1922, pp. 192–5.
[5] *Official Report, Punjab Legislative Council*, 26 October 1923, p. 368.

at the attitude of the Hindu members of the Swarajist party). At the local government level communal feeling was rampant. In 1916 the leading Hindu politicians of the province, including Motilal Nehru (1861–1931, the father of Jawaharlal Nehru, the first prime minister of independent India), had agreed to separate representation for Muslims with weightage (that is a number of seats in excess of population proportion) on the municipal boards of the United Provinces – a principle extended to district boards in 1922. In 1916 it had been hoped that this concession would bring about Hindu–Muslim co-operation in all-India politics. The upshot was an entrenched Muslim position in local government in the United Provinces, much stronger than any system of joint electorates without weightage would have been likely to produce. In 1925–6, 33.7 per cent of the membership of the forty-eight district boards of the United Provinces was Muslim.[6]

The post-dated cheque upon a bank that, after 1922, had failed, namely that of Hindu–Muslim co-operation at the all-India level against the British, counted for nothing in the currency of local politics in the town wards and rural districts of the United Provinces. In the words of the Simon Commission, 'Generally speaking there has been a sad lack of a wider outlook on questions like the existence of slaughter-houses, use of the Urdu script in the boards' offices and the appointment of Muhammadans in the service of the boards'.[7] Then, at the street level, serious communal riots occurred at Agra, Saharanpur and Shahjahanpur in 1923, at Allahabad and Lucknow in 1924, at Aligarh in 1925, at Lucknow and Allahabad in 1926 and at Bareilly and Cawnpore in 1927. Between 1923 and 1927 there were eighty-eight communal riots in the United Provinces, in which eighty-one people were killed and 2,301 injured.[8]

The hatreds of the street might have been kept in check if the resentments and bitternesses of school, office and shop had not been sharpened by the disappointment of rising expectations. The reforms of 1919 were operated in a period of economic stagnation, inelastic if not declining revenue and intense middle-class competition. By the middle of the nineteen-twenties the number of Muslims with

[6] Paul R. Brass, 'Muslim Separatism in the U.P.', *Economic and Political Weekly Annual Number*, January 1970, p. 184.

[7] *Report of the Indian Statutory Commission*, vol. IX (London, 1930), p. 507.

[8] *Report of the I.S.C.*, vol. IX, p. 66.

modern educational qualifications was rising rapidly. According to the 1921 census in the United Provinces, the percentage of Muslims literate in English surpassed that of Hindu similarly literate. Taking British India as a whole, the number of Muslims in educational institutions recognised by the government increased from one and a half million in 1917 to two and a half million in 1927.

The improvement in the Panjab was particularly striking. The number of Muslim boys at school rose from 242,000 in 1921–2 to 543,000 in 1926–7 and exceeded the number of Hindu and Sikh boys put together.[9] Between March 1921 and March 1923 the number of Muslim students at Government College, Lahore, the premier men's college, increased from 133 to 171. In Bengal, although the total number of Muslim pupils rose from 880,374 to 1,139,949, an increase of 29.4 per cent, wastage at the secondary stage was such that the proportion of Muslim pupils to the whole actually declined between 1921–2 and 1926–7. Nevertheless, the absolute total of Muslims in universities and colleges rose from 2,175 in 1921–2 to 3,419 in 1926–7, and in professional colleges from 440 to 886, an increase for which the existence of Dacca University, with its Muslim Hall, and the Calcutta Islamia College was mainly responsible.

In the Bombay Presidency, Muslims again were as forward in primary as they were lagging in secondary and higher education, but the proportion of Muslims undergoing education to the total Muslim population of the Presidency was, at 9.6 per cent, the highest in British India, despite the backwardness in education of the Muslim majority in Sind, then part of the Bombay Presidency.[10] The Bombay government's scheme for special scholarships for 'backward classes including Muhammadans' meant that there was one scholarship for every 2,100 Muslims of the Presidency proper and one for every 3,600 in Sind, as compared to one for every 7,000 and 5,700 of the population in those areas respectively for intermediate and backward Hindus.[11] It should be emphasised that this improvement in the absolute number of educated Muslims tended to come from those classes enfranchised by the 1919 reforms and directly interested in their material advantages.

[9] *Report of the I.S.C.*, vol. x, *Memoranda submitted by the Government of the Panjab*, p. 124.   [10] *Report of the I.S.C.*, vol. vii, p. 40.
[11] *Report of the I.S.C.*, vol. vii, p. 43.

The early years of the reforms were marked by a decline in the level, both agricultural and industrial, of production in India and an overall decline in current expenditure on goods and services in the public sector. Kshitimohon Mukerji's estimate of the agricultural production of India in terms of constant 1924–9 (average) prices is 13,959 million rupees in 1921–2, declining to 13,086 million in 1927–8.[12] The author's index for industrial activity 'corrected for deflated cheques clearance', which stands at seventy-seven for 1920–1, dropped to sixty-five in 1922–3 before rising to eighty-five in 1927–8. It dropped again to eighty in 1931–2.[13] The current expenditure on goods and services in the public sector in real terms (most likely to affect contractors and the employment of officials), which stood at 345.61 *crore* of rupees in 1920–1, rising to 371.40 *crore* in 1922–3, sank to 324.33 *crore* in 1924–5; it did not recover to the level of 1922–3 until 1929–30 before sinking as a consequence of the depression to 292.24 *crore* in 1933–4.[14] Attempting to see the question in provincial terms, the yield in the Panjab of income tax declined from Rs. 75 *lakh* in 1922–3 to Rs. 71 *lakh* in the following year. The revenue from income tax of course went to the central government, but this drop in yield is an indication of the falling off of income of the wealthier classes.

The middle classes were disappointed with the financial consequences of provincial dyarchy. The Montagu–Chelmsford Report had recognised that 'if the popular principle in government is to have fair play in the provinces', some means of separating the financial resources of the central and provincial governments and thus of reducing the control and interference of the centre, should be found. The Report suggested assigning the whole of the proceeds of main sources of taxation (for example, customs, land revenue, income tax) either to the centre or to the provinces. It was expected at the time of the Report that the result of such a distribution of the sources of revenue would produce a deficit in the central budget and that consequently the provincial governments would have to make contributions from their own tax resources to the central budget.

Objections to the Report's proposals for the allocation between

---

[12] Kshitimohon Mukerji, *Levels of Economic Activity and Public Expenditure in India* (London, 1965), table 1, p. 83.

[13] Mukerji, *Levels of Economic Activity*, table 4, p. 88.

[14] Mukerji, *Levels of Economic Activity*, table 8, p. 93.

particular provinces of such contributions led to a Financial
Relations Committee being appointed to devise a system of contributions acceptable to all the interests concerned. Its report of March
1920 became the basis of the 'Meston Settlement' (so named after
Lord Meston the chairman of the Financial Relations Committee),
the principles of which were embodied in the 'Devolution Rules'
subsequently promulgated under the powers granted by the Government of India Act of 1919. Under the 'Meston settlement', revenue
from income tax, customs, the excise on salt and the income from
railways, posts and telegraphs was assigned to the centre; income
from land revenue, excise on alcoholic liquors and narcotics, and
from stamp duties was assigned to the provinces. The authors of the
'Meston Settlement' anticipated that the provincial governments
would have ample resources for 'nation-building' activities, which
the freedom and ability of Indian provincial ministers to undertake
was generally accepted as a future touchstone of the success of the
Montagu–Chelmsford reforms. But the authors of the settlement
proved to be over-sanguine in their anticipations. Official salaries
had to be increased to meet the increased cost of living, and with the
substantial landholding electorate it proved politically impossible to
increase the yield of the land revenue, the provinces' principal
source of income. Expenditure on the transferred departments was
actually therefore decreased between 1921–2 and 1923 from 352
lakh to 314 *lakh* in the U.P., from 307 to 282 *lakh* in the Panjab,
from 352 to 321 *lakh* in Bengal and from 561 to 478 *lakh* in
Bombay. The Panjab, indeed, was obliged to increase taxation
between 1922 and 1928 by sixty-four *lakh*, mainly by an increase in
stamp duties, occupiers' rates in canal colonies and court fees, all
measures which tended to affect the rural population with, broadly
speaking, its majority of Muslim voters, as against the urban areas
with their comparatively large Hindu vote.

The Bengal government complained bitterly that, although a commercial and industrial province, Bengal was denied revenue from
industrial and commercial profits, as income tax and railway income
went to the centre. During the nineteen-twenties, Bengal was barely
able to devote the equivalent of one million pounds per annum to
education of all kinds for a population of forty-one million. Although
the Bombay Presidency was one of the wealthier provinces, it was
able to increase its expenditure on 'nation-building' activities by only

thirty-four *lakh* between 1920–1 and 1927–8, the smallest increase among the provinces under dyarchy.[15]

These cuts in the real order of public expenditure meant fewer building, road or drainage contracts for local contractors, fewer teaching posts relative to the increasing number of those sufficiently qualified to hold them, fewer posts relatively in the administration and fewer opportunities for patronage. The demand for education became an effective demand for many small landholders who had benefited by the higher prices for agricultural commodities during the war years. In so far as those landholders were Muslim they often found their sons repulsed from spheres of employment hitherto largely monopolised by Hindus. India was a prey in the nineteen-twenties to the tensions generated by the respectable classes finding that a stagnant or lagging economy was thwarting their rising expectations.

Rivalry among the educated for scarce loaves and fishes – or merely loaves – was not allowed to become merely personal or even nepotic; there were continual reminders from all over India that Hindus were Hindus and that Muslims were Muslims. The forcible conversion of Hindus by the Muslim Mappillas was followed by the conversion of Muslim by Hindus through the *shuddhi* (purification) and *sangathan* (consolidation) movements. The latter were founded to reclaim half-converted (and indeed any other) Muslims to the Hindu fold and to harden the Hindu for militant action by drill and physical culture. (C. V. Vaidya's *Downfall of Hindu India*, published in 1926, an 'academic' study of how the Ghaznavids and Ghurids conquered northern India, is an interesting contemporary revelation of the Hindu sense of physical inferiority before the meat-eating Muslim conqueror from Central Asia). Muslims riposted by founding the *tabligh* (education) and *tanzim* (organisation) movements in 1924 with converse intentions. These movements were led by the *°ulama*, but even such a 'modern' Khilafatist as Dr Saif al-din Kichlu (Kitchlew 1884–1963) gave them his support.

The *Hindu Mahasabha* (the Great Assembly of Hindus), founded in 1919, aimed to defend Hindu interests politically as well as religiously. Swami Shraddhanand (1856–1926), the founder of the *shuddhi* movement, concentrated on reconverting the Malkana Rajputs to Hinduism, and thirty thousand are said to have been

15 *Report of the I.S.C.*, vol. VII, p. 600.

reclaimed. The *Arya Samaj* was equally active in the Panjab. In 1924 one Rajpal published a scurrilous attack upon Muhammad the Prophet from Lahore. The Lahore High Court first acquitted and then convicted him for conduct 'wounding to his Majesty's subjects', before he was murderously assaulted by a Muslim in September 1927. Swami Shraddhanand was murdered in December 1926 at Delhi by a Muslim.

Communalism appeared to have affected even the top echelons of the Indian National Congress itself. Motilal Nehru wrote to his son Jawaharlal in November 1926, when the former was campaigning in the United Provinces for the Central Assembly elections, 'communal hatred and bribing of the voter was the order of the day...Publicly I was denounced as an anti-Hindu and pro-Mohammedan but privately almost every individual voter was told that I was a beef-eater in league with the Mohammedan to legalize cow-slaughter in public places at all times.'[16] Gandhi continued to preach communal affection and harmony at all times and in September 1924 fasted in penance for communal hatred, which had recently been inflamed by a Hindu–Muslim outbreak at Kohat in the North-West Frontier Province, when 155 persons were killed or wounded and the whole Hindu population fled from this predomin-antly Muslim town. Gandhi never quite established that bond with the modern-educated Muslim, concerned with employment and position, of which he was capable in his relationships with the more traditional and religious Muslim.

The combination of rising Muslim fears and expectations under the reforms of 1919, the deflation of emotion by the abolition of the Caliphate and the growing communal antagonism, at least in the towns, began to show its effects on Muslim political thinking. Not that, in the period immediately following the collapse of the *Khilafat* movement, there were any *all-India* Muslim leaders or political organisations worth the name. Congress in 1916 had taken the significant step of recognising the All-India Muslim League as a representative all-India Muslim organisation, with which it was possible to conclude the Lucknow pact. The 'young Muhammadan party', among which Muhammad ʿAli Jinnah, a Karachi lawyer, was prominent, appeared so far in command of the League that conservative Muslim landlords formed an All-India Muslim

[16] Jawaharlal Nehru, *A Bunch of Old Letters* (Bombay, 1958), p. 49.

Association in opposition to the joint Congress–League proposals for constitutional advance. Men like Jinnah, Mazhar al-Haq and Hakim Ajmal Khan were members both of the League and of Congress and, although Jinnah withdrew from Congress in 1920 in protest against the non-co-operation campaign, the others merely doffed their League for their Congress clothing for a time.

In December 1918, carried along by the tide of emotion and events, the League passed a resolution in favour of responsible government for the provinces at once; in 1920 it came into line with Congress in declaring its objective to be 'the attainment of Swaraj by all legitimate and peaceful means'. In 1923 the League was still ready to demand 'full responsible government' for India, though few had paid any attention to it since 1920. Conservative Muslims had lain low during the heady enthusiasms of non-co-operation, and the younger Muslim leadership had been too busy building bridges to the *ʿulama* and to Congress to attend to a League which added nothing to their political standing.

THE SEARCH FOR SECURITY IN STRONG MUSLIM PROVINCES WITHIN A WEAK INDIAN FEDERATION

By 1924, however, the collapse of the non-co-operation and *Khilafat* movements had weakened Muslim confidence in all-India political deals with Congress. It was far better to build up a Muslim political position in the Muslim majority provinces. In 1924 Jinnah proposed a revision of the Lucknow pact, which would give Muslims more seats in the Panjab and Bengal Legislative Councils. The 1924 session of the All-India Muslim League (with Jinnah present) resolved that under any future constitutional reforms India must be reorganised as a federation, with full provincial autonomy, with full expression being given constitutionally to the Muslim majority position in the Panjab, Bengal and the North-West Frontier Province, with separate electorates retained and the powers of any central government kept to a minimum.

It is significant that in 1925 Maulana Muhammed ʿAli complained of the reluctance of Hindus to allow the Muslims their majority in the Panjab and Bengal. Some of his statements in 1924 and 1925 show that even he was becoming sensitive to the communal atmosphere of politics. In 1924 he expressed to Jawaharlal Nehru his apprehensions that Pandit Malaviya (1861–1946) and others were trying to turn Congress into a Hindu organisation[17] and in March 1925 he publicly held a fallen Muslim to be better than Mr Gandhi. These emotional outbursts were substitutes for clear objectives and clear vision; uneasily aware that the British were ready to surrender real power, though in penny packets, Muslims had no political philosophy with which to face the future. The current Western shibboleths of self-determination and democracy, of which the Treaty of Versailles, with all its faults, expressed the temporary triumph, appeared to them to lead straight to majority rule, which they were convinced that, as a permanent minority, they had no hope of ever reversing.

In the twentieth century they could not assert the innate superiority of the Muslim over the non-Muslim as a ground for political privilege. Though the *ʿulama* might preach the virtues of life under the *shariʿa* as administered by themselves, the modern-educated Muslim could not see how jurisprudential federalism could be introduced into modern India. Certainly the 'Muslims of the Council Chamber', such as Fazl-i Husain or Fazl al-Haq, were demonstrating how dyarchy could be turned to the advantage of Muslims in the Muslim majority provinces. In the Muslim minority provinces, however, the Muslim landlords were well represented in the Councils, and gave colour to the later denunciations of them by the Congress left wing as a selfish and self-important reactionary coterie, owing their position to the British, who needed 'stooges' to act as a brake upon Congress dynamism and who would vanish from the Indian scene 'like snow on the desert's dusty back' once freedom of political expression was granted to their oppressed tenants. The revelation of their divisions and factious impotence merely encouraged the Congress leadership to brush them aside as men who had no political goods to deliver and who therefore could be discounted as a force in India.

This Muslim impotence and confusion does much to explain the abortiveness of all efforts to solve the communal political problem in the five years of intense political discussion of the future of India that opened in 1927, as a result of the appointment of the all-British Simon Commission to review the workings of the 1919 reforms and

[17] Nehru, *A Bunch of Old Letters*, p. 37.

of the Secretary of State for India Lord Birkenhead's (1872–1930) challenge that the Commission's membership had to be all-British because Indians could not agree on a constitution among themselves.

Already in March 1927 thirty Muslim members of the central and provincial legislatures decided at Delhi that they were ready to concede joint electorates if the number of Muslim seats in the Bengal and Panjab legislatures was made proportionate to the provincial Muslim population; if Sind, where there was a large Muslim majority, was made a separate province; if the North-West Frontier Province was given a legislative council and if Muslims were allowed one-third of the seats in the Central Legislature. Although this proposal was accepted by the Congress Working Committee in May 1927 and was ratified by the plenary session of December 1927, presided over by a Muslim, M. A. Ansari, this agreement, strongly challenged by the *Hindu Mahasabha* and other communal groups, such as the Sikhs, was washed away in the flood of Indian feeling against the Simon Commission.

The Muslim League split on whether the Statutory (Simon) Commission should be boycotted, one section, meeting at Lahore and led by Sir Muhammad Shafiʿ, deciding not to boycott, and another, meeting at Calcutta and led by Jinnah, deciding to join Congress in boycotting the Commission. Congress called an All-Parties Conference to show the British that they were wrong in their belief that Indians could never agree among themselves on a constitution for an independent India. A drafting committee produced a draft constitution but the members of the Jinnah group of the Muslim League did not attend. The report of the drafting committee (called the Nehru Report, after its chairman and secretary, Motilal and Jawaharlal Nehru) recommended joint mixed electorates, with reservation of seats for Muslims in the Muslim minority provinces, but no such reservation in the Muslim majority provinces, on the ground that it was unnecessary. It was agreed that Sind should become a separate province.

The reaction of Muslims to the Nehru Report was mixed. Muslim members of Congress, such as Abu'l Kalam Azad, M. A. Ansari, the Raja of Mahmudabad and Dr Saif al-din Kichlu, were ready to accept the report; the old Khilafatists, such as Maulana Mahammad ʿAli, were divided but mostly hostile; the Shafiʿ section of the Muslim League rejected the Report outright and Jinnah was ready to give a conditional acceptance. An All-Parties Muslim Conference, excluding the Jinnah section of the League, met to reiterate the proposals of March 1927, that is to reaffirm that it did not altogether reject joint electorates. In December 1928 Jinnah's section of the Muslim League sent a delegation to an All-Parties Convention to discuss the Nehru Report, as did a minority of the Khilafatists. Jinnah argued strongly for reservation of seats in Bengal and the Panjab on a population basis, one-third Muslim representation in the Central Legislature and the vesting of residual powers in any Indian federation in the provinces. The All-Parties Convention, overwhelmingly Hindu in composition, rejected all these proposals, whereupon Jinnah withdrew.

In March 1929 Jinnah formulated his famous 'Fourteen Points' (actually fifteen) on behalf of the All-Parties Muslim Conference, which now contained delegates from a reunited Muslim League. The 'Fourteen Points' proposed *inter alia* that India's future constitution should be federal, with residual powers vested in the provinces; that majorities in particular provinces should not, in the provincial legislatures, be reduced to minorities or even to an equality with other groups in the population; that separate electorates be maintained in the absence of agreement by the community concerned to give them up; that Muslims should have one-third of the seats in the Central Legislature, and that various other safeguards for Muslim culture, law and religion be adopted. But Jinnah failed to carry all Muslim opinion with him, the Shafi[e] section of the Muslim League sticking to the Muslim Conference demands, and some wishing to accept the Nehru Report. The latter constituted themselves, in July 1929 at Allahabad, into an All-India Nationalist Muslims' Conference; they included Maulana Abu'l Kalam Azad, M. A. Ansari, some Muslim Leaguers such as Dr Muhammad 'Alam and such Khilafatists as T. A. K. Sherwani.

Much has been made[18] of the failure of Congress and the Muslim parties to agree over the Nehru Report and of the rejection of Jinnah's 'Fourteen Points' as a significant milestone along the way to the partition of India. A great opportunity was lost, it is thought, for the abandonment of separate electorates by voluntary Muslim agreement. The price of that abandonment should, however, be

[18] By, for example, S. Gopal, *The Viceroyalty of Lord Irwin* (Oxford, 1957), p. 37.

measured. It was constitutional acknowledgement by the Hindu parties of the Muslim majority position in not only the Panjab and Bengal, but also in Sind and the North-West Frontier Province. If Muslims were afraid for their interests in the Hindu majority provinces, Hindus were equally afraid for their interests in Muslim majority provinces, given that any central government would have only very limited powers over the people and governments of the provinces. Acceptance of the various Muslim conditions for the abandonment of separate electorates would not have eliminated a Muslim political identity from India, it would merely have given it an earlier resting place in the Muslim majority provinces.

In the event, the failure of the Hindu and Muslim politicians to agree left the British government free for what Dr Spear has described as 'the last major constructive achievement of the British in India' – the Government of India Act of 1935 – but which might equally well be described as their last and, in the event, most portentous essay in balancing and ruling in India. In May 1930 the Simon Commission had reported and recommended the grant of provincial autonomy, but had emphasised the scepticism of its members about the development of full, responsible parliamentary government at the centre. The British government in London summoned a large number of hand-picked prominent Indians to a Round Table Conference to discuss the Simon Report.

Congress was not represented at the opening sessions in November 1930, as it was conducting a non-co-operation campaign in India, in protest against the British government's refusal to accept the goal of immediate dominion status as the presupposition of all discussions at the Round Table Conference. (Lord Irwin (1881–1959), the Viceroy had persuaded the new Labour government to allow him to declare, on 31 October 1929, that Dominion status was the goal of British policy in India.) After the Gandhi–Irwin direct talks (the occasion of Churchill's description of Gandhi as 'a half-naked *fakir*') in February and March 1931, ending in the Gandhi–Irwin 'pact', Gandhi attended the second session of the Round Table Conference in 1931 as the sole representative of Congress. At the Conference Muslim delegates made demands similar to those of Jinnah's 'Fourteen Points' and refused to commit themselves to the principle of resonsible government at the centre, unless their demands for guaranteed majority representation in the Muslim majority provinces were accepted. Agreement between the Muslim delegates and Gandhi proved impossible.

The British went ahead with their own plans for an Indian Federation, which would balance Congress against the Muslims and the princes against elected Indians in the legislature of British India; a federation in which there would be a centre strong enough to protect British economic interests in India until such time as the accession of Indian princes to the federation would permit the introduction of fully responsible government at the centre, a consummation which the Conservative government in Britain hoped and believed would not be swift. The provinces would be virtually autonomous, with provision for Governor's rule or overriding Governor's powers in constitutional emergencies.

These plans for a federation in India did not allay Muslim fears of Hindu domination, but did provide some means for abating them. Although a strong centre was foreshadowed, in the short and medium terms the British would remain to safeguard minority interests (or so it seemed to all parties in the early nineteen-thirties); the army would, at the then rate of Indianisation, remain under British control; Muslims would be in a majority in four provinces, excluding Baluchistan, even if the 'Communal Award' by Ramsay MacDonald (1866–1937) in August 1932 still failed to give Muslims an overall majority of seats in the legislatures of the Panjab and Bengal. (Muslims were to have 47.6 per cent as against a population proportion of 56.5 per cent in the Panjab.) However, given the representation of special interests in both provinces, even if Muslims were denied the power to do good, at least non-Muslims were denied the power to do harm. This negative power did not, of course, satisfy many Muslims. They lamented that like the gadfly they could make the horse twitch and kick, or perhaps even gallop, but not in any direction they could control. Not that in the circumstances of the early nineteen-thirties Muslims had much idea where they did want to go; most of them only knew that they wanted to go in company with fellow Muslims, though some Muslim supporters of Congress did not always want even that.

THE MUSLIM SEARCH FOR A POLITICAL IDEOLOGY

The bewilderment of Muslims within the circle of council, assembly and conference was matched by the confusion of political outlook and goals among educated Muslims outside that circle. It is desirable to depict that confusion on the eve of the first provincial elections under the Government of India Act of 1935, partly in order to help in the explanation of the poor showing of Muslim political parties in those elections, but also to help in the understanding of the popular appeal, after 1937, of Jinnah's and the Muslim League's one agreed goal of power for the Muslims. Earlier, politically-conscious Muslims had been unable to formulate a political, social and economic goal which all Muslims could accept or which they could visualise being achieved, so long as the acquiescence or the support of the non-Muslim majority was felt to be necessary.

In December 1929 a number of Muslim supporters of Congress, mainly from the Panjab, met at Lahore under the leadership of Chaudhuri Afzal Haq (d. 1942) to devise a more radical social programme than the Indian National Congress was then prepared to adopt – for example, that land with an income below Rs. 500 per annum should be exempted from land revenue, that there should be primary education for all and, a specifically Muslim plank, that the taking of interest should be banned.[19] Although this *Ahrar* movement co-operated politically with Congress and joined the non-co-operation movement of 1930, it stood for an India of federated religiously-inspired radicalisms rather than for a national and secular state; it was bitterly hostile for doctrinal reasons to the *Ahmadiyya* and called for obedience to the *shariᶜa*.

A radicalism of feeling, which, however, failed to express itself in a coherent political programme, was a characteristic of the *Khaksar* (humble) movement, organised by ᶜInayat-Allah Khan Mashriqi (1888–1963). Mashriqi was a middle-class Panjabi who, after a brilliant career at Cambridge before the First World War, became a member of the Indian Educational Service. He attended the 1926 Khilafat Conference in Cairo, went to Europe and met Hitler, whose storm-trooper movement, with its symbolism of the spade, he claimed to have inspired.[20] In 1931 he organised the *Khaksar* movement among skilled Muslim artisans and small in-

[19] Tufail Ahmad Mangalori, *Mussalmanon ka Raushan Mustaqbil* (Delhi, 1945), p. 548.
[20] J. M. S. Baljon, *Modern Muslim Koran Interpretation (1880–1960)* (Leiden, 1961), pp. 11–12.

dependent cultivators. Its members underwent military drill in uniform and armed with spades in order to become soldiers for Islam. The rank and file were not supposed to know specifically what they stood for and it is doubtful whether their leaders themselves knew. Mashriqi himself was hostile to Congress more on account of its philosophy, under Gandhi, of non-violence than because it was composed mainly of Hindus. The *Khaksar* movement succeeded in generating a fervour for direct action among lower-middle-class Muslims hitherto politically inert, upon which the All-India Muslim League was able to capitalise when it too aimed to become a mass movement under Jinnah's new leadership after 1937.

A third popular movement among Muslims with repercussions far outside the Muslim community was the *Khuda'i Khidmatgar* (Servant of God) Redshirt movement, led by Khan ꜥAbd al-Ghaffar Khan (1890–). It was the only organised body of Muslims in the twentieth century to fight for Indian freedom. Essentially a Pathan movement confined to the North-West Frontier Province, it was first organised in 1929 as a nationalist anti-British force, pledged to non-violence. In April 1930 British efforts to suppress the movement led to riots, considerable loss of life and a temporary British military withdrawal from Peshawar. In August 1931 the Redshirts were formally affiliated with Congress. The Redshirt movement dressed up Pathan unruliness and manly independence to look like a modern political programme – issuing a call to withhold land revenue and to redistribute landed property in the name of social justice. Its existence was used by Congress to justify its boast that it was a genuinely national and secular organisation. This was a myth. The Redshirt movement was nationalist only in that it stood for independence from Britain. In the North-West Frontier Province Muslims were 92 per cent of the population and Hindus were in effect the *zimmis* or protected people, with a subordinate place in Pathan society, of which they, the Hindus, knew the permissible limits very well. The North-West Frontier Province could no more be cited as an archetype for a secular national India than could Madras with its Muslim minority.

By the time of the passage of the Government of India Act in 1935, most Muslims still saw no political means of resolving the dilemma that Maulana Muhammad ꜥAli, with his customary verbal fire and force (though he was then a dying man), had stated so dramatically at the fourth plenary session of the Round Table Conference in 1930.

Where God commands. . .I am a Muslim first, a Muslim second and a Muslim last and nothing but a Muslim. . .My first duty is to my Maker, not to HM the King nor to my companion Dr Moonje [a Hindu delegate from the *Mahasabha*] and that is the case with Dr Moonje also. . .But where India is concerned, where India's freedom is concerned, where the welfare of India is concerned, I am an Indian first, an Indian second, an Indian last and nothing but an Indian. . .I belong to two circles of equal size but which are not concentric. One is India and the other is the Muslim world. . .we belong to these circles . . .and we can leave neither.[21]

Maulana Muhammad ʿAli could have added that Muslims could also reconcile neither. Muslim dilemmas were expressed in another way by an anonymous Muslim writing to the Turkish lady journalist, Halidé Edib (1883–1963), who toured India in 1935. The writer asked how patriotic Muslims, who wished to see the backs of the British, could play a constructive *rôle* in nation building. If they worked for the welfare of their own community, they were dubbed communalist; if they tried to join Gandhi's spinning project they were out of place as meat-eaters, and if they worked for the abolition of untouchability, they incurred the displeasure of Gandhi himself.[22] Halidé Edib noticed the attraction of socialism for the younger Muslim intelligentsia (the Muslim factory labour force was growing rapidly in this period and it was easy for Muslims to be against capitalists as the latter were mainly Hindu). She wrote that Muslims were obtaining popular support when they stood for the economic uplift of the masses. In 1936 in Bengal, A. K. Fazl al-Haq organised the *Krishak Proja Samiti* (Peasant–Tenant Party) with a programme of abolition of landlordism. The party won thirty-five seats in the first Bengal elections under the 1935 Act. The appeal of Jawaharlal Nehru's socialism was particularly strong. Nevertheless, the Muslim masses, a Muslim socialist explained to Halidé Edib, wanted both religion and economic betterment and

[21] Afzal Iqbal (ed.), *Selected Writings and Speeches of Mohomed Ali* (Lahore, 1944), p. 465.
[22] Halidé Edib, *Inside India* (London, 1937), p. 341.

in the mind of the Muslim intelligentsia acquainted with Marxist anti-religious doctrines the two clashed.[23]

Although some younger Muslims saw socialism as the great hope for a growing feeling of nationhood in India, Halidé Edib reported that the idea of there being two nations in India was gaining ground among communalists both Hindu and Muslim. Writing of the 'extreme communalist' Halidé Edib said,

As to his attitude towards the Hindus he deludes himself that by the mere fact of calling himself a Muslem...and by the capacity he has both for dying and for killing more readily than the Hindu, he will easily dominate the Hindu in the future. Though he seriously believes that Muslem India is a separate nation, he has never thought out whether it is possible or not to have two nations living in the same country in a modern state. Hence the moment it comes to a communal settlement on communal lines there seems to be two alternatives: either admit that a third power must be there to keep the peace, or consider that India is face to face with an everlasting impasse. But no one in India can declare openly that he stands for foreign domination, though he may think it necessary and inevitable under the circumstances.[24]

Two Muslim voices before 1935 had, however, called out for a bulldozer to break down the impasse. In December 1930 Sir Muhammad Iqbal, in his Presidential Address at the Muslim League session at Allahabad, had stated that he would like to see 'the Punjab, North-West Frontier Province, Sind and Baluchistan amalgamated into a single state'.[25] In January 1933 a Cambridge law student, the Panjabi Chaudhuri Rahmat ʿAli (1897–1951), in a pamphlet *Now or Never*, put forward a scheme for a fully independent territorial Muslim state consisting of the Panjab, the Frontier province, the princely state of Kashmir (where there was an over two-thirds majority) and Baluchistan.[26] This area, he argued, was already the home of a nation, the Muslims of Pakistan. In conversation with Halidé Edib some years later he claimed an ancient history for that nation: 'the Moslems have lived there as a nation for over twelve hundred years, and possess a history, a civilization

[23] Edib, *Inside India*, pp. 343–4.   [24] Edib, *Inside India*, p. 348.
[25] Relevant extracts from text of speech in: Wm. Theodore de Bary (ed.), *Sources of Indian Tradition* (New York, 1958), pp. 763–7.
[26] Text of *Now or Never* reprinted in: Syed Sharifuddin Pirzada, *Evolution of Pakistan* (Lahore, 1963), pp. 263–9.

and a culture of their own. The area is separated from India propei [Hindustan] by the Jumna and *it is no part of India.*'[27]

Rahmat 'Ali did not choose to regard his proposal as one for the vivisection of India, but merely as a severance of an artificial connection made by the British. In Hindustan, i.e. in the Hindu majority region east of the Jumna, Muslims had been present only as conquerors when Hindustan had been the colonial territory of the Pakistan nation living west of the Jumna in the area of their national home. 'But when they lost this Colonial Empire, as distinct from Pakistan, the Muslems who settled in these Muslem Imperial dominions of Hindustan became a minority community in Hindustan.'[28] As Pakistanis do not claim that Hindustan is now theirs merely because they once ruled it, so Hindus should not claim that the area of Pakistan is theirs merely because they once ruled it. Moreover, 'if Hindustan is theirs because they form three-quarters of its inhabitants Pakistan is ours because we constitute four-fifths of its population. We have acquired our title to Pakistan by the same canons of international law which have given them theirs to Hindustan.'[29] In sum, Chaudhuri Rahmat 'Ali claimed that the Muslims of the Muslim majority areas of the west and north-west already constitute a nation by reason of their distinct culture and historical occupation of territory and then, employing the logic of nineteenth-century Western doctrines of self-determination, concluded that these Muslims must therefore have their own independent state. Not until 1937 did Rahmat 'Ali demand a separate state for the Muslim majority region of Bengal.

In 1933 Muslim politicians giving evidence before the Parliamentary Joint Select Committee on Indian Constitutional Reform dismissed the Pakistan idea as 'only a student's scheme' or as 'chimerical or impractical'. They were not prepared to treat the Muslims of the United Provinces, Bihar, the Central Provinces, Madras, Bombay, and at that stage of Bengal and Assam also, as Kenyan or Rhodesian whites left high and dry by the ebb tide of empire. They still hoped that an honourable settlement of India's problems could be reached, that would give the Muslims of the sub-continent as a whole security and equal rights and opportunities. They did not see moreover any rapid approach of indepen-

---

[27] Edib, *Inside India*, pp. 352–3.
[28] Edib, *Inside India*, p. 353.   [29] Edib, *Inside India*, p. 359.

dence. Chaudhuri Rahmat ʿAli had not claimed Pakistan so that Muslims might obey God better; to abandon the Muslims of the minority provinces in the worldly interests of the Muslims of the majority provinces appeared an act of betrayal for no better cause than the accident of birth towards members of a faith of whom the poet Iqbal said 'Our Essence is not bound to any Place'.[30] To accept this accident as determining a man's temporal status was to deny the teachings of religion.

It is tempting to see the Muslim politicians' demand for a weak federation and for some constitutional expression of the Muslim majority status in the north-west and Bengal, for example in Jinnah's 'Fourteen Points', as steps leading straight to Pakistan. Indeed, J. Coatman (1889–1963), a former information officer of the Government of India, wrote in 1932,[31]

It may be that the die is already cast and that no united India as we understand it today will ever emerge. It may be that Moslem India in the north and north-west is destined to become a separate Moslem state or part of a Moslem empire. There is no reason yet to believe that this is so, but unless the processes that we have been watching at work are checked and reversed, there is good reason for believing that this might be the ultimate outcome.

But when Muslim politicians came to fight the first elections to be held under the 1935 Act, they fought them with the same assumptions as did the other parties to those elections, namely that India would remain constitutionally united, albeit under a federation, and that Muslims would continue to live as fellow-citizens of non-Muslims all over the sub-continent. Indeed, in many spheres of policy Muslim politicians went into the elections determined to prove how much Muslims shared with their fellow-countrymen. In 1935 an individual and distinct Muslim political identity, yes; a separate independent state, no. But how, in the logic of the territorial national state and majority rule, were Muslims to conceive and claim their distinct political personality, and what if others wished to deny it to them and, in the day of mass movements and weakening British control, appeared to have the power to deny it to them?

[30] *The Mysteries of Selflessness (Asrar-i Bekhudi)*, trans. A. J. Arberry (London, 1953), p. 29.

[31] J. Coatman, *Years of Destiny: India 1926–1932* (London, 1932), p. 376.

9

THE TWO PARTITIONS: OF BRITISH INDIA AND OF THE MUSLIM COMMUNITY

By its provisions, the Government of India Act of 1935 was certain to transform the grammar and syntax of Indian politics. At one stroke, the lowering of the franchise qualifications increased the electorate to over thirty millions. The increase in the number of general seats in the provincial legislative assemblies enabled untrammelled expression to be given, in the Hindu majority provinces, to a Hindu majority will – untrammelled, that is, except by the reserve powers in the hands of the British provincial governor and ultimately, through the Viceroy, of the Secretary of State.

In the United Provinces, the number of seats in the Assembly was increased to 228, of which 140 were general, including 20 for scheduled castes, and 66 Muslim. In Bihar there were 86 general to 40 Muslim seats, out of a total of 152 seats. In Bombay, of 175 seats, 114 were general, including 15 for scheduled castes, and 30 were Muslim. In Madras, 146 of the total of 215 were general, with 30 of those general seats reserved for scheduled castes; there were 28 Muslim seats. In the Muslim majority provinces of the Panjab and Bengal, however, a majority will was denied full constitutional expression; in the Panjab there were 42 general seats, 86 Muslim seats, 31 Sikh seats and the remaining seats were to represent special interests. In Bengal, with its 250 seats, 78 were general, of which 20 were reserved for scheduled castes, 119 were Muslim and there were 19 for representatives of commercial, industrial, mining and planting interests.

Both in the general and in Muslim constituencies, the day of the old conservative and oligarchic landlord politics was, except in the new province of Sind, nearly done. In the United Provinces, dyarchy had been worked in the provincial legislative assembly by groups of landlords, enjoying British favour and sure of their tenants' votes through their position as landlords. To meet the new mass electorate, in 1934 U.P. landlords had with difficulty gathered themselves into a National Agriculturist Party, but the province was notorious for agrarian unrest, and in 1937 at the provincial elections the party won only nine seats.

Muslim politicians were not oblivious to the challenge presented by a mass Muslim electorate, but could not agree upon a common response. In the Panjab, Sir Fazl-i Husain thought that for all the eighty-six Muslim seats, the only chance for Muslim power lay in a joint party, the Unionist Party, with Hindu and Sikh agrarian interests, presenting a programme of agrarian reform. Fazl al-Haq in Bengal, leader of the *Krishak Proja Samiti*, which enjoyed some mass support, was similarly to advocate a popular welfare pro-gramme which both Muslim and Hindu cultivators could support. Both these prominent Muslim politicians of the two great Muslim majority provinces believed that an inter-communal programme was the best way to protect and further specifically Muslim interests in those provinces, in the constitutional conditions created by the Communal Award of 1932 and the 1935 Act. Neither of them was immediately concerned with the Muslim position outside their provinces. Sir Fazl-i Husain's son, ʿAzim Husain (1913–), portrays his father was in favour of an Indian nationalism of religiously and culturally distinct communities on a footing of equality co-operating in policies of mass uplift, with the Panjab as the shop window for such political goods.[1]

Jinnah, however, posed the alternatives of Muslims organising themselves effectively as an all-India force for the first elections to be held under the 1935 Act. Jinnah had settled in England in 1931, in bitterness and dudgeon at his rebuffs from both Congress and the Muslim parties. As Halidé Edib's *Inside India* reveals, in 1935 he was a nonentity in Indian politics. The All-India Muslim League was in decay, unable even to collect annual subscriptions. No one foresaw the transformation of the arrogant, proud, cold-blooded logician and lawyer Jinnah into the charismatic Muslim leader of the nineteen-forties and the transformation of the de-crepit Muslim League into a mass movement. At the age of sixty, Jinnah returned to India in 1935, to try to bind the moribund Muslim political splinter-groups into a Muslim political *fasces*. Only if the Muslims had a powerful all-India organisation, with mass

[1] Azim Husain, *Fazl-i Husain* (Bombay, 1946), pp. 249, 381–3.

Muslim electoral support, could they influence the future constructively. In 1936, his aim was co-operation with Congress in a common programme of mass uplift; he wished to rebut the allegation that Muslim politics were the politics of stooges and wealthy sybarites.

Jinnah tried to form a Central Parliamentary Board under the aegis of the Muslim League, to approve a list of candidates to fight the elections as an all-India party standing for an economic and social programme similar to that of Congress – calling for full democratic self-government, free and compulsory primary education, the relief of rural indebtedness, the development of cottage industry and the state regulation of currency and prices in such a way as to promote a production 'take-off'. But Jinnah was too late in the field and the longer established provincial Muslim organisations largely ignored the Central Parliamentary Board. Men like Fazl al-Haq and Sir Fazl-i Husain, Saiyid ʿAbd al-ʿAziz (of the United Party, Bihar) and the Nawwab of Chhattari (1888–) of the U.P. did not wish to limit their freedom of action in their own provinces by submission to a Central Board formed by someone like Jinnah, who was without political backing in his own provinces of Bombay and who had had no practical experience of local politics under dyarchy. In the event, the provincial Muslim parties went their own way and Jinnah's Muslim League was not able even to put up candidates for all the seats reserved for Muslims.

The results of the elections in 1937 showed that neither Congress nor the All-India Muslim League could claim to represent Muslims as such, and that Muslim politics remained obstinately provincial. The Muslim League won only 109 of the 482 seats reserved for Muslims. It failed utterly in the Panjab, winning only two seats of the mere seven it contested. In Bengal it fared rather better, winning thirty-nine of the 117 Muslim seats, but was in no position to form a ministry. In the United Provinces, the League contested thirty-five of the sixty-six Muslim seats, winning twenty-nine. Congress Muslims did no better. They were rejected in the United Provinces where the Congress organisation was strong; no Muslim was returned on the Congress ticket. Nor was any Muslim elected on the Congress ticket for a Muslim seat in Bengal, Sind, Panjab, Assam, Bombay, the Central Provinces and Orissa. Congress won only twenty-six of such seats, mainly in the North-West Frontier Province, Bihar and Madras. Muslims had preferred to be represented by their provincial Muslim parties, acting in alliance with or sharing a common platform with such non-Muslims as did not follow the Congress line.

The elections of 1937 did reveal, however, the strength of Congress as an all-India movement in the general constituencies. It won 716 of the 1,161 'open' constituencies it contested. Of the eleven provinces of British India, Congress secured a clear majority in six and emerged as the largest single party in three others. Muslims were left to contemplate the fact that while Hindus would dominate in all the provinces where Hindus were a majority of the population, Muslims could not dominate the two biggest Muslim majority provinces, namely the Panjab and Bengal. If ever the British implemented the federal provisions of the 1935 Act, under which Muslims would have one-third of the seats in the Central Legislature, Congress would be likely to win a dominating position in the central government as well. The outlook for Muslim politicians who aspired to play a major *rôle* in all-India politics was bleak indeed.

Congress proceeded to read the Muslim politicians of the United Provinces, the province where historically Muslims had considered themselves the natural aristocracy, a lesson in the power of elected majorities. There Congress had secured 134 of the 144 general seats and was in a position to form a ministry of its own. Some Muslim Leaguers, led by Chaudhuri Khaliq al-Zaman (Chaudhry Khaliquzzaman (1889–), had conversations with Congress leaders in April and May 1937, proposing a coalition on roughly the same platform of social and economic reform as Congress. Jinnah tried to halt the discussions, saying that it was no use dealing with those who were in and out of Congress and in and out of the Muslim League as it suited them, and appealed to the Muslims of the United Provinces not to betray the Muslims of India. Other Muslim Leaguers in the United Provinces also objected to Khaliq al-Zaman's dealings.

The leaders of Congress in the United Provinces, including Jawaharlal Nehru himself, aware of Muslim dissensions and unenthusiastic about coalition with conservative men of little political weight, were only prepared for an understanding under certain conditions: the Muslim Leaguers must cease to function as a separate group, the Muslim League Parliamentary Board in the

United Provinces must be dissolved and the existing members of the Muslim League in the Assembly must accept Congress discipline. This was indeed the kiss of death to any separate Muslim political personality in the United Provinces. Negotiations were therefore broken off. The Muslim League in the United Provinces was given a new lease of life and Muslims were humiliated by the revelation of their impotence after the elections of 1937.

THE RISE OF THE MUSLIM LEAGUE AND THE DEMAND FOR PAKISTAN

The 1937 elections then had (to the dismay of the British as well as of Muslims) shown that there were only two real foci of power in India, the British-dominated central government, and Congress. Jinnah quite deliberately set out to establish that there was a third, the Muslim League. His determination was no mere response to the experience of Congress rule in the provinces; it had already been expressed in his Muslim League Parliamentary Board of 1936 and in his reaction to Chaudhuri Khaliq al-Zaman's approaches towards Congress in 1937. He merely spelt it out in his address to the October 1937 session of the Muslim League at Lucknow:

No settlement with [the] majority community is possible as no Hindu leader speaking with any authority shows any concern or any genuine desire for it. Honourable settlement can only be achieved between equals and unless the two parties learn to respect and fear each other, there is no solid ground for settlement. Offers of peace by the weaker party always mean confession of weakness and invitation to aggression. Politics means power and not relying only on cries of justice or fair-play or goodwill.[2]

By reorganising the Muslim League, reducing the membership fee to two annas and ensuring that the members of the Council of the League were elected from among local district or *tahsil* Leaguers, Jinnah aimed to win it a mass following rivalling that of Congress, and to establish it in the eyes of the British government and of Congress as the only representative and authoritative Muslim political organisation.

---

[2] Jamil ud-din Ahmad (ed.), *Some Recent Speeches and Writings of Mr Jinnah*, 5th ed., vol. 1 (Lahore, 1952), p. 33.

Jinnah's campaign to popularise the Muslim League among Muslims met with a response which surprised both the British and Congress. It is said that one hundred thousand new members were recruited in the months immediately after the Lucknow session of 1937. In the United Provinces the League was able to capitalise upon the class fears of Muslim landlords. The elections of 1937 had killed the Agriculturist party and landlords faced the prospect of Congress-inspired tenancy legislation. In 1938 the Governor-General disallowed a bill passed by the United Provinces Legislative Assembly which would have reduced the rental income of landlords by about half, but in 1939 an Act was passed improving the security of tenure of tenants. Socially too, the Muslim gentlemen of the United Provinces were threatened by the Congress victory. The new active 'grass-roots' Congress workers were hardly Westernised; with their homespun clothes, Gandhi caps, aggressive vegetarianism and Hindi speech they reminded the Muslim with any pretensions to gentility – and U.P. Muslims had most pretensions to gentility – of all the values that he did not share with the humbler Hindu.

In other Congress-ruled provinces the policies of Congress governments, however innocently conceived for the welfare of the masses, jarred upon Muslim sensibilities. The Wardha scheme for elementary education, associating book learning with craft learning, with its emphasis on spinning, on textbooks in Hindi which glorified Hindu heroes and on self-supporting schools living on the sale of their handicrafts, looked too much like a Gandhi *ashram* on a national scale to be acceptable to Muslims. As the scheme was drawn up by a committee headed by a prominent Muslim educationalist, the late President of India, Dr Zakir Husain, and was implemented in Bihar by a Muslim education minister, Dr Saiyid (Syed) Mahmud, charges of efforts deliberately to 'hinduise' Muslims were misplaced, but in the Muslim minority provinces any Congress attempt to come closer to the mass of the population was in the nature of things likely to adopt a Hindu idiom.

Congress blundered too in its 'mass contact' campaign in 1937–8. In an attempt to reach over the heads of Muslim politicians to the rank and file Muslim voter, Congress gave the Muslim League just the occasion for mass campaigning it needed. The aim of Congress was to convince the ordinary Muslim voter of the common interests of all the poor of India and to win him for the Congress policies of agrarian reform. With separate electorates, this was seen as an attempt to deprive the Muslim politician of his constituents and also, since the appeal was secular in terms, as an attack upon Islam. Both Muslim politicians and the village ʿ*ulama* joined to repulse it. Old Khilafat leaders such as Shaukat ʿAli and Maulana Hasrat Mohani joined with politicians like Khaliq al-Zaman, and ʿ*ulama* such as Maulanas Jamal Miyan, ʿAbd al-Hamid Bada'uni (d. 1969), Siddiq Hasan and Sibqat-Allah in touring the countryside campaigning against 'Congress Raj'.

The task of the League's propagandists was undoubtedly helped by the Hindu idiom of Congress political expression, a not unnatural phenomenon where the rural population was overwhelmingly Hindu and where, as in Islam, religion was the oxygen of the daily social atmosphere. Hindus were charged in the so-called Pirpur and Sharif (Shareef) Reports[3] with forcing cow-protection upon Muslims, pushing the use of Hindi and interfering with Muslim worship. Whether or not these allegations were justified – and certainly the *khadar*-clad Congress worker did not share the respect for Muslim culture of Nehru or Gandhi – they were believed. By the outbreak of war in 1939 the Muslim League stood forth as the strongest single Muslim political organisation in the Muslim minority provinces.

As a local force in the politics of the Muslim majority provinces of the Panjab and Bengal, the All-India Muslim League was able to make little headway between 1937 and 1939. Sir Fazl-i Husain died in 1936 and his successor as leader of the Unionist Party in the Panjab, Sir Sikandar Hayat Khan (1892–1942), concluded a 'pact' with Jinnah, after negotiations in the autumn of 1937, whereby the Muslim members of the Panjab Unionist Party joined the Muslim League and submitted themselves to the Panjab Muslim League Parliamentary Board. Since the Parliamentary Board was now composed overwhelmingly of Muslim Unionists, the Muslim Unionists were in effect merely submitting to themselves. Under the pact, however, Sir Sikandar Hayat Khan undertook to follow

---

[3] *Report of the Inquiry Committee appointed by the Council of the All-India Muslim League to inquire into Muslim grievances in Congress Provinces*, 1938. (Chairman the Raja of Pirpur); *Report of the Enquiry Committee appointed by the Working Committee of the Bihar Provincial Muslim League to inquire into some grievances of Muslims in Bihar*, 1939. Draftsman: S. M. Shareef.

agreed Muslim League policy on all-India questions.[4] In Bengal Fazl al-Haq advised his Muslim followers in his *Krishak Proja* party to act similarly, thus enabling him to bring the forty Muslim Leaguers into a coalition government. In Sind the Muslim members of the Assembly were split into at least four factions and it was only possible for the leading Sind Muslim politicians, Sir Ghulam Husain Hidayat-Allah (1879–1948) and Allah Bakhsh (1897–1943), to form governments with Hindu help. When in October 1998 Jinnah himself came to Karachi to preside over the Muslim League session, his efforts to convert the Sind government into a Muslim League government failed utterly. In the politics of these Muslim majority provinces, the League was no more than a convenient stalking-horse.

The undertaking by Fazl al-Haq and Sir Sikandar Hayat Khan to follow League policy in all-India questions was, however, a significant step towards converting the League into a 'third force'. By 1939 all sections of the League rejected any advance to an all-India federation, as planned under the 1935 Act. With Congress ministries in six provinces and with the proposal that the federal representatives of the princely states should be elected by the (overwhelmingly Hindu) populations of the states, a responsible federal government leaving Muslims in a hopeless minority at the centre held no charms for the League. In August 1938 Lord Zetland (1876–1961), the Secretary of State for India, noted that Sir Sikandar Hayat Khan was just as hostile to federation under the 1935 Act as Jinnah, and he himself in the course of 1938 'could not resist a steadily growing conviction that the dominant factor in determining the future form of the Government of India would prove to be the All-India Muslim League'.[5] By the summer of 1939 he was very doubtful whether Muslims would consent to work the federal portion of the Act of 1935.

The outbreak of war in September 1939 rapidly raised the status and the bargaining power of Jinnah and the Muslim League. The British naturally wanted an effective Indian contribution to the war, but did not wish to pay Congress too much for it. The Panjab was

---

[4] An interesting account of this period in Panjab politics is given in: ʿAshiq Husain Batalawi, *Iqbal ke Akhiri Do Sal* (Karachi, 1961). For the Sikandar–Jinnah pact negotiations see pp. 521 *et seq.*

[5] Marquess of Zetland, *'Essayez'* (London, 1956), p. 247.

the major army recruiting area and the Panjab was a Muslim majority province; in military terms Muslim support appeared more worthwhile than that of the Congress politician and party worker. The League was a useful counterweight to Congress, which was now only too likely, if the influence of Subhas Chandra Bose grew, to take advantage of British embarrassments. Lord Linlithgow (1887–1952), the Viceroy, was in no hurry to terminate the British Raj, and with a war on his hands there was no reason why he should have been. Jinnah found himself seeing the Viceroy on 4 September 1939, only one day after Linlithgow declared war on Germany for India, on a footing of equality with Gandhi. On 11 September Linlithgow announced the suspension of all moves towards federation. In October 1939 the Congress ministries in the provinces resigned in protest against India being pitchforked into a war not of her making without any consultation.

On 1 November 1939 the Viceroy, in interviews with Gandhi, Jinnah and Rajendra Prasad (1884–1963), stipulated that any expansion of the Viceroy's executive council to include more representative Indians and any return to popular government in the provinces was conditional upon the Congress and the Muslim League reaching agreement. Jinnah had been presented with a veto upon any further constitutional advance and indeed upon any attempt to return to the position in the provinces between 1937 and 1939. On 5 November 1939 he demanded assurances from Linlithgow that the 1935 Act would be wholly reconsidered and that no constitution for India would be enacted without the consent of the two major parties, Congress and the League. In February 1940 Zetland wrote of British realisation that any yielding to Congress demands for a constituent assembly might mean civil war in India.[6] The British were now ready to concede to Jinnah the bargaining power he had sought. Not so Congress, which still saw the weaknesses of the League position in the very provinces which should have been its principal strongholds, namely the Panjab and Bengal. Could the League find a platform which would fire the imagination of Muslims in the majority provinces and define a clear political objective? Jinnah now had power over the British; how would he use it?

On 23 March 1940 the answer was publicly given. On that day,

[6] Zetland, *'Essayez'*, pp. 284–5.

the All-India Muslim League passed the famous 'Pakistan' resolution. After Jinnah had declared in his presidential address that 'the Mussulmans are a nation by any definition with the need for a homeland, territory and state if we are to develop to the fullest our spiritual, cultural, economic, social and political life' the League resolved that:

> no constitutional plan would be workable in this country or accept-
> able to the Muslims unless it is designed on the following basic prin-
> ciples, viz. that geographically contiguous units are demarcated into
> regions which should be so constituted, with such territorial adjust-
> ments as may be necessary, that the areas in which the Muslims are
> numerically in a majority should be grouped to constitute 'independent
> states' in which the constituent units should be autonomous and
> sovereign.[7]

This was, for all the ambiguities of the resolution, to put the issue of partition at the top of the agenda of Indian politics.

The idea of a Muslim state composed of the Muslim majority areas was by no means a bolt from the blue. Pakistanis have compiled anthologies showing the respectable ancestry of the idea.[8] Iqbal's prognosis of 1930 has already been quoted. Chaudhuri Rahmat 'Ali's ideas were well known to responsible Muslim leaders; in the summer of 1939 Sir Sikandar Hayat Khan published a scheme for the loosest of federations, with regional or zonal legislatures dealing with common subjects; also in the summer of 1939 Nawwab Sir Muhammad Shah Nawaz Khan (1883–?) published[9] a confederal scheme anonymously attributed to 'a Punjabi'. This would have divided India into five autonomous units each with a federal government and all coming together in a confederal association with undefined common links; a Dr Saiyid 'Abd al-Latif (1893–1972) of Hyderabad (Deccan) also published a plan for a minimal federation of homogeneous cultural zones, but this would have required the migration of the Muslim and Hindu populations; the north-central Muslim zone was eventually to be a permanent home

---

[7] C. H. Philips (ed.), *The Evolution of India and Pakistan, 1858–1947, Select Documents* (London, 1962), pp. 354–5.

[8] See, for example, Syed Sharifuddin Pirzada, *The Evolution of Pakistan* (Lahore, 1963).

[9] 'A Punjabi', *Confederacy of India* (Lahore, 1939). The actual author is thought by some to have been one Miyan Kifayat 'Ali.

for all the Muslims then living in the United Provinces and Bihar.[10]
No doubt the desire not to give the Muslims of the minority provinces the sensation of having been abandoned, as well as the need
to find the highest common factor of Muslim agreement and leave
Jinnah room for manoeuvre, helps to account for the absence of
precise territorial definition in the Lahore resolution. It was enough
to cry that Islam and Muslims could only be safe in their own
state.

Whether or not as Professor Tinker has suggested,[11] most British
statesmen regarded the partition resolution as a deliberate over-bid
to ensure proper attention for Muslim demands and interests, they
spoke and acted as if partition was henceforth one of the options to
be kept open in Indian politics. It was noticeable that Linlithgow
did not rush to condemn the Lahore resolution. On 18 April 1940,
in the House of Lords, Zetland said that he could not believe that
any parliament or government in England would force a constitution for India upon unwilling Muslims. In the declaration of 8
August 1940, reiterating the goal of Dominion status for India and
offering a War Advisory Council and an expanded Viceroy's
Executive Council, the British government stated that it could not
contemplate the transfer of its responsibilities in India to any government whose authority was denied by large and powerful elements in
Indian national life. Jinnah was now being told, in effect, that
Britain would not join with Congress to deny him 'Pakistan' by
force.

A further intimation of British willingness to concede Pakistan
if it was certain Muslims wanted it occurred during the Cripps
mission of March 1942, when, with the destruction of British naval
power in the eastern seas by the Japanese, the loss of Malaya, the
capitulation of Singapore (in February 1942) and the retreat from
Burma in progress, it was decided to send Sir Stafford Cripps
(1889–1952) with new political and constitutional proposals designed, in Churchill's words, 'to rally all the forces of Indian life
to guard their land' against the feared Japanese invasion. Cripps
offered, in return for Indian (and particularly Congress) support for
the war effort, representation of the major parties in the central

---

[10] Taken from R. Coupland, *Indian Politics 1936–1942* (Calcutta, 1944),
pp. 201–2.
[11] Hugh Tinker, *Experiment with Freedom* (London, 1967), p. 24.

government, and at the end of the war independence and full Dominion status for a Union of India. Any provinces (and the Muslim majority provinces were clearly intended) which did not wish to accede could stay out of the Indian Union and yet enjoy the same status. Again, Jinnah was being informed in effect that if he could win mass Muslim support for the Pakistan resolution, the British would accept partition.

Congress itself, for all its indignant repudiation of the notion of forcibly vivisecting 'Mother India', was far from meeting the Lahore resolution with a steely negative. In an article in *Harijan* of 13 April 1940, Gandhi stated that although he could never be a party to the division of India and would employ every non-violent means to prevent it, nevertheless as a man of non-violence he could not forcibly resent the proposed partition if the Muslims really insisted upon it.[12] Again, in the course of rejection of the Cripps offer, the Congress Working Committee said it could not contemplate forcing the people of any territorial unit to remain in an Indian union against its will.[13] On 1 April 1942 the Congress members of the Madras legislature, prompted by Rajagopalachari (1878–), passed a resolution recommending acceptance of the Muslim League's partition demand and in a series of meetings with Jinnah in September 1944 Gandhi, though refusing to accept that Muslims formed a separate nation, expressed willingness to concede separation to those areas of India all of whose inhabitants, irrespective of religion, decided by plebiscite that they wished to form a separate state. On the other hand, the 'Quit India' resolution and rebellion of August 1942 were in fact, though not in form, partly an effort to destroy the power of the Muslim League, by removing the British as the third party preventing a direct confrontation between Congress and the League.

The years following the Lahore resolution saw a steady consolidation of the Muslim League's power and of Jinnah's personal position. In June 1940 the Working Committee of the League resolved that Jinnah alone should conduct negotiations with the Viceroy, and that no Muslim Leaguer should serve on any war committee without his consent. When in July 1940 the Muslim premiers of the Panjab, Bengal and Assam joined the Viceroy's

---

[12] Quoted in: Sachin Sen, *The Birth of Pakistan* (Calcutta, 1966), p. 121.
[13] V. P. Menon, *The Transfer of Power in India* (Calcutta, 1957), p. 132.

Defence Council without his permission, Jinnah called upon them to resign; they either did so or were expelled from the League. The resignation of the Congress ministries in October 1939 and the proscription of Congress by the British after the 'Quit India' resolution of August 1942 enabled the League to operate in a political vacuum. It gradually strengthened its support in the Muslim majority provinces, which it had to win to give reality to the Pakistan demand. In Bengal, after some very involved political infighting, Fazl al-Haq, who had refused to toe the local Muslim League line, was forced to resign and in March 1943 a Muslim League ministry was formed under Khwaja Nazim al-din (1894–1964). In Sind, the pro-Congress Allah-Bakhsh was dismissed by the British governor in September 1942 and his successor, Sir Ghulam Husain Hidayat-Allah expediently joined the Muslim League and managed to hold office with League support. Even in the Congress Redshirt North-West Frontier Province, the resignation of the Congress ministry in the autumn of 1939 enabled the local League leader, Sardar Aurangzib Khan to gather support so that he was able to form a ministry in May 1943. In Assam too the League took over.

Only in the Panjab did the Muslim League receive a rebuff. Sir Sikandar Hayat Khan died in 1942, to be succeeded as Chief Minister and leader of the Unionist party by Khizr Hayat Khan Tiwana (1900–). In April 1944 Jinnah demanded of Tiwana that he change the name of the Unionist Party to 'The Muslim League Coalition Party'. Dependent upon Hindu and Sikh support, Tiwana refused and in a public manifesto charged Jinnah with breaking the 'Sikandar–Jinnah' pact. Despite an affirmation of faith in the Pakistan idea, Tiwana was expelled from the League. As, however, he had not lost his majority in the Panjab Legislative Assembly, he remained Chief Minister in the Panjab. It was this open challenge from a Muslim head of a Hindu–Muslim coalition party that impelled Jinnah to break up the Simla Conference in June 1945. After the end of the war in Europe, the Viceroy, Lord Wavell (1883–1950), proposed to form an interim government composed of the nominees of the major parties in India. Jinnah rejected any suggestion that Congress should include a Muslim among its nominees and held firm to his stand that all Muslim nominees must be Muslim Leaguers. It was essential to deny to the Unionist

Muslims of the Panjab, and to Tiwana in particular, all status as a separate and parallel organisation of, and spokesman for, any group of Muslims in India. If the Muslim League was to conquer the heartland of 'Pakistan' it must give no quarter to the Muslims of the Panjab Unionist Party, and it could afford no 'quislings' to weaken its confrontation with Congress at the all-India level (however miscast the Muslims of the Panjab Unionist Party were for that *rôle*).

During these war years the League was able to bring into its fold not only the Muslim provincial politicians but also many hitherto non-political Muslims. The experience of war contracts awarded by Muslim provincial governments, or by governments wishing to mollify Muslims, sweetened the thought of a Muslims' state for the growing number of Muslim industrial and commercial magnates. 'A Panjabi' in *Confederacy of India* had argued powerfully that there would be no hope of the industrialisation of the Panjab under a centre dominated by existing Hundu financial interests.[14] Such business families as the Ispahanis and Habibs were persuaded to contribute to Muslim League funds. A Federation of Muslim Chambers of Commerce was founded in 1944. A Planning Committee of the League was set up after the League session of 1943 at Karachi to devise plans for the economic development of the areas intended to form part of Pakistan. Muslim university students were enrolled to take the Pakistan idea to the ordinary Muslim voter and indeed to the unenfranchised. Jinnah was able to convert *Dawn*, a rather drooping weekly, into a flourishing daily. By 1942 the now well-known commentator on Islam in India, Wilfred Cantwell Smith, then living in India, reckoned that the League's 'Pakistan' demand had conquered the Muslim middle class by which he meant the professional, clerical and salaried Muslim).[15] By the end of the war in 1945, as the elections of the winter of 1945–6 were to show, the Muslim League was a mass movement.

As soon as the Labour leaders in Britain came to power as a result of their landslide victory at the polls in July 1945, they determined to seek a settlement of the 'Indian question'. They decided to test Indian opinion (and to discover with whom they had to deal) by holding the first provincial elections since 1937. The Muslim

---

14 *Confederacy of India*, pp. 100–2.
15 Wilfred Cantwell Smith, *Modern Islam in India* (Lahore, 1943), p. 312.

League, all over India, fought the election campaign on the sole issue of 'Pakistan', that is upon the extended plan which would have included the two undivided Muslim majority provinces of Bengal and the Panjab with their large non-Muslim minorities. The League won a famous victory. It won all the thirty Muslim seats in the Central Legislative Assembly. It won 439 of the 494 seats reserved to Muslims under separate electorates in the provincial assemblies. In the Panjab it emerged with seventy-five seats, the largest single party; the Unionist party was reduced to ten seats. In Bengal the Muslim League won 113 of the 119 Muslim seats. In the Muslim minority provinces the League's triumph was equally great. In the United Provinces it won fifty-four of the sixty-four Muslim seats and in Bombay and Madras it won all the Muslim seats contested.

In the general constituencies the Congress victory was equally overwhelming. It won 930 seats and gained an absolute majority of places in the provincial assemblies in eight provinces. There is no doubt how the sentiments of political and enfranchised India had aligned themselves. The League was indeed the 'third force' which Jinnah had striven for the past ten years to make it. Muslim India had pronounced in favour of political separatism for the free expression of an independent Muslim political personality.

From a cabal of self-interested office seekers condescendingly seeking the suffrages of their social inferiors to the chosen shepherd of a nation in the making and on the march – this was the transformation of the All-India Muslim League between 1936 and 1946. The transformation was so dramatic that unbelieving observers have held that the position of the League in 1946 was created by factors extrinsic to the League and to the Muslim community: to the miscalculations of Congress in requiring its provincial ministries to resign in October 1939 and in rebelling in August 1942, thus leaving the political field open to the League, or in being neither willing to coerce minorities to remain in a united India nor willing to make them a realistic offer; or to the manoeuvres of the British, who accorded Jinnah on the outbreak of war political parity with Gandhi and Nehru and who, in the August 1940 offer, gave him a veto on future constitutional change, by insisting that no change was possible unless it was accepted by all the main elements in Indian life. No one would deny the strategic and tactical advantages that these actions offered Jinnah, the supreme political strategist and tactician, but they do not explain the ability of the League's leaders to bring out the Muslim vote in 1945–6 or to topple the Unionist ministry of Khizr Hayat Khan Tiwana in the Panjab by a non-co-operation movement in February and March 1947, or, indeed, so to inspire the Muslims of the minority provinces that they voted for the establishment of a separate homeland which would not be theirs to inhabit.

The political 'lift-off' of the League occurred in the United Provinces between 1937 and 1939. It was here that the threat of the homespun-clad Hindi-speaking Congress activist to the Muslim and Urdu-speaking bearer of Mughal culture was most felt. It was here that, with a growing proportion of Muslims knowing English and having college qualifications, middle-class competition for government and professional careers was keenest: it was noticeable that the League vote was greater in urban than in rural areas. It was here that Muslim landlords had the wealth and standing to resist tenancy legislation. It was here that Muslims felt most strongly that they were the natural aristocracy of the country and it was here, at Aligarh University, that the League found an eager band of young propagandists and election workers. The United Provinces first gave Jinnah that provincial *pied à terre* which as an all-India politician he had previously lacked; it also provided the League with its 'natural' leaders, able to meet British politicians and administrators on socially equal terms. Even in 1946, when the destiny of the Muslim majority provinces was immediately at stake, the United Provinces had four members of the Working Committee of the League to three each for Bengal and Panjab.

The creation of Pakistan in August 1947 left U.P. Muslims high but far from dry in a Hindu-dominated province. Why then did so many U.P. Muslims vote for a Pakistan in 1945–6? Some certainly, among the sophisticated landlords and their supporters, voted mainly in the belief that Jinnah, sure of support for extremes, would be able to settle for a very loose all-India federation with safeguards for the Muslim minority provinces. Others believed in the hostage theory – that the threat of Muslim ill-treatment of non-Muslims in the Panjab, say, would prevent non-Muslim ill-treatment of Muslims in the United Provinces. Others believed that the 'big Pakistan' for which the League campaigned would give the United

Provinces a common frontier with a Pakistani Panjab. Some no doubt thought that Pakistan, any Pakistan, would give them employment, for were they not, as U.P. Muslims, born to rule? Outside these more pretentious circles, however, religious fervour undoubtedly played its part.

In the Panjab, which the League had to win if the Pakistan demand was to have any credibility, the Muslim League gained its electoral victory by making a religious appeal over the heads of the professional politicians. Between 1937 and 1945, as long as there were no general elections, first Sir Sikandar Hayat Khan and then Khizr Hayat Khan Tiwana were able to control the province through the inter-communal Unionist party. But the Muslim Unionists of the Panjab were undermined by the revelation at the Simla conference that Jinnah's influence, even before the central and provincial elections, was such that he could bar the appointment of non-League Muslims to the Viceroy's Executive Council. Before his death, Sir Sikandar Hayat Khan, fearing that the League might appeal to Muslim religious emotions in the Panjab, had felt obliged to accept Jinnah's all-India strategy.

During the provincial election campaign of 1945–6 the League did enlist such religious leaders in the Panjab as the Pir Sahib of Manki Sharif, Pir Jamaʿat ʿAli Shah and Makhdum Riza Shah of Multan, *inter alios*, to campaign on the slogan that a vote for the League and for Pakistan was a vote for Islam. The League also relied on the fervour of young students, many of whom were attracted to the League, as the veteran Panjabi Muslim socialist, Miyan Iftikhar al-din (1908–62), had been attracted, by the socialist programme put forward by the Provincial Muslim League in 1944. It may well be, too, that with high prices prevailing for food and large remittances of military pay and allowances still flowing into the province, the Muslim rural voter was optimistic about the economic future of an independent Panjab.

In Bengal the victory of the Muslim League at the polls came after the province had been ruled for more than two years by a Muslim League ministry, supported by the votes of the resident European community. The experience of power, with all that it meant in the award of contracts to Muslim war and other contractors, won over many middle-class Muslims to the Pakistan idea. It should also be remembered that in 1945–6 it was hoped and believed that Calcutta would form part of a Muslim-dominated Bengal. The negotiations of Husain Shahid Suhrawardi (1893–1964) in early 1947 for the maintenance of a united Bengal of Hindus and Muslims suggested that many Bengali Muslims had not necessarily committed themselves to the partitioned Bengal of August 1947 when they had voted in 1945–6. It is also important to recall that although Fazl al-Haq, the Muslim politician with the most popular following in the province, had been estranged from the League since 1943, during the election campaign he did not withhold his support for the League at the grass roots.

The strength of the Muslim League's programme was that it was not a programme but a promise. The League of the nineteen-forties was a chiliastic movement rather than a pragmatic political party. It was all things to all of British India's Muslims – socialist to the socialist, capitalist to the capitalist, and Islamic to the pietist. Its Pakistan was to be a panacea for the ills of Muslims of each and every class. Its slogans were unity, discipline and faith: creativity was to be postponed until after the day on which the faithful should enter the promised land. Jinnah deliberately kept not only the future character and constitution of Pakistan in heaven, but its very boundaries too. In the winter of 1945–6 the Muslim voter did not vote for the truncated Pakistan of August 1947, nor for a future which held emigration, massacre and personal destitution. He voted for the creation of a haven for Muslims and for Islam which should extend over six provinces or regions of British India: Baluchistan, Sind, Panjab, the North-West Frontier Province, Bengal and Assam, with such minimal subtractions as his *Qaid-i A°zam* (Great Leader) could not deny to the Hindus.

THE IDEA OF PAKISTAN

Many Muslims had voted for Pakistan so that a distinct way of life could take political command over its future. For some this was expressed in terms of nineteenth-century European nationalism – that independent cultures should be independent polities. This was how Jinnah himself saw it in his Muslim League presidential address before the passing of the Lahore resolution of March 1940.[16]

---

[16] Jamil ud-din Ahmad (ed.), *Some Recent Speeches and Writings of Mr. Jinnah*, vol. I, (Lahore, 1952 ed.), pp. 177–8.

The Hindus and Muslims belong to two different religious philosophies, social customs, literature. They neither intermarry nor interdine together and, indeed, they belong to two different civilizations which are based mainly on conflicting ideas and conceptions. . .It is quite clear that Hindus and Mussalmans derive their inspiration from different sources of history. They have different epics, different heroes, and different episodes. Very often the hero of one is a foe of the other and, likewise, their victories and defeats overlap. To yoke together two such nations under a single state, one as a numerical minority and the other as a majority, must lead to growing discontent and final destruction of any fabric that may be so built up for the government of such a state. . .The present artificial unity of India dates back only to the British conquest and is maintained by the British bayonet. . .Mussulmans are not a minority as it is commonly known and understood. . . Mussulmans are a nation according to any definition of a nation, and they must have their homelands, their territory, and their state. . . We wish our people to develop to the fullest our spiritual, cultural, economic, social and political life in a way that we think best and in consonance with our own ideals and according to the genius of our people.

Jinnah's vision was of a state whose constitution and political life would be Muslim because its people were Muslim.

But during the elections of 1945–6 the Muslim voter had been asked to cast his vote for the Muslim League in order to further the mission of Islam in the world as much as his own worldly interests. No doubt many middle-class Muslims voted for the League to free themselves from Hindu competition. But many active workers for the League, students and intelligentsia, saw in Pakistan a chance to restore not only the physical but also the moral authority of Islam in a world where, in 1945, non-Islamic values were looking rather shoddy. They wanted the divine law of Islam to be the law of the new Muslim state.

The poet and seer, Sir Muhammad Iqbal (1876–1938), had, in his lectures on *The Reconstruction of Religious Thought in Islam* (1930), proposed a reconstruction of Muslim society by the exercise of a free *ijtihad* or 'effort' by Muslims to understand what God wanted them to do when confronted by the novel challenge of the twentieth century. Rejecting the *ijma*ᶜ or consensus of the orthodox schools of jurisprudence, he wished to see the authority of *ijma*ᶜ transferred to regional Muslim legislative assemblies.[17]

Let the Mussulman of today appreciate his position, reconstruct his social life in the light of ultimate principles and evolve out of the partially revealed purpose of Islam, that spiritual democracy which is the ultimate aim of Islam.[18]

But in his lectures Iqbal noted that 'In India, however, it is doubtful whether a non-Muslim legislative assembly can exercise the power of Ijtihad.' The logic of *ijma*ᶜ modernism, as Professor Leonard Binder has called it, led to a demand for independent statehood for Muslims. Writing to Jinnah on 28 May 1937, Iqbal said,

After long and careful study of Islamic Law I have come to the conclusion that if this system of law is properly understood and applied, at last the right to subsistence is secured to everybody. But the enforcement and development of the Shariat of Islam is impossible in this country without a free Muslim state or states.[19]

The growing influence by 1939 of the idea that Muslims should be politically independent in order to introduce the reign of Islam is betrayed in the *Confederacy of India* by 'a Panjabi', already referred to. 'A Panjabi' wrote,

A Muslim state may not mean a state in the Western sense of the word to which the Indian Muslims have been accustomed. It may mean a state governed by the Islamic Law as contained in the Holy Quran. It may mean the purging of the Indian Muslims of all the un-Islamic influences which they have contracted on account of their close contact with the non-Muslim communities in India.[20]

Other Muslim writers, opinion- rather than policy-makers, wrote of Pakistan as necessary as an example to, rather than as a refuge from, the non-Muslim world. F. H. Khan Durrani of the Panjab, who had spent his life as a missionary for Islam, proclaimed:

We are here not for political privileges or economic concessions, but to fight the battles of Allah and His Apostle, to fight against wrong

[17] Sir Muhammad Iqbal, *The Reconstruction of Religious Thought in Islam* (Lahore, 1962 reprint), p. 174. The lectures were first published from Lahore in 1930.
[18] Iqbal, *Reconstruction*, p. 180.
[19] *Letters of Iqbal to Jinnah* (Lahore, 1963 reprint), p. 18.
[20] *Confederacy of India* (Lahore, 1939), pp. 198–9.

and oppression and injustice and to uphold those values which are essential for the maintenance of the world society in health and order and without which civilizations must perish.

Those of our brethren who have joined the Congress say that religion is out of date, that it is a medieval practice to found political groupings on religious distinctions. It may be true of other religions which supply cheap and spurious passports to heaven, which are but 'schemes of salvation' in the hereafter. But Islam is a polity, a complete plan of life in which there is no salvation in the thereafter unless one has worked one's salvation in the sphere by toiling for the salvation of one's fellow beings.[21]

Some of the *ʿulama*, including notably Shabbir Ahmad ʿUthmani (1887–1949), an *ʿalim* from Deoband, supported the Pakistan demand so that Muslims should be free to live according to the Holy Law of Islam, enforced as the orthodox *sunni* scholars understood it. In November 1945 at Calcutta, such *ʿulama* founded the *Jamʿiyyat al-ʿulama-i Islam* to campaign in support of the All-India Muslim League. They included Mufti Muhammad Shafiʿ, Maulana Ihtisham al-Haq Thanvi (both now in Pakistan) and Maulana ʿAbd al-Hamid Bada'uni (d. 1969). Several years earlier (probably in 1942) Maulana Shabbir Ahmad ʿUthmani had published an important pamphlet *Hamara Pakistan*, in which he looked forward to a Pakistan where the *shariʿa* ruled. He countered the argument that Pakistan would be run by irreligious Muslims, Westernised members of the Muslim League, by calling for religious men to join the League and thus ensure that Pakistan would be in the right hands.[22] He assured Muslims in the minority provinces who would remain in Hindustan that they would be safe, since the presence of substantial minorities on both sides of the Hindustan–Pakistan border would ensure fair treatment by the majority community.[23] Maulana ʿUthmani and his followers were undoubtedly of great assistance in winning over the Urdu-educated Muslim voter for the League. But even *ʿulama* opposed to Pakistan had helped condition Muslim voters in favour of the League.

[21] F. H. Khan Durrani, *The Future of Islam in India* (Lahore, 1946), pp. 73–4.
[22] Shabbir Ahmad ʿUthmani, *Hamara Pakistan* (Lahore, n.d.), pp. 65–6.
[23] ʿUthmani, *Hamara Pakistan*, pp. 44–5.

THE FAILURE OF THE ʿULAMA HOSTILE TO 'PAKISTAN'

The majority of Muslim voters were unsophisticated if not illiterate. They belonged to that stratum of society virtually untouched by Westernisation and by English education. They were susceptible to religious emotion and indeed had traditionally looked to *maulawi* and *mulla, pir* and *shaikh* for guidance. Now they listened to the Western-educated leadership of the Muslim League and to its supporters among the ʿ*ulama*, rather than to the ʿ*ulama* of Deoband, mustered under the banner of the *Jamʿiyyat al-ʿulama-i Hind*, who were opponents of partition and of Pakistan and supporters of the Indian National Congress. The election results of 1946 were a defeat for these ʿ*ulama*, religiously the most prestigious in British India.

It does not seem enough to ascribe the Muslim League's victory to the unscrupulous use by Muslim League campaigners of such slogans as '*Allahu Akbar*' or cries that a vote for Pakistan was a vote for Islam or that an opponent of the League was a *kafir*. Why could not the *Jamʿiyyat* offer more effective religious counter-slogans, more effective because coming from men of greater piety? Was it because only an educated and well-read person could detect the difference by 1946 between the programme of the *Jamʿiyyat* and that of the Muslim League?

Led by Maulana Husain Ahmad Madani (1879–1957), Mahmud al-Hasan's successor at Deoband, the *Jamʿiyyat al-ʿulama-i Hind* had campaigned against the Pakistan demand from the moment of the Lahore resolution. An 'Azad Muslim Conference' in April 1940, convened on behalf of the *Jamʿiyyat* and other organisations, declared 'India will have geographical and political boundaries of an individual whole and as such is the common homeland of all its citizens irrespective of race and religion who are joint owners of its resources... From the national point of view every Muslim is an Indian'.[24] Earlier, in 1938, in an exchange of letters with Sir Muhammad Iqbal, Madani said that the word *qaum* (community) could be applied to any collectivity whether its common characteristic was religion, common habitat, race, colour or craft. It should

---

[24] Quoted in: Ziya-ul-Hasan Faruqi, *The Deoband School and the Demand for Pakistan* (Bombay, 1963), p. 97.

The Muslims of British India

be distinguished from *millat*, which refers to a collectivity with a *shariᶜa* or din.[25] Indian Muslims were fellow-nationals with other communities and groups in India, though separate from them in religion. At present, he said, nations are made by homelands, as for instance England, where members of different faiths make up one nation.[26] Madani argued that freedom from British rule was necessary for the welfare of Islam, so that Muslim religious duties could be properly performed. The Muslims were not strong enough to win this freedom for themselves but needed the help of other and non-Muslim communities. He wanted independence for India in order that Muslims could freely express their religious personality, enjoy a really Islamic system of education and remove corruptions from their social life by abolishing British-made laws.[27] The *ᶜulama* would oppose Hindu Raj as fiercely as anyone.

Madani was violently critical of the claim that Pakistan would be an Islamic state. He castigated Jinnah and other leading Muslim Leaguers as men who not only were ignorant of Islam but also had displayed indifference to its Holy Law by not supporting the Shariat Act of 1937 giving preference in the courts of British India to the *shariᶜa* over local custom, and by not opposing interference with the Holy Law in the Dissolution of Muslim Marriages Bill of 1939.[28] He cited Jinnah himself as saying that Pakistan would have not a religious but rather a wordly government.[29] The *Jamᶜiyyat al-ᶜulama-i Hind* regarded the Muslim League's 'hostage' theory, that is that the presence of a minority of their co-religionists in the other's country was a guarantee of good treatment by the majority of the minority on both sides of the border, not only as political nonsense but also as contrary to the Muslim Holy Law. Furthermore, the hatred of Muslims which, in the nineteen-forties was already being generated by the demand for partition, together with the stirring up of feelings of contempt and fear towards Hindus, would render the peaceful spread of Islam by the *ᶜulama* impossible. Madani believed that the large increase in the Muslim population of India since the

[25] *Millat aur Qaum* (Multan, 1938), p. 9.
[26] *Millat aur Qaum*, p. 7.
[27] *Maktubat-i Shaikh al-Islam*, vol. II (Delhi, 1954), pp. 70–3, *passim*.
[28] Husain Ahmad Madani, *Congress, Muslim League aur Jamiᶜat al-ᶜulama ki Siyasi Position* (Lucknow, 1945), p. 15.
[29] Husain Ahmad Madani, *Pakistan Kya Hai*, part II (Delhi, 1946), p. 11.

end of Muslim rule – he put it at 400 per cent – was attributable to this peaceful missionary activity.[30]

The *ulama* of the *Jam'iyyat* then did not lack a case to argue against Pakistan. Yet they failed to put it across to the mass of Muslim voters. Partly this was because they found it difficult to speak and write other than as scholars. With their sincere and simple faith that as Islam had not been suffered to fail among men in British India so it would not be suffered to fail among men in independent India,[31] they did not fully enter into the fears of the ordinary Muslim, faced daily with the realities of Hindu exclusiveness. Nor were they masters of modern methods of publicity and propaganda. Moreover, from the collapse of the *Khilafat* movement onwards, their political activity was spasmodic. In the middle nineteen-twenties the energies of many *ulama* were diverted to the *tanzim* and *tabligh* movements and in the early nineteen-thirties into sectarian *sunni–shi'a* controversy. In Lucknow there was a series of bloody *sunni–shi'a* riots. The *sunni 'ulama* founded in Lucknow in 1931 a militant seminary, the *Dar al-Mubalighin*, in order to controvert *shi'i* doctrines. The *'ulama* were drawn from and were supported mainly by the poorer sections of Muslim society; what funds they did possess were divided between religious and political activity. Dependence upon Congress funds only brought charges of selling their souls for a mess of Hindu pottage.

By 1945–6 the unsophisticated Muslim voter might well wonder whether what the *'ulama* of the *Jam'iyyat* and the Muslim League were offering him differed only in the wrapping. The Muslim League was offering him the physical and mental partition of India; the *'ulama* were offering him the mental partition of India. The former was prepared to cut through the map of British India, the latter to scarify it. During the *Khilafat* movement the *'ulama* had stood for the nomocratic partition of India, for an India whose peoples would live under their own religious law and have little life in common. By 1927 the *Jam'iyyat al-'ulama-i Hind*'s stand on communal electorates, the creation of a separate province of Sind, Muslim representation at the centre and a constitutional bar to

[30] Maulana Muhammad Miyan, *'Ulama-i Haq*, vol. II (Delhi, 1948), pp. 340–1.

[31] Impression gained from remarks made by leading Deobandi *'ulama* to the author at Deoband in December 1960.

discussion of any subject objected to by three-quarters of the representatives of any community, was the same as that of the modern Muslim politician.[32] In August 1928, the *Jamᶜiyyat* rejected the Nehru Report on the grounds that it did not give enough autonomy to the provinces, did not safeguard adequately the Muslim majority position in Bengal and the Panjab, and did not give Muslims sufficient representation at the centre. In December 1928 their fourteen-point reply to the Nehru Report was in terms almost identical to those of Jinnah's fourteen points. In August 1931 at Saharanpur the *ᶜulama* spelt out their religious *imperium in imperio*. The government of independent India would have no power to interfere with the culture of the various *millats*, their places of worship and religious endowments; a supreme court must be set up to safeguard the rights of the different *millats*; an independent system of courts under *qazis* must be set up to administer Islamic law.[33] The *ᶜulama's* specific was a 'Pakistan' of *fiqh* and *shariᶜa*.

Fiercely though the *Jamᶜiyyat al-ᶜulama-i Hind* resisted the partition resolution of March 1940, they gradually edged nearer the Muslim League's position. Although at the time of the Cripps offer in March 1942 the *Jamᶜiyyat* joined with Congress in demanding independence for India at once, they also demanded complete autonomy for the provinces. In supporting the Congress 'Quit India' resolution, they declared their bitter opposition to 'Hindu Raj'. In May 1945 in again demanding complete independence for India they stood out for a minimal federal government and practically complete autonomy for the provinces.[34] The ordinary Muslim voter could be forgiven for thinking that if the so-called nationalist *ᶜulama* so lacked confidence themselves in the majority community as to demand these extreme safeguards for his religion and culture, then he might as well have Pakistan. The *Jamᶜiyyat al-ᶜulama-i Hind* had themselves publicly proclaimed that they considered Muslims' religious freedom to keep their own distinctive culture to be more important than Muslims' political freedom.[35]

[32] *Jamᶜiyyat al-ᶜulama Kya Hai?*, pt. II, p. 146.
[33] *Jamᶜiyyat al-ᶜulama Kya Hai?*, pt. II, pp. 179–80.
[34] *Jamᶜiyyat al-ᶜulama Kya Hai?*, pt. II, pp. 273–4.
[35] *Jamᶜiyyat al-ᶜulama Kya Hai?*, vol. II, (Delhi, n.d.), p. 15.

THE YEARS OF POLITICAL DECISION 1946-7

The negotiating hand with which Jinnah confronted the British and Congress in 1946 after his victory at the polls was a strong one. He believed, correctly as is now known, that the British really intended to go and that they would not use force to deny him Pakistan. He had complete control of the League in both the Muslim minority and majority provinces and could enter into binding commitments. Moreover he was operating in a situation where the options that were open (on the assumption that the British did not mean to stay) had been narrowed down to two – either a very loosely-federated free India with most powers inhering in the provinces, or some form of Pakistan. As early as April 1942 Congress had declared that it could not think in terms of 'compelling the people of any territorial unit to remain in an Indian Union against their declared and established will'. During the Gandhi–Jinnah talks of 1944, Gandhi had shown himself willing, in the last resort, to concede the 'maimed, mutilated and moth-eaten' Pakistan of Sind, Baluchistan and the North-Western Frontier Province, with only the Muslim majority areas in Panjab, Bengal and Assam.

The principal weakness in Jinnah's negotiating position was the Lahore resolution of March 1940 itself, which conceded the necessity of territorial adjustments to and the demarcation of geographically contiguous areas for any Pakistan that might be agreed. The two-nation theory itself was a two-edged sword, for every argument which could be advanced to demand a homeland for a distinct Muslim nation could also be advanced to deny that members of the other nation should be included in the territory of that Muslim nation. Away from the conference room, Jinnah's weakness was the fact that Muslims were a minority in British India and though he might be able to deny others the kind of settlement they wished, he was unable to impose his own on them.

In March 1946, when the British government in London sent a Cabinet Mission composed of Lord Pethick-Lawrence (1871–1961), Sir Stafford Cripps and A. V. Alexander (1885–1965) to seek an agreed plan for handing over power, Jinnah uncompromisingly demanded the full six-province Pakistan. Finding Congress adamant in its opposition to this demand, the Cabinet Mission went ahead with proposals for a three-tiered federation in which the six

'Pakistan provinces' would, as two eastern and western groups of provinces, be but minimally subordinate in foreign affairs, defence and communications in an Indian Union. On 11 May 1946, the Muslim League proposed a Union of a Pakistan group and of a Hindu group of provinces, which would have parity of representation in a confederal Union authority limited to just those subjects. Jinnah was determined to avoid being forced into a cul-de-sac.

On 16 May 1946 the Cabinet Mission published its own plan for a three-tiered Indian Union in which provinces would be free to form sections and to determine what subjects should be under the jurisdiction of a section government. A constituent assembly would be formed of representatives drawn from the existing provincial assemblies, which would immediately divide into a Section A including Madras, Bombay, the Central Provinces, the United Provinces and Bihar, a Section B including the North-West Frontier Province, Panjab and Sind, and a Section C which would include Bengal and Assam. Each section would decide both upon the constitution of each of its provinces and upon a constitution for the section as a whole. In a subsequent statement the Cabinet Mission laid down that no province could opt out of its section *before* the provincial and sectional constitutions had been drawn up. In effect, the proposed sections B and C would have given the Muslim League two semi-autonomous 'big' Pakistans, within a minimal federation in which there would be strong barriers to encroachment by the Union authority upon the powers of the sections. This constitutional plan was coupled with a proposal to form an interim government at the centre, representative of the major political organisations of British India.

On 6 June 1946 the Council of the Muslim League accepted the Cabinet Mission plan, after Jinnah had obtained an assurance from Lord Wavell that if the League accepted the plan and Congress subsequently rejected it, the League would, in terms of the statement of 16 May 1946, be brought into the new interim government. Jinnah's motives in apparently resiling from the full Pakistan demand have been convincingly explained by M. A. H. Ispahani (1902–) a prominent member of the Working Committee of the League.[36] The Cabinet Mission plan yielded the substance of a

[36] M. A. H. Ispahani, *Qaid-e-Azam Jinnah As I Knew Him*, second ed. (Karachi, 1967), p. 221.

'big' Pakistan with sufficient safeguards against interference by the Union authority, which would be confined to foreign affairs, defence and communications. Any constitution drawn up under the plan, whether for the Union, for the sections or for the provinces, would be open to revision at the end of ten years, which implied freedom for provinces and sections to leave the Union. The Muslim majority in sections B and C would be in a position to obtain safeguards for the Muslims of the Hindu majority provinces – a consideration which doubtless made the Cabinet Mission's plan attractive to the League's U.P. leaders.

The Indian National Congress also accepted the plan, with reservations, but rejected the proposal to join an interim government. Then, on 10 July, Nehru repudiated any compulsory grouping of provinces into sections. Earlier, on 25 June 1946, the Cabinet Mission had informed Jinnah that the League would not be invited into an interim government as Congress was not willing also to join it. Jinnah decided that the time had come to read both Congress and the British government a lesson in the realities of power; he believed that the latter had gone back on Wavell's undertaking, that parties accepting the Cabinet Mission plan and the interim government proposal would be invited to enter an interim government even though other parties had not accepted, because they formed a Congress rebellion. On 29 July 1946 the Council of the Muslim League formally withdrew acceptance of the Cabinet Mission plan and decided on (undefined) 'direct action', calling upon Muslims to observe 16 August 1946 as 'direct action day'. Jinnah himself publicly said his farewell to constitutional methods.

There followed the Great Calcutta Killing from 16 to 20 August 1946, when in a hysteria of communal hatred at least 4,000 were killed and 15,000 wounded. The killing of about 7,000 Muslims in Bihar and a smaller number of Hindus in the Noakhali district of Bengal ensued. British India was on the brink of civil war. Meanwhile, in August 1946, Nehru had formed an interim government which the League declined to join. In October 1946, however, fearing that Congress in office would steal a march on the League, Jinnah consented that his right-hand man, Liaqat ʿAli Khan (1895–1951), and other members of the League should enter the interim government. But with Jinnah refusing to participate in a Constituent Assembly under the Cabinet Mission plan, and Congress refusing to accept compulsory grouping of provinces, progress towards a constitutional settlement was completely blocked.

On 20 February 1947 the British Prime Minister, Clement Attlee (1883–1967), in an attempt to break the deadlock, announced that Britain would transfer power in India in any event by June 1948 and that Lord Louis Mountbatten (1900–) was to be sent out as the last Viceroy of India. By the time of his arrival at Delhi on 22 March 1947, a sea-change had taken place in the political situation in India. Wearied by the frustrations of trying to govern in harness with the League in the interim government, and dismayed by the revelation of the potential for disruption of a determined minority in a united India, on 5 March the Working Committee of Congress had come round to an acceptance of partition of the Panjab and of Bengal as a *pis aller*. The Congress attitude was now that if partition had to be conceded, it should leave Pakistan the minimum compatible with the principle of separate statehood for contiguous Muslim majority districts – the 'maimed, mutilated and moth-eaten' Pakistan. Although Jinnah publicly protested against any suggestion of the partition of Bengal and the Panjab, his attitude in March 1947 was probably that expressed in a reported remark to Lord Mountbatten at their first interview: 'I do not care how little you give me as long as you give it to me completely'.[37] Events in the Panjab had underlined the problems of ruling a province which Muslims would in a 'big' Pakistan have to share with non-Muslim minorities of over 40 per cent.

Following Attlee's announcement of 20 February 1947, which portended a possible demission of power to the provincial governments of the time of such demission, the Muslim League in the Panjab, by a campaign of non-co-operation, had forced the resignation on 2 March of the coalition government of Khizr Hayat Khan Tiwana, supported by Congress, the Sikhs and the remaining handful of Muslim Unionists. But with seventy-nine of the eighty-six Muslim seats in an assembly of 175 seats, it was impossible for the Muslim League to form a government and, amid anti-Muslim riots by Sikhs and Hindus, Governor's rule had to be imposed. Even if, after a Pakistan was created, Muslims acquired a dominant position in the political machinery of the Panjab, this violent Sikh and Hindu reaction was a foretaste of political life in an undivided Panjab.

Lord Mountbatten quickly discovered that the Cabinet Mission plan was beyond resuscitation and that all major parties were ready for a deal. He rapidly drew up a plan for the devolution of power to provinces initially independent, with provision for the Muslim and Hindu majority districts of the Panjab and Bengal to determine their future. This scheme was shown privately to Nehru after it had already been taken to London, and produced a horrified reaction. Nehru felt that it was tantamount to the Balkanisation of India and an encouragement to any and all separatist tendencies. Lord Mountbatten promptly changed course and, with the aid of the Reforms Secretary to the Government of India, V. P. Menon (1894–1966), drew up a new plan for the transfer of power to two successor Dominions of the Commonwealth, India and Pakistan, each with a centre government constituted with the powers (until such time as new constitutions should be formulated) of the centre under the Government of India Act of 1935. Bengal and the Panjab would be partitioned, should one of the two groups of the representatives of the Muslim and Hindu majority districts in the Panjab Provincial Assembly, sitting separately, so decide. The actual line of demarcation between Hindu and Muslim majority districts would be determined later by a boundary commission.

This partition plan, presented to the Indian political leaders by Lord Mountbatten on 2 June 1947, was a bitter pill for Jinnah to swallow. It represented the disappointment of all those hopes of a 'big' Pakistan which had beguiled many Muslim voters in the elections of 1945–6. Opposition to acceptance within the League appears to have been considerable, for Jinnah would not record his acceptance in writing but only by a silent nod when Lord Mountbatten, on 3 June 1947, said in the presence of the Congress and Sikh leaders that he had received verbal assurances of acceptance from Mr Jinnah. Since then surviving leaders of the Muslim League have maintained a studied silence. Their bitterness against Congress and the British for denying them the full six-province Pakistan is perhaps a measure of their disappointment.

For Jinnah, who played the game of politics with the men actually on the chess board, acceptance of a 'moth-eaten' Pakistan was recognition that in the circumstances of June 1947 that was all he could expect to obtain. He knew that the Muslim League Premier of undivided Bengal, H. S. Suhrawardi, was putting out feelers to the provincial Hindu leaders for an independent and united Bengal and he knew that without a League government in the Panjab, and in the absence of agreement with Congress, a Pakistani Panjab might have to be fought for. As a lawyer he recognised that the partition plan gave the two wings of Pakistan a legally strong central government. The British were determined to go without fighting for anyone or anything except the safe evacuation of their nationals from India; if he did not grasp the power they still had to offer, there might soon be no power to grasp. With the Indian army in June 1947 still undivided into Muslim and non-Muslim units, he had no means to seize the 'big' Pakistan by force. In the end the great negotiator and constitutionalist had to accept the limits of negotiation and decision by agreement imposed upon those who must perforce enter the conference chamber naked of military power. Paradoxically, it was a supreme bargainer, the son of Muslim traders, who won statehood for those whom so many, Hindus as well as British, believed to be the fighters of British India.

By 1947, then, the enfranchised Muslims of British India had recorded their conviction that the things which they did not share with their non-Muslim neighbours were more important than the things which they did share, and that this conviction required political expression in the partition of the sub-continent and the creation of Pakistan. Pride of past power (even among those whose ancestors had not shared that power), religious revivalism and fear of the Hindu had done their work. The British and the Hindus between them had destroyed the illusion that the Muslim in pre-British times had been able to cherish – that India was a Muslim land. The modern Muslim refused to accept the reality and the implications of that reality, that under the shibboleths of democracy and majority rule the whole of British India could never be a *dar al-Islam*. In the abstract he might have forgotten what it meant to be a Muslim except on Fridays and on feast days, but his own religious teachers, whether the *ʿulama*, the revivalists or the modernists, would not let him do so. Nor would the British, who needed him as an 'interest' to be balanced against other 'interests' in British India. Nor, in the last resort would the Hindu with his own revivalist movements and his social exclusiveness.

A sense of equal commitment to and equal participation in a society with a steadily widening area of common concern was not allowed to grow; perhaps it could never have grown – we shall never know. Medieval precedents were of little relevance. Power had not been popular in its foundation and neither government nor law had assumed a dynamic society in which men would jointly will to change their social environment. The British taught much that proved fearsome, notably the Austinian notion of legal sovereignty, which they exemplified in their own parliament at Westminster and in their own codes of law in India; it was too late in the nineteen-twenties and thirties, with socialism and communism in the air, to teach the legal limitation of powers and the diffusion of authority, perhaps the only safeguard of minority cultures in plural societies. Moreover Muslims in British India themselves were not content to be a minority, however secure; the most educated of them knew that their faith required them to be in command of history and, with the vicarious memory of empire behind them, most of them were confident enough to seize the opportunity to be so.

Only time could tell whether the religious passions, the ethical aspirations, the economic and social egoisms and the fears and hatreds which compounded Pakistani nationalism in 1947 would suffice to mature that nationalism into nationhood. The exclusion from the new state of about thirty-six million Muslims (including those in the Indian States) left in the Dominion (later Republic) of India, confronted thinking Pakistanis with dilemmas of their own identity and of their relationship with their past. Other than the fact of their inhabiting contiguous Muslim majority areas, what exactly was it that had conferred independent statehood upon them? Classical doctrines of the Islamic religious community living independently under divine law and with rulers of its own determination, and modern doctrines that culturally distinctive peoples should enjoy political self-determination could be deployed to justify independent statehood for all the Muslims of British India. Yet some had been granted statehood and others denied it, apparently for no other reasons than those of political expediency.

Although beset by uncertainty as to why they were as they were, and, in varying degrees, conscious of the paradoxes inherent in separate statehood for less than the totality of British India's Muslims, most Pakistanis were ready to react fiercely, and to support their rulers in reacting fiercely, as any proud newly-independent people would, to any outside challenge to what they were, namely possessors of political independence within one state embracing two wings, in the west and in the east. But for those landowning, military and bureaucratic elements which, with support drawn mainly from the west wing, dominated between 1947 and 1971 the two-wing Pakistan of the Mountbatten deal, the possession and retention of the political independence of that Pakistan were ends sufficient unto themselves to be secured by every and any means, including the use of violence against fellow Muslim citizens. These elements acted, whether under the charismatic régime of Jinnah which ended with his death in September 1948, or under the quasi-parliamentary, bureaucratic-military régimes thereafter until General Yahya Khan's fall in December 1971, as though the Pakistan of 1947 was created to serve only their interests.

The majority of the Muslims of the east wing gradually refused to acknowledge that they must accept a version of statehood which suited only the ideas and the interests of the ruling elements in the west wing. Before the new state was ten years old the Bengali-speaking Muslims of Pakistan discovered that a political independence of non-Muslims, nourished initially on religious beliefs and antipathies which they believed they shared with the Muslims of the west wing, was not a prelude to a true community of hearts and interests across the thousand miles physically separating both wings. In 1971 the majority of the politically conscious Muslims of the east wing demonstrated that they considered the price of maintaining the Pakistan of 1947 to be too high at the level of continued acquiescence in the political, economic and social inequalities between the two wings of that Pakistan. By welcoming the very-ready assistance of the Republic of India in securing their independence from the west wing of Pakistan (and by turning on Muslims from outside), the Muslims of the east wing have added yet another dimension to the question of what are the political implications of being a Muslim in the sub-continent in the twentieth century. The quest for identity satisfying in spiritual and temporal terms remains today as agonising as most thinking Muslims found it before 1947.

For the Muslims of the new Dominion (after 1951, Republic) of India, Pakistan was not even a Pyrrhic victory, it was a victory which turned into defeat at the very moment of being gained. They had, by their votes in 1945-6, proclaimed that Islam and Muslims must, in the twentieth-century, have their own state in order to be fulfilled. But after 1947 the Muslims of India have been obliged to live a version of Islam and of Muslim life in which that fulfilment is denied to them.

Whatever the history of the Muslims of British India in general and the events leading to the partition of 1947 in particular have settled, it is not the problem of how God is to be obeyed in the modern world in the idiom nearly all Muslims agree He has commanded – that is, in and through the public and social life of a world-wide community of believers. History has denied to Muslims, and nowhere more brusquely than in what is now called, outside the Republic of India, 'the Indo-Pakistan sub-continent', the political unity and the exclusive political power which most instructed Muslims have taken to be (whether rightly or wrongly in Allah's sight is not for the non-Muslim to judge) the necessary condition for obedience in this idiom. The question still exercising the aspiring Muslim in the Republic of India, namely whether in wanting to be accepted as a fellow citizen on equal terms with his non-Muslim compatriots, he is obeying or disobeying Divine Command, is one to which, twenty-five years after the partition of British India, no answer appears to have emerged which is acceptable to a consensus of his islamically-informed and concerned leaders and guides. Perhaps, as has happened before in Muslim history, the Muslims of the Republic of India will show forth the answer in their lives, doubtless for a considerable time before that answer is recognised as such.

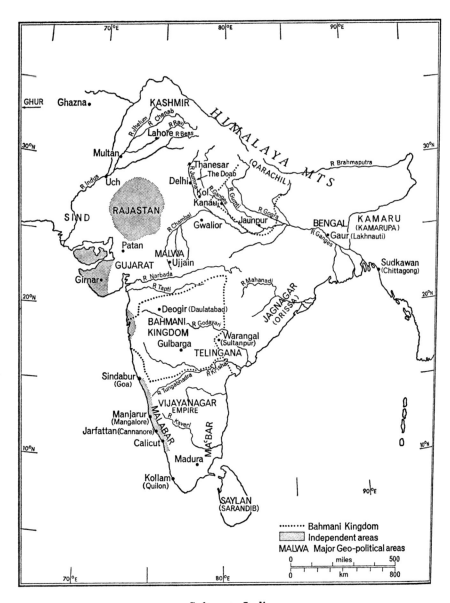

Sultanate India

NOTE: the Jaunpur sultanate is indicated by the dotted line in the north.

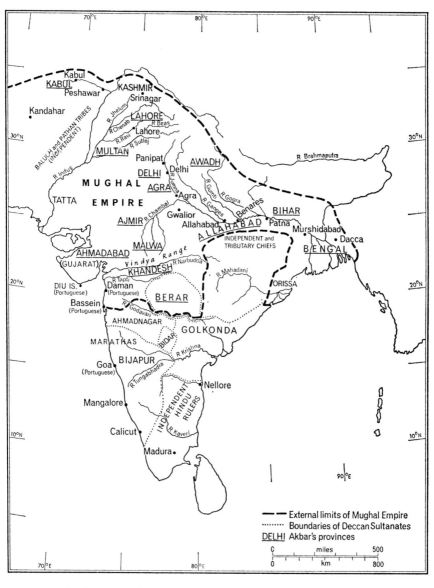

Muslim power in Mughal times at its widest effective extent

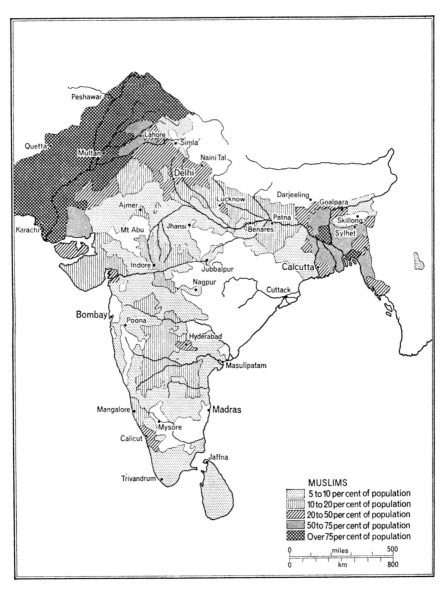

Muslim population-proportions in British India (1931)

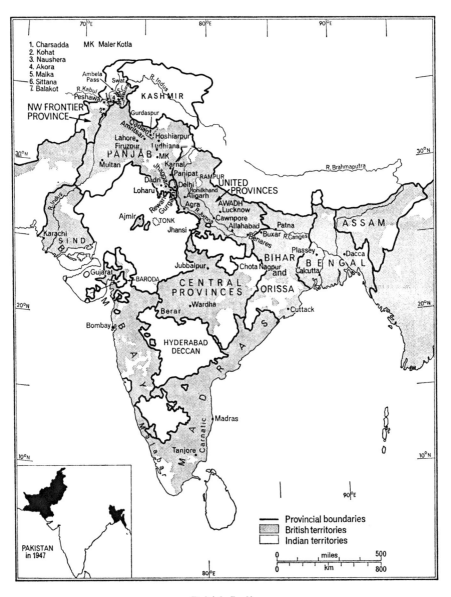

British India

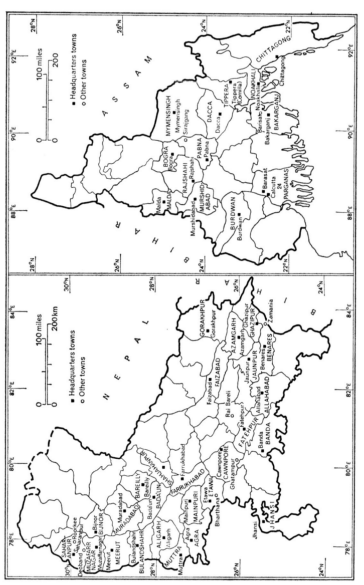

The North-Western Provinces and Bengal (showing principal districts and headquarters towns mentioned in the text)

A DESCRIPTIVE BIBLIOGRAPHY
OF WORKS IN EUROPEAN LANGUAGES

Largely for political reasons – the British urge to establish the superior quality of their rule over Muslim, the Muslims' own search for their identity in modern South Asia and the Hindu debate whether to regard Muslims as brother freedom fighters or as deposed conquerors – the study of Islam and of Muslims in South Asia is as yet neither as disciplined, dispassionate nor as sophisticated as the study of Islam and of Muslims in the classical lands of Islam. Thus no bibliographical work equivalent to J. Sauvaget, *Introduction à l'histoire de l'orient musulman* has been published specifically for Islam in South Asia. The source material in Persian histories and biographies has been exhaustively catalogued in C. A. Storey, *Persian Literature: A Bio-Bibliographical Survey*, Section 11, fasciculus 3 M. *History of India*, London, 1939 and *Biographies, Additions and Corrections, ibid.*, vol. II, part 2, London, 1953. A conspectus of the administrative literature for the earlier Mughal period is to be found in Irfan Habib, *The Agrarian System of the Mughal Empire (1556–1707)*, London, 1963, which also contains a first-rate bibliography of the European travellers' accounts in the period. Ishtiaq Husain Qureshi, *The Administration of the Sultanate of Delhi*, Lahore, 1942, contains a valuable list of the medieval Muslim writing on polity and administration. Recent attempts to catalogue the resources in languages other than Persian have been made in P. Saran, *Descriptive Catalogue of Non-Persian Sources of Medieval Indian History*, London, 1965 and D. N. Marshall, *Mughal India: A Bibliographical Survey*, vol. I, *Manuscripts*, London, 1967. For periodical literature J. D. Pearson, *Index Islamicus 1906–1955*, Cambridge, 1958, with the two supplements for 1956–60 and 1961–5 (Cambridge, 1962 and 1967) is indispensable.

For the modern period Muin ud-din Ahmad Khan, *A Bibliographical Introduction to Modern Islamic Development in India and Pakistan 1700–1955*, Appendix to the *Journal of the Asiatic Society of Pakistan*, Dacca, 1959, is useful though incomplete.

GENERAL HISTORIES AND SURVEYS

The best-balanced accounts of Muslim fortunes and problems by British scholars writing general histories of India are to be found in W. H. Moreland and A. Chatterjee, *A Short History of India*, London, 1936 (Moreland wrote the portion on the medieval Muslim period); Percival Spear, *India, Pakistan and the West*, first edition, London, 1949, *India: a Modern History*, Ann Arbor, 1961 and *A History of India*, vol. 11, Harmondsworth, 1965.

The following are indispensable to an understanding of the different ways in which modern Muslims have viewed Muslim history and destiny in South Asia:

Ishtiaq Husain Qureshi, *The Muslim Community of the Indo–Pakistan Subcontinent (610–1947)*, 'S-Gravenhage, 1962.

M. Mujeeb, *The Indian Muslims*, London, 1967.

Aziz Ahmad, *Studies in Islamic Culture in the Indian Environment*, Oxford, 1964.

S. Abid Husain, *The National Culture of India*, Bombay, 1956; *The Destiny of Indian Muslims*, London, 1965.

Examples of different Hindu approaches to Muslim history may be found in:

R. C. Majumdar (ed.), *The Delhi Sultanate*, Bombay, 1960; Tara Chand, *History of the Freedom Movement in India*, vol. 1, Delhi, 1961, vol. 11, Delhi, 1967, and *The Influence of Islam on Indian Culture*, Allahabad, 1936, and in the many works by A. L. Srivastava on the Muslim period.

MUSLIM POLITICAL HISTORY BEFORE THE BRITISH PERIOD

Following the traditions of the Persian medieval histories themselves, most political histories of medieval India under Muslim rule have followed the narrative genre, with occasional bows in the direction of administrative and social history. Although such a work as *The Delhi Sultanate* (see above) includes chapters on religious, legal, literary and aesthetic history, it does not achieve a genuine synthesis. The methods of Marx and Weber are known, perhaps understood, but in political history, with the exception of 'the Aligarh school', not applied. The 'rulers of India' approach of a well-known British series of the late nineteenth century is still much in evidence.

On the period of conquest, A. B. M. Habibullah, *The Foundation of*

Muslim Rule in India, second ed., Allahabad, 1961, is much the best. The remainder of the political history of the 'sultanate' period in north India is covered in narrative form in K. S. Lal, *History of the Khaljis* (1290–1320), Allahabad, 1950; Agha Mahdi Husain, *Tughluq Dynasty*, Calcutta, 1963, and K. S. Lal, *The Twilight of the Sultanate*, Bombay, 1963. The principal provincial sultanates are treated in M. S. Commissariat, *A History of Gujarat*, vol. 1, London, 1938, vol. 11, Bombay, 1957; H. K. Sherwani, *The Bahmanis of the Deccan*, Hyderabad, 1953, Upendra Nath Day, *Medieval Malwa*, Delhi, 1965; Sir Jadunath Sarkar (ed.), *History of Bengal*, vol. 11, *Muslim Period*, Dacca, 1948 and Mohibbul Hasan, *Kashmir under the Sultans*, Calcutta, 1959.

The political history of the Mughal period broadly follows dynastic chronology. The best attempt to see Babur against the Central Asian social background is in F. Grenard, *Baber*, Paris, 1930, but still worth reading on his campaigns in India is L. F. Rushbrook Williams, *An Empire Builder of the Sixteenth Century*, London, 1918. Humayun is effectively depicted in Ishwari Prasad, *The Life and Times of Humayun*, Bombay, 1955. The Afghan 'comeback' under Sher Shah Sur is described by K. R. Qanungo, *Sher Shah*, Calcutta, 1921.

Akbar has not yet found a biographer or historian to match his genius. Vincent Smith, *Akbar the Great Mogul*, Oxford, 1927, just manages to place him at about the level of the average British viceroy and is ill-informed on Islam. A. L. Srivastava, *Akbar the Great* (two vols), Agra, 1962 and 1967 is more sympathetic to Akbar though not to Islam and covers Akbar's political institutions also. On Jahangir, Beni Prasad, *Jahangir*, London, 1922 and on Shah Jahan, Banarsi Prasad Saksena, *History of Shahjahan of Dihli*, Allahabad, 1932, are pedestrian. Aurangzib is a figure of controversy in that his orthodoxy has been blamed for the decline of the Mughal empire. Sir Jadunath Sarkar's monumental *History of Aurangzib* in five volumes (Calcutta, 1912–24) depicts Aurangzib as failing to live up to Victorian standards, while Zahir ud-din Faruki, *Aurangzeb and his Times*, Bombay, 1935 is an apologetic, important in that it brings arguments for Aurangzib already expressed in Urdu writings to the notice of the English reader. The religious issue between him and his eldest brother Dara Shikuh is discussed in K. R. Qanungo, *Dara Shikoh*, second ed., Calcutta, 1952.

Irvine has painstakingly chronicled the events of the period 1707 to 1740 in his *Later Mughals*, two volumes, London and Calcutta, 1922 and Sir Jadunath Sarkar has finished off the chronicle of woe in his *Fall of the Mughal Empire*, four volumes, Calcutta, 1932–50. Rather more analytical is Satish Chandra, *Parties and Politics at the Mughal*

Court, 1707–1740, Aligarh, 1959. W. Irvine's edition of Nicolao Manucci's *Storio do Mogor,* four volumes, London, 1907–8, conveys the atmosphere of the Mughal court circle better than any of the narrative histories listed. The personalities of Babur and Jahangir come to life in their personal memoirs, the *Babur Nama,* translated in two volumes by Annette Beveridge, London, 1921 (reprinted in one volume, 1969) and in the *Tuzuk-i Jahangiri,* translated by A. Rogers and edited by H. Beveridge in two volumes, London, 1909 and 1914.

RELIGIOUS HISTORY IN THE MEDIEVAL PERIOD

Apart from chapters in T. W. Arnold, *The Preaching of Islam,* second edition, London, 1913, there has been little British contribution to this area of study. The outstanding contributions have been made in recent years by Indian and Pakistani scholars, who, however, have not been altogether free from political prepossessions. Some have regarded Pakistan as an inevitable expression, under modern conditions, of Muslim religious urges, others have regarded political separatism as the outcome of only one strand of thought and that not the dominant strand, in medieval Indian Islam. Central to the whole field of study has been Muslim mysticism, treated by some as the Muslim version of Hindu urges towards *ahimsa* and as responsible for most conversions to Islam, and by others as the Trojan horse within Islam in South Asia. In addition to the works by Mujeeb, Abid Husain, Aziz Ahmad and Ishtiaq Husain Qureshi already mentioned, the following should be consulted:

Murray T. Titus, *Islam in India and Pakistan,* Calcutta, 1959.

Khaliq Ahmad Nizami, *Some Aspects of Religion and Politics in India during the Thirteenth Century,* Aligarh, 1961.

Burhan Ahmad Faruqi, *The Mujaddid's Conception of Tauhid,* Lahore, 1940.

J. Spencer Trimingham, *The Sufi Orders in Islam,* Oxford, 1971.

Saiyid Athar Abbas Rizvi, *Muslim Revivalist Movements in Northern India in the Sixteenth and Seventeenth Centuries,* Agra, 1965.

Yusuf Husain, *L'Inde mystique au moyen âge, Hindoues et Musalmans,* Paris, 1929.

Dr Rizvi's work contains an exhaustive bibliography for the area of study.

THE GOVERNMENT AND RELIGION IN THE MEDIEVAL WORLD

The general background of Muslim legal and 'political' ideas needs to be studied as a prelude to Muslim thinking in South Asia. N. J. Coulson, *A History of Islamic Law*, Edinburgh, 1964, Louis Gardet, *La Cité musulmane*, Paris, 1954, T. W. Arnold, *The Caliphate* Oxford, 1924, E. I. J. Rosenthal, *Political Thought in Medieval Islam*, Cambridge, 1958 and W. Montgomery Watt, *Islamic Political Thought*, Edinburgh, 1968 will be found useful. Some indications of the main lines of thought in medieval India are given in P. Hardy, 'Islam in Medieval India' in *Sources of Indian Tradition*, ed. W. Theodore de Bary, New York, 1958, while the ideas of Ziya al-din Barani are presented by M. Habib and Afsar Umar Salim Khan, *The Political Theory of the Delhi Sultanate*, Allahabad, 1960. The connection between Indo-Persian historical writing and the dominant 'pious sultan' theories of the pre-Mughal period is discussed in P. Hardy, *Historians of Medieval India*, London, 1960. The religious activities and policies of the Mughals have been authoritatively treated in Sri Ram Sharma, *The Religious Policy of the Mughal Emperors*, second edition, London, 1962, and in Makhanlal Roychaudhuri, *The Din-i-Ilahi*, Calcutta, 1941 and *The State and Religion in Mughal India*, Calcutta, 1951.

ECONOMIC HISTORY IN THE MEDIEVAL PERIOD

Except perhaps for office holders and those receiving largesse from government, it is impossible to separate the economic fortunes of Muslims from those of the other peoples of India in the medieval period. Most works on economic history are in fact works on the history of political economy, specifically of agrarian policies, during the period of Muslim domination. By reason of the continuing concern with the standard of life of the rural population, some distinguished work has been accomplished in this sphere. The great pioneer was W. H. Moreland, with his *Agrarian System of Moslem India*, Cambridge, 1929. He has had a brilliant successor in Irfan Habib, *The Agrarian System of the Mughal Empire 1556–1707*, London, 1963 (in which, incidentally, the exhaustive bibliography includes a useful list of European travellers' accounts of the Mughal empire). For the period 1700–50 see the recent Noman Ahmad Siddiqi, *Land Revenue Administration under the Mughals (1700–1750)*, London, 1970, which curiously does not refer to Irfan Habib's work. W. H. Moreland has also pioneered the wider study of Mughal economic history in his

India at the Death of Akbar, London, 1920, and *From Akbar to Aurangzeb*, London, 1923. All these works convey more of the spirit and organisation of Muslim governments than do most of the political and administrative histories.

SOCIAL HISTORY IN THE MEDIEVAL PERIOD

Social history is very popular these days among scholars of medieval India in the Muslim presence, but the output of significant monographs is negligible. Kunwar Muhammad Ashraf, *The Life and Conditions of the People of Hindustan 1200 to 1556*, second edition, New Delhi, 1970, deals only with Muslim society; it contains valuable reflections on the institution of the sultanate. Mohammad Yasin, *A Social History of Islamic India 1605–1748*, Lucknow, 1958 is rather discursive and contains ideological matter not suited to social history. However inaccurate in details and however given to the repetition of bazaar tittle-tattle, travellers' accounts best convey the social atmosphere of medieval times. The Indian portion of Ibn Battuta's *Rihla*, translated by Agha Mahdi Husain in one volume, Baroda, 1953, is good reading; for the Mughal period see Irfan Habib's bibliography referred to above.

POLITICAL AND MILITARY INSTITUTIONS OF THE MEDIEVAL PERIOD

For the Delhi sultanate see: Ishtiaq Husain Qureshi, *The Administration of the Sultanate of Delhi*, Lahore, 1942; the author is somewhat inclined to assume the ideal to have been the actual and that it is possible to argue from practice in the Muslim world outside India to practice inside India. The work includes a most valuable bibliography. For the Mughal period, Ibn Hasan, *The Central Structure of the Mughal Empire*, London, 1936, P. Saran, *The Provincial Government of the Mughals (1526–1658)*, Allahabad, 1941, Jadunath Sarkar, *Mughal Administration*, Calcutta, 1920 are all authoritative accounts of the structure of the administration. The *mansabdari* system is described in Abdul Aziz, *The Mansabdari System and the Mughal Army*, Lahore, 1945, while Athar Ali, *The Mughal Nobility under Aurangzeb*, Aligarh, 1966, has transformed our knowledge of the office-holding classes and their *rôle* in the political life of Aurangzeb's time and provides an important index to current economic and social interpretations of the stresses of the later Mughal empire. For the organisation of the later Mughal army as a fighting force, W. Irvine, *The Army of the Indian Mughals*, London, 1903, still holds the field.

As the Jaipur and Hyderabad (Deccan) archives are mined so know-ledge of the administrative history of the later Mughal period is likely to be transformed.

MUGHAL CULTURE

Useful comments, particularly on Persian and Urdu literature, and bibliography are given in Aziz Ahmad, *Studies in Islamic Culture in the Indian Environment*, Oxford, 1964 and *An Intellectual History of Islam in India*, Edinburgh, 1969. Percy Brown, *Indian Painting under the Mughals A.D. 1550 to A.D. 1750*, Oxford, 1924 and *Indian Architecture (Islamic Period)*, fourth edition, Bombay, 1964 are classics in their respective fields. To them should be added: Ivan Stchoukine, *La Peinture indienne a l'époque des grands moghols*, Paris, 1929 and S. C. Welch, *The Art of Mughal India*, New York, 1963. Muhammad Sadiq, *A History of Urdu Literature*, London, 1964 is the best of the general accounts, though its literary judgements are far from being shared by other scholars of Urdu literature. Ralph Russell and Khurshidul Islam, *Three Mughal Poets*, London, 1969, convey the flavour of medieval Indo-Muslim society in a manner many historians of the period have failed to do. The atmosphere of the court of Awadh in the period before annexation in 1856 is conveyed by Mrs Meer Hassan Ali, *Observations on the Mussulmauns of India*, second edition, edited by W. Crooke, London, 1917, and by William Knighton, *The Private Life of an Eastern King*, ed. S. B. Smith, London, 1921.

MUSLIMS IN BRITISH INDIA

Before 1947, the fortunes of Muslims in British India were treated as an aspect of the history of British India as a whole and although some more specialised work has been published since independence, scholarly output has been small. Many materials are situated in the Republic of India and have been almost impossible of access by Pakistanis, and Indian Muslims have not felt able to draw attention to themselves in the climate prevailing in India since partition. Few European scholars have as yet worked in the Urdu materials available, although a number of young researchers in England and America are now preparing to do so. The passions generated by partition have made it difficult for all concerned to exercise that empathy which historians should extend to those the consequences of whose actions they personally lament. The study of the economic history of British India is still young and little work on the economic fortunes of Muslims as such has been attempted.

THE IMPACT OF BRITISH CONQUEST UPON MUSLIMS

Little advance in terms of research in depth has been made since 1947, but S. A. A. Rizvi's general analysis 'The Breakdown of Traditional Society' in the second volume of the *Cambridge History of Islam*, edited P. M. Holt *et al.*, two vols, (1971), is a small gem. Azizur Rahman Mallick, *British Policy and the Muslims in Bengal 1757–1856*, Dacca, 1961, does little more than embroider Hunter's *The Indian Musalmans*, while ignoring contemporary official *caveats* at Hunter's findings. There is no published monograph on how Muslims fared in the upper provinces, but Bernard S. Cohen, 'The Initial British Impact on India: A Case Study of the Benares Region', *The Journal of Asian Studies*, XIX, 4, August 1960, provided some valuable leads which the author has tried to follow up as far as was possible within the scope of a general work. Thomas R. Metcalf, *The Aftermath of Revolt: India 1857–1870*, Princetown, 1965 should be consulted. No monograph has yet been published on the effect of British rule upon the Muslims of the Punjab. S. S. Thorburn, *Musalmans and Money-lenders in the Punjab*, Edinburgh, 1886, should be treated with the same reserve as Thorburn's views were treated by his fellow Panjab officials. The fortunes of Delhi after 1803 have been recounted in P. Spear, *The Twilight of the Mughuls*, Cambridge, 1951. On British agrarian and land revenue policies in India in general readers should consult: S. Gopal, *The Permanent Settlement in Bengal and its Results*, London, 1949; N. K. Sinha, *The Economic History of Bengal*, vol. I, Calcutta, 1857; Ranajit Guha, *A Rule of Property for Bengal*, 'S-Gravenhage, 1963; Sulekh Chandra Gupta, *Agrarian Relations and Early British Rule in India*, Bombay, 1963.

MUSLIM REVIVALIST MOVEMENTS

There is no worthwhile published monograph on Shah Wali-Allah in a European language, but the following articles or references should be consulted: Alessandro Bausani, 'Note su Shah Waliullah di Delhi', *Annali del Instituto Universitario di Napoli*, X, 1961; Fazl Mahmud Asiri, 'Shah Wali-Allah', *Visva-Bharati Annals*, IV, 1951; Muhammad Daud Rahbar, 'Shah Wali-ullah and Ijtihad'. *Muslim World*, XLV, 4, October, 1955; Fazle Mahmud, 'Philosophy of Shah Wali-ullah', *Oriental College Magazine*, XXXIII, 3, May, 1957.

On the movement of Saiyid Ahmad Bareilly the most recent valuable work has been in Urdu, but the following material in English should be consulted: Qeyamuddin Ahmad, *The Wahabi Movement in India*,

Calcutta, 1966; K. K. Datta, *History of the Freedom Movement in Bihar*, Patna, 1957; Hafeez Malik, *Muslim Nationalism in India and Pakistan*, Washington, D.C., 1963; Muin-ud-din Ahmad Khan, *Selections from Bengal Government Records on Wahhabi Trials (1863–1870)*, Dacca, 1961; M. A. Bari, 'A Nineteenth Century Muslim Reform Movement' in G. Makdisi (ed.), *Arabic and Islamic Studies in Honour of H. A. R. Gibb*, Leiden, 1966; Muhammad Hedayetullah, *Sayyid Ahmad*, Lahore, 1970.

THE MUSLIMS AND 1857

Again no monograph specifically on the Muslim *rôle* has been written, but S. N. Sen, *Eighteen Fifty-Seven*, Delhi, 1957, Metcalf's *The Aftermath of Revolt* already mentioned, S. A. A. Rizvi and M. L. Bhargava (eds.), *Freedom Struggle in Uttar Pradesh*, five vols., Lucknow, 1957–8, the work on the freedom struggle in Bihar and *Source Material for a History of the Freedom Movement in India*, vol. 1, published by the Government of Bombay, Bombay, 1957, should be read.

THE MUSLIM RELIGIOUS RESPONSE TO BRITISH RULE

Aziz Ahmad's indispensable handbook, *Islamic Modernism in India and Pakistan 1857–1964*, London, 1967, with its excellent bibliography, has obviated the need for an extensive bibliography here. He has not, however, listed Kenneth Cragg, *Counsels in Contemporary Islam*, Edinburgh, 1965, which has conveniently classified material under the names of principal thinkers within appropriate chapters. A companion volume of readings to Aziz Ahmad's book is now available: Aziz Ahmad and G. E. von Grunebaum (eds.), *Muslim Self-Statement in India and Pakistan 1857–1968*, Wiesbaden, 1970. Readers should not neglect Wilfred Cantwell Smith, *Modern Islam in India*, Lahore, 1943 (London, 1946). It was a remarkable pioneering effort and most subsequent authors are indebted to it whether they acknowledge (as the author does) the debt or not. The best bibliography on Sir Muhammad Iqbal has been compiled in Annemarie Schimmel, *Gabriel's Wing*, Leiden, 1963. A useful corrective to romantic views of the ᶜulama as freedom fighters is provided by Mushir U. Haq, *Muslim Politics in Modern India 1857–1947*, Meerut, 1970.

MUSLIM POLITICAL HISTORY 1858—1906

Ram Gopal, *Indian Muslims: A Political History (1858–1947)*, Bombay, 1959, is the most convenient introduction to this period and is better balanced than many Pakistanis will allow. Khalid bin Sayeed, *Pakistan: the Formative Phase, 1857–1948*, 2nd ed., London, 1968, is very brief for this period. Most work by Muslims published so far is content to gild W. W. Hunter's lily. K. K. Aziz, *Britain and Muslim India*, London, 1963, is an interesting addition to the expanding study of the history of attitudes and it also contains sidelights upon political history. Anil Seal, *The Emergence of Indian Nationalism*, Cambridge, 1968, deals with the crucial break between Muslims of upper India and the Indian National Congress; it has a most useful bibliography. H. B. Tyabji, *Badruddin Tyabji: A Biography*, Bombay, 1952, is an attractive picture of a key figure. This and the Bombay Government's publication *Source Material for a History of the Freedom Movement in India* contains well-chosen quotations from the Tyabji papers, now in the National Archives in Delhi. M. S. Jain, *The Aligarh Movement*, Agra, 1965, although useful for its extensive references to the *Aligarh Institute Gazette* (of which the only near-complete run is to be found at Aligarh), gives a very jaundiced interpretation of Sir Saiyid Ahmad Khan's and his supporters' motives.

MUSLIM POLITICS 1906–47

Ram Gopal's and Khalid bin Sayeed's works have not been superseded for this period as general accounts. S. R. Wasti, *Lord Minto and the Indian Nationalist Movement 1905–1910*, Oxford, 1964, is indispensable for the negotiations which led to the grant of separate electorates. Accounts of the early days of the Muslim League are to be found in Matiur Rahman, *From Consultation to Confrontation: A Study of the Muslim League in British–Indian Politics 1906–1912*, London, 1970; Muhammad Noman, *Muslim India: the Rise and Growth of the All-Indian Moslem League*, Allahabad, 1942 and Allah Buksh Rajput, *The Muslim League Today and Yesterday*, Lahore, 1948.

The history of the *Khilafat* movement has not been rewritten since independence, but the accounts in A. J. Toynbee, *Survey of International Affairs 1925*, vol. 1, *The Islamic World and the Peace Settlement*, London, 1927, and in E. Sell, *The Khilafat Agitation in India*, Calcutta, 1932, have worn well. The author has not seen P. C. Banford, *Histories of the Non-Co-operation and Khilafat Movements*, New Delhi, 1925, said to have been published under the aegis of the Government of India's Intelligence Bureau. Mohamed Ali, *My Life: a Fragment*, ed. A. Iqbal, Lahore, 1942, is a moving personal document, by a principal in the whole movement. A recent analysis of the political ideas of Abu'l Kalam Azad and the *Jam'iyyat al-'ulama-i Hind* has been attempted in P. Hardy, *Partners in Freedom and True Muslims*, Lund, 1971.

For the politics of the 1920s and 1930s see: J. Coatman, *Years of Destiny: India 1926–1932*, London, 1932; G. T. Garratt, *An Indian Commentary*, London, 1928 and W. R. Smith, *Nationalism and Reform*, New Haven, 1938; Azim Husain, *Fazl-i-Huzain: a Political Biography*, Bombay, 1946; Waheed-uz-Zaman, *Towards Pakistan*, Lahore, 1964; S. Gopal, *The Viceroyalty of Lord Irwin, 1926–1931*, London, 1957; Reginald Coupland, *Report on the Constitutional Problem in India*, Part 1: *The Indian Problem 1833–1935*, London, 1942; His Excellency the Aga Khan, *Memoirs*, London, 1954.

There is a flood of literature on the politics of the decade before partition, though little whose authors have had access to first-hand evidence of Muslims' decisions. The recently-published volume of seminar papers, *The Partition of India: Policies and Perspectives 1935–1947*, (ed.) C. H. Philips and Mary Doreen Wainwright, London, 1970, contains a useful introduction suggesting further lines of inquiry. Many of the papers by eyewitnesses, however, merely defend entrenched positions with a bitterness that time has only served to make more acrid. M. Mujeeb's paper, 'The Partition of India in Retrospect', deserves none the less to be singled out as an attractively rueful account of the reactions to the Congress victory of 1937 in the United Provinces by a Muslim who is himself a bearer of Mughal culture. The first two volumes of British official documents on the transfer of power: *The Cripps Mission*, London, 1970 and *Quit India*, London, 1971, jointly edited by Nicholas Mansergh and E. W. R. Lumby, do not contain any momentous secrets hitherto concealed from contemporary historians. Hector Bolitho, *Jinnah*, London, 1954, and M. H. Saiyid, *Mohammad Ali Jinnah*, Lahore, 1945, are unlikely to survive the throwing open of the Jinnah papers – whenever that may come about. The second of Professor Coupland's reports, *Indian Politics, 1936–1942*, London, 1942, has not been superseded or indeed much improved upon. Chaudhry Khaliquzzaman, *Pathway to Pakistan*, Lahore, 1961, though unreliable, suggests much that many would rather have forgotten. Notices of some of the lesser-known Muslim figures are to be found in S. M. Ikram, *Modern Muslim India and the Birth of Pakistan 1858–1951*, 2nd ed., Lahore, 1965. Maulana Abu'l Kalam Azad's view of events is expressed in retrospect in *India Wins Freedom*, Bombay, 1959.

The most important accounts of the period between the end of the Second World War and independence and partition are: V. P. Menon, *The Transfer of Power in India*, Bombay, 1957; Hugh Tinker, *Experi-*

ment with Freedom, London, 1957; Penderel Moon, *Divide and Quit*, London, 1961; H. V. Hodson, *The Great Divide*, London, 1969; Leonard Mosley, *The Last Days of the British Raj*, London 1961. To these may be added: Michael Brecher, *Nehru: A Political Biography*, London, 1959; Alan Campbell-Johnson, *Mission with Mountbatten*, London, 1951; E. W. R. Lumby, *The Transfer of Power in India, 1945–47*, London, 1954.

GLOSSARY

System of transliteration of words in Arabic, Persian and Urdū

The Arabic definite article (al-) which undergoes certain vowel or other changes according to syntax has, both in the text and here, always been rendered al-. Hence, for example, Faẓl al-Ḥaq (not Faẓlul Ḥaq or Faẓl u'l-Ḥaq), dār al-ḥarb (not dārul-ḥarb or dār u'l ḥarb).

The hamza in an initial position supported by alif is not shown separately from its vocalization, e.g. amīr; nor is it shown in a final position without bearer, e.g. zinā. In a vowelled medial position, or when it is used to indicate a junction of vowels, it is rendered by ', e.g. nā'ib or musta'min, farā'iẓ or (in the text) Bada'un.

Words belonging to other languages found in South Asia have the long vowels only indicated.

Letter	Transliteration
alif	as supporting an initial vowel or hamza, or as bearer of a medial vowelled hamza, it has not been given a separate value; as alif al-maqṣūra ('the abbreviated alif') at the end of an Arabic word, it is shown as 'a' – e.g. fatwa
bā or be	b
pe (Persian and Urdū)	p
tā or te	t
ṭa (Urdū)	ṭ
thā or the	th often found in other works relating to Persia and India as ṣ
jīm	j
che (Persian and Urdū)	ch
he	ḥ
khā or khe	kh
dāl	d
ḍa (Urdū)	ḍ

zāl	ẕ
rā or re	r
ṛa (Urdū)	ṛ
zā or ze	z
zhe (Persian and Urdū)	<u>zh</u>
sīn	s
shīn	<u>sh</u>
ṣād	ṣ
ẓād	ẓ
ṭā	ṭ
ẓā	ẓ
ʿain	ʿ
ghain	<u>gh</u>
fā or fe	f
qāf	q
kāf	k
gāf	g
lām	l
mīm	m
nūn	n
wāw	w (often found in other works as v)
hā or he	h
yā or ye	y

Short vowels

fatḥa (Persian zabar)	a
kasra (Persian zīr)	i
ẓamma (Persian pī<u>sh</u>)	u

Long vowels

represented by alif and alif madda	ā
represented by yā	ī
represented by wāw	ū

Diphthongs

fatḥa yā	ai e.g. <u>sh</u>ai<u>kh</u>
fatḥa wāw	au e.g. maulānā

There are certain vowel sounds in the Persian of South Asia and in Urdū, which are unknown to Arabic and are only occasionally found in the classical and modern Persian of Iran. Where they occur as the South Asian pronunciation of Arabic and Persian vowels, they are transliterated according to the above system, e.g. Aurangzīb not Aurangzeb (Aurangzib in the text), or S͟hīr (S͟hir) S͟hāh, not S͟her S͟hāh. Where however they represent sounds peculiar to South Asian languages (including Urdū), the two most important are usually rendered in the text by e and o – e.g. Deoband, Nānotawī, Gangohī. Complete consistency may not have been attained in this respect however.

The glossary includes the titles of certain works and institutions the English renderings of which were unfortunately omitted at their first appearance in the text. Some words or phrases, the meaning of which has been given in or is sufficiently defined by the text and which appear but once, have not been included in the glossary.

ahimsā: non-harming, non-injury; the relinquishing of all acts causing physical, mental, emotional or moral harm.

Ahl al-ḥadīth: (in India, Ahl-i ḥadīth), the partisans of Prophetic tradition (*see* ḥadīth); in India and Pakistan a sect preferring the authority of Prophetic tradition over that of a conflicting ruling accepted by one of the schools (maẕāhib q.v.) of Islamic jurisprudence.

ahl al-kitāb: (ahl-i kitāb): people of a revealed book or scripture; in Islamic law such non-Muslim peoples are to be publicly tolerated in the dār al-Islām (q.v.) on their acceptance of the status of ẕimmī (q.v.).

Aḥrār: 'the free'; name of a largely Panjāb-based Muslim political party founded in the nineteen-thirties.

Ā͟khirī Maẕāmīn: 'last essays or articles'; title of a collection of such by Sir Saiyid Aḥmad K͟hān published in the year of his death (1898).

ᶜāmil: a Mug͟hal official who collected the revenue of a pargana (q.v.) or sarkār (q.v.).

amīr al-mu'minīn: 'the commander of the faithful'; a title of the sunnī (q.v.) caliph or of a sulṭān (q.v.) appearing to himself or to others to have the necessary qualifications for k͟hilāfat (*see* p.25).

anjuman: assembly, meeting; used of confessional, professional and political associations of Muslims.

ātman: life breath, microcosmic life principle, often equated with the macrocosmic life principle brahman (q.v.).

auqāf: pl. of waqf (q.v.).

bābū: originally a term of respect, but often used disparagingly by the British in India for the English-educated Bengali and for Indian clerks who used English.

Baḥr al-ʿulūm: 'sea of sciences'; one of the madrasas (q.v.) of the Farangī Maḥall, the famous dār al-ʿulūm (q.v.) at Lucknow.

bait al-māl: 'house of wealth'; the public treasury in Islamic lands.

bania (banya): Hindu trader, merchant, broker; often acted as a moneylender.

bidʿa: a reprehensible innovation in religion.

bohrā (bohorā): 'trader, merchant'; name of a shīʿī (*see* shīʿa) Muslim community in western India, mainly of Hindu descent but with some Yemenite Arab blood, upholding the claims of al-Mustaʿlī (1094–1101) as Fāṭimid imām (*see* imām).

brahman: prayer, the sacred word and its magical force, the macrocosmic ultimate ground of the universe; brāhman, priest, the first of the four ranks or classes (varnas) of the ideal Hindu social order.

chamār: in northern India the caste traditionally occupied as tanners and menial labourers.

chaudharī (chaudhurī, chaudhrī): an honorific; title of the local pargana (q.v.) headman charged with the collection (under the control of the ʿāmil q.v.) of land revenue.

Chauhan: name of former ruling Rājput sept; a class of Rājput landholders in northern India.

crore (kror): one hundred lākhs or ten millions.

daftar: a stitched or bound booklet, register or letter-book; commonly used in British India for an office or place of administration and business.

dār al-ḥarb: 'the abode of war'; territory not under Islamic law which, according to classical Muslim jurisprudence, should be made so, if necessary by force.

dār al-Islām: 'the abode of Islam': territory where Islamic law and, classically, a properly constituted or functioning Islamic ruler were supreme.

Dār al-mubālighīn: 'the abode of preachers'; a sunnī (q.v.) seminary in Lucknow founded to combat shīʿī (*see* shīʿa) doctrines.

dār al-ʿulūm: the abode of sciences'; a Muslim establishment for higher religious learning.

darbār (durbar): the court or levée of a ruler; a formal occasion for consultation between a ruler and his officers and advisers or for the ceremonial performance of a public act.

dārūgha (dārogha): a superintendent; a subordinate court of police officer; in Bengal under Warren Hastings a petty magistrate presiding over district criminal courts.

Dasehra: the Hindu festival in September–October lasting nine nights or ten days; also called Durgā-pūjā in Bengal.

dhotī: the form of loin cloth worn by 'respectable' Hindu castes of upper India.

Dīwālī: the Hindu festival of lights in October–November, originally a fertility rite.

dīwān: a collection of poetry or prose, a register, an office; in Mughal times the name of the chief revenue official at the centre and in each province.

faqīh: a specialist in the science of Islamic jurisprudence.

farẓ (pl. farā'iẓ, hence farā'iẓī): a religious duty the omission of which will be punished and the performance of which will be rewarded.

fatwa (pl. fatāwa): an opinion on a point of Islamic law given by a muftī, a person qualified to do so.

faujdār: under the Mughals, the military and executive officer in charge of the sarkār (q.v.); he enjoyed certain penal powers.

fiqh: 'understanding, knowledge, intelligence'; the technical term for the science of Islamic jurisprudence, that is of the religious law (sharīʿa q.v.).

ghadr (ghadar): 'perfidy, ingratitude; mutiny, rebellion'; used in Urdū speech and writing for the Mutiny and Rebellion of 1857; name given to the various conspiratorial movements against the British, principally among Muslims and Sikhs in the Panjāb during the war of 1914–18.

ghair-muqallid: one who does not regard himself as necessarily bound by the doctrines of the schools of Islamic law; a term applied to the Ahl-i ḥadīth (q.v.) in India and Pakistan.

ḥadīth: 'talk, narrative'; al-ḥadīth, an account of what the Prophet Muḥammad said, did or tacitly approved.

hajj: the pilgrimage to Mecca; the fifth of the five 'pillars' of Islam.

ḥanafī: belonging to the school (maẓhab q.v.) of Islamic jurisprudence named after its eponymous founder, Abū Ḥanīfa al-Nuʿmān (c. 699–767).

Holi: Hindu festival in February–March, once a fertility festival.

ʿīd: Muslim festival, especially ʿīd al-fiṭr, the breaking of the fast of Ramaẓān, and ʿīd al-aẓha, the sacrificial festival on 10 Ẓū al-ḥijja.

ijmāʿ: 'agreement, consensus'; one of the bases (uṣūl) of the Islamic religious law. Theoretically the unanimous agreement of the Muslim community (umma) as to a divine mandate (ḥukm), in the sphere of jurisprudence in practice ijmāᶜ represents the unanimous doctrine and opinion of the ᶜulamā at any given time. The nearer an ijmāᶜ approaches to unanimity, the surer Muslims are of divine guidance in arriving at that doctrine.

ijtihād: 'exerting oneself'; in Islamic jurisprudence, technically the effort to form an opinion as to a rule of law; among 'modernists' it may denote the effort, free from traditional religious and legal criteria, to reinterpret the Islamic revelation to the modern world. A person qualified to exercise ijtihād in the technical sense is known as a mujtahid.

imām: a person exercising supreme leadership of the Muslim community after the death of Muhammad the Prophet; used specifically (but not exclusively) for s͟hīᶜī (*see* s͟hīᶜa) claimants; also honorifically for the founders of the four sunnī (q.v.) schools of jurisprudence; title of a prayer-leader in the mosque.

Ismaᶜīlī: a member of the s͟hīᶜī sect which believes that the descendants of Ismaᶜīl ibn Jaᶜfar al-Ṣādiq (died *c.* 765) the seventh in the line of s͟hīᶜī imāms should lead the community and communicate both the exoteric and the esoteric truths of divine revelation to mankind.

jāgīrdār: an assignee of the right to collect the state revenues from a specified area, in Mughal times in lieu of a salary from the royal treasury.

jajmānī: a system of prestations and counter-prestations within a patron–client relationship, embracing different castes within a village and related to religious concepts of interdependence and hierarchy within an ordered social whole.

jamᶜdār (jemadar): in British India the title of the second rank of Indian officer in a sepoy company or of certain officers of police, customs, etc.

jihād: according to Islamic law, the religiously obligatory effort, violent if necessary, to establish the sway of Islam over the world, or to defend the dār al-Islām (q.v.); mujāhid (pl. mujāhidīn), one who is engaged in jihād.

jizya: the poll tax which, according to Islamic law should be levied in dār al-Islām (q.v.) from ẕimmīs (q.v.).

jumᶜa (jumᶜat): Friday, the day of congregational prayer for Muslims.

kāfir: one who is ungrateful to God for His gifts, hence an unbeliever.

kāyasth: member of a caste traditionally occupied as writers or accountants.

khādar, khādī: a thick and coarse variety of cotton cloth, hand-spun and hand-woven.

Khān-Bahādur: an honorific title in British India; compounded of the Mughal title meaning 'gallant officer' and of a title earlier applied to Mongol rulers, and to high officers of the Delhi sultanate and the Mughal empire.

khattrī: (khatrī): derived from kshatriya (q.v.); name of a mercantile caste or class, originally of the Panjāb but found widespread in the sub-continent.

khoja: from Persian khwaja, 'lord, master'; name of a (principally) trading community or caste of Muslim converts found mainly in the Sind and Bombay areas, the great majority of whom are Isma^cīlīs (q.v.) of the Nizārī sect, but including some Sunnīs and Ithnā-^casharī shī^ca (*see* shī^ca). The Nizārīs, followers of the Āghā Khān. regard Nīzār (elder brother of al-Musta^clī, *see* bohrā), and his descendents as the true imāms (q.v.).

khuṭba: a bidding prayer or sermon delivered in the congregational mosque on Fridays, in which God's blessings on the reigning prince are invoked, thus constituting a symbolic acknowledgment of soverignty.

kshatriya: the second, warrior, class of the ideal Hindu social order.

lākh: one hundred thousand.

lā-kharāj: 'without kharāj', land freed from the payment of revenue.

madrasa: a higher Islamic school or college; a collegiate mosque.

majlis: gathering, assembly.

majlis-i shūra: consultative assembly.

maktab: a school for teaching children the elements of reading, writing and Qur'ānic recitation.

manṣabdār: the holder of a civil and/or military appointment, graded according to a decimal ranking system, within the Mughal imperial service.

maulānā: 'our tutor, trustee, helper or lord' (the Qur'ānic sense of maula); title applied to scholars of the Islamic religious sciences.

maulawī: 'my tutor, helper or lord'; title applied to a Muslim religious scholar; *see also* maulānā.

mazāhib: *see* mazhab.

mazhab (pl. mazāhib): a school of sunnī (religious) jurisprudence.

millat: religion, religious community; sometimes used in the modern Muslim world as a synonym for 'nation'.

mīr ^cadl: a Mughal provincial judicial officer with wide powers of inquisition, if necessary outside the formal procedures of the Islamic law.

miyān: in India a term of respect; 'master', 'good sir'.

mu‘āfīdār: a holder of land exempted (mu‘āfī) from the payment of revenue, a privilege granted in lieu or by way of a pension.

muftī: one qualified to give a fatwa (q.v.).

mujāhid: *see* jihād.

mujtahid: *see* ijtihād.

mullā: Hindī corruption of maula (*see* maulānā); learned man; often used in British India for a Muslim schoolmaster.

mu'minīn: 'those who are believing and faithful'; Muslims.

munṣif: 'one who adjusts equitably'; lowest grade of Indian judge in British India, with jurisdiction in minor civil suits.

muqallid: one deeming himself bound by the principle of taqlīd (q.v.).

musta'min: a non-Muslim entering and living in dār al-Islām (q.v.) under amān or safe-conduct or a Muslim having similar status *vis-à-vis* dār al-ḥarb (q.v.).

Mu‘tazilites: a group of thinkers largely responsible for the appearance, in the eighth century A.D., of speculative dogmatics in Islam, i.e. 'the discussion of Islamic dogmas in terms of Greek philosophical concepts'.

Nadwat al-‘ulamā: 'an assembly or meeting place of Muslim scholars'; name of the seminary founded by Maulānā Shiblī Nu‘mānī at Lucknow.

nā'ib-dīwān: deputy to the chief revenue officer of a Mughal province.

nā'ib-nāzim: deputy to the governor of a province in later Mughal times, charged with military and penal responsibilities.

Nau-rūz: 'New Year's Day', according to the Persian solar calendar.

nawwāb (nawāb, corr. nabob): pl. of nā'ib, 'deputy, vicegerent'; a style assumed by governors of provinces in later Mughal times.

nazr: an offering or gift as from an inferior, or as between persons of equal rank, or on paying respects to a prince.

nizāmat ‘adālat: the chief court of the later Mughal province of Bengal and Bihar, presided over by the governor (nāzim) or his deputy and exercising criminal powers.

parda (purda): 'a curtain, screen or veil'; the seclusion of women in respectable Muslim households.

pargana: a traditional grouping of villages for revenue purposes; in British India smaller in area than a tahṣīl (*see* tahṣīldār).

paṭṭā: a document specifying the conditions on which land is held; a lease or other document securing rights in land or house.

pīr: a ṣūfī (q.v.) teacher or director.

qānūngo: keeper of the records of the revenue district known as the pargana (q.v.).

qaum: tribe, kinship group, religious community, nation – according to period and context.

qāẓī: a Muslim judge according to the religious law (sharīᶜa, fiqh q.v.).

ṣadr-amīn: 'head officer'; title of an Indian judge empowered to try civil suits, ranking between Principal ṣadr-amīn and munṣif.

saiyid: 'prince, lord, chief, owner'; used to denote a descendant of the Prophet Muḥammad.

sarkār: the first grade of subdivision of a Mughal province (ṣūba q.v.).

shab-i barāt: the eve of the fourteenth day of the month of Shaᶜbān, on which Indian Muslims make offerings to their ancestors.

shaikh: 'old man, elder, chief'; ṣūfī (q.v.) leader or head of mystical order; title enjoyed in many parts of British India by those Muslims possessing or wishing (as converts perhaps) to suggest Arab descent.

sharīᶜa: the path to be followed; the totality of the exoteric revelation of Islam; the divine law.

shīᶜa: 'party', the party of ᶜAlī; general name for all those Muslims who regard the son-in-law of the Prophet Muḥammad, ᶜAlī, and his descendants as the only legitimate leaders (imāms q.v.) of the Muslim community after Muḥammad's death. The majority of the shīᶜa, the Ithnā-ᶜashiriyya, accept a line of twelve imāms ending with Muḥammad al-Muntaẓar ('the awaited') who, it is believed, went into occultation *c.* 874 but who will reappear at a pre-ordained time to fill the earth with justice.

shirk: associating a partner with God, worshipping other than God, polytheism.

ṣūba: a Mughal province, presided over by a ṣūbadār, the more usual term for provincial governor in earlier Mughal times.

ṣūbadār: governor of a Mughal province (ṣūba q.v.); in British India the title of the first rank of native officer in a company of sepoys.

ṣūfī: a Muslim mystic, so called after the early ascetics in Islam who wore garments of coarse wool (ṣūf).

sulṭān: 'power, authority'; used under the Ummayads and ᶜAbbāsids of persons to whom authority was delegated by the caliph, then of self-made warlords, becoming the Muslim equivalent of 'monarch' or 'king'.

sunnī: 'one who follows the trodden path'; i.e. the model practice of the Prophet and of the early Muslim community; one who does not deviate from the beliefs and practices of the catholic Muslim community (as distinct from the shīʿa q.v.).

swarāj: rule over self, self-government, political independence.

taʿaiyūnī: 'one who identifies himself'; used of those nineteenth-century Muslim reformers in Bengal who wished to identify themselves with a particular Islamic school of law.

taʿalluqdār: in Bengal, an engager for, or collector of revenue paid through a superior zamīndār (q.v.); elsewhere, as in Awadh and Allāhābād, a superior zamīndār who engaged with the state for the payment of revenue from his own and other (inferior) zamīndārīs; after 1858 the British endowed taʿalluqdārs of the latter sort with proprietory rights to conciliate them to British rule.

tafsīr; the science of Qur'ānic exegesis.

Tagas: a cultivating or landholding tribe of the upper Ganges region and Rohilkhand, having Hindu and Muslim branches.

tahsīldār: chief Indian revenue officer of a tahsīl or subdivision of a British-Indian district, larger than a pargana (q.v.).

taqlīd: 'imitation'; the principle of following the established doctrines of the schools (mazāhib) of Islamic law.

Taqrīr-i dil-pazīr: 'an agreeable utterance'; the title of a work of Muslim–Christian controversy written by Maulānā Muhammad Qāsim Nānotawī of Deoband.

tarīqa: a way, the term for the sūfī (q.v.) path, a mystical method, or school of guidance along that path.

Taṣfiyya al-ʿAqā'id: 'Clarification of Religious Tenets'. Title of a polemical work by Maulānā Muhammad Qāsim Nānotawī of Deoband against Sir Saiyid Ahmad Khān's doctrines.

tauba: repentance, turning to God.

tauhid: the divine unity and unicity.

thākur: a term of respect, 'lord'; a minor Rājput chief; a class of Rājput landholders; in form 'Tagore' used in Bengal as a 'surname'.

ʿulamā: (sing. ʿālim): learned men, scholars in the Islamic religious sciences.

wahdat al-wujūd: the unicity of Being, existential monism.

wahhābī: name given by opponents to followers of Muhammad b. ʿAbd al-Wahhāb (1703–87) an Arabian reformer; often incorrectly used of the followers of Saiyid Ahmad of Rai Bareilly in India.

waqf: a pious foundation; an irrevocable settlement of property under which ownership is immobilised and the usufruct is to be devoted to purposes meritorious in God's sight.

zamīndār: 'landholder'; under the Mughals, a term applied loosely to the possessor of a variety of interests in land, as hereditary chief, engager for land revenue, as agent for the latter's collection under official control and as a claimant to an hereditary or prescriptive cess. In British India, a landholder who individually or jointly engaged to pay revenue; the holder of a right of property in land with the right to collect rent and to regulate the occupancy of all other tenures on his estate (zamīndārī).

zamīndārī: *see* zamīndār.

ẓilaᶜ (corr. zilla): the district in British India, presided over by a Collector or Deputy-Commissioner.

ẓimmī: in Islamic law, one whom, as a non-Muslim, the Muslim state undertakes to protect in the practice of his religion on certain conditions, notably the payment of jizya (q.v.).

zinā: the Islamic legal term for fornication, i.e. sexual relations between those who are not in a state of legal matrimony or legal concubinage.

INDEX

285

Index 305

of name, 234; loses office in 1947, 250; position under 'Sikandar–Jinnah pact', 228–9
United Patriotic Association, 136–7
United Provinces, the, 27, 131; anti-cow-killing riots in, 140–1; communal feeling in, 203–4; Congress rejects coalition with Leaguers in, 225–6, under dyarchy, 200, (communal riots) 204; (finances) 207; government prefers representation of interests, 160; Hindu literacy in, 144, 205; landlord politics in, 222–223; local government: (communal position in) 160, 203–4; (separate electorates in) 204; (statistics of Muslims and) 144; Muslim literacy rising in, 144, 205; Muslims: (decline in services and law) 144–5; (and 'Lucknow Pact') 187; (support League after 1937) 227; (why voters support Pakistan idea) 237–8; number of seats after 1935 Act, 223; results of elections: (in 1937) 224; (in 1945–6) 236; Urdu issue in, 142–143, 153; 'young muslims' in, 153, 186, 187–8, (conservative Muslim opposition to) 188; *see also* North-Western Provinces
Upanishads, 28
'Urabi, Pasha (*anglice*, wrongly, 'Arabi), 120
Urdu, 61, 138; development of, 18; gains ground, 143; Hindi–Urdu issue in United Provinces, 102, 142–143, 153; loses ground, 143–4; *Urdu-i Mu'alla*, 18
Uttar Pradesh, *see* United Provinces

Vaidya, C. V.: *Downfall of Hindu India*, 208
Vijayanagar, empire of, 1
Vivekananda, Swami, 140

wahdat al-wujud, 27, 28
Waheed al-Haq, 46n, 80n, 81n
Waheed-uz-Zaman, 271
'Wahhabis', Indian (so-called), 83; detention under Regulation III, 84; in Panjab (1876), 174; trials of, 80, 84; *see also mujahidin*
Wa'iz al-Haq, 65

Wainwright, Doreen Mary, 271
Wajid 'Ali Shah, 64
Wali-Allah, Shah, 51, 58, 84; doctrines, 28–9; enlisted by Sir Saiyid, 100; *Hujjat Allah al-Baligha*, 29
waqfs: Privy Council decision on (1894), 180, (Muslim League and 'ulama combine against) 180–1
Wasti, Syed (Saiyid) Razi, 166n, 270
Watt, W. Montgomery, 265
Wauchope, S., 90
Wavell, Archibald Percival, 1st Earl, 234, 248
Wazir Hasan, Saiyid (1874–1947), 153
Welch, S. C., 267
Wellesley, Richard Colley, 1st Marquess of, 32
Wellhausen, J.: *Das arabische Reich und sein Sturz*, 175
Wheeler, J. Talboys, 87n
Wilayat 'Ali, Maulawi, 54, 59
Williams, F., 76n
Williams, L. F. Rushbrook, 263
Wingfield, Sir Charles John, 66
Wiqar al-Mulk, 143, 153
Wright, F. V., 48n
Wyllie, John, 87

Yahya 'Ali, 84
Yahya Khan, General (b. 1917), 254
Yasin, Mohammad, 266
yogis, 28
Young, Sir William Mackworth (1840–1924), 141n
'young Muslims': alliance with 'ulama, 167, 180–5, 186, 187, 188, 189; British policy towards, 154, 159–160, 167, 183, 185, 186; leading personalities among, 153
Yusuf Husain, 103n, 264

Zafarul Islam, 80n
Zahir Dihlawi (Saiyid Zahir al-din), 70–1; *Dastan-Ghadar*, 70
Zahur Ahmad, Saiyid, 153
Zaidi, Zawahir Husain, 149n, 150n, 151n
Zakir Husain, Dr (1897–1969), 227
zamindars: in Bengal, 39, 43–5; in North-Western Provinces, 46, 78; in Panjab, 23; in pre-British India, 15–16, 20, 21, 23, 39, 42

Printed in the United Kingdom by
Lightning Source UK Ltd., Milton Keynes
137281UK00001B/61/A